THE OXFORD SH.

General Editor · Stanley Wells

The Oxford Shakespeare offers new and authoritative editions of Shakespeare's plays in which the early printings have been scrupulously re-examined and interpreted. An introductory essay provides all relevant background information together with an appraisal of critical views and of the play's effects in performance. The detailed commentaries pay particular attention to language and staging. Reprints of sources, music for songs, genealogical tables, maps, etc. are included where necessary; many of the volumes are illustrated, and all contain an index.

ROGER WARREN, the editor of *Henry VI, Part Two* in the Oxford Shakespeare, has also edited *Cymbeline* and co-edited *Twelfth Night* with Stanley Wells for the series.

FEB 09

ED

THE OXFORD SHAKESPEARE

Currently available in paperback

The rest of the plays are forthcoming

OXFORD WORLD'S CLASSICS

WILLIAM SHAKESPEARE

Henry VI, Part Two

Edited by
ROGER WARREN

OXFORD
UNIVERSITY PRESS

OXFORD

UNIVERSITY PRESS

Great Clarendon Street, Oxford OX2 6DP

Oxford University Press is a department of the University of Oxford.
It furthers the University's objective of excellence in research, scholarship,
and education by publishing worldwide in

Oxford New York

Auckland Bangkok Buenos Aires Cape Town Chennai
Dar es Salaam Delhi Hong Kong Istanbul Karachi Kolkata
Kuala Lumpur Madrid Melbourne Mexico City Mumbai Nairobi
São Paulo Shanghai Taipei Tokyo Toronto

Oxford is a registered trade mark of Oxford University Press
in the UK and in certain other countries

Published in the United States
by Oxford University Press Inc., New York

First published 2003
First published as an Oxford World's Classics paperback 2003
Reissued 2008

British Library Cataloguing in Publication Data

Data available

Library of Congress Cataloging in Publication Data

Data available

ISBN 978–0–19–953742–6

1

Typeset in Photina MT
by SNP Best-set Typesetter Ltd., Hong Kong
Printed in Great Britain by
Clays Ltd, St Ives plc

PREFACE

I WAS fortunate to encounter this play, and the other parts of *Henry VI*, first in performance, in a television series of Shakespeare's histories made by the BBC in 1960 under the general title 'An Age of Kings', and then in an overwhelming production by Peter Hall and John Barton at Stratford-upon-Avon in 1963–4 which decisively established the plays in the modern theatre. I have also benefited from subsequent productions, especially Jane Howell's BBC television version in 1983. But inevitably I have learnt most about how the plays work by rehearsing them, participating in the preparation of Edward Hall's production at the Watermill Theatre, Newbury, and on its subsequent tour and London season. Edward and his company have made a crucial contribution to this edition.

I also owe much to my predecessors in the Oxford Shakespeare. When R. B. McKerrow died in 1940, his Oxford Shakespeare remained unfinished, a sad loss to scholarship; but his admirable edition of *2 Henry VI* exists in the archives of Oxford University Press, and my debt to him will be evident from the frequency with which his views are quoted in this edition. I am glad to have the opportunity to give them wider circulation, and I thank Martin Maw and Jenny McMorris of Oxford University Press for facilitating my access to McKerrow's papers. My debt to William Montgomery is greater still. He edited the play for the Oxford *Complete Works*, and the 1594 Quarto for his Oxford D.Phil. thesis and for the Malone Society Reprint (both 1985). I have reached different conclusions about the relation of the Folio and Quarto texts, so that my text differs in several respects from his, but without the clarity and thoroughness of his editorial work, mine would have been very much harder.

For expert help of widely varying kinds, ranging from palaeography to falconry, I thank Duncan Cloud, Anne Marie D'Arcy, Barbara Jefford, Emrys Jones, Randall Martin, Richard Pearson, Maurice Pope, Elaine Treharne, Geoffrey Wheeler, and the library staff of the Shakespeare Centre, the Shakespeare Institute, the University of Bristol Theatre Collection, and the BBC Information and Archives Commercial Service.

I have been supported at every turn by the generosity and friendship of the general editor, Stanley Wells, of Frances Whistler at Oxford University Press, and of Christine Buckley, whose expertise makes the phrase 'copy-editor' seem bleakly inadequate. And I owe a very special debt to Angie Kendall for helping to prepare this edition through all its stages.

The completion of this edition was facilitated by a semester's leave from the University of Leicester, complemented by a further period of leave made possible by a grant from the Arts and Humanities Research Board. To all, my thanks.

ROGER WARREN

CONTENTS

LIST OF ILLUSTRATIONS

A NOTE ON TITLES

In this edition, the three parts of *Henry VI* are always referred to by their titles in the 1623 Folio of Shakespeare's plays: *Henry VI*, Parts 1, 2, and 3 (or abbreviations of those). The titles *The First Part of the Contention betwixt the two Famous Houses of York and Lancaster* and *The True Tragedy of Richard Duke of York* (sometimes abbreviated as *Contention* or *True Tragedy*) are exclusively reserved for the two texts from which they derive, the Quarto of *2 Henry VI* (1594) and the Octavo of *3 Henry VI* (1595). They are *never* used to refer to the Folio texts. The point needs emphasis because the Oxford Shakespeare *Complete Works* uses the Quarto and Octavo titles to identify the Folio texts, partly because these were probably the titles under which they were originally performed. The plays must, however, have become known as 'Parts' of *Henry VI* by 19 April 1602, as that is what they are called in an entry on the Stationers' Register; and in any case to call them *Henry VI*, Parts 2 and 3 is an unambiguous way of identifying the Folio texts, especially desirable when discussing complicated textual issues.

INTRODUCTION

THE three plays dramatizing the reign of King Henry VI, which the First Folio of Shakespeare's works in 1623 entitled *Henry VI*, Parts 1, 2, and 3, belong to the theatre of the early 1590s. They also belong, in an important sense, to the modern theatre, since they have come fully into their own since the end of the Second World War. The timing is surely significant. In a blood-soaked century, after two world wars, the uncompromising violence of these plays, from which earlier generations had shrunk, have clearly struck a chord with modern performers and audiences. The *Henry VI* plays dramatize contemporary as much as Elizabethan issues: the struggle for power, the manoeuvres of politicians, social unrest; and, for the last decade of the twentieth century, they provided a dark mirror to the unnerving spectacle of civil war erupting in the former Yugoslavia, at the heart of Europe. It is small wonder that these plays have struck such a chord; they are plays for today.

There is evidence that they were popular in their own day, too. In March 1592, a play called *Harry VI* (probably *Henry VI, Part 1*) was a great success at the Rose Theatre in Southwark, south London; that same year a rival dramatist, Robert Greene, attested to the success of *Henry VI, Part 3* by enviously parodying a line from it; in 1594 and 1595, versions of Parts 2 and 3 were published, suggesting that there was a market for the texts of plays that had proved popular; and at the end of *Henry V* in 1599, the Chorus alludes to the events of Henry VI's reign, 'Which oft our stage hath shown': he also asks the audience to show appreciation of *Henry V* itself 'for their sake', a phrase which implies that the *Henry VI* plays had been well received. The complex issues of dating and textual relationship raised by the facts baldly stated in this paragraph will be discussed more fully later in this introduction.

Three Plays or a Trilogy?

The modern theatre has usually presented the *Henry VI* plays as a group; so far as I know, *Henry VI, Part 2* has not been staged on its own, as an independent work, since it was given at the Birmingham

I

Repertory Theatre in 1951—and in any case its success there led to stagings of the other two parts in subsequent years, with linked casting. Often, too, the *Henry VIs* have been performed as part of a complete cycle of all Shakespeare's history plays that follow one another chronologically from the deposition of Richard II in 1399 to the defeat of Richard III at the battle of Bosworth and the establishment of the Tudor dynasty in 1485. But they were not written in that order. We know from the contemporary allusions just mentioned that the *Henry VIs* existed by 1592, and *Richard III* probably followed shortly afterwards;[1] but the four plays that dramatize the earlier events, *Richard II*, *Henry IV*, Parts 1 and 2, and *Henry V*, were written subsequently, roughly between 1595 and 1599.

What are the advantages of regarding and performing the three parts of *Henry VI* as a trilogy, not three independent plays? The obvious advantage is narrative continuity, with several major characters continuing from one play to the next. Part One opens with the funeral of Henry V, and subsequently deals with the loss of his French conquests, largely because of disunity between the English nobility, and especially because of the quarrel between the Dukes of York and Somerset, vividly dramatized in the fictional episode in which they pluck the white and red roses which become the symbols of the civil war that subsequently develops. Their inability to work together is directly responsible for the death of Lord Talbot, heroic leader of the English forces in France and arguably the central character of Part One, opposed by Joan la Pucelle (Joan of Arc); her burning at the stake is juxtaposed with the capture of Margaret of Anjou by Suffolk, whose passion for her leads him to engineer her diplomatic marriage with Henry VI. Part Two opens with Margaret's arrival in England, where she acts as a catalyst for the political tensions between the ambitious politicians who surround Henry VI, and for the destruction of Henry's Lord Protector, Duke Humphrey of Gloucester. The removal of his strong government creates a dangerous political vacuum, providing the opportunity for the rise of York, the rival claimant to the English crown, and his agent Jack Cade, whose popular rebellion anticipates, and parodies, York's aristocratic one. The Wars of the Roses break out at the end of Part Two, and rage destructively throughout Part Three: they involve the deaths of York and his ally

---

[1] See John Jowett's edition of *Richard III* (Oxford, 2000), p. 3.

the Earl of Warwick, of Margaret's son, and of Henry VI himself. Out of this chaos arises the figure of Richard of Gloucester, the future Richard III, who embodies in his own self the anarchy into which the country has fallen. It is an exciting story, packed with dramatically interesting events and incidents. It is not surprising that it was popular in the 1590s and remains so.

Another advantage of presenting the three plays as a group is that it allows those characters who appear in more than one of them to develop beyond the limitations imposed by appearing in one play only. The greatest beneficiary of this approach is Queen Margaret. Peggy Ashcroft, who played the part at Stratford-upon-Avon in 1963–4, describes its range: 'an amorous princess . . . , an adulterous wife, a scheming politician, a cruel and dauntless soldier';[1] but that range is fully apparent only when the actress appears in all the plays. The 'adulterous wife' and the 'scheming politician' are powerfully dramatized in Part Two, but not the other characteristics.[2] The 'amorous princess' emerges only in Margaret's single appearance in Part One (5.5), but it establishes her relationship with Suffolk in a brilliantly theatrical way. Its tone is perfectly caught by Peggy Ashcroft, who calls it a 'daringly contrived scene, witty, sensual, and comic, . . . a small glimpse of what is in store with Katherine the Shrew and Beatrice [in *Much Ado*]'.[3] The 'daring' of the scene is that the start of a relationship which has such serious political and human consequences in Part Two should be dramatized by means of high comedy: as each character talks directly to the audience, the other tries to get a word in edge-ways; and as the scene becomes more intimate, Suffolk moves from the polite Elizabethan form 'you' to the familiar 'thee' and 'thou':

> I'll undertake to make thee Henry's queen, . . .
> If thou wilt condescend to be my—
> MARGARET   What?
> SUFFOLK His love.   (5.5.73–7)

[1] 'Margaret of Anjou', *Shakespeare Jahrbuch* (West) 109 (1973), 7–9; p. 7.

[2] Not everyone believes that Margaret is presented as an 'adulterous wife', but the intensity of the scene in which they are forced to part, and especially Suffolk's lines about dying in her lap (3.2.393–4; see the Commentary), seem to me to put this beyond doubt.

[3] Introduction to *King Henry VI Part One*, the Folio Society (1967), p. 7. *The Taming of the Shrew* was probably written just before 1 *Henry VI* rather than after it (*Textual Companion*, pp. 109–12), but this does not affect Peggy Ashcroft's point about their close relationship.

The monosyllabic 'What?' with which Margaret completes Suffolk's verse line, emphasizing their collusion, reveals that she knows exactly what Suffolk is suggesting, and, in agreeing to become Henry's queen, plays along with it. But she is already in control of the relationship: after Suffolk has agreed to cede the counties of Anjou and Maine to her father, the decision that is so bitterly resented at the start of Part Two, they exchange a kiss, ostensibly to be sent as a token to Henry; but as she says,

> That for thyself; I will not so presume
> To send such peevish tokens to a king.
> (5.5.141–2)

In one short scene, the basis for their relationship in Part Two is established: the immediately mutual attraction of two clever, ambitious people who will put their personal desires above every-thing, but who, when they overreach themselves in contriving Duke Humphrey's murder and are forced to part, are desolated; and when Suffolk himself is murdered, Margaret's grief hardens into the desire for revenge.

That revenge, however, is not achieved in Part Two itself; it has to wait until the extraordinary scene of Margaret's tormenting and slaughter of York in Part Three (1.4). Peggy Ashcroft stresses the relation between that scene and the equally extraordinary one in Part Two where Margaret enters cradling Suffolk's severed head in her arms (4.4):

I came to realise why this scene [in Part Two] was of paramount impor-tance—for later in what is one of the greatest and certainly most horrific scenes . . . when Margaret wipes the blood of York's son on the Duke's face . . . , I found that seemingly impossibly bestial act to be credible as the result of the violence that has been perpetrated on her lover.[1]

Of course, Part Two does not *require* the scenes in parts One and Three in order to make sense. The opening of Part Two is clear enough as it stands, but it is enriched if the audience has seen the first meeting of Margaret and Suffolk; equally, Margaret's dedicat-ing herself to revenge at 4.4.3 is a perfectly comprehensible motive in itself, not 'incomplete' in that sense; but again, the experience of both audience and actress is enhanced if she goes on to achieve her

---

[1] *Shakespeare Jahrbuch* 109 (1973), pp. 7–8.

revenge in Part Three—which is then to recoil upon her when her son is murdered at the end of that play (5.5.38–41).

Other advantages of what might be called the plays' long-range view of events are that the allusions in Part Two to the loss of France are clearer if the audience has seen it happen in Part One, and that York's repeated use of his feud with Somerset as an excuse to seize the crown in Part Two is more effective if we have seen their quarrel in the rose garden and their betrayal of Talbot in Part One. Somerset is in general rather ill-defined in Part Two; here Part One helps.

On the other hand, each of the plays needs to stand on its own in performance, and has its own structure. Part One is based on the opposition between Talbot and Joan of Arc, leaders of the English and French forces. The structure of Part Two is quite different, built upon the fall of Duke Humphrey and the rise of York. Part Three is more diffuse, depending upon several major climaxes: Margaret's slaughter of York (1.4), the battle in which King Henry witnesses the twin tragedies of civil war, a father who has killed his son and a son who has killed his father (2.5), and the scheming and rise of Richard of Gloucester in the second half of the play, especially his long soliloquy at 3.2.124–95. The relation of the three plays is best summarized by Emrys Jones: 'Shakespeare could not have expected an identical audience for each of the three plays', any more than a theatre company can today:

A man might drop in for *3 Henry VI* on one day and return for *1 Henry VI* a few days later and on each occasion expect to find what he did find—a more or less unified theatrical experience that certainly referred outwards to a larger mass of historical information but which he did not expect to find represented within his afternoon's entertainment.[1]

So far, I have set the three individual plays against the idea of a trilogy; but there are other ways of regarding them. When Part Two first appeared in print in 1594, its title was *The First Part of the Contention betwixt the two Famous Houses of York and Lancaster*; that '*First Part*' anticipated the continuation of the story with the publication in 1595 of *The True Tragedy of Richard Duke of York*. These texts presented versions of what the First Folio calls *Henry VI*, Parts 2 and 3, not as the concluding parts of a trilogy, but as a two-part play without reference to the Folio's *Part 1*. This has led to the

[1] *The Origins of Shakespeare* (Oxford, 1977), pp. 129–30.

influential current view, discussed on pp. 67–71 below, that Part One was written *after* Parts Two and Three. Yet another view regards the *Henry VIs* not as a trilogy but as part of a tetralogy, a sequence of *four* plays culminating with *Richard III*. The chief argument in favour of this view is that when the characters in *Richard III* allude to past events, as they often do, the play is made more comprehensible if the audience has seen those events on stage in the *Henry VI* plays. It is also true, as Jane Howell said when directing all four plays for the BBC television series in 1983, that when the plays are given in sequence Richard is the logical product of the society of *Henry VI*: 'you know where he came from and . . . why he is as he is.'[1] Against these advantages may be set Robert Speaight's view that when the plays were performed in sequence in 1963, '*Richard III*, *as a play*, seemed far less significant than . . . its precursors'.[2] I think that was because *Richard III* is a different kind of play. In the *Henry VIs*, the interest is divided between a large number of major characters, almost all of them interesting: *Richard III* is really a play built around one mighty figure. That helps *Richard III* to stand on its own more successfully than any of the three parts of *Henry VI*, as its much more extensive stage history shows; but the rise of a single character, however magnetic, can also come as an anti-climax, rather than a climax, after the sheer variety of *Henry VI*.

Theatricality and Modernity

Since almost all the productions of *Henry VI* since the 1590s have occurred within the last fifty years, an initial survey of them should provide a context of theatrical experience which will help to focus the principal issues to be developed later in the introduction and in the commentary.[3]

After the Restoration of the monarchy in 1660, the *Henry VIs* had to wait another twenty years before they were revived in 1681, in a two-part adaptation by John Crowne. His first part was drawn

---

[1] *Henry VI Part 3*, BBC TV Shakespeare edn. (1983), p. 31.
[2] *Shakespeare on the Stage* (1973), p. 287.
[3] Apart from the brief reference to eighteenth- and nineteenth-century productions, and the account of Douglas Seale's in 1951–3 and 1957, I have only drawn on productions that I have seen and whose details I could therefore verify for myself. Luckily, most of these productions were recorded, enabling me to refresh my memory.

from the first three acts of *2 Henry VI*, focused on the downfall of Duke Humphrey of Gloucester, and his *Misery of Civil War* drew on the Jack Cade scenes from *Part 2* and on *Part 3*. Two other adaptations followed in 1723: Ambrose Phillips's *Humfrey Duke of Gloucester* used a mere thirty lines of *Part 2*, and Theophilus Cibber's *Henry VI* drew on Act 5 of *Part 2* and Acts 1 and 2 of *Part 3*.[1] In 1817 the famous actor Edmund Kean played the title role in J. H. Merivale's *Richard Duke of York*, which drew on all three parts to provide Kean with a central star role.[2] In 1864 the first known revival of *2 Henry VI* since Shakespeare's day took place at the Surrey Theatre in London, a house known for performing melodramas. The director, James Anderson, doubled York and Jack Cade. So far as one can judge from this distance, these productions seem to have been what Prospero in *The Tempest* would call insubstantial pageants; but they interestingly emphasize aspects of the structure of *2 Henry VI*, Crowne and Philips concentrating on the fall of Duke Humphrey, Crowne and Anderson on the rise of York and Cade.

As the nineteenth century drew to a close, *2 Henry VI* was revived at the Shakespeare Memorial Theatre, Stratford-upon-Avon, in 1899.[3] At that time, the brief (three-week) Stratford season in April was presented by a company run by the actor/director Frank Benson, who played Cardinal Beaufort. Benson revived the play in 1906, together with Parts One and Three, in the context of an (incomplete) cycle of Shakespeare's histories, and this seems to have been the first time that the three plays were presented together in England, unadapted, since Shakespeare's day. With seventeen plays to be performed by the company in three weeks, one should beware of making any great claims for the significance of this event;[4] but it had at least one important consequence.

Looking back to Benson's cycle in 1953, Sir Barry Jackson

---

[1] George C. D. Odell, *Shakespeare from Betterton to Irving*, 2 vols. (New York, 1920), i. 63–6, 248–52.

[2] A review by Keats's friend J. H. Reynolds is reprinted in Stanley Wells's anthology *Shakespeare in the Theatre* (Oxford, 1997), though, as Wells says, some of the phrasing (and one might add the extensive Shakespearian allusion) sounds like Keats himself. Wells also reprints Keats's description of Kean as a Shakespearian actor (pp. 50–5).

[3] The original theatre was largely destroyed by fire in 1926. It occupied the space the modern Swan Theatre now occupies. The rebuilt Memorial Theatre, now the Royal Shakespeare Theatre, was opened in 1932.

[4] See J. C. Trewin's account in Trewin and T. C. Kemp, *The Stratford Festival* (Birmingham, 1953), 47–9, 72–4.

recalled that it was the 'Second Part of *King Henry VI* that made the greatest impression on my mind',[1] and it was with Part Two that he began his cycle of the *Henry VI* plays at his Birmingham Repertory Theatre in 1951. Part Three followed in 1952 and Part One in 1953; all three parts were then given at the Old Vic theatre in London that summer. Jackson arranged the text; the plays were actually staged by Douglas Seale, a director particularly admired for his work on Shakespeare's histories. Seale directed them again at the Old Vic in 1957. This was a completely different production, spread over two evenings rather than three: Parts One and Two were given on the first evening, though Part One was virtually eliminated. In his 1953 article, Jackson asked: 'why has no major actress ever discovered the tremendous character of Margaret of Anjou, surely one of the greatest feminine roles in the whole [Shakespearian] gallery?' That discovery was certainly made by Barbara Jefford in Seale's 1957 production, to judge from Mary Clarke's description:

Her arrogance and increasing power were underlined by her cruel humour. The insult to the Duchess of Gloucester, who is 'accidentally' struck in the face for not retrieving the Queen's fan, was made more humiliating by the false, mocking apology, 'I cry you mercy, madam! Was it you?' (1.3.140). . . . Her supreme moment of triumph came with [Duke Humphrey's] disgrace when, her arms stretched upwards exultantly, she cried, 'Why now is Henry King and Margaret Queen' (2.3.39) . . . and in the tragic farewell to Suffolk (3.2.304–416) was apparent all the passion in this woman so absurdly, so fatally united with poor Henry. [See figs. 1 and 9.][2]

This sketch usefully emphasizes aspects of the dramatic impact of *2 Henry VI* which subsequent performances have confirmed.

Perhaps one can glimpse something of what Seale's productions were like from a BBC television version made in 1960, when Peter Dews directed all the histories from *Richard II* to *Richard III* in fifteen hour-long episodes under the general title of 'An Age of Kings', with several of Seale's actors in the *Henry VI* episodes. Like many Shakespeare productions of the 1950s, these were vigorous, straightforward stagings, strong and clear in narrative, without perhaps probing very deeply into the meaning of the text or the

---

[1] 'On Producing *Henry VI*', *SS* 6 (Cambridge, 1953), 49–52; p. 49.
[2] *Shakespeare at the Old Vic 1957–8* (1958), no page numbers. Clarke also describes both the adaptation and the staging in detail, with numerous photographs.

1. Queen Margaret (Barbara Jefford) 'accidentally' strikes Duchess Eleanor (Margaret Courtenay) in Douglas Seale's production, Old Vic theatre, London, 1957.

language in which it is expressed.[1] At any rate, valuable though both Seale's and Dews's productions were in making audiences aware of the *Henry VI* plays, neither succeeded in establishing them as an important part of the Shakespearian repertoire. That was achieved by a remarkable production at Stratford-upon-Avon

---

[1] Videos of this series are available for hire, at moderate rates, from the BBC Information and Archives Commercial Service.

in 1963, where the *Henry VIs* were given with *Richard III* under the general title of *The Wars of the Roses*.

When in 1960 Peter Hall became Director of what was then still called the Shakespeare Memorial Theatre (renamed the Royal Shakespeare Theatre the following year), he aimed to create a long-term company, the nucleus of which would continue from one year to the next, performing in both Stratford and London; and he succeeded in doing this so quickly that by 1963 he had assembled a versatile group of actors equipped to deal with the challenges of the *Henry VI* plays and led by Peggy Ashcroft, whose views on playing Queen Margaret have already been cited. Another of Hall's aims was that his company should not only be trained to play Shakespeare, and especially to handle Shakespearian verse, but should be alert to contemporary issues, and how these illuminated the plays and vice versa. In 1963, the Second World War had been over for eighteen years, but Europe was divided by an 'iron curtain' into communist and non-communist spheres of influence, and in the years preceding the productions there were two major international crises. In August 1961, the East Berlin communist authorities constructed the 'Berlin Wall' which cut the city in half, so reinforcing the image of Germany as a divided nation (the Wall was not dismantled until 1989); and October 1962 saw the Cuban missile crisis, when a face-off between America and Russia brought the world to the very brink of nuclear war. This was the context of tense international division in which *The Wars of the Roses* was created; and during its run there followed a third crisis: the assassination of President Kennedy at Dallas in November 1963. No one could say that the atmosphere of international crisis and civil war in Shakespeare's histories was a thing of the past. As Peter Hall said at the time: 'We live among war, race riots, revolutions, assassinations . . . and the imminent threat of extinction. The theatre is, therefore, examining fundamentals' in staging the *Henry VI* plays.[1]

There was not, however, any attempt to force modern parallels on to the actual staging, as there was, for instance, in Michael Bogdanov's cycle under the same title in 1987, as we shall see; instead, contemporary issues were used to help the company

---

[1] 'Shakespeare and the Modern Director', *Royal Shakespeare Theatre Company 1960–1963*, ed. John Goodwin (1964), 41–8; p. 47.

explore the political and psychological meaning of the plays. Above all, these productions were an analysis of power, and the time-honoured, or dishonoured, behaviour of politicians, contrasted with the political innocence and religious idealism of King Henry VI himself. Peter Hall summarized this contrast in his introductory talk to the company.[1] 'In theory [Henry] should be a good king; he applies Christian ethics to government. But he is up against men who don't.' Henry tries to live by his Christian beliefs, and many of his speeches are coloured by echoes of the Bible, noted in the commentary to this edition. When Henry uses such phrases, they are an expression of his convictions; but when the politicians use them, they become mere slogans. The most notorious example is Cardinal Beaufort, and the difference between his lip-service to Christianity and the King's conviction is precisely caught in their contrasted echoes of Christ's Sermon on the Mount at 2.1.34–6. But it is not only religious slogans that the politicians abuse. As Hall continued: 'They justify their behaviour by invoking the great sanctions—God, the King, Parliament, the People—that unscrupulous statesmen, motivated by the naked desire to be on top, have used throughout the ages.' He added that these politicians 'team up in packs in order to fight, just as wolves unite to hunt': this catches the way in which the court turns upon and destroys Duke Humphrey, the Lord Protector, in the first half of *2 Henry VI*, and how that leads to anarchy and civil war as the rival packs of York and Lancaster set out to destroy one another.

To express the contrast between the apolitical Henry and the politicians, Hall ran the risk of casting an inexperienced actor, David Warner, as the King. The risk paid off, and it established the character as much as the actor, as Harold Hobson reported:

He and Mr Hall between them discover in Henry one of Shakespeare's greatest parts. The discovery is the more exciting for being improbable, since drama gives its principal opportunities to active men. Henry is never active. . . . He suffers only, and endures, never resisting, never striking back. . . . Yet [Warner's] sad, distressed face, meeting each new misfortune with an absolute absence of protest or indignation, spreads over the darkest waters of the play a quiet and persistent golden glory. (*Sunday Times*, 21 July 1963)

[1] Partly reprinted in the published text of *The Wars of the Roses*, BBC publications (1970), pp. xii–xiv. For further information on this production, see Richard Pearson, *A Band of Arrogant and United Heroes* (1990).

But such personal qualities have disastrous political consequences when Henry evades the responsibilities of government. As Hall summed it up: 'here is the central irony of the plays: Henry's Christian goodness produces evil.' This conflict was reinforced by the physical staging. John Bury designed a menacing steel set, whose central feature was an oval council table placed at the very front of the stage, which served brilliantly to focus the ambitions and intrigues of the individuals who sat around it, with Duke Humphrey vainly trying to keep their attention, and the King's, on the need to govern the country rather than to pursue their own aims. T. C. Worsley pointed out how 'the play is admirably produced to show us how behind-the-scenes decisions are cooked up to be ratified later at this table' (*Financial Times*, 18 July 1963)—for example, the plot to destroy Duke Humphrey himself (fig. 2).

On certain occasions the *Henry VIs* and *Richard III* were presented in a single day, with morning, afternoon, and evening performances, and this began a modern theatrical tradition of all-day performances of Shakespeare's histories. But it necessitated adapting *Henry VI* into two plays rather than three; and whereas Douglas Seale had achieved this by combining Parts One and Two in his first play, Hall's collaborator John Barton divided Part Two in the middle, after the death of Cardinal Beaufort (3.3); his second play, renamed *Edward IV*, began with the later scenes of Part Two, Jack Cade's rebellion and the rise of York, and then continued into a shortened Part Three. But this version was reshaped as well as cut, and Barton added about 1,400 lines of pastiche Elizabethan verse to bridge the gaps created by the cuts. This inevitably aroused controversy; but the overwhelming reaction of press and public was that the adaptation, the ensemble acting, and the way in which the plays reflected the contemporary world, constituted a theatrical triumph, summed up by Irving Wardle when the productions transferred to London as 'a revival in the true sense of the word—the restoration of a work of the past to the understanding of modern audiences' (*The Times*, 13 January 1964). The plays returned to Stratford in 1964 as part of a complete cycle of the histories from *Richard II* to *Richard III* and were televised by the BBC.[1] This production decisively established the *Henry VI* plays in the

---

[1] A copy of the television recording is held at the Shakespeare Centre Library, Stratford-upon-Avon.

2. Queen Margaret (Peggy Ashcroft) tries to turn Henry (David Warner) against Duke Humphrey at the council table, watched by Suffolk (Michael Craig), the Cardinal (Nicholas Selby), Exeter, incorporating some of Salisbury's part (Clifford Rose), York (Donald Sinden), and Warwick (Brewster Mason), in Peter Hall's production, Stratford-upon-Avon, 1963.

modern theatre, and, as one reviewer of a more recent Stratford history cycle pointed out, it 'remains still the benchmark in terms of political and psychological elucidation and drive' (Carole Woddis, the Glasgow *Herald*, 19 December 2000). Its outstanding success also emboldened others to attempt further revivals.

In 1977, for example, the Royal Shakespeare Company risked giving the *Henry VIs* at Stratford unadapted and only minimally cut. The achievement of *The Wars of the Roses* raised hopes that an unadapted version would shed further light on the plays, and for some commentators it did;[1] but for others, including myself, Terry Hands's production was a great disappointment, especially when compared directly with *The Wars of the Roses*, a comparison actively encouraged by Hands when he said in the theatre's publicity at the time that he aimed 'to show the plays simply as they are, without excessive rewriting and cutting' in order 'to tell the story as simply as possible'. To this end, he used a bare, steeply-raked stage, covered with a green carpet for Part Two; the common people watched the great events, cordoned off from the court, until, in Jack Cade's rebellion, they burst out in a parody of the violence and greed of the aristocrats.

But a bare stage and a simple narrative throw the entire burden of responsibility on to the actors, and most of the parts were undercast or miscast or both, especially Duke Humphrey, whose shifty, eccentric manner robbed Part Two of its great positive force. Jack Cade was strangely interpreted as a zealot, a kind of perverted John the Baptist; and Helen Mirren at that stage in her career lacked the emotional range and scale that Margaret had been shown to need in Seale's and Hall's productions. Henry himself was played by Alan Howard, who had scored a great success as the hero in Terry Hands's production of *Henry V* which immediately preceded the *Henry VIs*: it was clearly a part of Hands's plan to use the same actor in order to contrast the son and the father. Alan Howard offered an alternative to David Warner's saintly innocent, creating a complex portrait of a well-intentioned man who suffered from periodic bouts of madness, a point emphasized by York as he spoke the phrase 'Henry put apart' (3.1.383), tapping his forehead as if to suggest that when he became king he would have Henry incarcerated as a madman. This interpretation interestingly raised the

[1] For example, Homer D. Swander, 'The rediscovery of *Henry VI*', *SQ* 29 (1978), 146–63.

question of how much Shakespeare knew about the historical Henry's periods of madness, and how far they are allowed for in the plays (see below, pp. 34 and 44). But Henry appears too infrequently for Alan Howard to carry these productions, as he had done Hands's *Henry V*; and in general this *Henry VI* was weakest just where Peter Hall's had been strongest—politically and psychologically. It is not enough to 'tell the story as simply as possible'. This production did not, at any rate for me, demonstrate that these plays can work unadapted.[1]

Luckily, however, that demonstration *was* made in 1983. There is general agreement that Jane Howell's productions of *Henry VI* and *Richard III* for the complete BBC television Shakespeare are a high point, if not *the* high point, of the series. Part of their success derives from their skilful integration of the techniques of theatre and television. All four plays are performed on the same set, a circular acting area surrounded by a balustraded balcony with swing doors underneath to speed exits and entrances. Made of rough wood, it initially suggests a children's playground, but as the plays' mood darkens it is gradually broken up to reflect the disintegration of the realm during the Wars of the Roses. Part of it is set alight during Jack Cade's rebellion, and books, manuscripts, and even characters are hurled on to the fire: Cade's face, laughing hysterically as he becomes more drunk with power, is superimposed on the flames.

The precision and clarity of Jane Howell's direction can be illustrated from her handling of the opening of Part Two, where the relation of the numerous characters and the political and psychological cross-currents are vividly communicated. When Suffolk says that he has married Margaret on Henry's behalf, a glance between Suffolk and Margaret instantly makes it clear that this proxy marriage is an image of their private relationship. When Duke Humphrey, reading the terms of the marriage contract negotiated by Suffolk, hesitates slightly at the phrases 'Marquis of Suffolk' and 'ambassador for Henry, King of England' (1.1.44–5), the tension between the Lord Protector and the man who is usurping his authority is palpable. When later in the scene Buckingham says of Duke Humphrey 'Why should he then protect our sovereign' (1.1.164), a quick glance of reaction from York registers that

[1] I have analysed Hands's productions in greater detail in *SS 31* (Cambridge, 1978), 148–51.

the plot to destroy Humphrey is beginning to take shape; and in the line in which York agrees to work for the good of the country, 'And so says York, (*aside*) for he hath greatest cause' (1.1.206), the aside is economically expressed by a change of shot and by York glancing at the camera, as asides are handled throughout. This treatment not only helps identify characters and makes the narrative crystal clear, it also brings out the quality of the writing, the skill with which so much information is communicated in a relatively short exposition.

A consistently strong cast is dominated by Julia Foster's Margaret. She begins Part Two as a demure, softly-spoken bride, but soon develops a fierce resentment against Henry and especially Duke Humphrey. At the start of 3.1, Henry is placed in the foreground of the shot so that both he and the viewer receive the full impact as Margaret, backed by the court and all of them held within the same shot, begins her attack on Humphrey with a sweet reasonableness that gives way to angry impatience at Henry's 'fond affiance' (3.1.74) and sheer contempt for his 'foolish pity' (3.1.225). This develops in her huge speech at the discovery of Humphrey's murder (3.2.73–121), which she plays as a furious attack on Henry, who sits hunched and broken on the floor, for preferring Humphrey before herself. It is a tour de force; but I will return to its details when I consider that central speech later in this introduction. When Henry banishes Suffolk, her face becomes a mask contorted with fury, but she modulates from this to the tenderness of her lyrical farewell to Suffolk; and in the scene with Suffolk's head (4.4), placed uncompromisingly close to the camera, Julia Foster makes it plain that, once Suffolk is killed, Margaret 'becomes intent on revenge . . . for the rest of her life', motivating her savagery in Part Three.[1]

Although this production left no doubt that each of the *Henry VI* plays can work unadapted, the productions given later in the decade by the English Shakespeare Company and the RSC reverted to the broad lines of John Barton's two-play adaptation, dividing Part Two in the middle and occasionally using some of Barton's new lines.[2] The English Shakespeare Company was founded by the

---

[1] *Henry VI Part 2*, BBC TV Shakespeare edn. (1983), p. 25.
[2] The RSC's 1988 version was attributed to the dramatist Charles Wood (see Adrian Noble's introduction to *The Plantagenets* (1989), p. xii), but this claim is placed in perspective by Ralph Fiennes, who played Henry VI: 'I thought (as did

director Michael Bogdanov and the actor Michael Pennington to tour large-scale Shakespeare productions, beginning with *Henry IV* and *Henry V* in 1986; in subsequent years they added the other history plays so that they could tour the complete cycle from *Richard II* to *Richard III* under the general title of *The Wars of the Roses*.[1] Michael Bogdanov is a director keen to bring out modern parallels, not merely by implication, but by presenting them specifically on stage; in *Henry VI* the chief examples were his handling of Queen Margaret and Jack Cade.

At the time of Bogdanov's production, Britain had had eight years of the Conservative government of Margaret Thatcher, who was notorious for her inflexibility and her dictatorial attitude and manner. Bogdanov seized his opportunity, and presented Queen Margaret as an equivalent figure, casting in the part a middle-aged 'character' actress, the company's Mistress Quickly in *Henry IV*, June Watson. Severely dressed and with a stiff coiffure resembling Thatcher's, she asserted Margaret's dominance from the moment she met Henry: in a novel interpretative twist, she responded to his attempt to give her 'this kind kiss' (1.1.19) by making him kiss her *hand*. She instigated the plot to kill Humphrey with relish, and as she delivered her reaction to Suffolk's brutal practical details, ''tis resolutely spoke' (3.1.266), her eyes gleamed with a kind of misplaced idealism that cruelly resembled Thatcher's. Still more telling was her handling of Margaret's transparently unconvincing line after Humphrey's murder that Suffolk 'most Christian-like laments his death' (3.2.58): she invested 'Christian-like' with the voice of official religion, cold and meaningless. She delivered her rebuke to Suffolk

> Fie coward woman and soft-hearted wretch!
> Hast thou not spirit to curse thine enemies?
> (3.2.311–12)

as if to say 'Pull yourself together, man!' The drawback to such a slanted interpretation was that it was powerful but monotonous: no wit, no variety. And yet, as often happens, the text asserts itself

many of the actors) that his adaptation . . . was disappointing . . . so the first part of the rehearsals became a process of realigning the script, of putting lines back in' (*Players of Shakespeare 3*, ed. R. Jackson and R. Smallwood (Cambridge, 1993), p. 100).

[1] Their cycle is available on video, *Henry VI* on ITEL 625 PAL.

over directorial reductiveness: even with such a Margaret, the parting with Suffolk was as moving as ever. But perhaps that is not so surprising: even Thatcher showed signs of emotion when her party finally got rid of her in manoeuvres worthy of the politicians in *Henry VI*.

Against this Margaret, and considering Bogdanov's marked left-wing credentials, he might have been expected to make whatever case can be made for Jack Cade's rebellion. But not at all. He simply seized upon a variety of negative influences: 'punk' rock stars, the National Front, football hooligans. Michael Pennington's Cade, with a carrot-orange 'punk' hair-style and wearing a union-jack vest with a white rose in the middle, rather unconvincingly addressed a political meeting in, as it might be, the local Town Hall (fig. 3): the real purpose of this was to present the Clerk of Chatham as a middle-class figure who had attended the meeting out of interest in politics, only to be torn to pieces. The actor had played Duke Humphrey earlier: both characters were figures of moderation destroyed by negative forces, Humphrey by political manoeuvre, the Clerk by mindless violence. My final impression of Bogdanov's *Henry VI* was of a world that believed in nothing—a chilling reflection of contemporary Britain perhaps, but also defining the limitation of relating the plays too specifically to contemporary society: for all their cruelty and violence, the world of the *Henry VI*s is not, I think, as bleakly negative as in Bogdanov's production.

There was no risk of excessive modernity in Adrian Noble's *The Plantagenets* (*Henry VI* reduced to two parts, followed by *Richard III*) for the RSC in 1988, as Robert Smallwood reported: 'At much the same time as the English Shakespeare Company was making its point about the contemporary relevance of these plays through a succession of twentieth-century stage allusions . . . the RSC remained ostentatiously historical in its approach.' And although he admired the productions, as I did, he also felt that the very 'splendour of the staging and scenic effects' tended 'to blunt the cutting edge of the texts' trenchant political vision', while allowing 'some remarkable performances' to emerge.[1] The most striking of these were Ralph Fiennes's Henry and David Waller's Duke

---

[1] Introduction to *Players of Shakespeare 3* (Cambridge, 1993), pp. 14–15. Ralph Fiennes (Henry VI), Penny Downie (Margaret), and Anton Lesser (Richard of Gloucester) provide very full and interesting accounts of their roles on pp. 99–159.

3. Michael Pennington as Cade harangues his supporters in Michael Bogdanov's production, English Shakespeare Company, 1987.

4. A harvest of heads. Oliver Cotton as Cade in Adrian Noble's production, Stratford-upon-Avon, 1988.

5. Duke Humphrey (David Waller), Henry (Ralph Fiennes) and Margaret (Penny Downie) at the council-table in Adrian Noble's production, Stratford-upon-Avon, 1988.

Humphrey. In his review in *The Times* of 24 October 1988, Irving Wardle said that Fiennes 'communicates the sense of a real moral alternative to his faction-riven court: without sacrificing the character's gentleness, he has moments of spectacular strength'—that is, he occupied a middle ground between David Warner's and Alan Howard's interpretations.

One of his 'moments of spectacular strength' came in his passionate delivery of 'How irksome is this music to my heart!' (2.1.54)—i.e. 'how can I hope to govern when my court is riven with factions?'—but they mostly arose from his relationship with Duke Humphrey. For the scene of Humphrey's arrest (see fig. 5), the production followed the lead of the Hall/Barton *Wars of the Roses* by introducing a long council table to its otherwise empty stage: as Suffolk arrested Humphrey, Henry actually rose to intervene, but was restrained by Margaret, who pulled him back down into his chair, and thereafter Henry let events take their course, overwhelmed it seemed by sheer force of numbers. So after Humphrey had been removed, his answer to Margaret's 'will your highness leave the Parliament?', 'Ay Margaret, my heart is drowned with grief', was a great cry of pain: he had wanted to save Humphrey but had failed to do so. The long speech that follows was beautifully controlled, the comparison of Humphrey to a calf led to a 'bloody slaughterhouse' bitterly directed at Humphrey's enemies, the reference to his 'sad *unhelpful* tears' pointedly acknowledging his own failure to help his uncle, and the concluding 'Who's a traitor? Gloucester, he is none' a tremendous affirmation of faith (3.1.197–222). All this intensified his reaction to the discovery of Humphrey's dead body. He turned on Suffolk, and on Margaret for defending him—but really he turned on himself for his failure as a nephew and as a king: when he swore an oath to banish Suffolk before God 'Whose far unworthy deputy I am' (3.2.289–90), the word 'unworthy' was packed with a deep self-accusation; his rejection of Margaret's attempt to plead for Suffolk, 'No more, I say!' was almost frenzied, as he physically rejected her; and his assertion 'when I swear, it is irrevocable' was another of those 'moments of spectacular strength' to which Irving Wardle refers (3.2.295–8)— but it was both authoritative and near-hysterical, the admission of a man who knows that something terrible has happened, largely through his own fault.

The intensity of Fiennes's relationship with his uncle was greatly helped by David Waller's Humphrey, at once impassioned— as in his fury at the terms of Margaret's marriage settlement or his tears of frustration when his wife 'hath dishonoured Gloucester's honest name' (2.1.194)—and yet delivered with all the ease and variety that comes from decades of experience in playing major roles of this kind in Shakespeare. With two such performances in these central roles, 3.1 and 3.2 were far and away the most effective of the material drawn from *2 Henry VI*. By contrast, the Jack Cade scenes were so severely curtailed that they hardly got off the ground, and here Robert Smallwood's reservations about the spectacular element in the production seemed most apposite, when the text's two heads on poles (4.7.121.1–2) were transformed into a veritable forest of them. Michael Ratcliffe's overall verdict was that while Noble's staging was in the honourable tradition of the Hall/Barton version, it added 'little individual of its own' (*Observer*, 30 October 1988), though of course a generally strong, clear production like this is always of value in introducing audiences to unfamiliar plays. But the two most recent productions at the time of writing certainly did break new ground, containing striking theatrical features not encountered in earlier versions.

In the winter of 2000–1 Michael Boyd staged the three parts of *Henry VI* unadapted and only slightly cut at the Swan Theatre, Stratford-upon-Avon, as part of another complete cycle from *Richard II* to *Richard III* for the Royal Shakespeare Company, though the other plays were divided between different directors and given in different theatres. *Henry V*, for example, was directed by Edward Hall, and it was he who simultaneously directed another staging of *Henry VI* with his own company at the Watermill Theatre, Newbury, and on a subsequent international tour. This adapted the plays into two parts though not, this time, divided half-way through Part Two, which was given on the first evening with a much abbreviated Part One; Part Three occupied the second evening.

To appreciate certain aspects of Michael Boyd's staging of Part Two, it was necessary also to have seen his Part One. This introduced a red-clad character called 'the Keeper', who reappeared throughout the three plays as each of the major characters died, rose from death, and followed him to a mysterious, smoke-filled other world. He was in league with the similarly red-clad female forces who accompanied Joan of Arc in Part One. In the text, Joan's 'fiends' do not appear until just before she is burnt; here they attended her from the start. Joan was doubled with Margaret: with a little textual rearrangement, Joan's burning was followed by Margaret's first appearance. The suggestion made in earlier productions that one French destroyer of the English was giving way to another was carried much further by Boyd, since Margaret's father was played by that red-clad 'Keeper': he was something more than the King of Naples; the implication was that he was sending his daughter to bring about the destruction of England. A danger of introducing Margaret like this might have been to deprive her and the other characters in Part Two of their independence of action, making them mere puppets of malign external forces; but in fact the first half of Part Two was played perfectly straightforwardly. The influence of another world, however, reappeared with a vengeance in the second half of Part Two, from the Cardinal's death scene (3.3) onwards.

The ghost of Duke Humphrey appeared to the dying Cardinal, whose body was then hoisted in mid-air, while his bed became the deck of the ship where Suffolk is beheaded in 4.1. From below deck, the ghost of Lord Talbot, commander of the English forces in Part One, emerged as the 'Lieutenant', followed by that 'Keeper' to play Walter Whitmore and so to 'waft' Suffolk to his death (4.1.116). There were some interesting advantages in using Talbot's ghost like this. The strange over-writing in the Lieutenant's opening speech, discussed on p. 50 below, seemed less strange when spoken by Talbot, whose style it resembles; the Lieutenant's concern for the loss of France at 4.1.86–90 came naturally from the betrayed Talbot of Part One; and Suffolk's odd description of his pirate killers as 'soldiers' (see the Commentary to 4.1.133) seemed less odd in these circumstances. With the ghost of Duke Humphrey overseeing the deaths of the Cardinal and Suffolk, the far-reaching consequences of his murder were spelt out; and the possibility, suggested on pp. 50–1 below, that the grotesqueness and violence of Suffolk's death scene deliberately prepare for those of Cade's rebellion was emphasized when the ghosts of Humphrey, the Cardinal, and even the headless body of Suffolk, joined Cade's rebels. That red-clad 'Keeper' inevitably played Dick the Butcher, disembowelling Stafford's brother at 4.3.0.2. The grotesque aspects of the writing in these scenes were the elements in Part Two most suited to Michael Boyd's 'expressionist' style as a director, but they did not unduly dominate the performance; Cade's rebellion, played at a brisk pace, was not given more prominence than the text allows it, so that the proportions of the play were preserved: the Cade scenes were a comment upon, and a parody of, the behaviour of the court.

Reviewing Boyd's production in *The Times* on 15 December 2000, Benedict Nightingale described the world it presented as 'an abattoir England'. That aspect of *Henry VI* was carried further in Edward Hall's production at the Watermill Theatre, which sought a social context and a theatrical environment in which to communicate the extremes of violence in these plays. 'An abattoir England' was here actual rather than metaphorical, since Michael Pavelka's

6. Michael Pavelka's set design for Edward Hall's production, Watermill
Theatre, Newbury, 2001.

set design (fig. 6) was based on an abattoir at Smithfield meat market dating back to Victorian times: the floor was tiled, and the acting area surrounded by metal spikes, meat-hooks upon which
severed heads (or their symbolic representation) could be displayed. But the design also drew on another aspect of Victorian
tradition. One of the influences on the production was Lindsay
Anderson's 1968 film *If . . .* , in which the brutality ingrained in
the traditional public school system leads to violent rebellion—
hence, in part, the vaulting-horse in the middle of the set, which
was put to a variety of practical uses: when broken into sections, it
served as the coffin of Henry V at the start of Part One; the English
throne; London Stone for Cade to sit upon at 4.6.1–2; and most
important, as a chopping-block for executions.

This block offered a novel solution to the acts of violence. Members of the company, wearing white butchers' clothing and masks,
and using cleavers, severed pieces of meat on that chopping-block
as characters were killed, or—for the heads that needed to be displayed—they chopped red cabbages in half while the actor mimed
the moment of death. For the (onstage) decapitation of Lord Saye

and his son-in-law by Cade's rebels, the cabbages representing the severed heads were not sliced in half but smashed in pieces which flew all over the stage; into this messy chaos York arrived to 'claim his right' (5.1.1), and out of it grew the climactic battle of St Albans. This both emphasized the link between Cade's rebellion and York's ambitions, and vividly conveyed the chaos of civil war to which those ambitions lead, an impression reinforced by the nauseating stench of crushed cabbage, now indelibly associated with the severed heads. This was an interesting variant on the customary attempts to present violence 'realistically' on stage, and it raised questions about audience response to such overtly theatrical devices. There was of course some (nervous) laughter when a cabbage was placed on the block next to the actor's head; but when the cleaver sliced it and the actor simultaneously slumped to the floor, the laughter (mostly) died: as one audience member put it, the deaths were 'symbolic, but had all the impact of physical violence'—more, arguably, than the usual expedient of daubing actors liberally with stage 'blood'.

While the English theatre was slow to revive *Henry VI*, a complete cycle of Shakespeare's histories was given at the Pasadena Playhouse, California, in 1935. Similar cycles had already been given in Germany, directed by Franz Dingelstedt at Weimar in 1864 and at Vienna in 1873–4. *Henry VI* Parts 2 and 3 were performed on a 'Shakespeare stage' at the Munich court theatre between 1889 and 1906. Another complete cycle was directed by Saladin Schmitt at Bochum in 1927 where the lavishly historical visual presentation seems to have had a blurring effect: 'The many battles and political conferences repeat themselves till one cannot tell one from the other. Imperceptibly one Henry begins to slide into the next' (*Frankfurter Zeitung*, 18 June 1927). The experience of the Second World War, as well as the influence of Bertolt Brecht's dramatic techniques, which advocated both a 'socialist' attitude to politics and an 'alienatory' approach to characterization, in which actors were asked to 'present' rather than to embody the roles they played, meant that the next major German production, Peter Palitzsch's *Der Krieg der Rosen* at Stuttgart in 1967, was a very different affair. Palitzsch said that the aristocrats 'hang on to the wheel of power as long as it carries them upward, and they try to cut off the heads, or at least the fingers, of anyone they feel to be a competitor'. Duke Humphrey was apparently robbed of his unselfish motives, and more surprisingly, perhaps, in this context, Jack Cade was denied any revolutionary fervour, but was as brutal a butcher as his aristocratic opponents.[1]

Palitzsch acknowledged the influence of another major European version, Giorgio Strehler's *Il gioco dei potenti* ('The Play of the Mighty') at the Teatro Piccolo in Milan in 1965. I saw this production at the 1973 Salzburg Festival, now in German, but by comparison with Strehler's imaginative staging of Mozart's operas in Salzburg and elsewhere, and of *The Tempest* in Milan and Paris, his *Henry VIs* were a disappointment. The ultimate effect was monotonous. Like Palitzsch and several English directors, he reduced the three plays to two, but also made some unhelpful additions, adding a commentator whose part was 'based on monologues of the chorus in *Henry V*, the reports of messengers in *Henry VI*, and on passages from *Richard II*, *Henry IV*, *Macbeth*, and *Timon of Athens*', to cite the programme—for no reason that I could appreciate. Still more tiresome were two Germanic gravediggers, called 'Bevis' and 'Holland' after the Folio's names for the two rebels at 4.2.0.1, commenting gloomily as they tipped one after another of the 'Mighty' into their graves. Their last victim was King Henry himself who, as the programme put it, 'becomes a puppet and a clown like Cade the rebel'. The effect was to reduce the plays to a mere pessimistic catalogue, perhaps under the influence of the then fashionable Jan Kott's *Shakespeare our Contemporary* (1965) which similarly reduces history to a relentlessly repetitive mechanism.

Since the three parts of *Henry VI* have usually been staged together, this survey has had to speak of 'plays', while attempting to keep the focus on Part Two. This is not difficult, since, as Michael Billington put it when reviewing Michael Boyd's cycle, 'Part Two is the trilogy's undisputed high point' in which 'Shakespeare displays that ability to embrace court and commoners that he was later to deploy, with even greater genius, in the *Henry IV* plays' (*Guardian*, 15 December 2000). But Billington's comment raises once again the question of a 'trilogy'—or of a 'tetralogy'.

---

[1] Simon Williams, *Shakespeare on the German Stage 1586–1914* (Cambridge, 1990), 155–6; Wilhelm Hortmann, *Shakespeare on the German Stage: The Twentieth Century* (Cambridge, 1998), 226–30. For subsequent stagings in Europe and America, see Judith Hinchcliffe, *King Henry VI, Parts 1, 2, and 3*, Garland Shakespeare Bibliographies (1984), and the annual theatre reviews in *SQ*.

Origins

A tetralogy, or rather two tetralogies, including the subsequently written *Richard II–Henry V* series, was certainly how the plays were seen by their most influential critic in the first half of the twentieth century, E. M. W. Tillyard.[1] He interpreted them as presenting a providential view of history in which the Wars of the Roses were England's bloody expiation of Henry IV's crime in deposing an anointed king, Richard II, an expiation that was not completed until Richard III was destroyed by the Lancastrian Earl of Richmond (King Henry VII) whose marriage to the Yorkist princess Elizabeth finally united the houses of York and Lancaster in the Tudor dynasty, and so brought about peace and stability. For Tillyard, Shakespeare adopts and dramatizes this 'Tudor myth' that he found in the chronicles which he used as sources, especially that of Edward Hall. Hall's title *The Union of the Two Noble and Illustre Families of Lancaster and York* (1548) makes his position clear; but was Shakespeare's so simple? It is true that his histories reflect aspects of Tudor political orthodoxy because, as John Jowett puts it, 'it was virtually impossible to do otherwise'. Shakespeare 'would have been aware that he was negotiating troublesome ground that was critical to the Tudor claim to the right to govern. His freedom to vary the received accounts was limited'.[2] In addition, he was writing about issues that aroused both interest and anxiety in his audiences. Although Queen Elizabeth I had another decade to live, by the early 1590s she had been on the throne for over thirty years yet was unmarried and childless: the succession was not determined, and there were natural fears that on her death civil war between rival claimants might break out—the Wars of the Roses all over again.

The *Henry VI* plays, therefore, presented their audiences with matters of real relevance to them, just as they have in different ways to audiences of today. But that is not at all the same thing as saying that Shakespeare uncritically accepted what A. P. Rossiter

---

[1] *Shakespeare's History Plays* (1944). For a survey of Tillyard's supporters, and of the reaction against him which has become 'a new orthodoxy', see Robin Headlam Wells, 'The Fortunes of Tillyard: Twentieth-Century Critical Debate on Shakespeare's History Plays', *English Studies* 5 (1985), 391–403, and Judith Hinchcliffe, *King Henry VI, Parts 1, 2, and 3*, Garland Shakespeare Bibliographies (1984).

[2] Introduction to *Richard III* (Oxford, 2000), p. 11.

calls the 'rigid Tudor *schema* of retributive justice' that he found particularly in the chronicle of Edward Hall.[1] As Rossiter implies, this 'Tudor myth' is too reductive for the varied theatrical experience that the plays offer.

But Shakespeare found in Hall something much more dramatically useful than a providential or mythical pattern, and that was the striking contrast between the personalities of King Henry and Queen Margaret, which it is worth quoting at length:

During the time of this truce [in 1444–5, mentioned at 1.1.40–2], ... while there was nothing to vex or trouble the minds of men, within the realm a sudden mischief ... sprang out suddenly, by the means of a woman: for King Henry ... was a man of a meek spirit, and of a simple wit, preferring peace before war, rest before business, honesty before profit, and quietness before labour. And to the intent that all men might perceive that there could be none more chaste, more meek, more holy, nor a better creature, in him reigned shamefastness, modesty, integrity, and patience to be marvelled at, taking and suffering all losses, chances, displeasures, and such worldly torments, in good part, and with a patient manner, as though they had chanced by his own fault or negligent oversight; yet he was governed of them whom he should have ruled, and bridled of such whom he sharply should have spurred. He gaped not for honour, nor thirsted for riches, but studied only for the health of his soul, the saving whereof he esteemed to be the greatest wisdom, and the loss thereof the extremest folly, that could be.

But on the other part, the Queen his wife was a woman of a great wit, and yet of no greater wit than of haut stomach [pride], desirous of glory and covetous of honour, and of reason, policy, counsel, and other gifts and talents of nature belonging to a man, full and flowing; of wit and wiliness she lacked nothing, nor of diligence, study, and business she was not unexpert.[2]

Hall's vivid juxtaposition of the opposed—indeed, irreconcilable—natures of the King and Queen was surely the immediate inspiration for the writing of Part Two itself, since Shakespeare pins down the essence of Hall's contrast in one incisive line at the start of the play: welcoming Margaret, Henry thanks God for the blessings she brings him, 'If sympathy of love unite our thoughts' (1.1.23); it is from the absence of such 'sympathy' that all the subsequent disasters derive.

---

[1] *Angel with Horns*, ed. Graham Storey (1961), p. 2.
[2] 1809 reprint, p. 208.

Hall's chronicle was one of the sources for Raphael Holinshed's *Chronicles of England, Scotland and Ireland*; but while he carries over Hall's contrast between the King and Queen into his own account, Holinshed modifies it in the first edition of his chronicle (1577), and still further in the second (1587), which Shakespeare certainly used for other plays: the positive, saint-like qualities in Hall's description of Henry, which so clearly influenced Shakespeare's conception of the character, are wholly omitted; and whereas Hall places the main responsibility for the civil strife on the Queen, Holinshed blames

overmuch mildness in the King, who by his authority might have ruled both parts and ordered all differences betwixt them, but that indeed he was thought too soft for governor of a kingdom. The Queen contrariwise, a lady of great wit and no less courage, desirous of honour, and furnished with the gifts of reason, policy, and wisdom.[1]

Holinshed's abbreviated version of Hall's contrast *might* have been enough to spark Shakespeare's imagination, but Hall's seems positively to invite dramatic treatment. And Hall may also have provided a hint for the Margaret/Suffolk relationship. There is no evidence that the historical Margaret and Suffolk were lovers, but their affair in the play may have been suggested by two phrases of Hall: 'the Queen, which entirely loved the Duke' and 'the Queen's darling, William Duke of Suffolk' (Appendix B, 3.2.293–303). The first phrase is in both Hall and Holinshed, but the second, arguably more intimate, occurs only in Hall. Even there, of course, 'darling' need not imply a sexual relationship, but the warmth of the phrase may have suggested the dramatic potential to Shakespeare.

Even so, there is evidence that Shakespeare consulted Holinshed as well as Hall, notably in a passage about the animosity between York and Somerset. Hall merely says that, in the dispute over the regentship of France which the play dramatizes in 1.3, Somerset was appointed Regent and York was discharged. Holinshed, however, offers background and motivation for Hall's bald statement of fact:

The Duke of York was established Regent of France . . . to continue in that office for the term of five years, which being expired, [York], as a man most meet to supply that room, [was] appointed . . . again as Regent of France.

[1] 1808 reprint, p. 210.

. . . But the Duke of Somerset, still maligning the Duke of York's advancement, . . . now wrought so, that the King revoked his grant made to the Duke of York. (pp. 208–9)

This passage underlies the dispute at 1.3.102–207, and Holinshed's phrase about York 'as a man most meet' for the office is specifically used by Duke Humphrey in the play: 'York is meetest man | To be your regent' (161–2). Again, at the end of the play, when the King and York negotiate before the battle of St Albans, the King sends Buckingham to York as his ambassador (4.9.37–8), as in Holinshed (p. 240); Hall has no reference to Buckingham here.

Shakespeare probably went to Holinshed for the details of the Peasants' Revolt against Richard II in 1381 which he introduces into the Jack Cade scenes, but which Hall does not describe because he begins his chronicle in 1399, at the end of Richard II's reign. But this information was also available in Richard Grafton's *A Chronicle at Large* (1569), which also reproduces entire stretches of Hall's narrative with only minor verbal variants. Geoffrey Bullough calls this 'plagiarism',[1] but in fact all the sixteenth-century chroniclers borrowed extensively from one another, often word for word, as Holinshed does from Hall; and despite some differences of emphasis here and there, they interpret the major events and crises in the same way, interpretations often carried over into the play, for example that the murder of Duke Humphrey had catastrophic consequences for those who contrived it, and that the removal of his strong government created a vacuum in which York could claim the throne. This is Hall's version:

the public wealth of the realm of England, by the unworthy death of this politic prince, sustained great loss and ran into ruin, for surely the whole weight and burden of the realm rested and depended upon him. . . . If this Duke had lived, the Duke of York durst not have made title to the crown; if this Duke had lived, the nobles had not conspired against the King, nor yet the commons had not rebelled; if this Duke had lived, the house of Lancaster had not been defaced and destroyed, which things happened all contrary by the destruction of this good man. (p. 210)

This passage lies behind Shakespeare's general conception of Duke Humphrey, and particularly behind his speeches at 3.1.142–94. After giving a condensed version of it, the 1587 Holinshed refers

[1] *Narrative and Dramatic Sources of Shakespeare*, 8 vols., vol. iii (1960), p. 12.

the reader to John Foxe's *Acts and Monuments* (1583) for a further example of Duke Humphrey's wisdom. If Shakespeare followed that reference up, he would have found the story of Duke Humphrey's exposure of the false miracle at St Albans, which he dramatizes in 2.1. But he could equally well have found it in Grafton (see Appendix B, 2.1.57–155); and since Grafton includes almost everything that Hall does, together with the false miracle episode and the information about the Peasants' Revolt of 1381, neither of which occurs in Hall, it could be argued that Grafton rather than Hall should be regarded as Shakespeare's principal source. Against that is the evidence of York's genealogy.

Since, as we have seen, Hall's aim is to show how the divisions of civil war were resolved in the 'union' of the two rival houses of York and Lancaster, he begins by setting out a genealogy of each house, tracing the origins of each back to the sons of King Edward III. He lists Edward's seven sons; he explains that Henry VI's claim to the crown derived from the fourth son, John of Gaunt, Duke of Lancaster; and that York could claim the throne because, although his father was only descended from the fifth son, Edmund Langley, Duke of York, his mother was descended from Edward III's *third* son, Lionel, Duke of Clarence, giving him, arguably, a prior claim. This is essentially what York argues at 2.2.10–52; and that the play's account derives from Hall is established by some near-identical phrasing: in lines 35–8, York says that Edward III's third son

> had issue Philippa, a daughter,
> Who married Edmund Mortimer, Earl of March;
> Edmund had issue Roger, Earl of March;
> Roger had issue Edmund, Anne, and Eleanor.

Hall says that Edward III's third son 'had issue Phillipe his only daughter, which was married to Edmund Mortimer, Earl of March, and had issue Roger Mortimer, Earl of March, which Roger had issue Edmund Mortimer, Earl of March, Anne, and Eleanor' (p. 2).[1] Grafton sets out the children of Edward III in tabular form, which is even clearer than Hall's version, but he doesn't include the crucial information that York's mother was descended from the third son of Edward III as Hall does.

---

[1] Holinshed inserts an extra 'Roger Mortimer' into the last line (p. 266), so it is clear that Shakespeare is following Hall here, not Holinshed.

The two principal modifications to the chronicle accounts in Part Two concern the Duchess of Gloucester's witchcraft and the battle sequence in Act 5. The disgrace and exile of the Duchess took place in 1441, four years before Margaret arrived in England; so the rivalry between them, and the fact that in the play the Duchess's disgrace is engineered by Suffolk as part of a larger plan to destroy Duke Humphrey, are invented for obvious dramatic reasons. The Duchess's fall is only briefly described by the chroniclers, and the dramatist may have supplemented it with her lament in the expanded version (1578) of *The Mirror for Magistrates* (1559), a series of verse-histories in which historical characters who came to unfortunate ends instruct rulers to profit from their example.[1] Apart from some smaller adjustments—as when Suffolk's banishment and death are made an immediate consequence of his arranging the murder of Duke Humphrey, rather than happening three years later—the other principal departure from Hall and Holinshed is the compression of a series of events taking place between 1451 (York's return from Ireland) and 1455 (the first battle of St Albans) into a continuous sequence as the climax of Act 5; but the idea for this treatment may have come from the earliest of the chronicles in English, Robert Fabyan's brief *New Chronicles of England and France* (published in 1516), which similarly condenses the events of these years.

The evidence is far from clear-cut, but I think it likely that Shakespeare read Hall and/or Grafton early in his career, perhaps while he was still 'a schoolmaster in the country' (see p. 69 below). When he came to write *2 Henry VI*, he probably consulted the most recent chronicle, the 1587 Holinshed. This simple procedure would account for the debts to the various chroniclers in the play; and in accordance with it, Hall is cited in Appendix B as the principal chronicle source, with Holinshed, Grafton, and to a much lesser extent Fabyan and *The Mirror for Magistrates*, as subsidiary sources.

History and Pseudo-history

How far do the Tudor chronicle accounts upon which Shakespeare drew present what modern historians might recognize as historical

---

[1] See Appendix B, 1.2.35–44. Many of the other characters in *The Mirror* also appear in *2 Henry VI*, but this material was taken from the chronicles, and so was already available to the dramatist.

fact? In the second edition of his book *Shakespeare's English Kings*, Peter Saccio says: 'One fascinating result of recent [historical] research and reinterpretation is that Shakespeare's account of the kings now seems closer than before to history as we now understand it.'[1] The main departures from historical 'fact' seem to lie in the chroniclers' and Shakespeare's treatment of Henry VI himself and of Duke Humphrey of Gloucester. The deeply religious, almost saint-like, image of Henry was, if not created, then actively encouraged by Henry VII, the victorious Richmond of *Richard III*. 'Once Henry VII ascended the throne in 1485, what he wanted for propaganda purposes was an ancestor worthy to have carried the precious blood of Lancaster: so, if Henry VI could not be portrayed as a successful ruler (as clearly he could not), then he must at least be a saintly one';[2] and Henry VII pressed the Pope unsuccessfully for his predecessor to be canonized. The image of Henry VI's sanctity as presented in the passage from Edward Hall quoted on p. 28 above ultimately derived from the Latin life of Henry by John Blacman, a Carthusian monk who had been Henry's chaplain. Most of the Tudor chroniclers, with the partial exception of the 1587 edition of Holinshed, followed Blacman in emphasizing Henry's saintliness and playing down his political incompetence and his periodic attacks of madness.

As noted above, Holinshed significantly modifies Hall's view of Henry, placing the blame for the Wars of the Roses much more squarely on the fact that Henry was 'too soft for governor of a kingdom', a view shared by most modern historians to a greater or lesser degree. But the contributors to the 1587 Holinshed go further.[3] Hall says that after Jack Cade's rebellion had been suppressed, the King 'mitigated his justice with mercy and compassion' (Appendix B, 4.9.15–21), and Shakespeare follows him. At first Holinshed appears to echo Hall: the King punished only the 'disordered ringleaders' and 'pardoned the ignorant and

---

[1] Oxford, 2000; p. vii. For historical information I have relied upon R. A. Griffiths, *The Reign of King Henry VI*, second edn. (Stroud, 1998). Bertram Wolffe offers a more disenchanted view of the King in his *Henry VI* (1981). Keith Dockray's *Henry VI, Margaret of Anjou and the Wars of the Roses: A Source Book* (Stroud, 2000) usefully reprints original documents in accessible form.

[2] Dockray (see previous note), p. xxiv.

[3] Holinshed died before the 1587 edition was completed, and other writers contributed to it; Abraham Fleming, for example, provided the passage quoted casting doubt on the King's compassion to the rebels, as the marginal annotations attest.

simple persons, to the great rejoicing of all his subjects'; but then the 1587 edition adds: 'But saith another, the King sent his commissioners into Kent, and caused enquiry to be made of this riot in Canterbury, wherefore the same eight men were judged and executed, and in other towns of Kent and Sussex was done the like execution' (p. 227). This hints at the historical fact that in 1451 the King personally presided over a retributive commission which sentenced so many to execution that it was known as the 'harvest of heads'.[1] This dents the image of the compassionate King.

Again, Holinshed, but not Hall, mentions the King's illness in 1453, 'which was so grievous, as it was said, that he lay senseless, and was not able for a time either to go or stand' (p. 238). As a marginal note acknowledges, the source here is a graphic account by Abbot Whethamsted of St Albans, a contemporary of Henry VI:

A disease and disorder of such a sort overcame the king that he lost his wits and memory for a time, and nearly all his body was so uncoordinated and out of control that he could neither walk, nor hold his head upright, nor easily move from where he sat. . . . [Henry VI was] his mother's stupid offspring, not his father's, a son greatly degenerated from the father, who did not cultivate the art of war . . . a mild-spoken, pious king, but half-witted in affairs of state.[2]

It is likely that Henry inherited his bouts of mental illness from his maternal grandfather, King Charles VI of France; they caused a serious constitutional crisis in 1453, and they modify the impression of Henry's saintly remoteness from political affairs, which may be attributable to another kind of 'innocence'. But if Shakespeare grasped the full implication of the account of the King's illness in the 1587 Holinshed, he seems to have made little or no use of it (but see the Commentary to 3.2.46–55). Rather, he followed Hall's view of Henry as a man of deep religious conviction but no political acumen, fatally married to his polar opposite.

If one of the Tudor chroniclers, at least, shows awareness of the less saintly side of Henry, they present a unanimously positive image of 'the good Duke Humphrey', as in the passage from Hall quoted on p. 30 above. It is true that the historical Humphrey had genuine virtues. He was a man of learning; but he was not the

---

[1] Griffiths, p. 649; Dockray, pp. 53, 58.
[2] Cited in Dockray, p. 6.

altruistic upholder of the well-being of the kingdom as in the play and in the chronicles. Though he was named Protector of the realm by the dying Henry V (see the Commentary to 2.3.34), his authority was less than that shown in the play, and it declined further after 1439, because he vigorously opposed Henry's policy of making peace with France; as the two of them increasingly grew apart, Cardinal Beaufort's influence over the King increased. After 1439, Humphrey was 'never again to return to the king's innermost counsels, even though until his death he remained heir presumptive to Henry's throne'.[1] The breach between Henry and Humphrey grew so great that the King almost certainly connived in his arrest at the Parliament of Bury St Edmunds in 1457, dramatized in 3.1, though not necessarily in his murder there. The suspicious circumstances of his death, however, seem to have been the chief reason why the myth of 'the good Duke Humphrey' grew up shortly afterwards. The Elizabethan chroniclers appear to have derived it, as they did much else, from the *Brut*, a history of England named after Brutus, the legendary first king of Britain, from those legendary times to 1475 and first printed by Caxton in 1480. This provides an uncompromising summary of Humphrey: 'This duke was a noble man and a great scholar, and had honourably ruled this realm to the king's advantage. No fault could ever be found in him.'[2] This is essentially Shakespeare's view, though he also emphasizes the destructive, or self-destructive, aspect of Humphrey, his turbulent temper and his feud with the Cardinal; but it is not the view of 'history'.

Shakespeare, however, is not primarily concerned with historical fact, but with a dramatic interpretation of it. But why, Robert Smallwood pertinently asks, choose to write plays about history at all? The 1623 Folio of Shakespeare's works divides the plays into comedies, tragedies, and histories; but by 1623 the 'history play' had become established largely because Shakespeare himself had written ten of them: in the early 1590s, as he was starting his writing career, there was no such genre. As F. P. Wilson points out, 'there is no certain evidence that any dramatist before the [defeat of the Spanish Armada in 1588] dared to put upon the public stage a play based upon English history. . . . So far as we know Shakespeare was the first popular dramatist to give dignity and

---

[1] Griffiths, p. 238.   [2] Cited in Dockray, p. 43.

coherence to the play on English history'.[1] Why did he do it? The answer, writes Smallwood, lies

in the man's fascination with politics . . . History is above all an exploration of human political behaviour, of the desire for power, of men's response to gaining it and to being deprived of it. . . . Shakespeare's 'use of history' consists, then, in selecting, shaping, amplifying, . . . chronicle material in order to intensify concentration on political issues and on their human consequences.[2]

That is why it is more accurate to speak of 'political plays' than 'history plays', and why Shakespeare's Henry and Humphrey are only partly the Henry and Humphrey of 'history'; Shakespeare takes what he needs from the chronicles of his time in order to create a bond of love and loyalty between the two characters which does not seem to have existed historically, so as to establish a strong positive force in *2 Henry VI*, to contrast with the more destructive elements, the incompatible marriage of Henry and Margaret, and the manoeuvres of the corrupt politicians against Humphrey. In doing so, he creates a complex theatrical experience which this introduction will try to focus a little further.

The Fall of Duke Humphrey

Even the titles of *2 Henry VI* in both the 1623 Folio and the 1594 Quarto point us in the right direction. The first page of text in each edition may have a different main title (*The Second Part of Henry the Sixth* in the Folio, *The First Part of the Contention of the Two Famous Houses of York and Lancaster* in the Quarto) but both agree about the sub-title: '*with the death of the good Duke Humphrey*'. Both texts recognize the centrality of this cataclysmic event to the first half of the play. But the Quarto's title-page goes further: '*And the banishment and death of the Duke of Suffolk, and the tragical end of the proud Cardinal of Winchester, with the notable rebellion of Jack Cade; and the Duke of York's first claim unto the crown.*' This is not simply a synopsis of the plot, though it is that; it emphasizes the structure of the play, which is that of a fall and a rise: the destruction of 'the good Duke Humphrey' leads inexorably to the destruction of those

---

[1] *Shakespearian and Other Studies*, ed. Helen Gardner (Oxford, 1969), pp. 9, 23.
[2] 'Shakespeare's use of history', in *The Cambridge Companion to Shakespeare Studies*, ed. Stanley Wells (Cambridge, 1986), 143–62; pp. 146–7.

who contrived it, Suffolk and the Cardinal; and the removal of Humphrey's strong central government leads to the rise of York, prepared for by the rebellion of Cade, and ultimately to the outbreak of the Wars of the Roses in Act 5.[1]

As John Barton put it when he was preparing the performing text of *The Wars of the Roses* in 1963, 'The central action concerns Henry's relationship with [Duke Humphrey of] Gloucester and their ultimate failure to help one another. Gloucester himself is the principal character . . .; he is conciliatory, unselfish, clear-sighted and able [but] he has a turbulent temper which is self-destructive and ultimately undoes him.'[2] Emrys Jones develops two implications of these points. The fall of Duke Humphrey comprises 'a tragedy in little, which, given its narrower dimensions in keeping with its place within the *Henry VI* trilogy, can be compared with the fully extended actions of such formal tragedies as *Titus Andronicus*, *Lear*, and *Coriolanus*'.[3] Part of his tragic stature derives, Jones continues, from the way he is dramatized as 'a *passionate* man, one subject to strong, even violent, feeling', from the opening moments of the play. When he realizes the cost of the marriage between Henry and Margaret agreed by Suffolk, he breaks off from reading the marriage articles in mid-word: 'the duchy of Anjou and the county of Maine shall be released and delivered to the King her fa—' (1.1.50–2). That interrupted 'fa—' is the Quarto's reading; the Folio text expands it to 'father', probably because the compositor took a manuscript 'fa.' for an abbreviation, thus muffing a powerful dramatic point which performance reveals. At the Old Vic in 1957, for example, Humphrey's 'spluttering fury' drew an instant reaction from Barbara Jefford's Margaret, who made it clear, 'from the mere flash of her eye, the tightening of her mouth, that he was doomed'.[4] When the King asks him what is wrong, he replies 'Some sudden qualm [illness] hath struck me at the heart' (1.1.54); later, after his wife is accused of witchcraft, he tells the Cardinal to stop 'afflict[ing] my heart' (2.1.177). The words 'qualm' and 'afflict' suggest a man taken ill, struck to the heart

---

[1] This structure is so strong that even when the three plays are reduced to a two-part version, with the Folio's *Second Part* split across the two evenings, its impact survives: the destruction of Duke Humphrey then becomes the climax of the first of the two plays thus created, while the rise of Cade and York makes a powerful start to the second.

[2] *The Wars of the Roses* (1970), p. xviii.　　[3] Jones, *Origins*, p. 35.

[4] Mary Clarke, *Shakespeare at the Old Vic 1957–8* (1958), no page numbers.

as if 'suffering from palpitations of painful grief'.[1] 'Qualm' can suggest mental as well as physical stress; *OED* gives another gloss, 'fit of sickening fear, misgiving . . .; a sudden sinking or faintness of heart' (*sb.*[3] 2 *transf.* a). In this respect Humphrey seems to anticipate, not only the intensity of the tragic heroes, but more specifically that of Leontes in *The Winter's Tale* when he is first struck down by a fit of jealousy: 'I have *tremor cordis* on me. My heart dances' (1.2.112). *Tremor cordis* ('palpitation of the heart') is a seventeenth-century medical term, representing 'some involuntary palpitation within the heart, a sign that something is wrong and, so it was thought, could be a sign of mental stress'.[2] Duke Humphrey seems to be suffering from something of the kind here, and like Leontes he is unable to control his passion even in public.

One way in which he attempts to control his temper is to leave without a word at 1.3.138.1: it is as if he simply does not trust himself to say anything at all. What has provoked this reaction is Margaret's suggestion that, for accepting bribes during the war with France, he runs the risk of execution, the climax of a series of charges hurled at him by Suffolk, the Cardinal, and Buckingham. As soon as he has left the stage, 'the explosive violence latent in the stage situation is at once converted into physical terms' as Margaret 'accidentally' strikes his wife.[3] The sense of the Queen and the nobles turning like a pack of dogs or wolves on Humphrey crops up again in the scene of his arrest (3.1), first before he appears, as the Queen and the court try to persuade Henry that he is a dangerous traitor, and then to his face when he appears and is arrested. The charges are the same in all three cases—misappropriation of public funds, accepting bribes leading to the loss of France, exceeding the laws of the land in executing offenders. The charges are so blatantly trumped-up and lacking in evidence that even a political innocent like the King is not taken in by them, and Duke Humphrey himself is easily able to dispose of them (3.1.104–35). Is the fact that such preposterous charges come three times a sign of dramatic weakness, the repetition a mark of an inexperienced dramatist? Peter Hall appears to have thought so when preparing *The Wars of the Roses* in 1963: 'I am a little foxed by

---

[1] Jones, *Origins*, p. 39.

[2] Private communication from Vivian Nutton of the Wellcombe Institute for the History of Science, cited in my *Shakespeare's Late Plays* (Oxford, 1990), p. 105.

[3] Jones, *Origins*, p. 41.

Gloucester's impeachment. It seems so very arbitrary.' But Hall then realized that this is the point of the accusations, and that he had resolved his own doubts: 'Perhaps this is good. Perhaps it will be like the praesidium suddenly accusing somebody of activities against the people without much need of backing. All the wolves join the pack.'[1] The threefold statement of the charges is not, therefore, a sign of dramatic incompetence, but is there to underline the very arbitrariness of which Hall speaks, as the politicians destroy their opponent under the guise of legality 'without much need of backing'—except, of course, the backing of force.

Because the charges are so obviously contrived, as even the conspirators themselves admit (3.1.241–2), they realize that they will have to use the force that is in their power to kill Duke Humphrey, and in a particularly pointed dramatic episode (3.1.223–81), they plot to do so. As at the start of the scene, Queen Margaret takes the initiative, insinuating that for the general good 'This Gloucester should be quickly rid the world' (3.1.233). The Cardinal thinks that he should 'be condemned by course of law' (l. 237), but Suffolk, who at *1 Henry VI* 2.4.7–9 had declared

> Faith, I have been a truant in the law,
> And never yet could frame my will to it,
> And therefore frame the law unto my will,

thrusts that argument aside, and, after an extended circumlocution comparing Humphrey to a fox killing lambs, comes to the point in dialogue that 'reaches an extreme point of callousness and blatancy':[2]

> do not stand on quillets how to slay him:
> Be it by gins, by snares, by subtlety,
> Sleeping or waking, 'tis no matter how,
> So he be dead.
>
> (3.1.261–4)

Those last four monosyllables pack a terrific punch.

The conspiracy is interrupted by a messenger with news of rebellion in Ireland. York is invited to lead an army to suppress it; and one of the most brilliantly ironic aspects of the scene is that the other conspirators are so obsessed with arranging Humphrey's murder that they fail to see the danger of providing York with

---

[1] *The Wars of the Roses* (1970), p. xix.   [2] Jones, *Origins*, p. 45.

soldiers, a danger he himself points out in the soliloquy that ends the scene: ''Twas men I lacked, and you will give them me' (3.1.345). So the mid-point of the play prepares for the climax, York's return to claim the crown. And because of the context, it is inseparably linked with the proposed death of Duke Humphrey: its consequences are beginning to be felt even before his death has happened.

As soon as it has happened, the consequences for those who engineered it are powerfully dramatized in the scenes that follow. By the end of 4.1, Suffolk and Margaret have been forced to part, the Cardinal has died in 'phantasmagoric guilt and terror', and Suffolk 'by malignant popular justice'.[1] What is more, in the scene of Suffolk's murder, we are made aware of wider consequences: the Lieutenant points out that 'the commons here in Kent are up in arms' (4.1.100); in the next scene they swarm on to the stage and the second half of the play, the rise of Cade, and through him York, has begun. This bold, simple structure of a fall and a rise gives 2 *Henry VI* its strong shape, and focuses the dramatic significance of the events.

Dramatic Style: Henry and Margaret

That dramatic significance is also brought out by the language, which has considerable range. Whereas the other two *Henry VI* plays are entirely in verse, here the extended verse speeches in the court scenes are set against the equally elaborate prose of Jack Cade's rebellion. This range helps to provide variety in a very long play (roughly three and a half hours in an uncut version). It is also, of course, an early play, and Shakespeare is still learning his craft as he goes along: the momentum is not sustained at every moment, and if the scenes vary in style, they also vary in accomplishment, from the sustained power of 3.1 throughout to the very elementary dialogue between York and Buckingham at 5.1.12–34 (see below, p. 57). Both the achievements and problems of that style can be demonstrated by considering two extended speeches: Henry's reaction to the arrest of Humphrey (3.1.202–22) and Margaret's to the discovery of the body (3.2.73–121).

To express his sense that his uncle is the 'map of honour, truth,

[1] Philip Brockbank, 'Shakespeare: His Histories, English and Roman', in *English Drama to 1710*, Sphere History, 3, ed. C. Ricks (1971), 166–99; p. 172.

and loyalty' (3.1.203), the 'harmless' victim of the Queen and the powerful lords who surround him, Henry uses one of the extended similes that occur often in this play. Humphrey is likened to a calf being slaughtered by a butcher (which vividly communicates Henry's instinct that his uncle's life is in danger even before the plot to kill him has been hatched):

> And as the butcher takes away the calf,
> And binds the wretch, and beats it when it strains,
> Bearing it to the bloody slaughterhouse,
> Even so remorseless have they borne him hence.
>
> (3.1.210–13)

He then develops the simile further to apply to himself:

> And as the dam runs lowing up and down,
> Looking the way her harmless young one went,
> And can do naught but wail her darling's loss,
> Even so myself bewails good Gloucester's case
> With sad unhelpful tears, and with dimmed eyes
> Look after him, and cannot do him good,
> So mighty are his vowèd enemies.
>
> (3.1.214–20)

In one way, this is a formal, 'artificial' speech, in that it is constructed upon an epic simile that runs through eleven lines; but a great deal of work is done in it. First, the choice of the simile of the calf and its mother beautifully catches the tenderness of Henry's relationship with his uncle, similar to the comparison used by Orlando in *As You Like It* to express his love for his old servant Adam: 'like a doe, I go to find my fawn | And give it food' (2.7.128–9). And when Henry develops it in the later part of the speech, he vividly conveys his feeling of helplessness: but that helplessness also contains an awareness that he is failing in his responsibilities as a king as well as a nephew. He ought to assert himself and protect his uncle whom he knows to be innocent (3.1.141), but he fails to do so; and this greatly increases his sense of guilt when Humphrey's murder is discovered. He is, in an important way, responsible for it.

That is why his reaction in 3.2 is so emotional, in the near-hysteria of his attack on Suffolk (3.2.39–55). When Margaret tries to defend Suffolk by implying that it is as absurd to accuse him as it would be to accuse herself of causing Humphrey's death, Henry ignores her and keeps his attention fixed on his uncle: 'Ah, woe is me for Gloucester, wretched man!' (3.2.72). This is the cue for the fifty-line speech in which Margaret argues that she is more wretched than Humphrey because Henry effectively rejects her in lamenting so much for his uncle. This speech is by far the longest in the play; it is central in its positioning (roughly half-way through) and its length suggests that it should also be central in significance and impact. But it constitutes perhaps the greatest puzzle in the play, since its dramatic purpose is far from clear. Perhaps it is simply a miscalculation by an inexperienced dramatist, and it is often drastically shortened in performance on that assumption, a process that may have begun in the Elizabethan performances, since only seven lines of it occur in the Quarto text.[1]

If Henry's speech is built upon an extended simile, Margaret's is more formal still, constructed out of traditional rhetorical devices. Lines 74–8 use three rhetorical questions, each one emphasizing Henry's neglect of her, or worse, that he wants her dead. Lines 82–113 conjure up an elaborate picture of her arrival in England during adverse weather: three more rhetorical questions follow (ll. 82–91) as the weather itself appears to be warning her against coming to England; but the tempest did not drown her, 'Knowing that thou wouldst have me drowned on shore' (l. 95). In lines 101–13 she stands on the storm-swept deck, trying to glimpse the 'chalky cliffs' of the south coast; then she throws a characteristically Elizabethan jewel—a heart 'bound in with diamonds'—into the sea, as an elaborate and artificial image of how she wished Henry's body might receive her own heart. Finally, in ll. 114–19, she uses a classical comparison typical of the play: before she came to England, she had often asked Suffolk to talk about Henry, as Ascanius talked about his heroic father Aeneas' exploits at the sack of Troy and after; the point is that Ascanius was at that stage in the story impersonated by the love-god Cupid, who tricked Queen Dido of Carthage into falling in love with Aeneas, as, Margaret implies, Suffolk tricked her into falling in love with Henry. And she ends as she began by emphasizing Henry's unkindness in preferring Humphrey to her: 'Die Margaret, | For Henry weeps that thou dost live so long' (120–1).

---

[1] But see the Textual Introduction, p. 97.

It is a rhetorical tour de force, but what is it for? Does it have a dramatic function? L. C. Knights proposes that its rhetoric is an indication of Margaret's insincerity: the rhetoric 'virtually tells us how to take the speech'.[1] One of her motives would then presumably be to try to deflect Henry from his instinctive awareness of Suffolk's complicity in the murder of Humphrey, an early, uneconomical version of Lady Macbeth's behaviour as she tries to distract attention from the risk of Macbeth's indiscretions revealing their complicity in the murder of Duncan (*Macbeth* 2.3.86–7, 118–19).

Another possibility is that the rhetoric is not 'insincere', but is an attempt to express Margaret's turbulent state of mind: the plot against Humphrey is not turning out at all in the simple way she and Suffolk had hoped; the King has reacted against Suffolk in a quite unexpected fashion, and it may be that her fear of losing both her lover and her control over the King is expressed in this speech. It is frustrating that most of it was cut in the playing text for *The Wars of the Roses* in 1963, since it would have been especially interesting to see Peggy Ashcroft handle it. In the absence of such evidence, I asked Peter Hall if he had tried out the whole speech with her in rehearsal, and if so what had emerged. He had, and felt that 'the speech is there to establish the emotional, hysterical side of Margaret's nature. I think that is why the language gets so extremely elaborate—it is an attempt by Margaret to contain her turbulent emotions by expressing them in such a strange way.'

On the other hand, in the BBC television production, where the speech is given uncut, Julia Foster uses it to intensify, rather than to contain, her emotion. She unleashes tremendous power at the start: 'Be woe for *me*' is blatantly selfish; 'I am no loathsome leper, look on me!' is furious with Henry. As she proceeds into the tempest passage, she colours the language ('nigh *wrecked* upon the sea', 'this *unkind* shore', '*cursed* the gentle gusts') to make the most of her resentful accusation: the god of the winds would not kill her, 'But left that hateful office unto *thee*'. It is a performance of great courage and conviction, watched in amazement by the court: by the end it seems clear that her marriage to Henry is, to borrow the language of the speech, on the rocks. For all its intensity, though,

---

[1] 'Rhetoric and insincerity', in *Shakespeare's Styles, Essays in honour of Kenneth Muir*, ed. P. Edwards, I.-S. Ewbank, and G. K. Hunter (Cambridge, 1980), 1–8; p. 4.

we remain aware of the effort involved, and of the length and difficulty of the speech.

Perhaps the most intriguing treatment came in Terry Hands's 1977 production. The speech was not given complete even there; some twenty lines were cut. But what remained was ingeniously handled. This production used the historical fact that Henry was subject to bouts of mental illness to interpret some difficult passages, beginning with his collapse at the news of Duke Humphrey's death. When he recovered consciousness, the extreme phrasing of the speech in which he rejects Suffolk (3.2.40–55) was interpreted as the utterance of a man in the grip of an attack of raging madness, perhaps following the belief that the insane have insights denied to the sane. In the face of that, Margaret's long speech became a desperate attempt to bring him round by talking him out of his fit. Henry sat staring in front of him, Alan Howard using his mannerism of a drooping lower lip to help suggest Henry's temporary loss of control, as Helen Mirren moved round him, delivering the speech (fig. 7). She paused several times, to give him the opportunity to react to her;[1] and his failure to respond made her ever more desperate, so that she added point after point in a frantic attempt to rouse him from his stupor. This was an ingenious interpretation of both the length and the style of the speech; but it depended upon a view of Henry for which director and actor had to look beyond the text. As always with this speech, the ultimate impression was one of strain.

Suffolk and Margaret

It is unfortunate that such an important dramatic consequence of Duke Humphrey's death as Margaret's long speech should involve uncertainty about how it should be interpreted; but there is nothing uncertain about the other consequences, least of all '*the banishment and death of the Duke of Suffolk*', to cite the Quarto's title-page. Too late to save Humphrey, Henry at last asserts his authority and banishes Suffolk. The power of the language in which he does so gives a glimpse of the king he might have been:

---

[1] Pauses are marked in the prompt-book, held at the Shakespeare Centre Library, Stratford-upon-Avon, after lines 73, 75, 81, 96, 100, and 109.

7. Margaret (Helen Mirren) tries to talk Henry (Alan Howard) out of an attack of madness (3.2.73–121) in Terry Hands's production, Stratford-upon-Avon, 1977.

> by his majesty I swear,
> Whose far unworthy deputy I am,
> He shall not breathe infection in this air
> But three days longer, on the pain of death. . . .
> Had I but said, I would have kept my word;
> But when I swear, it is irrevocable.
>
> (3.2.289–98)

From a man of such deep religious conviction, the allusions to the divine right of kings and the sacred, binding quality of an oath are solemn statements. When he leaves, there follows the great scene of the parting between Margaret and Suffolk, a high point in any performance. The King's banishment of Suffolk sets the seal on the incompatibility of his relationship with Margaret, as her furious reaction (ll. 304–8) attests. From this point, they are emotionally irreconcilable, both driven by their strong feelings for others: Henry's for his uncle, Margaret's for Suffolk.

At the start of their parting scene, Margaret turns her fury with the King on to Suffolk himself, upbraiding him for lacking the spirit to curse his enemies; but when he does so, it is with such venom that she has to restrain him, as the scene modulates from one extreme to another, from extended cursing to the quietness of Margaret's

> Give me thy hand,
> That I may dew it with my mournful tears;
> Nor let the rain of heaven wet this place
> To wash away my woeful monuments.
>
> (3.2.343–6)

In the lines that follow, she contradicts herself, urging him to be gone, yet immediately telling him not to, expressing the desperation she feels (3.2.356–9); and she concludes with one poignantly simple, summarizing line: 'Yet now farewell, and farewell life with thee.' Suffolk catches her tone:

> where thou art, there is the world itself, . . .
> And where thou art not, desolation.
>
> (3.2.366–8)

That final word seems to summarize the bleakness of their situation, caught in the trammels of what they have done in conspiring Humphrey's death.

That point is reinforced when their parting is interrupted by the news that Cardinal Beaufort is dying in agony, imagining that he sees Duke Humphrey's ghost (3.2.372–82), a situation that is graphically dramatized in the following scene. As the messenger leaves, Margaret speaks a line which refers to the news she has just heard, yet also seems to look beyond that situation: 'Ay me! What is this world? What news are these?' (3.2.384). As Julia Foster finely communicates in the BBC television version, Margaret momentarily glimpses the wider consequences of their plot to destroy Humphrey, both for the Cardinal and for themselves. But Margaret characteristically returns to her own situation in the following lines, urging Suffolk to be gone in order to save his life. He answers with special intimacy:

> If I depart from thee, I cannot live.
> And in thy sight to die, what were it else
> But like a pleasant slumber in thy lap?
>
> (3.2.392–4)

The primary meaning of 'die' here is the usual one: Suffolk would rather be killed in the Queen's presence than part from her. But

46

'die' and 'lap' could also have sexual connotations in Elizabethan English (see the Commentary), so this is the most overt allusion in the play to their affair, intensifying it at the very moment when it is coming to an end. The scene concludes with speeches which juxtapose elaborate language and great simplicity in a way characteristic of Shakespeare's later work. Margaret alludes to the classical messenger of the queen of the gods:

> wheresoe'er thou art in this world's globe
> I'll have an Iris that shall find thee out.

Then they share an utterly simple line: 'I go.'—'And take my heart with thee.' Suffolk's following description of her heart as

> A jewel, locked into the woefull'st cask
> That ever did contain a thing of worth

and of their parting as a 'splitted barque', a ship split in half in a storm, may recall the elaborate artifice of Margaret's long speech earlier in the scene, but in this condensed form it is surely a much more effective expression of feeling; and in any case its impact is enhanced by being set against the moving finality of their final, shared line: 'This way fall I to death.'—'This way for me.' (3.2.410-16)

It was at this point in the Stratford-upon-Avon production of 1963 (see fig. 8) that I felt the full force of Harold Hobson's comment in his review of it: 'one's mood is neither of judgement nor condemnation of these ambitious, unscrupulous, unhappy characters, but rather of sympathy . . . for people we have come to know' (*Sunday Times*, 21 July 1963). Hobson's reaction is supported by Mary Clarke, writing about the Old Vic's 1957 production: 'the scenes of human anguish . . . often roused in the audience an almost unwilling compassion'.[1] Whether the compassion was willing or not, the significant fact is that it was aroused (see fig. 9). There is nothing sentimental in the portrayal of Suffolk and Margaret: they have behaved as badly as anyone. But that is no reason for writing them off as characters, and Shakespeare doesn't do so. Even in this early play he shows the breadth of his compassion for his creations: while presenting them with analytic clarity, he also shows them from their own point of view, and does not pass external 'moral' judgements upon them.

---

[1] See p. 8 n. 2.

8. The parting of Margaret (Peggy Ashcroft) and Suffolk (Michael Craig)
in Peter Hall's production, Stratford-upon-Avon, 1963.

It is worth pausing to look back on the achievement of these
two scenes. Act 3 Scene 1 is a masterly scene, perhaps the most
effective in the play. It moves with great sense of purpose from
stage to stage: after the Queen and the lords have attempted to
poison Henry's mind against Humphrey, Somerset reports the
loss of France, so that a disaster in foreign policy is linked to the
imminence of another disaster at home as the court turn on
and arrest Humphrey; after his exit, the King laments his loss;
Margaret and the lords plot his death; then York is left alone to plan
his seizure of the crown. The scene is very skilfully laid out: some
of the speeches (e.g. the King's discussed above) are long, but
are sustained. The structure of 3.2 is even more ambitiously
planned to bring out the consequences of Humphrey's murder: the
King's hysteria; Margaret's huge speech reacting to it; Warwick's
description of Humphrey's dead body and his dispute with Suffolk,
during which the Cardinal is (probably) taken ill and has to be

9. The parting of Margaret (Barbara Jefford) and Suffolk (Derek Godfrey)
in Douglas Seale's production, Old Vic theatre, London, 1957.

helped off stage (see the Commentary to 3.2.185.1); the intervention of the commons to demand Suffolk's banishment; and finally
the parting of Margaret and Suffolk. It is not quite so sustained as
the previous scene, and perhaps some of it is over-extended: not
just Margaret's speech analysed above, but even her parting
from Suffolk, moving though that is. But the scene contains a
tremendous amount of incident and activity, and in both scenes
the shaping of the smaller dramatic units is on the whole as
securely planned and carried out as the larger fall-and-rise structure of the play.

Jack Cade's Rebellion

Up to the end of Act 3, the play is almost exclusively concerned with intrigue within the court; thereafter, the action broadens to involve the population at large, first with the murder of Suffolk in 4.1, and then in Jack Cade's rebellion. These scenes are both a contrast and a mirror to those at court since, as Philip Brockbank says, 'the virulent ambition and hostility to law that characterized the barons . . . equally characterize the workmen'.[1]

The scene of Suffolk's murder is in some respects a transition from the court world to that of the rebels, both in material and in style. Its transitional nature may help to explain the curious language of some of the Lieutenant's speeches, beginning with his opening lines:

> The gaudy, blabbing, and remorseful day
> Is crept into the bosom of the sea;
> And now loud-howling wolves arouse the jades
> That drag the tragic melancholy night;
> Who with their drowsy, slow, and flagging wings
> Clip dead men's graves, and from their misty jaws
> Breathe foul contagious darkness in the air.
>
> (4.1.1–7)

This is a curiously 'written-up' description of sunset and the coming on of night: the 'gaudy, blabbing' day, and the wolves howling at the dragons that are drawing the chariot of night so slowly that their huge, beating wings seem almost to catch on the gravestones, border on the grotesque.[2] That style recurs in the Lieutenant's attack on Suffolk later:

> By devilish policy art thou grown great,
> And like ambitious Sulla, overgorged
> With gobbets of thy mother's bleeding heart.
> By thee Anjou and Maine were sold to France.
>
> (4.1.83–6)

This sounds almost like a parody of the court's indignation in the opening scene at the surrender of Anjou and Maine as part of

---

[1] 'Shakespeare: His Histories, English and Roman' (see p. 40 n. 1), p. 172. See also Brockbank, 'The Frame of Disorder—*Henry VI*', in *Early Shakespeare*, ed. J. R. Brown and B. Harris (1961), 72–99.

[2] See the Commentary to l. 6 for an alternative reading which, if anything, increases the grotesque effect.

Margaret's marriage settlement. Both the element of grotesquerie and the apparent concern about the abuses of government which lead to the brutality of Suffolk's decapitation and the displaying of his severed head and headless corpse, anticipate the way in which Jack Cade and his followers use a grotesquely comic style to express their grievances over misgovernment which then become the reason, or the excuse, for acts of extreme violence.

The central dramatic issue of the Cade scenes concerns the relative importance of the comic and violent elements. What exactly is the 'tone' of these scenes, which has sometimes seemed elusive in performance? Jonathan Bate says that the 'groundling' or member of an Elizabethan audience standing in the yard nearest the stage 'would have seen himself mirrored on the stage. He would have seen a plain man speaking of new-dressing the commonwealth of England from below. The Cade sub-plot is about a potential revolution'.[1] But what kind of mirror image did the scenes offer that 'groundling'? There are certainly echoes of the popular disturbances in Shakespeare's day. Cade himself, who is not given a trade in the chronicles, is said to be a 'clothier' (4.2.4) or 'shearman' (4.2.124), one who works in the Kent cloth-making trade; and cloth-workers were associated with social unrest in Elizabethan England. But, as Jean Howard says, 'interpreting Cade and his actions is a complicated business'.[2]

Much of the Cade episode is broadly comic. Before he first appears, two of his supporters use the proverb 'Labour in thy vocation' to argue that this 'is as much to say as "Let the magistrates be labouring men"; and therefore should we be magistrates' (4.2.17–18). The chop-logic here presents an inversion of the usual structure of society, such as was associated with periods of holiday or celebration like the twelve days of Christmas, when accepted norms were inverted, servants became masters, and 'Lords of Misrule' were allowed to preside over a kind of licensed Saturnalia. This association has led to a currently influential interpretation of the Cade scenes in terms of the 'carnivalesque'. Stephen Longstaffe, for example, cites the description of carnivalesque laughter given by the Russian critic Mikhail Bakhtin: it 'is festive; it

---

[1] *The Genius of Shakespeare* (1997), p. 109.
[2] *The Norton Shakespeare Based on the Oxford Edition* (New York, 1997), p. 206. Her bibliography lists several articles relating the Cade scenes to contemporary popular unrest.

is universal in scope; it is directed at all and everyone, including the carnival's participants; it is ambivalent, it is gay, triumphant, and at the same time mocking, deriding. It asserts and denies, it buries and revives.'[1] Longstaffe relates this to Cade's first appearance where, in response to his claim to be a Mortimer, his followers mock him—in most editions, as asides (4.2.31–58). But interpreting the episode in the light of Bakhtin's definition, the rebels' comments do not need to be asides, as the Watermill production in 2001 made clear: the comments were overt, mocking statements, heard and relished by all. Neither Cade nor his followers really believed in his claim to be Mortimer; it was just a convenient excuse for riot and rebellion. In view of this very effective treatment, I felt that to print the rebels' comments as asides would be unduly prescriptive, and so departed from the editorial tradition.[2]

The 'carnivalesque' interpretation can certainly accommodate a passage like Cade's self-contradiction 'All the realm shall be in common . . . and when I am king, as king I will be' (4.2.63–5). The best comment on Cade's view of himself here as the king of a realm where everything is in common is made by Shakespeare at the other end of his career, when Antonio in *The Tempest* says of Gonzalo's wish to be king of *his* ideal commonwealth: 'The latter end of his commonwealth forgets the beginning' (2.1.163–4). But if, as the quotation from Bakhtin seems to imply, the essence of carnival is all-inclusive laughter, then I don't think it takes us far enough into the scenes, especially in the way they develop. For if these scenes are comic, they are surely black comedy, and very disturbing, as soon becomes clear in the attack on literacy in the Clerk of Chatham and Lord Saye episodes (4.2.78–101, 4.7.29–43).

Like so much else in this play, the attack on literacy has its grim resonances in our experience of modern 'revolutions'. When, for example, the fanatical nihilistic regime of Pol Pot in Cambodia reduced the country to 'killing fields' in 1975, the national library of the capital, Phnom Penh, was turned into a pig-sty, a symbolic condemnation of literacy. Such associations arise continuously during the Cade scenes. Perhaps the remark that a tanner 'shall

---

[1] '"A short report and not otherwise": Jack Cade in *2 Henry VI*', in *Shakespeare and Carnival*, ed. R. Knowles (1998), 13–35; p. 27.

[2] They are not designated as asides in the Folio, but since many necessary asides are not indicated in that volume, no conclusion can be drawn from the absence of such directions.

have the skins of our enemies to make dog's leather of' (4.2.23–4) is intended as a cruel joke, but it is hard to ignore its echo in the barbarism of our own times, when in the Nazi concentration camp at Buchenwald the skins of prisoners were used to make gloves and lampshades. When the rebels plan to 'break open the jails and let out the prisoners' (4.3.14–15), the source may be Elizabethan—Cade 'broke up the jails . . . and set at liberty a swarm of gallants . . . meet for his service' (see Appendix B)—but that is a depressingly familiar habit of revolutions and civil wars: on 27 March 1999, for example, *The Independent* reported that the Serbians released violent criminals from jails and sent them to commit atrocities in Kosovo. And there are plenty of examples of Cade-like violence nearer home. The BBC television production of *2 Henry VI* was influenced by 'the riots in this country now', when during hot summer evenings in 1981 unrest and setting buildings on fire in several cities led to a spate of 'imitative violence' elsewhere in the country. Twenty years later, similar rioting occurred in Bradford and Oldham. Often there are genuine grievances, some arising out of local tensions; but these easily become exploited and developed into mindless violence, as happens in the Cade scenes. Trevor Peacock, who played Cade in the television version, concluded: 'Though the plays are historical, they are about continual processes in human beings.'[1]

I draw these uncomfortable modern parallels because I think it important not to allow the savage cruelty of the Cade scenes to get lost in laughter, carnivalesque or otherwise. What is needed is to strike a balance between humour and violence. A relevant point here is that the characterization of Cade himself develops, or at least changes. When York first mentions him as his agent at 3.1.357–70, the personality that he describes—valiant, a nimble morris-dancer,[2] and subtle double-agent—is rather different from the Cade we actually meet: crude, brutal, illiterate. In this respect, the play is probably taking its cue from Hall's chronicle, where there is an even greater contrast, from the first description of Cade as a 'young man of a goodly stature and pregnant wit' to the 'bloody butcher' that he later becomes. In the play, Cade maintains his grim humour to the end, but as the rebellion becomes more and

---

[1] BBC TV Shakespeare edn. (1983), p. 27.

[2] This aspect has led to speculation that Cade was originally played by the morris-dancing comic actor Will Kemp; for an alternative candidate, see p. 66 below.

more successful, even capturing London and forcing the King to flee to the security of Kenilworth Castle, so Cade himself becomes more and more carried away by his own ambitions and sense of power—a clear parallel to, and parody of, the behaviour of Suffolk, York, and the other nobles earlier on.

The development in Cade emerges most powerfully in the scene of the interrogation and decapitation of Lord Saye, and especially in his long speech of accusation (4.7.23–44), which is as much a challenge to the verbal dexterity of the actor as the long verse speeches in the court scenes are. It starts with more grotesque humour, punning on Saye's name, and accusing him of treacherously negotiating with the French 'Dolphin', a mocking anglicization of 'Dauphin', whom Cade also derisively calls 'Mounsieur Buss-my-cue' ('Kiss-my-arse'). Gradually the speech builds in intensity, or mock-intensity, into a far more extended attack on literacy than that directed against the Clerk of Chatham earlier. The climactic accusation is that Saye has wrongly executed people because they could not read, whereas, Cade concludes, in his inverted value-system 'only for that cause they have been most worthy to live'. We have heard such charges before: they are a parody of those brought against Duke Humphrey earlier. Like Duke Humphrey, Saye is (against historical fact) a true public servant who defends himself but is murdered for his pains. Unlike Humphrey's enemies, however, Cade admits that Saye has made a good case, though he cynically overrides it: 'I feel remorse in myself with his words, but I'll bridle it. He shall die an it be but for pleading so well for his life' (4.7.99–100); and from this point Cade becomes more and more extreme, commanding his followers to decapitate Saye and his son-in-law 'and bring them both upon two poles hither', and insisting on the prerogatives of a king, including the *droit de seigneur*, a lord's right to sleep with the bride of any of his vassals on the wedding night (4.7.113–17). The climax comes when the heads of Saye and Cromer are carried on, displayed on poles: Cade insists that they be made to kiss, and then adds the grotesque joke: 'Now part them again, lest they consult about the giving up of some more towns in France' (4.7.124–5). Cade is here at the height of his power, and at his most monstrous. In his chronicle account, Hall says that 'with these two heads this bloody butcher entered into the city again, and in despite caused them in every street kiss together, to the great detestation of all the beholders' (Appendix B, 4.7.18–128). The play does not dramatize this 'detestation', but if it can be suggested in performance, it has the double advantage of emphasizing Cade's power-mania and of helping to explain how Buckingham and Clifford in the next scene manage to win the rebels away from Cade so easily (i.e. not entirely through Clifford's jingoistic appeal to their patriotism by recalling the memory of Henry V at 4.8.10–17, 34–52).

This development in Cade very much depends upon the playing, and in particular upon the delivery of Cade's extended speeches, as two contrasting performances may illustrate. Trevor Peacock in the BBC television production is a powerful actor, but he tends to fragment his speeches by pausing after each sentence and sometimes within sentences, so that rhythm and continuity are lost; as a result the scene with Lord Saye especially seems to last too long. Tony Bell in the Watermill version, far from breaking up the speeches, delivered them at an extraordinary speed, building accusation upon accusation in his interrogation of Lord Saye in a sustained crescendo; but he didn't stop there: the speed, and the taut rhythm, were sustained through his speech insisting on having the maidenheads of all new brides, to the amazement of his followers. This performance gave shape to Cade's role and illuminated the technique of his speeches: they emerged at once as virtuoso opportunities for the actor and as a demonstration of the intensifying megalomania of the character. And it made a wider point about these scenes. They depend upon a combination of laughter and hideous violence, but finding a point of balance between these extremes is not to be achieved by compromise. The answer seems to be to push the humour as far as it will go, and then to choke the audience's laughter on the hideousness of, say, the episode where the severed heads are made to kiss.

Before leaving Cade, a word about his destroyer, the Kentish squire Alexander Iden. This character, whose pleasure in his rural retreat may have been suggested by his name even without Holinshed's spelling 'Eden', has provoked the most divergent reactions. For E. M. W. Tillyard, he is a symbol of order, 'entirely content with his own station in the social hierarchy';[1] for Peter Roberts, reviewing the RSC's 1963 production, his 'smug self-esteem' might represent 'bourgeois complacency' (*Plays and*

---

[1] *Shakespeare's History Plays* (1944), Penguin reprint (1991), p. 159.

10. Jack Cade (Tony Bell) and butchers in Edward Hall's production, Watermill Theatre, Newbury, 2001.

Players, September 1963, p. 42); for Philip Hope-Wallace, reviewing the same production on its transfer to London, 'Squire Iden's almost accidental destruction of Jack Cade' was 'utterly irrelevant and delightful' (*Guardian*, 13 January 1964); and for Michael Hattaway in his Cambridge edition, 'the sincerity of Iden's commitment to the happy life away from court may be judged by the alacrity with which he grasps at preferment at 5.1.81' (p. 196). That last judgement seems a bit hard, since the King specifically commands him to 'attend on us' (5.1.80), and even then it is not certain if he stays: the Quarto gives him an exit, the Folio doesn't. Jane Howell, in her BBC television production, characteristically turns this textual uncertainty to dramatic advantage. Having characterized Iden in 4.10 as a matter-of-fact country gentleman out for an evening stroll, smoking his pipe which he unhurriedly taps out before disposing of the troublesome intruder who turns out to be Cade, she has him remain to witness the outbreak of the Wars of the Roses in 5.1. This finely-handled sequence, with each of the rival combatants caught in close-up as they assemble, ends with a fade to the troubled face of Iden, one of the many who will become embroiled in those wars.

The Outbreak of War

This edition, like others, is divided for convenience into acts and scenes, but they derive from the eighteenth-century editors: there are none in the Quarto and Folio texts. And 'Act 5' here could easily be regarded as a single long final scene, since the action is continuous, building to the outbreak of civil war at the battle of St Albans. When war breaks out, it does so very quickly: and it can do that because the ground has been so carefully prepared throughout the four long preceding 'acts'. This last act draws all the threads together. After the destruction of Duke Humphrey's government and the chaos created by Cade's rebellion, the public declaration of what the Quarto's title-page calls '*the Duke of York's first claim unto the crown*' becomes inevitable. This is important if the play is not to end in anti-climax. A comparison, and a contrast, may be drawn with the later history play which *2 Henry VI*, in its variety, its breadth of incident, and its interweaving of verse and prose, most anticipates: *Henry IV, Part 1*. This play has arguably the strongest, most unerring structure in the Shakespeare canon. It never falters for a moment, and is based on the rivalry between Prince Hal and Hotspur: it alternates, roughly, a Hal scene and a Hotspur scene throughout the play; they never meet until they confront each other on the battlefield at Shrewsbury, which the audience recognizes as the natural climax for which they have been waiting, and which is therefore absolutely satisfying. So the play never seems incomplete, although its title makes it clear that there is in fact more narrative to come in *Henry IV, Part 2* (which has a totally different, extremely sophisticated structure). But in the case of the present play, the audience is already aware from the title—whether the Folio's *Second Part of Henry the Sixth* or the Quarto's *First Part of the Contention*—that this play cannot dramatize all of the Wars of the Roses: there is more to come. Shakespeare's task, therefore, is to ensure that this final sequence is a genuine climax and not, as it were, a mere stopping-point. How does he do it?

At first, none too securely. True, York's return with his Irish army is a big moment which always arouses fresh interest in performance after the destruction of Cade, and the essence of this final episode is announced clearly from the outset:

> From Ireland thus comes York to claim his right,
> And pluck the crown from feeble Henry's head.
>
> (5.1.1–2)

But then the scene runs into dramatic shallows. York's dialogue with Buckingham (5.1.12–34) is very lame, especially his question 'Art thou a messenger, or come of pleasure?' (l. 16), and his huge aside, as he tries to contain his fury at being called a subject (23–31), with its astonishingly feeble concluding apology for feeling 'melancholy' (l. 34). This is such a far cry from the confident movement of 3.1, the scene of Humphrey's arrest, as to seem like another play altogether. But the scene recovers when they get down to business and York as usual uses his feud with Somerset as a stepping-stone to making his claim to the crown. He suffers a setback when Buckingham assures him that Somerset is in the Tower, so that his bluff is called and he has to dismiss his army, or some of it (see the Commentary to 5.1.47.1, 109–10). Interestingly and ironically, it is his adversary Queen Margaret who in effect comes to his rescue.

As so often during this play, Margaret serves as the catalyst for a crisis or an act of violence (e.g. 1.3.138–9, 3.1.4–65, 223 ff.)—this time for the outbreak of war. By freeing Somerset, and bringing him on stage with her, she compromises Buckingham's and Henry's guarantees, and provides York with the excuse he needs to drop his pretence and attack the King directly, since he can now accuse him of bad faith (5.1.91–105). The challenge to Henry's authority has at last been made, and war is inevitable. Shakespeare dramatizes the build-up to it, and so ends his play on a climactic, upbeat note, by a striking theatrical device, the gradual summoning and assembling on stage of the rival houses of York and Lancaster.

This assembly has great theatrical impact, and there is more than one way of staging it. The Folio text brings on the individual protagonists without supporting troops. This may simply be authorial shorthand, giving the essentials without bothering to specify details that are thought to be obvious, but it may be a deliberate decision. Terry Hands at Stratford-upon-Avon in 1977 took the Folio at its word, and brought the rival principals on stage unat-

tended; what is more, they fought the battle of St Albans themselves, without any supporting armies. This made a surprisingly
effective climax to the play, and it had the additional advantage of
emphasizing how the Wars of the Roses originated from the squabbles of a small group of aristocrats, a kind of family quarrel. The
success of this aspect of Hands's staging, in fact, made me wonder
if I should retain the Folio's 'protagonists only' approach, especially in an edition based firmly on the Folio; but in the end I weakened
and included, from the Quarto, the more conventional but
arguably less interesting drummers and soldiers to back them up,
partly because the rhythm of the drums helps to underpin the
increasing menace of the arrival of combatant after combatant,
and partly because the Quarto probably reflects at least *an*
Elizabethan staging.[1]

In some respects, the formal assembly of the Yorkist and
Lancastrian leaders is a theatrically more powerful event than the
battle of St Albans itself, whose staging is complicated by the fact
that the Folio and Quarto texts present the incidents in a different
order, and provide completely different versions of the dialogue
between York and Clifford before their combat at 5.2.19–30. The
relative advantages and disadvantages of the Folio and Quarto
versions are discussed as part of my textual hypothesis (Textual
Introduction, pp. 93–5). The Quarto's version of the York/Clifford
dialogue, given in Appendix A, Passage G, is not negligible. It
emphasizes the mortal enmity of York and Lancaster; but the Folio
allows a greater contrast between the York/Clifford chivalrous
exchange of compliments, each combatant capable of recognizing
the qualities of his enemy, and the subsequent breakdown of such
chivalry as civil war intensifies in *3 Henry VI*. That intensification is
anticipated in this play by Young Clifford's apocalyptic vision on
finding his father's corpse (5.2.40–5), which has seemed to

---

[1] The lack of agreement between Folio and Quarto about how many characters
are on stage imperils the attempts that have been made to work out how many
actors were needed for *2 Henry VI* in the Elizabethan theatre. Having participated in
the preparation of a production of *Henry VI* with a company of only eleven actors, I
am convinced that the way in which multiple casting is done will depend entirely on
local circumstances. No production will ever follow another's pattern *exactly*,
whether in 1591 or 2001. It seems to me impossible therefore to reach any firm conclusions about what happened in 1591 (or 1592 or 1593, when no doubt circumstances kept changing, as they do today), and so this edition does not offer a
speculative casting chart, not even one drawing upon my own experience.

commentators more mature in style than the rest of the play:[1] it may be that Shakespeare revised the scene in order to prepare more emphatically for the important part played by Young Clifford in avenging his father's death in the next play. But for the moment, as Young Clifford himself admits (5.2.84–90), the Lancastrians have to flee the battlefield, and the play ends with the triumph of the Yorkists. Warwick's final lines invite the drums and trumpets to celebrate that victory, simultaneously bringing a single play to a resounding conclusion and preparing the way for the next stage in the dramatization of the Wars of the Roses.

Date and Chronology

Both the earliest surviving allusions to Shakespeare in London— one certain, one probable—concern the *Henry VI* plays.

At some time before his death in poverty on 3 September 1592, the playwright Robert Greene, in *Greene's Groatsworth of Wit*, published after his death, warned his fellow dramatists to beware of

an upstart crow, beautified with our feathers, that with his 'tiger's heart wrapped in a player's hide' supposes he is as well able to bombast out a blank verse as the best of you; and being an absolute *Johannes Factotum* [Jack-of-all-trades] is in his own conceit the only Shake-scene in a country.[2]

'Shake-scene' is an unmistakable reference to Shakespeare; but the extremity of Greene's resentment renders him incoherent, so that it is not clear whether he is accusing Shakespeare of appropriating other writers' 'feathers' (their lines) as an actor or as a plagiarizing dramatist or both. But Greene's allusion to Shakespeare's 'tiger's heart wrapped in a player's hide' parodies a line from the scene in *3 Henry VI* in which York accuses Queen Margaret, who is sadistically tormenting him prior to killing him, of having a 'tiger's heart wrapped in a woman's hide' (1.4.138); here, Greene surely specifically resents Shakespeare's success as a writer, and since he expects the allusion to be picked up easily, he testifies to the fact that the line had become well known: this suggests that *3 Henry*

---

[1] For example, E. K. Chambers, *William Shakespeare: A Study of Facts and Problems*, 2 vols. (Oxford, 1930), i. 286.

[2] Reproduced in S. Schoenbaum, *William Shakespeare: A Documentary Life* (Oxford, 1975), p. 115.

VI must have been performed at latest earlier in 1592, and in any case before 23 June, when all theatres were closed by the government for fear of unrest concerning foreign communities in London, and particularly because of a serious outbreak of plague. It is a reasonable assumption that *2 Henry VI* was performed at roughly the same time, or earlier. How much earlier must be considered shortly.

The other allusion is more problematic. In his 'diary' or account book, Philip Henslowe, theatrical impresario and manager of the Rose theatre, notes that on 3 March 1592 Lord Strange's Men staged 'harey the vj' [*Harry VI*] at the Rose.[1] He marked it 'ne', usually taken to mean a new play, though perhaps sometimes a newly revised or even newly licensed one. It was clearly very successful, receiving fifteen performances, with two more in January 1593 when the plague abated somewhat and the theatres reopened for about five weeks. *Harry VI* was performed more often than any other play that season, with correspondingly good receipts. Could this have been the production of *3 Henry VI* whose success Greene so envied? It seems unlikely: when a version of *3 Henry VI* was published in an Octavo edition of 1595, it was entitled *The True Tragedy of Richard Duke of York*; and since one motive for publication must have been to cash in on the play's success, it could only have done that if it had used the title under which it was performed—which cannot therefore have been *Harry VI*. And since *2 Henry VI* was originally published in 1594 as *The First Part of the Contention betwixt the two Famous Houses of York and Lancaster*, it seems to be ruled out for the same reason. So if Henslowe's play was one of the three parts of *Henry VI*, and not a different play entirely, it must have been Part One. It is just possible that the large number of performances given implies that Strange's company performed all three parts of *Henry VI* at the Rose, but that is unlikely for two reasons: Henslowe seems usually to have specified in his diary a 'second part' of a multi-part play, but not necessarily a 'first part',[2] and he always refers to 'harey the vj [or 6]', without further qualification; and in any case *2* and *3 Henry VI* seem to have belonged to a different company.

The title-page of the Octavo edition of Part Three says that it was

[1] *Henslowe's Diary*, ed. R. A. Foakes and R. T. Rickert (Cambridge, 1961), p. 16.

[2] He differentiates, for example, between *Tamburlaine* and 'the second part of *Tamburlaine*' (*Henslowe's Diary*, p. 26).

performed by the Earl of Pembroke's servants (commonly known as Pembroke's Men). The title-page of the Quarto edition of Part Two does not specify a company, but since both were published by Thomas Millington, and exhibit the same textual features, which suggest a theatrical provenance, it is a fair assumption that Part Two was also performed by Pembroke's Men.[1]

We now, therefore, have *Henry VI* associated with two companies: Strange's and Pembroke's. To explore their relationship further requires a summary of the complicated state of the Elizabethan theatre scene in the early 1590s, as far as it concerns the *Henry VI* plays. Theatrical conditions in 1590–4 were exceptionally fluid, with companies forming and reforming, and actors now appearing with one, now another; but in the Christmas season at court in 1591–2, two months before they performed *Harry VI* at the Rose, Lord Strange's Men were clearly held in special esteem, since they gave what Andrew Gurr calls 'an unprecedented six performances'.[2] Maddeningly, we do not know what they performed. From early in 1591, Strange's company had included the leading actor of his time, Edward Alleyn. He and the rest of Strange's Men seem to have been performing at The Theatre, built by James Burbage in 1576; but in May 1591, Alleyn quarrelled with James Burbage, and departed to Henslowe's Rose theatre. It is a reasonable inference that James Burbage's son Richard, soon to be the leading actor of the Chamberlain's Men and therefore of Shakespeare's plays, remained with his father at the Theatre.

'It was this quarrel in May 1591', speculates John Dover Wilson in his edition of *2 Henry VI*, 'which led . . . to the formation of Pembroke's men'. He continues:

That Alleyn induced all the players in [Strange's] company to cross the Thames [to the Rose] with him seems unlikely. . . . Richard Burbage, who had been a member of it, almost certainly remained behind [and probably] persuaded a number of players to stay with him. If so, it would be necessary for him to find a fresh patron. . . . I suggest that the second Earl of Pembroke consented to lend his name and badge to the newly formed company.

---

[1] Neither title-page identifies Shakespeare as the author; but this has no particular significance, since nor do any of the other quartos of Shakespeare's plays published earlier than *Love's Labour's Lost* (1598).

[2] *The Shakespearian Playing Companies* (Oxford, 1996), p. 259.

He concludes that *2* and *3 Henry VI* 'originated at [James] Burbage's Theatre, and were being played in 1591–2 by a company calling itself Lord Pembroke's men and including Richard Burbage' (pp. xii–xiii). Andrew Gurr develops Dover Wilson's theory, adding the supporting evidence that James Burbage may have applied to Pembroke to sponsor a new company at the Theatre in place of the departed Strange's Men because Pembroke had had close associations with Robert Dudley, Earl of Leicester, to whose company Burbage had once belonged; so Pembroke 'was the obvious choice for a former Leicester's player to turn to as a new patron who was a senior noble, a Privy Councillor, and a playgoer, but who was not currently patronizing any of the major London companies.'[1] This plausibly accounts for the sudden appearance of Pembroke's Men in 1592, and for their surprisingly swift rise to a prominence equal to Strange's; for in the Christmas season at court in 1592–3, only two companies were invited to perform: Strange's gave three performances, Pembroke's two.[2] Yet Pembroke's decline was as swift as their rise: by the summer of 1593 they were bankrupt. Henslowe reports in a letter to Edward Alleyn of 28 September 1593[3] that they had disbanded and were in such financial difficulties that they were forced to pawn their costumes. It was probably as a consequence of these difficulties that versions of their texts of *2* and *3 Henry VI* were sold to Thomas Millington and came to be printed in the Quarto of 1594 and the Octavo of 1595.

But where was Shakespeare at this time? If Henslowe's *Harry VI* is Part One of *Henry VI*, he seems to have been connected with Strange's Men at the Rose; yet the title-page of the 1595 text of Part Three links that play, and by implication Part Two, and by further implication Shakespeare himself, with Pembroke's Men, speculatively at the Theatre.[4] Luckily, a solution to this difficulty is provided by the title-page of the First Quarto edition of *Titus Andronicus* (1594). Like the Quarto and Octavo of *2* and *3 Henry VI*, this does not mention an author, but it does say that *Titus* 'was played by the right honourable the Earl of Derby (= Strange), Earl of Pembroke,

---

[1] Gurr, pp. 267–8.

[2] E. K. Chambers, *The Elizabethan Stage*, 4 vols. (Oxford, 1923), iv. 164.

[3] *Henslowe's Diary*, p. 280.

[4] Of course, as Chambers says, 'it may be that for a time he was not attached as an actor to any company at all' (*Elizabethan Stage*, ii. 130)—nor, perhaps, as a dramatist.

and Earl of Sussex their servants'.[1] This has led to speculation that *Titus* was performed by these three companies jointly,[2] but the title-page of the Second Quarto of *Titus* (1600) seems to disprove that fairly conclusively, since as well as mentioning Pembroke's, Derby's/Strange's, and Sussex's companies, it adds the Lord Chamberlain's, a company formed when the theatres reopened after the plague closure in 1594, and to which Shakespeare belonged from its inception. Although it is possible that *Titus* was played by all three companies jointly first, and later by the Chamberlain's Men, the natural inference seems to me to be that *Titus* was performed by each of these companies in turn. This inference leads naturally to another: someone who owned the play (Richard Burbage? Shakespeare?)[3] moved from Strange's to Pembroke's; then, after Pembroke's disbanded in 1593, to Sussex's; and thence to the Chamberlain's in 1594. It is probable that *Henry VI* followed a similar route. Perhaps Parts Two and Three (or even all three parts) were written, or at any rate planned, for Lord Strange's company. But when Alleyn and some of Strange's Men left the Theatre for the Rose in May 1591, they may have taken Part One with them, in its present form or partly written, while Parts Two and Three were retained by the Burbages at the Theatre; if Wilson and Gurr are correct and Pembroke's company was created to play at the Theatre, that would explain how Pembroke's Men came to be in possession of Parts Two and Three, but not Part One. When Pembroke's Men disbanded in 1593, Parts Two and Three may have gone to Sussex's company as it appears *Titus* did, and thence to the newly-formed Chamberlain's in 1594. Perhaps, finally, Part One also came to the Chamberlain's from the Rose with those members of Strange's Men who joined the Chamberlain's,[4] thus providing

---

[1] E. K. Chambers, *William Shakespeare*, 2 vols. (Oxford, 1930), i. 312.

[2] David George, 'Shakespeare and Pembroke's Men', *SQ* 32 (1981), 305–23.

[3] In the Elizabethan theatre, a dramatist did not necessarily own a play he had written: ownership passed to the company who performed it, or to one or more of the 'sharers' (senior actors with responsibility for running the company). Gurr comments: 'That the Chamberlain's acquired so many of Shakespeare's pre-1594 plays is either a tribute to his self-esteem and the high value he put on his own plays, or to his commercial acumen in keeping possession of them for himself and not selling them to the companies. Either that, or his patron or some other agent with influence in the new set-up [the Chamberlain's Men] valued them enough to take them from their various owners for the new company' (p. 281).

[4] They included George Bryan, John Heminges, Will Kemp, Augustine Phillips, and Thomas Pope (Gurr, p. 279).

the two members of the Chamberlain's Men who compiled the First Folio in 1623 with the three texts that they needed.

At this point, another contemporary allusion becomes relevant. The central character of Part One is Lord Talbot, the valiant defender of Henry V's conquests against the French armies led by Joan la Pucelle (Joan of Arc). To modern audiences, the brilliant dramatization of Joan—partly an inspiration to the French, partly a witty ironist, partly in league with devils—is a more interesting character than the rather monotonous militarist Talbot. But that was probably not how most Elizabethan audiences regarded him. In his *Piers Penniless*, Thomas Nashe defends the theatre against its critics by arguing that it is an 'exercise of virtue', providing such inspiring examples as Talbot:

How would it have joyed brave Talbot, the terror of the French, to think that after he had lain two hundred years in his tomb, he should triumph again on the stage, and have his bones new embalmed with the tears of ten thousand spectators at least, at several times, who, in the tragedian that represents his person, imagine they behold him fresh bleeding?[1]

Piers Penniless was entered in the Register of the Stationers' Company on 8 August 1592, and it seems certain that Nashe is referring to the successful performances of *Harry VI* at the Rose earlier in the year. A little later in *Piers Penniless* he says that not even the classical 'tragedians' 'could ever perform more in action than famous Ned Alleyn'. Nashe doesn't actually say that Alleyn played Talbot, but the use of the word 'tragedian' in both contexts is suggestive, and since Alleyn had been the leading actor at the Rose at least since February 1592,[2] it is likely that he played the leading role in *1 Henry VI* there.

Alleyn may have appeared in the other two parts of *Henry VI* as well, at the Theatre, before he quarrelled with the Burbages. In his edition of Part Three in this series, Randall Martin argues that the phrase 'big-boned', which describes Warwick in the Octavo text, deriving from a performance, is a reference to Alleyn, 'who was known for his large stature';[3] since Warwick is the longest role in Part Three, this is a probable part for the leading actor of the company. He may well have played Warwick in Part Two as well, and

---

[1] *Works*, ed. R. B. McKerrow, revised F. P. Wilson, 5 vols. (Oxford, 1958), i. 212.
[2] *Henslowe's Diary*, p. 16.   [3] *Henry VI Part 3* (Oxford, 2001), p. 128.

11. Edward Alleyn, who may have created the roles of Jack Cade and Warwick.

doubled it with Jack Cade. At *3 Henry VI* 5.1.54, Warwick's hair is described as 'coal-black'; in his death speech in the next scene, he refers to 'The wrinkles in my brows, now filled with blood' and his Kingmaker's frown: 'who durst smile when Warwick bent his brow?' (5.2.19–22). All these characteristics come together in a description of Cade's severed head in the Quarto of Part Two:

> A visage stern, coal-black his curlèd locks,
> Deep-trenchèd furrows in his frowning brow
> Presageth warlike humours in his life.
>
> (2022–4)

These two similar descriptions of characters so dissimilar sound as if they might be describing the characteristics of a particular actor.[1] The description of Cade does not occur in the Folio text, so perhaps the lines were deleted when the casting changed. But there is evidence that the doubling of Cade and Warwick in Part Two was a standard procedure. In the Quarto, Warwick does not appear in the Cardinal's death scene (3.3) as he does in the Folio: the actor was probably preparing for his first appearance as Cade in 4.2.[2] In the Folio's version, Warwick is able to appear in 3.3, since 4.1 is so much longer in that text, allowing the actor more time to change. If Alleyn did play Cade and Warwick, then Parts Two and Three at least must have been on stage before the split of May 1591. And perhaps all three were, Alleyn taking his starring role of Talbot with him to the Rose, whether by agreement with the Burbages or not, with enough tinkering with the text of Part One to enable Henslowe to describe it as 'new' in March 1592.[3]

But a different interpretation of the scanty facts is possible. The prevailing modern view is that Part One was written *after* Parts Two and Three, in order to exploit their success, and that much of its fifth act, especially the introduction of Margaret for only a single scene (5.5), was added to link up with the opening scene of Part Two. This is entangled with another prevailing theory, that Shakespeare wrote very little of Part One. Shakespeare's authorship of all three parts has been questioned since the eighteenth century, usually on the grounds of their supposed inferiority. As so often, Dr Johnson, who accepted Shakespeare's authorship, brought robust common sense to bear on this issue: 'From mere inferiority nothing can be inferred; in the productions of wit there will be inequality.'[4] The early work of a writer is likely to be uneven; and if he is also an actor, regularly learning and repeating

---

[1] The portrait of Alleyn in Dulwich Picture Gallery (fig. 11) shows a dark brown beard; most of the hair is covered by a hat. Perhaps by 1626, the date of the painting and of Alleyn's death, the hair may have been affected by ageing and greying.

[2] Scott McMillin, 'Casting for Pembroke's Men: The *Henry VI* Quartos and *The Taming of a Shrew*', SQ 23 (1972), 141–59; p. 151.

[3] There is another sliver of evidence for the doubling of Warwick and Cade in the early performances. Since Cade's line about Henry in Q, 'I'll have his crown, tell him, ere it be long' (ll. 1678–9), does not correspond to anything in F at that point, Hattaway (pp. 230–2) thinks it might reflect material originally in the play but cut by the censor and so absent from F. But Cade's Q line is simply a confused memory of Warwick's line at *3 Henry VI* 3.3.232: 'And therefore I'll uncrown him ere't be long.' As often in 'reported' texts (see the Textual Introduction), an actor appears to bridge a gap in his memory of one part from another that he has played.

[4] *Plays*, 8 vols. (1765), v. 225.

other men's lines, he is likely, consciously or otherwise, sometimes
to echo the work of those other men.[1] This is a strong argument
against the use of parallel passages or phrases in an attempt to
demonstrate multiple authorship, as for example in Dover Wilson's
edition of Part Two.[2] But doubts continue to linger about Part One
in particular, so Gary Taylor, in a detailed and closely argued article, attempts to apply 'objective' criteria, a kind of literary finger-
printing, to Part One in order to try to establish whether more than
one hand can be distinguished, and, if possible, whose.[3] He concludes that the play is collaborative, written by a syndicate of four
dramatists: Nashe in Act 1 (so that when he applauds a Talbot play
he may in part be applauding his own achievement); Shakespeare
in 2.4 (the quarrel in the rose garden) and 4.2 to 4.7.32 (the aftermath of the roses quarrel, when York's and Somerset's refusal to
work together causes the deaths of Talbot and his son); and two
other unidentified authors.

Even 'objective' criteria can only establish probability, not certainty, and I have some (subjective) reservations about Taylor's
conclusions, based on theatrical experience. Taylor's distribution
denies to Shakespeare the meeting between Margaret and Suffolk
(Part One, 5.5) which so clearly prefigures what is to come in Part
Two, whether it was written before Part Two or added later to refer
back to Part Two. The tone of this episode seems to me that of

[1] Proof that Shakespeare was an actor, not just a dramatist, is provided by his
inclusion in the list of actors given in the First Folio of 1623, and of those who had
performed in Jonson's *Every Man in his Humour* (1598) and *Sejanus* (1603) in the
Folio edition of Jonson's plays in 1616.

[2] pp. xxviii–xxxv. These 'parallels' are, in any case, more impressive when taken
in bulk than when scrutinized individually: some of them are commonplaces or
catch-phrases, as Dover Wilson admits (p. xxix).

[3] 'Shakespeare and Others: The Authorship of *Henry the Sixth, Part One*',
Medieval and Renaissance Drama in England 7 (1995), 145–205. When some of these
tests are applied to Part Two, the results are inconclusive. 'You' and 'ye', the differing use of which Taylor draws on to differentiate between Shakespearian and non-
Shakespearian material in Part One, are used interchangeably in Part Two, for
example in Margaret's 'Can you not see, or will ye not observe' (3.1.4). The test
based upon 'function words which Shakespeare uses relatively consistently' neither
confirms nor discountenances Shakespeare's authorship of Part Two (*Textual Companion*, pp. 81, 86). Ants Oras's test drawing upon pause patterns in verse is in my
view invalidated because based on punctuation, which is as likely to be compositor-
ial as authorial. The Oxford editors conclude that 'stylistic tests which seem to work
well for other parts of the canon are ambiguous, or break down altogether' for the
early plays (*Textual Companion*, p. 107). In the face of such uncertainty, agnosticism
seems the safest policy, and the focus best placed on the play itself rather than on its
authorship.

Shakespearian comedy, as it seemed to Peggy Ashcroft, whose opinion is cited on p. 3 above. Conversely, Taylor allocates to Shakespeare what seems to me the most suspicious area of Part One, the deaths of the Talbots in chinking couplets (4.5.16–4.7.32); this is not simply a dramatically disappointing passage: as Emrys Jones points out, Shakespeare never uses heroic couplets 'elsewhere in a tragic passage'.[1] But I concede that this may point less to non-Shakespearian authorship than to 'a lack of authorial conviction' in Talbot's death scenes, which Jones finds 'somewhat unmovingly "official"'—perhaps because Shakespeare may have been writing to a commission.

It has been conjectured that Shakespeare began his career with Lord Strange's company, as a dramatist or an actor or both. It must be emphasized that none of the surviving documents naming, or conjecturally associated with, Strange's Men mentions Shakespeare. With that reservation, however, we may discuss probabilities.[2] We have no record of Shakespeare's whereabouts in the 'lost years' between the baptism of his twins at Stratford on 2 February 1585 and Greene's attack on him in 1592. Of the various legends that have subsequently grown up around him, much the most plausible is that given by William Beeston, son of Christopher Beeston, an actor in Shakespeare's company, that he was 'a schoolmaster in the country'.[3] E. A. J. Honigmann claims that this was in Lancashire, where Shakespeare became acquainted with the Stanley family, and that this is how he came to be writing for Lord Strange's company in London in the early 1590s.[4]

---

[1] Jones, *Origins*, p. 158.

[2] A 'plot' or theatrical outline of a now lost play, *The Second Part of the Seven Deadly Sins*, has been connected with Strange's Men because it was originally found among Edward Alleyn's papers at Dulwich College which he founded, and because it lists several actors who were identified as members of Strange's company in a Privy Council licence of 6 May 1593. (For both documents, see Chambers, *Elizabethan Stage*, ii. 123–6.) Other actors listed in the 'plot' include 'J. Holland' and 'John Sincler'. A John Holland is mentioned in the opening direction of the first Jack Cade scene (4.2) in the Folio text, 'Sinklo' in that of the Folio's 3 *Henry VI*, 3.1, as identifications of otherwise unnamed minor characters. If Shakespeare was using actors' names for characters as he wrote, that may provide a tenuous link with Strange's company; but since John Sincler joined the Chamberlain's Men some time after 1594, his name could have been jotted down on the manuscript for a revival. And 'John Holland' may not in fact refer to an actor at all: see the Commentary to 4.2.0.1.

[3] John Aubrey, *Brief Lives*, ed. O. L. Dick (Harmondsworth, 1962), p. 335.

[4] *Shakespeare: the 'Lost Years'*, revised edn. (Manchester, 1998).

The patron of Strange's Men was Ferdinando Stanley, Lord Strange. Andrew Gurr notes that the Stanley family 'had a long history in the English chronicles, claiming in their ancestry the two Talbots who fought in France against Joan of Arc' (p. 258). The Stanleys inherited the title of Lord Strange of Knockin in Shropshire when George Stanley married the heiress of the Strange family in 1479.[1] The younger sons of the Stranges held the title of Lord Strange of Blackmere, also in Shropshire, and this was the title inherited by Talbot from his niece in 1421.[2] It is mentioned in the resounding list of Talbot's titles delivered at *1 Henry VI* 4.7.60–71, derived from his actual epitaph in Rouen Cathedral. So it is possible that Lord Strange may have commissioned a play about Talbot, an earlier Lord Strange, either from a syndicate of dramatists, or from Shakespeare alone,[3] perhaps specifically for performance at the Rose in 1592, with concluding scenes about the Henry/Margaret marriage to link up with the other two parts. But if I am right in suggesting that Alleyn played Cade and Warwick before he quarrelled with the Burbages in 1591, then Parts Two and Three were also originally performed by Strange's Men. That raises the possibility that Strange could have asked for a Talbot play before May 1591—and even that it was written, wholly or in part, before Alleyn's departure. It may even have been *performed* by Strange's Men at the Theatre.[4] It is possible, therefore, that Shakespeare and/or others planned or actually wrote all three *Henry VI* plays for Strange's company to perform at the Theatre, and that the scenes in Part One that look forward to the events of Part Two were written then, rather than later, as is the current orthodoxy. In

---

[1] George Stanley was held hostage by Richard III and narrowly escaped execution at the battle of Bosworth in 1485 (*Richard III* 4.4.425–7, 5.6.72–6). In dramatizing the politically equivocal behaviour of George's father in *Richard III*, Shakespeare presents Lord Stanley in a more favourable light, perhaps to appeal to his descendant Lord Strange, as John Jowett points out in his edition of *Richard III* in this series, pp. 4–5.

[2] *The Complete Peerage*, ed. G. H. White, vol. xii (1953), 340–57, 620.

[3] The list of Talbot's titles at Rouen was, so far as we know, first published in Roger Cotton's *Armour of Proof* in 1596, too late for a play performed in 1592. Was this information supplied by Lord Strange himself?

[4] Slight support for this is provided by Peter Alexander's point that when the Quarto text of Part Two was put together (see the Textual Introduction, pp. 78–9), it contained echoes of Part One, suggesting that it too had been performed by the same actors (*Shakespeare's 'Henry VI' and 'Richard III'* (Cambridge, 1929), pp. 190–1).

short, the Folio's (historical) chronology may correspond to the order of composition, and the three plays may have been planned as a trilogy. This does not conflict with a theory of multiple authorship, since, as Gary Taylor says, 'Elizabethan plays were sometimes written by several authors after being plotted by one' (p. 153).[1]

But how likely is it that anyone would plan three plays dramatizing the reign of Henry VI in the early 1590s? Gary Taylor makes the case against a trilogy:

The work which started the vogue for two-part plays, *Tamburlaine*, was an artistic accident, prompted by the enormous success of the original play (which 'became' the first of two parts); in the years that followed, whether an envisaged second part materialized always depended upon the theatrical fortunes of the first. No one could *depend* on being allowed even two plays to dramatize his themes—let alone three. Since the use of English chronicle material itself apparently departed from theatrical tradition, the play's chances of theatrical success must have been even less predictable. To have planned a two-part play, drawn from modern English history, was itself a daring and original ambition; to have set out to write a trilogy would simply have been unrealistic. (p. 149)

In this account, Taylor moves from saying that it was unrealistic to plan a two-part play to saying that in fact Shakespeare was 'daring and original' enough to do so. May he not, then, have been sufficiently 'daring and original' to plan a trilogy?[2] But it is not necessary to go so far: a planned two-part play might have become extended in scope to accommodate a third, perhaps commissioned by Lord Strange about his putative ancestor Talbot.

In his introduction to *1 Henry VI* for a projected Oxford Shakespeare that he did not live to complete, R. B. McKerrow writes: 'If *2 Henry VI* was originally written to continue the First Part, it seems utterly incomprehensible that it should contain no

---

[1] Even if Shakespeare alone was commissioned to write Part One, there is no need to suppose that he began writing it from the opening scene on; if he had only written some scenes at the time of the quarrel in May 1591, but remained with the Burbages at the Theatre, other writers may have been brought in to finish it for performance at the Rose. That offers another possible explanation for multiple authorship.

[2] There was, in any case, precedent for a trilogy: Thomas Legge's *Richardus Tertius* (1579). Though written in Latin and performed privately at Cambridge, not in the public theatres, Legge's work was well enough known for Francis Meres in his *Palladis Tamia* (1598) to mention him as among 'our best for tragedy'. See Jones, *Origins*, pp. 139–41, and G. K. Hunter, 'Truth and Art in History Plays', *SS 42* (Cambridge, 1990), 15–24.

allusion to the prowess of Talbot, especially when such an excellent opportunity for this is offered as the passage in which Gloucester recounts the sacrifices made by the English nobility in the conquest of France' (1.1.74–102). Dover Wilson independently makes the same point in his edition of Part One (p. xiii). But Emrys Jones provides an interesting answer by focusing the *dramatic* requirements of the speech:

As Dover Wilson says, it is strange that Talbot finds no place in this list—until one sees that there might be a good reason for leaving him out. . . . It suits Gloucester to assume that York and Somerset were heroes of the French wars: the fact that in Part One they had helped to seal Talbot's doom is not relevant here [and when it is relevant, at 1.3.168–73, York does refer to it]; it is certainly inconvenient to remember it. For they are present and Talbot is not. . . . The whole tendency of the speech is to assert the heroic solidarity of the English lords which is now being shamefully undermined by Suffolk. . . . Shakespeare's usual procedure, especially in his opening scenes, is to throw the attention *forward*, excite anticipation, engage interest in what is happening *now* between the persons on stage. It would run entirely counter to this forward movement if we were to be thrown back to 'brave Talbot' and the previous play. . . . Far from proving that Part Two was written before Part One, the omission of Talbot's name here helps to prove the opposite.[1]

To Jones's argument from dramatic requirements, I might add a still more practical one: Duke Humphrey's naming of each of the lords as he addresses them helps the audience to identify them, help that is very necessary at the opening of a play with the largest number of characters in the Shakespeare canon. Raising the spectre of Talbot would have distracted from this to no dramatic gain.

McKerrow raises another apparent difficulty. In Part One, the use of red and white roses as the symbols of Lancaster and York is established in the invented scene in which Somerset and York pluck the roses. Part Two, McKerrow says, makes 'very little use' of this symbolism, whereas Part Three makes 'a great deal of use' of it. The implication is that Part One is closer to Part Three than to Part Two in order of composition, and probably subsequent to it. The facts are these. In Part One, after the quarrel in the rose garden (2.4), there are three references to characters wearing roses

[1] Jones, *Origins*, p. 137. Jones answers Dover Wilson's other objections at pp. 130–6.

(3.8.29–30; 4.1.91–3, 152); in Part Two, one reference (1.1.253); in Part Three, two references (1.2.33; 2.5.97–101). The third hardly constitutes 'a great deal of use' of the roses; but it is true that in the opening scene of Part Three in the 1595 text, the Yorkists wear white roses 'in their hats', the Lancastrians red roses in theirs. (There are no such directions anywhere in the Folio texts.) After the quarrel in the garden, the text of Part One implies that the rival characters wear red or white roses, as in the opening stage direction of the Octavo of Part Three. In the single reference in Part Two, York says that he will 'raise aloft the milk-white rose' in claiming the crown. The remark is obviously more pointed if he is wearing his white rose, and the fact that the 1594 Quarto has no stage directions like the Octavo's doesn't mean that the characters aren't wearing their rival roses, as they do in most modern productions. It seems impossible to argue anything about chronology from this apparent discrepancy.

McKerrow raises a more substantial point when he comments on the verse of the rose-plucking scene. Like Gary Taylor (pp. 164–5), he draws attention to 'the high percentage of feminine line-endings' (his figure is 25.3, Taylor's 24) and he adds that 'we do not find anything like so high a percentage until we come to *Much Ado About Nothing* with 21 or 23', according to different calculations, in 1598–9. McKerrow suggests from this similarity that the scene may have been a late addition, or—more probably, since a version of the roses quarrel must have been in the play from the start in view of the later references to it—that it was revised, and by Shakespeare himself. This would accord with evidence for revision discernible in the Folio texts of the other two parts discussed by Randall Martin in his edition of Part Three in this series,[1] and in the Textual Introduction below, pp. 87–98.

A further possible link with 1598–9 occurs in the closing lines of *Henry V*, where the Chorus alludes to plays about the reign of Henry VI, 'Which oft our stage hath shown' (Epilogue, 13–14). *Much Ado About Nothing* and *Henry V* were probably written in 1598–9. Was it decided to revive the *Henry VI* plays in the winter of 1598–9, for which Shakespeare made his revisions, to accompany the new play about Henry V—in which case 'Which oft our stage

---

[1] pp. 113–23. See also his article '*The True Tragedy of Richard Duke of York* and *Henry VI Part Three*: Report and Revision', *RES* 53 (2002), 8–30.

hath shown' would refer to *recent* productions, rather than to those as far away as 1591–2? One other piece of evidence might offer (negative) support for this date. In his *Palladis Tamia*, Francis Meres lists all Shakespeare's plays which a modern consensus dates earlier than *Much Ado* except *Henry VI* and *The Taming of the Shrew*, perhaps because these had not been revived since the early 1590s, so that Meres may not have been aware of them. (He was still at Oxford in 1593, and is first recorded as living in London in 1597.)[1] The date of *Palladis Tamia* (September 1598) might help to date a possible revival and revision of *Henry VI* after that, perhaps in the winter of 1598–9. Such a revival might also have been the time at which they became known as *Henry VI*, Parts One, Two, and Three. If so, whatever may have been their original titles in 1591–2, that would explain the titles given to them when Heminges and Condell, members of Shakespeare's company, came to include them in the First Folio of 1623, since these would have been the titles by which Heminges and Condell knew and had performed in them.[2] The meagre facts point to a date of composition for the three *Henry VI* plays, in whatever order, of probably 1591–2, with a likely revision for revival in 1598–9. The question of revision conveniently brings us to the Textual Introduction.

---

[1] *Textual Companion*, p. 91.

[2] The plays must in any case have been known as *Henry VI*, and not the earlier titles, by 19 April 1602, when the Stationers' Register records the transfer of copyright from Thomas Millington to Thomas Pavier of 'The firste and Second parte of Henry the vj' (i.e. Parts 2 and 3, which Pavier eventually published in 1619).

TEXTUAL INTRODUCTION

THERE are two principal early texts of *Henry VI, Part 2*, that printed in a Quarto edition in 1594 under the title *The First Part of the Contention betwixt the two Famous Houses of York and Lancaster* (Q), and that in the First Folio of Shakespeare's plays in 1623 (F).[1] The relation between the Quarto and the Folio texts is complicated and still in dispute; but since an editor's view of that relation inevitably influences the text that is chosen, the textual situation needs to be discussed in some detail.

Q is roughly a third shorter than F, and differs from it in most of its readings, even though the basic material of each scene is the same. Only a handful of passages is identical in the two texts. Q's brevity is partly accounted for by the absence of short passages that involve figurative expressions or extended comparisons, for example those to the treachery of snakes and serpents that run like a motif through the Folio text, e.g. 3.1.228–30 / TLN 1530–2; 3.2.47 / TLN 1747; 3.2.76 / TLN 1776; 3.2.261–8 / TLN 1971–8.[2]

The Folio also contains several longer passages which are absent in the Quarto, and it will be useful to have a summary of them:[3]

---

[1] The publisher Thomas Millington entered *The First Part of the Contention* in the Register of the Stationers' Company to secure his entitlement on 12 March 1594. He reprinted it in 1600, but the Stationers' Register testifies that on 19 April 1602 he transferred his rights in the play to Thomas Pavier, who published the third Quarto in 1619. This was printed by William Jaggard, who four years later printed the First Folio.

[2] References to the Folio text use the through line numbering (TLN) in Charlton Hinman, *The Norton Facsimile: The First Folio of Shakespeare* (second edition, 1996), those to the Quarto the line numbering of *The First Part of the Contention (1594)*, ed. William Montgomery, The Malone Society Reprints (Oxford, 1985). The spelling has been modernized, since the arguments do not usually depend upon the original typography or layout. When they do, as at 4.1, the TLN numbers given precede those to the present edition; otherwise, for ease of reference, the line numbers of this edition are given first.

[3] In compiling this list, I have excluded anything of which there might be the slightest hint in Q. For example, although the King's F speech 3.1.66–73 / TLN 1360–7 seems to be completely absent from Q, a version of his phrase 'As is the sucking lamb or harmless dove' appears in his Q phrase 'as the sucking child or harmless lamb' in a later scene (Q, line 1207); and although half of Salisbury's message from the commons to the King (3.2.252–71 / TLN 1962–81) appears to be absent from Q,

(a) The first half of York's soliloquy ending the opening scene (1.1.213–34 / TLN 226–47).

(b) The King's long speech lamenting that he is unable to help Duke Humphrey (3.1.199–220 / TLN 1500–21).

(c) Margaret's huge speech after the discovery of Duke Humphrey's body from 3.2.87 / TLN 1787.

(d) The King's lament for Humphrey (3.2.136–48 / TLN 1838–51).

(e) The Lieutenant's accusation that Suffolk has caused the loss of France and imminent rebellion (4.1.79–103 / TLN 2247–71).

(f) All but five lines of Lord Saye's self-defence to Cade and the rebels (4.7.55–98 / TLN 2692–2737).

(g) Cade's soliloquy that opens his death scene (4.10.1–15 / TLN 2906–19).

(h) The passage that includes Salisbury's excuse for his oath-breaking (5.1.149–91 / TLN 3148–91).

(i) Almost all of Young Clifford's lament for his father's death (5.2.31–51 / TLN 3253–73).

Does the absence of these passages in Q suggest deliberate omission (perhaps cutting) in Q, or addition in F, or a mixture of the two?

There are also several occasions where F and Q present different versions of the *material*. These are as follows:

(a) Queen Margaret's first speech is completely different in the two texts (1.1.24–31; Appendix A, Passage A).

(b) In the witchcraft scene (1.4), Q adds a passage after the spirit's descent not in F (Appendix A, Passage B).

(c) The spirit's prophecies in 1.4 are read out by York in F, but by the King in the next scene in Q (Appendix A, Passage C).

(d) The plot to murder Duke Humphrey, and the plans to deal with the Irish rebellion, are differently handled in F and Q (3.1.223–330; Appendix A, Passage D).

(e) Duke Humphrey's murder at the start of 3.2 takes place on stage in Q, but is only reported in F (Appendix A, Passage E).

Q's odd phrase 'That they will err from your highness' person' (1326) seems to recall their declaration that, far from having 'a stubborn opposite intent, | As being thought to contradict your liking', they have a 'care of your most royal person' (3.2.253–6 / TLN 1963–6).

(f) The scene of Suffolk's murder (4.1) is considerably shortened in Q, which presents the text in a different order, and Q's 'Captain' is a 'Lieutenant' in F.

(g) After 4.7.117 in this edition, Q includes a passage mingling bawdry and violence that is not present in F (Appendix A, Passage F).

(h) In 4.10, Iden confronts Cade alone in F; in Q he is attended by five servants.

(i) In the course of apparently shortening F's version of 5.1, Q stages the assembly of the rival factions differently.

(j) In the battle sequence (5.2), the individual episodes are in a different order, and

(k) The combat between York and Old Clifford is completely different in each text (5.2.19–30; Appendix A, Passage G).

Not all the differences in these two lists are of equal importance; I focus the more significant in the discussion that follows.

The relation between the two texts has generated much speculation. There are two main arguments, both dating from the eighteenth century. In 1765 Dr Johnson, comparing the Quarto and Folio texts (and also the Octavo and Folio texts of *Henry VI, Part 3*), found the Quarto and Octavo versions 'so apparently imperfect and mutilated, that there is no reason for supposing them the first draughts of *Shakespeare*. I am inclined to believe them copies taken by some auditor . . . during the representation'.[1] Johnson here anticipates the influential modern view that the shorter texts are reports of fuller Shakespearian originals, except that actors have, more plausibly, replaced 'auditors' as the reporting agents. Edmond Malone initially shared Johnson's view, but, in his edition of Shakespeare in 1790, he included a 'Dissertation on the Three Parts of *King Henry VI*' which argued that the Quarto and Octavo did not contain 'an imperfect exhibition of the lines in the Folio', but indicated rather that 'Shakespeare wrote *two* plays' on the subject, 'a hasty sketch', and a 'more finished performance; or else . . . that he formed the [Quarto] on a foundation laid by another writer'.[2] Malone's view that the Quarto is a sketch, perhaps building upon the work of other Elizabethan dramatists (because those

---

[1] *Plays*, 8 vols. (1765), v. 225.
[2] *Plays and Poems*, 10 vols. (1790), vi. 412.

writers are so frequently echoed) broadly held the field until 1928–9, when Peter Alexander and Madeleine Doran independently argued that the Quarto is a 'reported' text, put together from memory by actors who had appeared in the play.[1] This view in its turn largely prevailed, and still prevails, though the whole theory of memorial transmission has been increasingly challenged in recent years, in favour of Malone's view that 'Shakespeare wrote *two* plays on the present subject', so that, for example, Q and F can be seen as texts of equal validity. The most vigorous exponent of this view is Steven Urkowitz, who derides the idea of the reporters' 'supposed desecrations of Shakespeare's supposedly perfect playscripts'.[2] In this contemptuous phrase, Urkowitz implies that belief in a reported text also involves belief in an unchanging original, a 'supposedly perfect playscript' by an author who never modified or revised what he wrote. This creates an entirely false antithesis; and I shall argue that while the textual features of Q are only explicable in terms of a reported text, features of F show unmistakable signs of Shakespearian revision.

Q as a reported text

Urkowitz focuses his attack on Peter Alexander's work; and since he accuses Alexander of 'ignoring surrounding contexts' (p. 232), I have attempted elsewhere to take up the challenge and to scrutinize complete scenes to establish whether or not Q's versions are reports.[3] There is insufficient space for such scrutiny here, but since the theory of memorial transmission has come under fire recently, it is necessary to cite the examples which demonstrate it most decisively.

The linchpin of Alexander's case (and of Urkowitz's attack on it) concerns the genealogy presented by York to show that his claim to the crown was better than Henry VI's because, while Henry was

---

[1] Peter Alexander, *Shakespeare's 'Henry VI' and 'Richard III'* (Cambridge, 1929); Madeleine Doran, *Henry VI, Parts II and III: Their Relation to the Contention and the True Tragedy* (Iowa, 1928).

[2] ' "If I mistake in those foundations which I build upon": Peter Alexander's textual analysis of *Henry VI Parts 2 and 3*', *English Literary Renaissance* 18 (1988), 230–56; p. 244.

[3] 'The Quarto and Folio Texts of *2 Henry VI*: A Reconsideration', *RES* 51 (2000), 193–207. Much of what follows draws upon this article, but considerably develops its central arguments.

descended from the fourth son of Edward III, York's mother was descended from the third (2.2.10–52). Both F and Q make this point. But Alexander pointed out that York's genealogy in Q also contains a factual error which is incompatible with the main thrust of York's argument. In Q, York mistakenly says that the second son of Edward III was 'Edmund of Langley, | Duke of York' (746–7), whereas F correctly identifies William of Hatfield as the second son, and Edmund Langley, Duke of York, as the fifth son (which was why York couldn't claim the crown from his York ancestors, his father's line, but had to do so through his mother's line, descended from the third son). But, Alexander comments, 'by making him declare his ancestor the Duke of York to be *second* son to Edward III', Q 'renders further argument superfluous; he had now no need to claim the throne through a daughter of the *third* son as he proceeds to do' (p. 62, my italics). Urkowitz disputes Alexander's point on the grounds that York in Q doesn't *specifically* 'mention his own lineal descent from Edmund of Langley' (p. 237), that is, he doesn't say something like 'The second son was Duke of York, and I am descended from him'. But any audience might reasonably be expected to draw the (historically correct) conclusion that one York was descended from the other, and if Q York's ancestor had been the second son, there would have been no need to make a case at all: his claim to the throne would have been established. The point is that Q, but not F, presents a contradictory account which no competent author would provide. The Oxford editors spell it out: 'No one who understood what he was writing— that is, no author—could have made this error, but someone parroting someone else's work, of which he himself had but a dim understanding—that is, a reporter—easily could' (*Textual Companion*, p. 175). Alexander's case stands.[1]

I have set out the evidence that the opening scene of Q is a report in my *RES* article; the case for 1.3 is clearer still, beginning with the Queen's long speech to Suffolk (1.3.43–65). This is the Quarto's version:

---

[1] The contradictions in Q1's genealogy were obvious to Pavier, the publisher of Q3 in 1619, who thought them important enough to have them corrected—by reference to Holinshed's account of Edward III's descendants, since the repeated phrase that some of Edward's heirs 'died young' is common to Q3 and Holinshed, but does not occur in Hall, Q1, or F. See R. B. McKerrow, 'A Note on *Henry VI, Part II*, and *The Contention of York and Lancaster*', *RES* 9 (1933), 157–69; p. 164.

> My lord of Suffolk, you may see by this
> The commons' loves unto that haughty Duke,
> That seeks to him more than to King Henry,
> Whose eyes are always poring on his book,
> And ne'er regards the honour of his name,
> But still must be protected like a child,
> And governèd by that ambitious Duke,
> That scarce will move his cap nor speak to us;
> And his proud wife, high minded Eleanor,
> That ruffles it with such a troop of ladies,
> As strangers in the court takes her for the Queen.
> The other day she vaunted to her maids,
> That the very train of her worst gown
> Was worth more wealth than all my father's lands:
> Can any grief of mind be like to this?
> I tell thee, Poole, when thou didst run at tilt,
> And stol'st away our ladies' hearts in France,
> I thought King Henry had been like to thee,
> Or else thou hadst not brought me out of France.
>
> (343–61)

In the Folio version of this speech, the Queen says nothing about 'The commons' loves unto that haughty Duke'; but in her next long speech of complaint in F, she describes how 'By flattery hath he won the commons' hearts' (3.1.28 / TLN 1322). Her complaint in Q that the King 'still must be protected like a child' has no equivalent at this point in F; but at F 2.3.28–9 / TLN 1083–4, she says:

> I see no reason why a king of years
> Should be to be protected like a child.

Again, her complaint in Q that Humphrey 'scarce will move his cap nor speak to us' has no equivalent at this point in F; but in her later complaint in F she says that

> He knits his brow, and shows an angry eye,
> And passeth by with stiff unbowèd knee,
> Disdaining duty that to us belongs.
>
> (3.1.15–17 / TLN 1309–11)

The Q speech then jumps from Humphrey to his wife Eleanor, introducing a shorter version of a passage that occurs in F four speeches later (1.3.76–88 / TLN 461–73), and only then includes

80

the material about Suffolk participating in a tournament and stealing away the ladies' hearts of France that comes much earlier in F (1.3.51–5 / TLN 436–40). Is Q's speech an example of what Urkowitz calls 'finely Shakespearean . . . first choices recorded in the Quarto' (p. 243), containing lines or material subsequently moved to different contexts; or is it a piece of cobbling, attempting to reconstruct a dimly remembered speech with material from disparate places?[1]

The rest of the scene supports the second alternative. When the King and the court arrive, there is a discussion, in both texts, about whether York or Somerset should be the regent in France; in F this leads to the first of several mass attacks on Duke Humphrey and his protectorship. The climactic accusation is characteristically delivered by the Queen:

> Thy sale of offices and towns in France—
> If they were known, as the suspect is great—
> Would make thee quickly hop without thy head.
> (1.3.136–8 / TLN 525–7)

This overt threat to Humphrey's life leaves him speechless with rage, and he storms offstage. Margaret presses her advantage, 'accidentally' giving his wife a box on the ear. Eleanor too storms off; Humphrey reappears, having calmed down 'With walking once about the quadrangle' (1.3.154 / TLN 548), and tries to get back to business by recommending York as regent of France; but Suffolk counters by producing the Armourer and his Man who accused him of advancing York's claim to the throne; so Humphrey recommends Somerset as regent instead, 'Because in York this breeds suspicion' (1.3.207 / TLN 603), and a date is set for the trial by combat between the Armourer and his Man.

In F, the sequence of events is absolutely logical, and the angry exit and calmer reappearance of Humphrey are adequately motivated. Q corresponds quite closely to F up to the point where the Queen and the court turn on Humphrey, when Suffolk abruptly switches back to the question of the regentship:

---

[1] Just as Margaret's Q speech here anticipates details from her F speech in 3.1, Q's version of that later speech reverses the process, drawing on lines spoken earlier in F: so Q 996–9, about the Commons calling Humphrey 'the good Duke', come from the Cardinal's speech at 1.1.157–61 / TLN 165–9.

> The common state
> Doth as we see all wholly go to wrack
> And millions of treasure hath been spent,
> And as for the regentship of France,
> I say Somerset is more worthy than York.
>
> (395–9)

Q then omits the accusations against Humphrey which culminate in Margaret's threat to his life in F, so that he has no reason to leave. Instead Suffolk introduces the Armourer and his Man at this point; Humphrey arranges for their trial by combat, and for no apparent reason leaves the stage. The Queen then strikes his wife, who departs. Humphrey reappears and announces:

> For that these words the armourer should speak
> Doth breed suspicion on the part of York,
> Let Somerset be regent over the French.
>
> (464–6)

It is not hard to conjecture how the Quarto's version came about. The conflicting claims of York and Somerset led to the Armourer and his Man being introduced too soon; whoever was compiling the Quarto text remembered that Humphrey left the stage though not why, but *did* remember that while he was offstage Margaret struck his wife. The utterly unmotivated exit and reappearance of Humphrey in itself rules out any possibility that the Quarto's scene is a legitimate alternative to the Folio version, rather than a confused report of it.

The witchcraft scene (1.4) provides a different kind of evidence for reporting, the borrowing of phrases from other plays known to the actors. The original scene probably grew out of the brief remark in Hall's chronicle that Eleanor 'by sorcery and enchantment intended to destroy the King' (p. 202) into a full-scale conjuring episode to exploit the popularity of Marlowe's *Dr Faustus* (though the relative dates of *Faustus* and *2 Henry VI* are not established with any certainty). But Q's version goes further, and uses actual phrases from *Faustus* as well as from Marlowe's *Tamburlaine*. When Bolingbroke in Q invokes Night

> Wherein the Furies mask in hellish troops,
> Send up I charge you from Cocytus' lake . . .
>
> (499–501)

he draws on two passages from *Tamburlaine*: 'Furies from the black
Cocytus lake | Break up the earth' (Part One, 5.1.218–19) and 'As
is the island where the Furies mask' (Part Two, 3.2.12); and when
he asks 'the spirit Ascalon' 'To pierce the bowels of this centric
earth' (502–3), he borrows 'centric earth' from *Dr Faustus* (A text,
2.3.37).[1] In F, the spirit who is raised is reluctant to co-operate with
the conjuror Bolingbroke, anxious to be gone: 'that I had said and
done' (1.4.28 / TLN 653–4). But in Q, he is calm and self-
possessed, assuming easy familiarity with the man who has conjured him up: 'Now Bolingbroke, what wouldst thou have me do?'
(508). A 'radically different conception'? It is in fact simply a borrowing from *Dr Faustus*, Mephistopheles' first line when Faustus
has conjured him up: 'Now, Faustus, what wouldst thou have me
do?'[2] One conjuring scene has become confused with another; and
together with the line, Q has borrowed the tone of intimacy and
familiarity that Mephistopheles uses to Faustus, presumably missing the point of the spirit's anguish in F.

Q's version of the end of 3.1, given at Appendix A, Passage D, as
well as providing further evidence of reporting, also raises the
issues of substantial omission and reshaping of the scene mentioned in the two lists given on pp. 76–7 above. The first half of this
episode deals with the plot to murder Duke Humphrey, the second
with sending York to deal with the rebellion in Ireland. The first
half reduces F's fifty-nine lines to twenty (Passage D, 1–20 / Q
1102–21). The numerical difference may suggest that the performance reported in Q was heavily cut at this point; but in fact there
are signs that Q's version recalls, distantly, most of F's scene. This
applies especially to Suffolk's lines 1107–16 in Q (Passage D, 6–15).
'It may be by policy he [Humphrey] works' seems a confused recollection of the discussion in F about whether it is good 'policy' or not
to condemn Humphrey legally. 'The fox barks not when he would
steal the lamb', which occurs much earlier in F's scene (3.1.55 /
TLN 1349), has been substituted for 3.1.252–60 / TLN 1554–62 in
F, in which Humphrey is compared to a fox guarding a sheepfold.

---

[1] The borrowing is made virtually certain since the *Faustus* passage is *OED*'s earliest citation for 'centric earth' (*a.* 1). Q's 'Ascalon' 'may derive from a confusion on
the part of the reporter between this spirit and the "Ascalon" mentioned in the plot
of 1 *Tamar Cam*, a play he may have known' (*Textual Companion*, p. 181.)

[2] A text, 1.3.36, ed. David Bevington and Eric Rasmussen, Revels Plays
(Manchester, 1993).

The reported nature of Suffolk's Q speech is confirmed when he says 'If our King Henry had shook hands with death', which borrows a line from *3 Henry VI* (1.4.103). Although this is a proverbial saying (Dent SS6), the near-identity of the phrasing surely confirms that the line is a report, especially since the scene from which it comes (Margaret's ritual slaughter of York) is probably the most striking and memorable in any of the three plays, if modern performance is anything to go by. Further evidence of reporting comes when the Messenger arrives from Ireland, and replaces F's speech with lines from Marlowe's *Edward II*, also in the repertory of Pembroke's Men:[1]

> The wild O'Neill, my lords, is up in arms,
> With troops of Irish kerns that uncontrolled
> Doth plant themselves within the English pale.
> (Passage D, 23–5 / Q 1125–7)

> The wild O'Neill, with swarms of Irish kerns,
> Lives uncontrolled within the English pale.
> (*Edward II*, 2.2.163–4)[2]

There is an interesting connection between this episode and the parting of Margaret and Suffolk in 3.2. Near the end of the scene Margaret says, in F:

> To France, sweet Suffolk. Let me hear from thee.
> For wheresoe'er thou art in this world's globe
> I'll have an Iris that shall find thee out.
> (3.2.409–11 / TLN 2122–4)

Q's version of these lines comes much earlier in the scene:

> No more. Sweet Suffolk, hie thee hence to France,
> Or live where thou wilt within this world's globe,
> I'll have an Irish that shall find thee out.
> (1384–6)

Q's lines replace an elaborate conceit by the Queen in F about

---

[1] See pp. 62–3 above.

[2] Alexander, p. 93. Gabriel Egan suggests privately that Shakespeare himself might be the borrower, in the course of writing an alternative version; this implies that *Edward II* was written before *2 Henry VI*, whereas, like most commentators, I believe that it was the example of the *Henry VI* plays that led Marlowe to move from writing plays based on a single central character to writing a play in which the interest is shared among several.

bedewing Suffolk's hand with her tears which the reporter presumably couldn't recall; and he replaces F's 'an Iris' with 'an Irish'. It is possible that this is a misprint, or a misunderstanding by the compositor of Q; but it seems much likelier to be a misunderstanding by the reporting actor. Nor is it difficult to see how it came about. Between the F speech that the reporter was trying to recall and the 'Iris' one comes the messenger's news that Cardinal Beaufort is dying. This is very close structurally to the second half of the previous scene when the messenger from Ireland interrupts Margaret, Suffolk, and the others plotting Humphrey's murder. The reporter muddled the two; he obviously didn't understand the classical reference to Iris, and with the Irish rebellion running in his head came up with a line in which an Irishman, rather than the messenger of the queen of the gods, would seek Suffolk throughout the globe. It is inconceivable that an *author* could have written this as an alternative version.

Despite the current scepticism about the principle of memorial transmission, I have only ever encountered one remotely cogent objection to it, made privately by Lois Potter: why should *actors* of all people, whose job is to memorize lines, remember the plays so badly as in some reported texts, including Q? I would focus a particular aspect of this question: why is a part (Suffolk or Warwick, for example) well reported in some scenes, raising the likelihood that actors of those parts were among the reporters, yet so dimly recollected in others?[1] The question is partly answered by recalling the theatre conditions of the early 1590s, usefully summarized by Scott McMillin. The Elizabethan actor

was playing a daily repertory of fourteen or fifteen different plays at the same time as he was committing the text of this roll [i.e. scroll, on which his speeches and the cues for them were written] to memory. The job was to memorize this roll and keep it separate from the other memorized rolls he was playing at the same time. Because parts were frequently doubled in production, an actor may have been playing fifty different parts a month in twenty-five different plays. . . . The memories of Elizabethan actors are among the unexplained phenomena of human history.[2]

[1] The reporters are variously conjectured to be Suffolk and Warwick (Alexander, pp. 73–82), and an actor who had played a series of roles: the Armourer, Spirit, Mayor, Vaux, and Scales (John E. Jordan, 'The Reporter of *Henry VI, Part 2*', *PMLA* 64 (1949), 1089–1113).

[2] 'Professional Playwrighting', in *A Companion to Shakespeare*, ed. David Scott Kastan (Oxford, 1999), 225–38; p. 231.

Considered in that context, perhaps the fallibility of (say) Suffolk's memory is more explicable, especially when the known financial plight of Pembroke's Men at their collapse by September 1593 is taken into account: some of them may have put together a text to raise some much-needed money, duly published in 1594. If so, as Peter Alexander says,

Lack of practice and the lapse of time must both have affected [an actor's] memory, and . . . he would naturally give a more imperfect report of his part than he was accustomed to do in the theatre; much would be remembered inexactly, and frequent confusions would not be surprising. (pp. 73–4)

That, at any rate, is what we find in the Quarto of *2 Henry VI*.

But if the Quarto is a reported text, precisely what is it reporting? The usual assumption is the Folio text. But the list given above of episodes where the material, not just the lines, differs in F and Q suggests that between composition and performance modifications were made, and that Q reports these. And the end of Q's version of 3.1, which I have already argued provides strong evidence of reporting, also testifies to apparent modification. After the exit of the King, the Queen says, in Q:

> Then sit we down again, my lord Cardinal,
> Suffolk, Buckingham, York, and Somerset.
> (Passage D, 1–2 / Q 1102–3)

The specific identifications in these lines seem to indicate a realization, perhaps in rehearsal, on someone's part—the author or the company or both—that much of F's scene appears to forget about the presence of Somerset and Buckingham (especially the latter, who has nothing to say) and to do something about it. This is still more noticeable in the discussion about the Irish rebellion, when there is at least an attempt made to integrate Buckingham into the scene (compare 3.1.321–30 with Passage D, 46–58). It is because of such variants that Oxford argues that the stage version which Q is reporting may contain 'authorial revision' of the original manuscript. Accordingly, Oxford adopts 'a number of Q passages or arrangements' into the text of the play in its *Complete Works* (*Textual Companion*, p. 177). But while it is true that 3.1 and perhaps other passages given in the second list on p. 76 above may be evidence of revision in rehearsal of the play as originally written, the situation is complicated by equally strong signs of a different kind of revision, to which I now turn.

Revision in the Folio text

Among the Quarto passages that Oxford includes in its text are some tiny, dramatically insignificant historical facts that occur in the Quarto but not in the Folio; and these details cannot easily be explained as part of the Quarto revision of the Folio that Q's version of 3.1, for example, may suggest. R. B. McKerrow has some relevant remarks about such tiny historical details which occur in one text but not in another:

> When a playwright undertook the revision of a play it is quite possible that he might look up the historical or other source on which it was based if he wanted to make important structural changes, correct or make more intelligible a genealogy, or insert a new incident; but it is surely most unlikely that he would go through the text with the original (especially when he was dealing with a historical play the sources of which were to be found in disconnected paragraphs scattered through a large volume and needing much looking for) only for the purpose of inserting in his revision a number of verbal reminiscences of the source which had no bearing on the plot and in no way improved the dialogue.[1]

Yet just such a detail occurs in the second scene of the Quarto, when the Duchess of Gloucester asks 'What, hast thou conferred with Margery Jourdayne, the cunning Witch of Ely' (261–2). At this point, the Folio has:

> What sayst thou, man? Hast thou as yet conferred
> With Margery Jourdayne, the cunning witch.
>
> (1.2.74–5 / TLN 349–50)

The Quarto's prose probably reflects a verse line in the text that it is reporting, rendered thus in Oxford: 'With Margery Jordan, the cunning witch of Eye' (1.2.75). The Oxford editors comment:

> Hall . . . , Shakespeare's probable source, calls this character 'Margerie Jourdayne surnamed, the witche of Eye' (Grafton and Holinshed agree substantively with Hall here). We presume that Q here preserves a corrupt version of a historical detail *added to the text* in the preparation of the

---

[1] See p. 79 n. 1; p. 160.

prompt-book, but absent from the foul papers upon which F is based. (*Textual Companion*, p. 180; my italics)[1]

But why, as McKerrow asks, should a dramatist, or a theatre company, go back to a chronicle source to *add* a detail (of Eye) which adds nothing of dramatic value to the scene? Moreover F's line 'With Margery Jourdayne, the cunning witch' is not only an absolutely regular iambic pentameter, but in my view a more incisive line than the one that Oxford reconstructs. It seems much likelier that someone cut the wholly redundant information 'of Eye' and so created a more effective line. And if that someone was Shakespeare, then the *Folio's* version of this passage, not the Quarto's, represents his revision of the original draft of the play.

It is possible that 'of Eye' was omitted by the Folio compositor, usually known as Compositor 'B', who set the page and who could be careless, especially as the phrase occurs at the end of a verse line; but that explanation does not seem possible for similar chronicle details within one of Jack Cade's prose speeches, although 'B' also set that page. When Cade orders Lord Saye's execution, he says, in the Quarto:

Go take him to the Standard in Cheapside and chop off his head, and then go to Mile End Green, to Sir James Cromer his son-in-law, and cut off his head too. (1823–5)

The Folio's version is:

Go, take him away, I say, and strike off his head presently; and then break into his son-in-law's house, Sir James Cromer, and strike off his head. (4.7.102–4 / TLN 2741–4)

The Quarto's details 'to the Standard in Cheapside' and 'go to Mile End Green' come from Hall; Oxford inserts them in its text, and William Montgomery, who edited that text, says in his unpublished Oxford D.Phil. thesis, which is a critical edition of the Quarto, that these details form 'one of the strongest pieces of evidence that a

---

[1] There are numerous villages called 'Eye', which means an island or dry ground in a marsh. This could well be a description of Ely (which means 'eel island'), so perhaps the dramatist altered Hall's 'Eye' to 'Ely', and Q is thus reporting an earlier version of the text correctly; on the other hand, Q's 'Ely' could be a simple misreporting of 'Eye'. For my spelling of the witch's name ('Iordane' in F, 'Iordaine' in Q), see the Commentary to 1.2.75.

chronicle history was consulted at some point between the manuscript which lay behind F, and Q' (ii. 171–2). But the details equally
provide one of the strongest pieces of evidence for those who, like
McKerrow and myself, find such consultation either by a revising
dramatist or a reporter an extremely unlikely proceeding. They are
so embedded within the speech that they must have been in the text
that is reported in Q (and Compositor 'B' is unlikely to have carelessly dropped two pieces of historical detail from the F speech); it is
much likelier that an author would omit unnecessary details of this
kind as he revised, or copied, his original manuscript.

Oxford inserts another passage from Q in the squabble between
Duke Humphrey and the Cardinal which precedes the false miracle
at St Albans. After the Cardinal's acceptance of Humphrey's
challenge to a duel, 'Marry, when thou dar'st' (2.1.38 / TLN 758),
Oxford adds, from Q:

> DUKE HUMPHREY   Dare? I tell thee, priest,
> Plantagenets could never brook the dare!
> CARDINAL BEAUFORT
> I am Plantagenet as well as thou,
> And son to John of Gaunt.
> DUKE HUMPHREY In bastardy.
> CARDINAL BEAUFORT I scorn thy words. (586–91)

Oxford thinks that these lines may have been 'added by the author
in the preparation of the prompt-book. They contain additional
historical matter (Beaufort's bastardy) unlikely to have been inter-
polated by the reporter, and of a kind which seems to have been
elsewhere similarly incorporated into the prompt-book', though
the editors acknowledge that A. S. Cairncross, who also includes
these lines in his Arden 2 edition, offers the alternative explanation
that 'these lines were censored from the manuscript behind F
at some time subsequent to their having been performed (and
so reported by Q)' (*Textual Companion*, p. 182). I do not find
Cairncross's arguments for censorship throughout the play very
convincing, for example that the reference to Beaufort's bastardy
was cut because he was 'one of Queen Elizabeth's ancestors'
(p. xxvii).[1] It seems to me less probable that this omission reflects

---

[1] This flimsy argument is further weakened by the fact that Humphrey calls
Beaufort 'Thou bastard of my grandfather' at *1 Henry VI*, 3.1.43, without any sign
of interference in F.

censorship than that Shakespeare, revising and/or copying his manuscript, cut the passage to shorten a scene that contains quite enough bickering between Humphrey and the Cardinal as it is; but whatever the explanation, a cut in F seems likelier than a consultation of the chronicles to *add* the historical detail of the Cardinal's bastardy.

If these historical details were not added to the original play during rehearsals for the performance reported in Q, but deleted from it in F, that must mean that the Folio is in some respects a revised version of the original manuscript. At this point, the larger variants between F and Q, and the longer passages present in F but absent in Q, set out in the two lists on pp. 76–7 above, become relevant. Are F's versions likely to be the originals, altered in rehearsal and so reported by Q, or do they represent substantial revisions of the original manuscript, which thus appear in F? And are the F passages of which there is no trace in Q likely to be cuts in Q or additions in F?

I find it hard to discern any qualitative difference, either stylistically or theatrically, between the two versions of Queen Margaret's opening speech (1.1.24–31; Appendix A, Passage A). Q obviously cannot be reporting F here, since the two speeches have nothing in common. Did the company have trouble with F's 'alderliefest' (see the Commentary to 1.1.28) and ask Shakespeare for a new speech, or write one themselves? Or did Shakespeare change his original, as reported in Q, to the 'alderliefest' version to make Margaret sound more formal, stilted even, perhaps more like a foreigner, as conjectured in the Commentary? The variants do not seem to provide compelling evidence either way.

The advantage of Q's moving the reading of the spirit's prophecies from York in 1.4 to the King in 2.1 is that it allows the King to react to his forecast deposition with a characteristic acceptance— 'God's will be done in all' (Appendix A, Passage C, l. 4)—and Suffolk to comment on the prophecy made about him, to be fulfilled later: 'By water must the Duke of Suffolk die?' (l. 7); but of course if York reads them, as in F, *he* can react to the possibility—the prophecy is ambiguous—that he might 'die a violent death'. And even if the production reported by Q moved the reading from York to Henry, the change need not have been authorial: it is not beyond the capacity of a group of intelligent actors to see the advantages for Henry and Suffolk in Q's arrangement. It is possible, then, that F's version is the original, left unrevised.

The murder of Suffolk (4.1) is in F a long, elaborate scene, hard to get into focus, as its frequent truncation or omission in modern performance indicates. That truncation may have begun early. In Q, the scene is not only shorter than in F, but presents its incidents in a different order, suggesting that it may have been reshaped as well as shortened in rehearsal.[1] In the process, the Lieutenant's long speech accusing Suffolk of losing France and preparing for Cade's rebellion may have been cut. But a quite different explanation is prompted by the signs of textual disturbance in the Folio text. A line is missing in F between TLN 2216–17, luckily supplied by Q (4.1.49 in this edition). Two lines later (TLN 2218 / 4.1.51), the Lieutenant appropriates a line of Suffolk's: and he probably does so again at F TLN 2300 / 4.1.133, although this is not quite certain (see the Commentary to this line). And at TLN 2237–9 / 4.1.70–1, F reads, in the original spelling and layout:

> Strike off his head.　　*Suf.*Thou dar'ſt not for thy owne.
> 　　*Lieu. Poole,* Sir *Poole?* Lord,
> 　I kennell, puddle, ſinke,whoſe filth and dirt

McKerrow and Alexander[2] independently demonstrated that F's Compositor B misread his copy in the second line, which was probably something like

Lieu. Poole, Su. [speech-prefix for 'Suffolk'] Poole? Lieu. [prefix for 'Lieutenant']

—in other words, it was a line squashed into the manuscript and hard to read. When two half-lines make up a single verse line, F usually sets them out on separate lines, so its unusual layout here

---

[1] But not reshaped to any apparent dramatic gain; for this reason, Q's version is not included in Appendix A.

[2] McKerrow in his draft edition for the Oxford Shakespeare that he did not live to complete, Alexander in 'Restoring Shakespeare: The Modern Editor's Task,' *SS* 5 (Cambridge, 1952), 1–9; pp. 7–8.

of the two half-lines that make up TLN 2237 / 4.1.70 also argues for some congestion in the manuscript.[1] What caused it?

The third line quoted above is the start of the Lieutenant's long speech of accusation against Suffolk. There are signs only of its first seven lines in Q, but the rest of the speech may not be a cut, but an addition in F. It refers back to the surrender of Anjou and Maine as part of Margaret's marriage settlement, and looks forward both to the rebellion of the Yorkists and to Cade's uprising. A further possible sign of revision is that the character called 'Captain' in Q and in the chronicle source is in F a 'Lieutenant'. McKerrow thought that 'Lieutenant' was 'a mere error', but it looks to me like a deliberate change, which helps to explain the textual difficulties. If the speech-prefix 'Captain' was altered to 'Lieutenant', or some abbreviation of it, throughout the scene, but its position was not always clear, non-alignment of prefix and line might explain the accidental dropping of line 49, the (possible) misattribution of l. 133, and the squashing and consequent muddle of l. 71. If so, 'Captain' at TLN 2233 / 4.1.66 is a survivor of the earlier version. But why should Shakespeare have made the change? A hint may be offered in the reference to Suffolk's killers as 'soldiers' in F (TLN 2300 / 4.1.133) but not in Q. In Q's version, the Captain might as well be a leader of a band of pirates, as indeed Suffolk calls them in both texts (TLN 2306 / 4.1.139; Q 1541). Perhaps Shakespeare changed the Captain to a Lieutenant (and added the reference to 'soldiers'?) to emphasize their military, not merely piratical, nature, perhaps that they are some of 'the ragged soldiers [sent] wounded home' (TLN 2258 / 4.1.90), who have turned pirate. This would help to explain the sheer resentment, and consequent savagery, shown towards Suffolk during the scene.[2]

One further F/Q variant in this scene may result from revision. At F TLN 2276 / 4.1.108, Suffolk likens the Lieutenant to 'Bargulus the strong Illyrian pirate'. At the same point Q's Suffolk likens him to 'mighty Abradas, | The great Macedonian pirate' (1518–19). Q's phrase also occurs in two works by Robert Greene: *Menaphon*

---

[1] The unusual layout here, with speech-prefixes and part-lines printed on the same line, recurs at TLN 2283–4 / 4.1.115–16:

> *Lieu.* Water: W. Come Suffolke, I must waft thee
> to thy death.

where 'W.' is almost certainly an abbreviated prefix for 'Whitmore'.

[2] For an interesting theatrical development of this idea, see p. 23 above.

5.197.19, *Penelope's Web* 6.77.27. Neither is a play, so, if the reporter of Q is echoing a play he was in, Greene may have used the phrase 'a third time, in a play, now lost, but which the reporter knew' (*Textual Companion*, p. 188). But it is also possible that F's phrase is a revision. Ronald Knowles in his Arden 3 edition suggests that Shakespeare, 'possibly self-conscious about his borrowing' from Greene, as reported by Q, substituted one exotic pirate for another in F (p. 370). See the Commentary to 4.1.108 and 111.

The other major variant involves the battle sequence in Act 5, beginning with the assembly of the rival factions in 5.1. Whereas in F York's sons and the Cliffords enter in sequence, in Q they appear at opposite doors simultaneously (2061–3), as, later, do Q's Warwick and Salisbury 'at one door' and Buckingham 'at the other' (2084–5), where in F Buckingham doesn't appear at all. And in Q's version of the battle, but not in F's, Buckingham is carried 'wounded to his tent' (2192), just before the entry of Henry and Margaret (5.2.71.2 in this edition). Like Q's introduction of Buckingham into the dialogue of 3.1, discussed above, this looks like an attempt during the rehearsals of the production reported by Q to tie up the loose ends involving Buckingham generally—though if so, Shakespeare seems to have been content to leave them untied in his revision of F, if in fact he had anything to do with the theatrical changes apparently reported in Q. Q's introduction of Buckingham to oppose Warwick and Salisbury in 5.1 seems connected with the absence of one of the substantial passages from F mentioned in the first list above, Salisbury's attempt to explain away his oath-breaking. Its absence in Q, taken together with Buckingham's entry, looks like reshaping in rehearsal: it seems safe to say that here, at least, the missing passage is a cut.

But what about the considerable differences in the battle scene itself? In F, the sequence is: York fights with and kills Old Clifford; Young Clifford finds the body and carries it away; Richard of Gloucester fights with and kills Somerset; the King, the Queen, and Young Clifford then fly, leaving the Yorkists victorious. But Q's sequence is: Richard kills Somerset; York kills Old Clifford; Young Clifford finds the body but fights with Richard before carrying it away; the King and Queen fly. Immediately before the battle, in both versions, comes an exchange between Richard of Gloucester and Young Clifford, quoted here from F:

RICHARD
   Fie, charity, for shame! Speak not in spite,
   For you shall sup with Jesu Christ tonight.
YOUNG CLIFFORD
   Foul stigmatic, that's more than thou canst tell.
RICHARD
   If not in heaven, you'll surely sup in hell.
               (5.1.213–16 / TLN 3213–17)

This seems to prepare for a combat between Richard and Young Clifford which does not materialize in F. In Q it does. After Young Clifford has discovered his father's corpse and lifted it on to his shoulders, Q has this direction:

Enter Richard, and then Clifford lays down his father, fights with him, and Richard flies away again. (2183–4)

The obvious gain in Q is that the 'flyting' dialogue between Richard and Young Clifford immediately before the battle leads somewhere—to their combat; it makes such logical sense that one might ask why Shakespeare didn't use it in the process of Folio revision that I am suggesting.

   A possible clue might be found in the completely different versions of the dialogue that precedes York's killing of Old Clifford in F and Q (5.2.19–30; Appendix A, Passage G). Both versions look forward to the events of *3 Henry VI*; but F's seems to me to do so in the more interesting way, since it allows a moment of generosity and chivalry before the full barbarities of civil war emerge in the next play, with Young Clifford's butchering of York's young son, and the ritual slaughter of York himself. Many commentators have felt that the style of Young Clifford's Folio speech suggests that it may have been a later addition, perhaps to give Young Clifford a more substantial profile in preparation for his major contribution to the following play;[1] if so, the Clifford/York dialogue in F may also have been an afterthought, designed to contrast Old Clifford's chivalry with his son's barbarity: ironically, the death of one who represented older, chivalric values leads directly to the barbarities at the start of the next play, to which Young Clifford contributes so strikingly, and after which he and Richard finally

---

[1] See p. 60 n. 1 above.

have the combat (3 *Henry VI*, 2.4) which is absent from F's version of 2 *Henry VI*.

The scene of Jack Cade's death (4.10) in Q is both shorter than, and somewhat different from, that in F. Cade's opening soliloquy in F is missing, and the scene begins with a simultaneous entry for Cade and Iden, similar to those for the competing factions in Q's version of 5.1, discussed above:

Enter Jack Cade at one door, and at the other master Alexander Iden and his men, and Jack Cade lies down picking of herbs and eating them. (1927–9)

The rest of Q's scene is quite close verbally to F's, and is essentially reporting it, except for one thing: in Q Iden is attended by five servants, whereas in F he is alone. The only hint of these servants in F comes at 4.10.38–9 / TLN 2943 5: 'come thou and thy five men, and if I do not leave you all as dead as a doornail . . .'. F makes sense as it stands: Cade may simply be defying Iden to bring 'all the men you have', may even be mocking him for keeping so small an establishment; and since Q omits the opening soliloquy and rearranges the entry, it is possible that Q also took F's reference to the five men literally and brought them on stage—though Iden orders 'stand you all aside' (1951) and fights Cade alone, as in F. It is equally possible that Q roughly represents the original, and that Shakespeare revised the scene in F, adding Cade's opening soliloquy but failing to expunge the reference to the five men. Or maybe—to risk multiplying hypotheses—the original version contained Cade's soliloquy *and* brought on the five men; the performance behind Q reshaped the opening but retained the five men; in revising F Shakespeare kept the original version but eliminated the five men, apart from the tell-tale reference at 4.10.38–9. I suspect that this last is in fact what happened, since it allows Iden's reflections on his rural contentment (4.10.16–23 / TLN 2921–8) to be a soliloquy, unhindered by the presence of servants. Cade's opening soliloquy is then balanced by Iden's and the scene becomes a dispute between the two characters, culminating in their duel and Cade's death. But of course this is sheer speculation, and underlines how difficult it is to evolve any simple, straightforward hypothesis that will cover all the differences between F and Q.

Of the longer passages which occur in F but not in Q, a major example is Lord Saye's plea to Cade and the rebels for his life, reduced from thirty-four lines to five. This looks like a cut; despite its structural function, discussed on p. 54 above, the episode is often shortened in modern performances, and may have been in the rehearsals of the 1590s. In exchange, as it were, Q *adds* later in the same scene an episode in which a sergeant seeks justice because Dick the Butcher has raped his wife, only to have his tongue cut out (off stage). Oxford includes this passage in its text, adducing several parallels with Shakespeare's acknowledged work (*Textual Companion*, pp. 190–1); some of these are noted in the annotations to Appendix A, Passage F. It may have been in the original version of the play, or it may have been added in the performance behind Q to allow more time for the executions of Lord Saye and his son-in-law, though if that was the motive, it could easily have been cobbled together by the actors. If Shakespeare did write it, he cut it when revising, since there is no corresponding passage in F.

In some ways the most interesting F passages absent from Q are those involving the King and Queen. While Warwick inspects Duke Humphrey's murdered body at 3.2.136–48 / TLN 1838–51, the King laments his death and prays characteristically to God: there is no sign of this speech in Q. And in the previous scene, the King's twenty-five line lament that he cannot help Humphrey (3.1.198–222 / TLN 1499–1523) is represented in Q by three lines:

> Ay Margaret. My heart is killed with grief,
> Where I may sit and sigh in endless moan,
> For who's a traitor? Gloucester, he is none.
>
> (1098–1100)

It is just possible that the F speech is an addition: it is surely crucially important for the actor playing Henry, as its impact in most modern performances attests. On the other hand, the Q lines don't look like a failed attempt to recall a longer speech, but rather a deliberate attempt to paper over a cut, the rewritten second line explaining the first, which closely corresponds to F's. And the style of F's speech, expressing Henry's grief and sense of impotence in an extended simile of a cow lamenting its calf which is carried off to slaughter, seems more characteristic of the earlier than the later Shakespeare: see the Introduction, pp. 40–1.

These considerations apply still more to Q's omission of the last thirty-five lines of the longest speech in the Folio text, in which Queen Margaret tries to distract Henry's attention away from the murdered Humphrey towards herself (3.2.87–121 / TLN 1787–1821). This passage is often omitted in modern performances, and it looks, on the face of it, like a cut in Q. Much of it elaborates the idea of the sea refusing to drown her, leaving it to Henry to murder her with his unkindness. The elaborate figurative style is the kind of language which Q often omits. Scott McMillin argues that a cut here is part of a larger process of Q's 'intentional abridgement' of Margaret's part:

> Margaret's 314 lines in *2 Henry VI* form one of the longest female roles among public-theater plays of the early 1590s . . . [Shakespeare] was pushing beyond the norm—perhaps because the company for whom he originally intended the plays[1] included a leading boy of unusual range who was not available for the performances of Pembroke's men and whose roles had to be reduced for another child actor.[2]

But again, as in Henry's 'calf' speech, it is just possible that F's longer version is a development of the shorter speech reported by Q, as part of the process of revision suggested earlier. The style, especially the close parallels with *Lucrece* and *Love's Labour's Lost* (see the Commentary to 3.2.107 and 113), is characteristic of Shakespeare's work in the early 1590s, so the possibility of an addition depends upon when one imagines such revision taking place. If it was shortly after the original composition, the style is not a barrier; but if, as suggested on pp. 73–4 above, it was for a revival in 1598–9, it surely is a difficulty — unless one regards such expansion as offering a virtuoso challenge to the obviously talented boy actor for whom Shakespeare wrote Beatrice in 1598 and (probably) Rosalind a year later. On balance, cutting seems likelier than revision; but since, as I have admitted on pp. 43–4 above, I find this speech of Margaret's the most difficult to account for theatrically in the entire play, I should prefer to leave the options open.

---

[1] See the Introduction, pp. 62–3.
[2] 'Casting for Pembroke's Men: The *Henry VI* Quartos and *The Taming of A Shrew*', *SQ* 23 (1972), 141–59; p. 152.

To summarize, Q and F show signs of two different kinds of revision of the play as originally written. Q seems to report changes to it made in rehearsal, F to reflect changes made in a later revision, probably for a revival. Whether or not Shakespeare was responsible for those reported in Q, he cannot have thought sufficiently well of them to include them in the revision detectable in F—unless, of course, all the material differences between Q and F were revisions made in F; but that does not seem probable, since Shakespeare is surely unlikely to have changed, for example, the 'tidier' Buckingham episodes of Q into the vaguer, untidier ones of F. Another possibility is that it was the company that made the Q changes (with or without Shakespeare's participation), and Shakespeare didn't want (or didn't bother) to adopt them when he made his own minor revisions of the original. He may have thought that such modifications as he made were sufficient to make *2 Henry VI* a pretty good play; if· so, it is hard to disagree with him.

The Folio text and this edition

The Folio text was printed from an authorial manuscript, as its vague and 'permissive' stage directions make clear: for example, Jack Cade's first entry is accompanied with the '*infinite numbers*' (4.2.30.2 / TLN 2351) characteristic of a dramatist writing impressionistically rather than with a strict regard for theatrical practicalities. But W. W. Greg, while agreeing that the copy was autograph, felt that it must have been a fair copy of the original manuscript or 'foul papers', since he thought the survival of foul papers from the early 1590s was unlikely.[1] Perhaps, then, Shakespeare prepared a fair copy either for presentation to a patron (Southampton?) or for a revival. E. A. J. Honigmann writes that, in making a fair copy of any play, Shakespeare might 'touch up . . . words and lines' as he went along, and so 'might introduce quite trivial variants'.[2] This seems to account perfectly for those small but tell-tale chronicle details which must have been in the performance reported by Q but were apparently deleted from the manuscript behind F.

---

[1] *The Editorial Problem in Shakespeare* (Oxford, 1942), p. 55.
[2] *The Stability of Shakespeare's Text* (1965), p. 129.

But there is, unfortunately, a serious objection to Greg's view that the source of the Folio text was an authorial fair copy. In 3.2, Henry calls Margaret 'Nell', the pet name Duke Humphrey uses for his wife Eleanor, and Margaret refers to herself as 'Eleanor' (TLN 1720, 1779, 1800, 1820): these are emended to 'Meg' or 'Margaret' in the present edition. Such slips are easily explained in the heat of composition; but they would surely have been corrected if Shakespeare made a fair copy—unless he was falling again into his original thought patterns. I think these slips tell against authorial fair copy, and that the only explanation compatible with the revisions is that, when a revival was contemplated, Shakespeare read through the original manuscript and made the small changes noted here and there, but left the bulk of the play as it was. That would apply particularly to Act 3, where the 'Nell' and 'Eleanor' problem occurs: by common consent and as performance regularly shows, the destruction of Humphrey and its aftermath is one of the most powerful sequences in the play—so why bother to alter it? He may simply have speed-read or skipped scenes that he knew worked especially well.

Greg's point about foul papers thirty years old by the time of the printing of the Folio in 1623, however, helps to focus the likelihood that an old and probably much used manuscript may have been damaged in places, so that the Folio editors or printers were compelled to supplement it with printed copy (i.e. a Quarto) in places, as McKerrow pointed out long ago.[1] So on the rare occasions when F and Q are identical, or virtually identical, that is not a sign that the reporters' memories improved spectacularly, but that the Folio editors, faced with damage or illegibility in the manuscript, turned to Q for their copy. There are three particularly clear examples of this: 2.1.112–149.2 / TLN 858–904; 2.3.58.1–2.4.0.2 / TLN 1115–70; and 4.5.0.1–4.6.0.2 / TLN 2598–2614. The extended stage directions in the first two passages, whose wording is almost identical in F and Q, would otherwise be difficult to reconcile with Q's status as a reported text. Once it is realized that the Folio editors drew on Q, the situation is easily explained.[2]

---

[1] 'A Note on the "Bad Quartos" of 2 and 3 *Henry VI* and the Folio Text', *RES* 13 (1937), 64–72.

[2] They may not, however, have used the *First* Quarto for this purpose. Q3, published in 1619, contains 176 substantive variants from Q1, twenty-five of which agree with F against Q1, according to William Montgomery, who analyses them and

The text in this edition is based firmly on that in the Folio, as representing Shakespeare's latest thoughts on the play, and unlike the Oxford *Complete Works* only incorporates material from the Quarto to correct obvious errors (for example, to supply the missing line at 4.1.49), with one important exception: since the Quarto reports an Elizabethan performance, its interesting and often extensive stage directions are incorporated into this edition where they supplement the rather meagre information given in the Folio ones (for example, at the opening of the play). Appendix A gives the principal passages where the Quarto appears to provide alternative treatments of Folio scenes or speeches, for the purposes of comparison, and to enable performers to use the alternative material where that seems preferable for a particular production.

suggests reasons for them (*Textual Companion*, pp. 176–7). The F editors drew 'probably' on Q3 rather than Q1 or Q2 to supply those passages damaged in the authorial manuscript, 'though the extent and frequency of consultation is uncertain'.

EDITORIAL PROCEDURES

THIS edition follows the Editorial Procedures established for the series by Stanley Wells and summarized in Gary Taylor's Oxford Shakespeare edition of *Henry V* (1982), pp. 75–81. In accordance with them, passages from Shakespeare's contemporaries quoted in the introduction and commentary are also modernized even when they are taken from editions using old spelling; as Taylor says, 'If modernizing is valid for Shakespeare's text it is equally valid for passages quoted only to illuminate that text'. Old spelling is reserved for the collations and for passages in the Textual Introduction where the original printing is relevant: the early use of u, v, i, and j is retained, but not long 's'.

Since this is an edition of the Folio text of *2 Henry VI*, the collations record Quarto readings only where these have been used for stage directions, and to correct obvious errors or replace lacunae in the Folio (e.g. at 4.1.49). Quarto passages which appear to offer significant alternative material to the Folio versions are included in Appendix Λ.

Stage directions such as 'aside' or 'to' a character are all editorial, and are not collated. All changes in directions for stage action are collated, but where the specified action is clearly implied by the dialogue, the change is neither bracketed in the text nor attributed to an earlier editor. Disputable directions (for example, who tears the petitions at 1.3.40.1) are printed in broken brackets. Titles are silently expanded in stage directions (e.g. '*Duke Humphrey of Gloucester*' for F's '*Duke Humfrey*' at 1.2.0.1, or '*Enter the Duke of Suffolk and Queen Margaret*' for F's '*Enter Suffolke, and Queene.*' at 1.3.5.1) to ensure consistency throughout the edition. Speech-prefixes are silently normalized.

References in the commentary to Shakespeare's extensive use of proverbs are to R. W. Dent's *Shakespeare's Proverbial Language: An Index* (Berkeley, 1981), which revises and expands that given in M. P. Tilley's *A Dictionary of the Proverbs in England in the Sixteenth and Seventeenth Centuries* (Ann Arbor, 1950), and uses references based on Tilley's. The identification of biblical allusions in the commentary is greatly indebted to Naseeb Shaheen's *Biblical References in*

Shakespeare's Plays (Newark, Delaware, 1999) and unless otherwise indicated follows the Geneva Bible of 1560. Quotations from classical works are from the Loeb editions. References to plays by Shakespeare's contemporaries are to the Revels editions, unless otherwise stated, and those to other works by Shakespeare to the Oxford *Complete Works*, Compact Edition (1988).

I have often adopted punctuation lighter than that required by strictly grammatical modern usage, in order to preserve the shape and rhythm of the verse lines as much as possible.

Abbreviations and References

The following references are used in the introduction, in the collations, and in the commentary. In all bibliographical references, the place of publication is London, unless otherwise specified.

EDITIONS OF SHAKESPEARE

F, F1	The First Folio, 1623
F2	The Second Folio, 1632
F3	The Third Folio, 1663
F4	The Fourth Folio, 1685
Q, Q1	The First Quarto, 1594
Q2	The Second Quarto, 1600
Q3	The Third Quarto, 1619
Alexander	Peter Alexander, *Works* (1951)
Cairncross	A. S. Cairncross, *The Second Part of King Henry VI*, The Arden Shakespeare, Second Series (1957) (Arden 2)
Cambridge	W. G. Clark and W. A. Wright, *Works*, The Cambridge Shakespeare, 9 vols. (Cambridge, 1863–6)
Capell	Edward Capell, *Comedies, Histories, and Tragedies*, 10 vols. (1767–8)
Collier	John Payne Collier, *Comedies, Histories, Tragedies, and Poems*, 6 vols. (1858)
Delius	Nicolaus Delius, *Werke*, 7 vols. (Leipzig, 1854–61)
Dyce	Alexander Dyce, *Works*, 9 vols. (1864–7)
Grant White	Richard Grant White, *Works*, 12 vols. (1857–66)
Hanmer	Thomas Hanmer, *Works*, 6 vols. (Oxford, 1743–4)

Hattaway	Michael Hattaway, *The Second Part of King Henry VI*, The New Cambridge Shakespeare (Cambridge, 1991)
Knowles	Ronald Knowles, *Henry VI Part 2*, The Arden Shakespeare, Third Series (1999) (Arden 3)
Johnson	Samuel Johnson, *Plays*, 8 vols. (1765)
Malone	Edmond Malone, *Plays and Poems*, 10 vols. (1790)
Malone 1821	Edmond Malone (ed. James Boswell), *Plays and Poems*, 21 vols. (1821)
Norton	Stephen Greenblatt (general editor), *The Norton Shakespeare Based on the Oxford Edition* (New York, 1997)
Oxford	Stanley Wells, Gary Taylor, John Jowett, and William Montgomery, *Complete Works* (Oxford, 1986 ; Compact Edition, 1988)
Pope	Alexander Pope, *Works*, 6 vols. (1723–5)
Pope 1728	Alexander Pope, *Works*, 10 vols. (1728)
Rann	Joseph Rann, *Dramatic Works*, 6 vols. (Oxford, 1786–94)
Riverside	G. Blakemore Evans (textual editor), *The Riverside Shakespeare* (2nd edn., Boston, 1997)
Rowe	Nicholas Rowe, *Works*, 6 vols. (1709)
Rowe 1709	Nicholas Rowe, *Works*, 2nd edn., 6 vols. (1709)
Rowe 1714	Nicholas Rowe, *Works*, 8 vols. (1714)
Sanders	Norman Sanders, *The Second Part of King Henry VI*, The New Penguin Shakespeare (Harmondsworth, 1981)
Singer	Samuel W. Singer, *Dramatic Works*, 10 vols. (1856)
Steevens	Samuel Johnson and George Steevens, *Plays*, 10 vols. (1778)
Steevens–Reed	George Steevens and Isaac Reed, *Plays*, 15 vols. (1793)
Theobald	Lewis Theobald, *Works*, 7 vols. (1733)
Warburton	William Warburton, *Works*, 8 vols. (1747)
Wilson	John Dover Wilson, *The Second Part of King Henry VI*, The New Shakespeare (Cambridge, 1952)

OTHER ABBREVIATIONS

Abbott	E. A. Abbott, *A Shakespearian Grammar*, 2nd edn. (1870) (cited by paragraph)
Dent	R. W. Dent, *Shakespeare's Proverbial Language: An Index* (Berkeley, 1981)

Grafton	Richard Grafton, *A Chronicle at Large* (1569)
Griffiths	R. A. Griffiths, *The Reign of King Henry VI*, 2nd edn. (Stroud, 1998)
Hall	Edward Hall, *The Union of the Two Noble and Illustre Families of Lancaster and York* (1548 ; reprinted 1809)
Henslowe	*Henslowe's Diary*, ed. R. A. Foakes and R. T. Rickert (Cambridge, 1961)
Holinshed	Raphael Holinshed, *The Chronicles of England, Scotland, and Ireland*, 2nd edn. (1587, reprinted in 6 vols., 1807–8)
Jones, *Origins*	Emrys Jones, *The Origins of Shakespeare* (Oxford, 1977)
McKerrow	R. B. McKerrow, unpublished papers for a planned Oxford Shakespeare, held in the archives of Oxford University Press
Montgomery	William Montgomery, 'The Contention of York and Lancaster : A Critical Edition', 2 vols. (unpublished D.Phil. thesis, University of Oxford, 1985)
Nashe, *Works*	Thomas Nashe, *Works*, ed. R. B. McKerrow, revised F. P. Wilson, 5 vols. (Oxford, 1958)
N&Q	*Notes and Queries*
OED	*The Oxford English Dictionary*, 2nd edn., 20 vols. (Oxford, 1989)
Onions	C. T. Onions, *A Shakespeare Glossary*, 2nd edn., with enlarged addenda (Oxford, 1953)
RES	*Review of English Studies*
Schmidt	Alexander Schmidt, *Shakespeare Lexicon*, 3rd edn., 2 vols. (Berlin, 1902 ; Dover reprint, New York, 1971)
Shaheen	Naseeb Shaheen, *Biblical References in Shakespeare's Plays* (Newark, Delaware, 1999)
SQ	*Shakespeare Quarterly*
SS	*Shakespeare Survey*
Textual Companion	Stanley Wells, Gary Taylor, John Jowett, and William Montgomery, *William Shakespeare : A Textual Companion* (Oxford, 1987)
Vaughan	H. H. Vaughan, *New Readings and New Renderings of Shakespeare's Tragedies*, 3 vols. (1878–86)
Williams	Gordon Williams, *A Glossary of Shakespeare's Sexual Language* (1997)

Henry VI, Part Two

THE PERSONS OF THE PLAY

Of the King's Party

KING HENRY VI

QUEEN MARGARET

DUKE HUMPHREY of Gloucester, the King's uncle, Lord Protector of England

DUCHESS ELEANOR of Gloucester

CARDINAL BEAUFORT, Bishop of Winchester, Gloucester's uncle and the King's great-uncle

William de la Pole, Marquis, later Duke, of SUFFOLK

Duke of BUCKINGHAM

Duke of SOMERSET

PERSONS OF THE PLAY] There is no comparable list in the early editions. One was first given by Rowe in 1709.

KING HENRY VI (1421–71) succeeded his father Henry V at the age of nine months. He was murdered in the Tower of London after the Yorkist victory at Tewkesbury (1471), according to *3 Henry VI* by Richard of Gloucester.

QUEEN MARGARET (1430–82), daughter of René, Duke of Anjou and titular King of Naples, Sicily, and Jerusalem, married Henry by proxy in 1445 at Nancy, Suffolk representing the King. She became the centre of opposition to the house of York until her son was killed at Tewkesbury in 1471. Historically, she died in poverty in France, but Shakespeare re-introduces her in *Richard III* to witness the destruction of many of her enemies.

DUKE HUMPHREY of Gloucester (1391–1447), youngest brother of Henry V, who appointed him Regent of England during the minority of Henry VI (until 1429).

DUCHESS ELEANOR (d. 1454) was Eleanor Cobham, first the mistress, and from 1428 the wife, of Duke Humphrey.

CARDINAL BEAUFORT (1374–1447) was the illegitimate son of Henry VI's grandfather John of Gaunt. The play's black-and-white presentation of his rivalry with Duke Humphrey simplifies a more complex historical situation.

Duke of SUFFOLK (1396–1450) married Margaret on Henry's behalf in 1445, but there is no historical basis for their presentation as lovers in the play.

Duke of BUCKINGHAM (Humphrey Stafford, 1402–60) was the grandson of the Thomas of Woodstock mentioned at 2.2.16, and therefore the King's cousin. He opposed Duke Humphrey and then supported the Queen against York. Killed at the Battle of Northampton (1460).

Duke of SOMERSET The play follows the chroniclers in conflating two historical figures, John Beaufort (1403–44) and his younger brother Edmund (1406–55), who succeeded York as Regent of France and was killed at the battle of St Albans (1455).

Old Lord CLIFFORD

YOUNG CLIFFORD, his son

Of the Duke of York's Party

Richard Plantagenet, Duke of YORK

EDWARD, Earl of March ⎤
                ⎬ his sons
RICHARD   ⎦

Earl of SALISBURY

Earl of WARWICK, his son

The petitions and the combat

Thomas HORNER, an armourer

PETER Thump, his man

Petitioners, Neighbours, Prentices

Lord CLIFFORD (1414–55) and his son (1435–61) were ardent supporters of Henry VI. Old Lord Clifford was killed at the battle of St Albans; in *3 Henry VI* his son avenges his death by killing York and his son Rutland. Young Clifford died at the battle of Ferrybridge just before the Yorkist victory at Towton (1461).

Richard Duke of YORK (1411–60) claimed the crown through his mother, descended from the third son of King Edward III, while Henry VI was descended from Edward's fourth son, John of Gaunt. York seems, however, to have been more patient in making his claim than the play suggests, and to have had no historical connection with Jack Cade's rebellion, as in the play. He and his sons were declared heirs to the crown after the Lancastrian defeat at St Albans, but Margaret refused to accept this, and York was killed at the battle of Wakefield (1460), dramatized in *3 Henry VI*.

EDWARD (1442–83), York's eldest son, appears only briefly in the play, but plays a major role in *3 Henry VI*. After York's death, he became King by defeating the Lancastrians at Towton (1461); Henry was briefly restored to the throne from 1469 to 1471, but Edward decisively defeated the Lancastrians at the battle of Tewkesbury (1471). His death is dramatized in *Richard III*.

RICHARD (1452–85) was historically only three at the time of the battle of St Albans, but the play introduces him in order to prepare for his major role as Yorkist leader in *3 Henry VI* and as King in *Richard III*. He was killed at the battle of Bosworth (1485) by the Lancastrian Richmond, later Henry VII. His nickname 'Crookback' derived from a probable minor deformity (one shoulder higher than the other) being exaggerated by his enemies.

Earl of SALISBURY Richard Neville (1400–60) inherited his title from his father-in-law. He only gradually sided with York, but fought for him at St Albans, and was executed after the Yorkist defeat at Wakefield (1460).

Earl of WARWICK Named like his father Richard Neville (1428–71), he became Earl of Warwick through his wife Anne Beauchamp. A major supporter of York's claim to the crown, he played a crucial role in the Yorkist victory at St Albans (1455). After York's death, supported Edward as King, but quarrelled with him in 1469 and restored Henry to the throne, thus gaining his nickname 'Kingmaker'. Defeated and killed by Edward at the battle of Barnet (1471).

HORNER and PETER are fictional names. The Elizabethan historian John Stow calls the armourer William Catur and the servant John David.

The conjuration

John HUM ⎫
⎬ priests
John SOUTHWELL ⎭

Margery Jourdayne, a WITCH

Roger BOLINGBROKE, a conjuror

A SPIRIT

The false miracle

Sander SIMPCOX

SIMPCOX'S WIFE

The MAYOR of Saint Albans

Aldermen of Saint Albans

A BEADLE of Saint Albans

Eleanor's penance

Gloucester's SERVANTS

SHERIFF of London

Sir John STANLEY

HERALD

The murder of Gloucester

Two MURDERERS

COMMONS

The murder of Suffolk

LIEUTENANT, commander of a ship

MASTER of that ship

The Master's MATE

Walter WHITMORE

Two GENTLEMEN

HUM, SOUTHWELL, JOURDAYNE, and **BOLINGBROKE** are named by the chroniclers as Duchess Eleanor's associates. Southwell at least is historical: he was a priest and canon of St Stephen's, Westminster.

Sander SIMPCOX Probably derived from the Tudor chroniclers (where he is anony-

mous) rather than from history, his name may be a combination of 'simpleton' and 'coxcomb', knave.

Sir John STANLEY Actually Sir Thomas (1406?–59), Governor of the Isle of Man.

Walter WHITMORE A fictional character. See the Commentary to 4.1.0.3.

The Cade Rebellion

Jack CADE, the rebel leader

Dick the BUTCHER ⎫
Smith the WEAVER ⎪
A Sawyer ⎬ Cade's followers
JOHN ⎪
REBELS ⎭

Emmanuel, the CLERK of Chatham

Sir Humphrey STAFFORD

William, STAFFORD'S BROTHER

Lord SAYE

Lord SCALES

Matthew Gough

Alexander IDEN, an esquire of Kent

CITIZENS of London

Others

VAUX, a messenger

A POST

MESSENGERS

A SOLDIER

Attendants, guards, servants, soldiers, falconers, drummers

Jack CADE, leader of the popular rebellion against Henry VI. Very little is known about him, and even his name may have been a pseudonym, although a John Cade in the Sussex household of Sir Thomas Dacre was indicted in 1450 for the murder of a pregnant woman.

Sir Humphrey STAFFORD and his BROTHER William were experienced soldiers who were lured into a trap by Cade and murdered in 1450.

Lord SAYE, Lord Chamberlain and Treasurer of England, was especially hated by Cade's rebels because associated with Suffolk's policies and especially the surrender of Anjou and Maine to Queen Margaret's father; he was murdered by them in 1450.

Lord SCALES (1399?–1460), a veteran of the French wars, left to defend the Tower of London from Cade in 1450; murdered by boatmen in 1460.

Matthew Gough, like Scales an experienced commander in the French wars, was murdered by Cade's rebels in 1450.

Alexander IDEN, sheriff of Kent after the murder of Sir James Cromer by Cade; he married Cromer's widow, daughter of Lord Saye.

VAUX may be Sir William Vaux who was killed at Tewkesbury: see the Commentary to 3.2.371.

The Second Part of Henry the Sixth, with the Death of the Good Duke Humphrey

1.1   *Flourish of trumpets, then hautboys. Enter, at one*
        door, King Henry the Sixth and Humphrey Duke of
        Gloucester, the Duke of Somerset, the Duke of
        Buckingham, Cardinal Beaufort, and others.
        Enter, at the other door, the Duke of York, and the
        Marquis of Suffolk with Queen Margaret, and the Earls
        of Salisbury and Warwick

SUFFOLK
As by your high imperial majesty

Title] F (*head title*) ; *The Second Part of Henry* [*King Hen. Catalogue*] *the Sixt.* (*running titles*) ; THE
FIRST PART OF THE CONTENTION OF THE TWO FAMOVS Houses of *Yorke & Lancaster*, with the
death of the good Duke *Humphrey*. Q (*head title*); *for Q's title-page, see p. 36.*   1.1] *Actus Primus.*
Scæna Prima. F (*which has no further act or scene divisions*)   0.1 *Flourish . . . hautboys*] F   0.1–7
Enter . . . Warwick] Q (*subs.*) ;   *Enter King, Duke Humfrey, Salisbury, Warwicke, and Beauford on the*
one side | The Queene, Suffolke, Yorke, Somerset, and Buckingham, on the other. F

1.1 The play opens with a formal state occasion, Suffolk's presentation to Henry VI of
the French princess Margaret of Anjou as
his queen. It took place in 1445; the
chronicle material for this and subsequent scenes is given in Appendix B.
The preparations for the marriage, arising out of a (fictional) chance encounter
between Suffolk and Margaret, and Duke
Humphrey's opposition to it, are dramatized in *1 Henry VI* 5.5 and 5.7.

0.1 *Flourish* Fanfare accompanying royal
entrances and exits.
    hautboys These were louder, with more
carrying power, than the modern oboe,
and were used as outdoor instruments.
They probably played a march accompanying the opening procession.

0.1–7 *Enter . . . Warwick* The court assem-
bles from the two doors set in the back
wall of the Elizabethan stage. The opening stage directions in the Quarto, followed here, and the Folio (see collation)
differ. Neither divides the characters
simply into Lancastrians and Yorkists; but
the Quarto's arrangement has a dramatic logic whereas the Folio's seems

haphazard: Suffolk brings Margaret
from France, so they are preceded by
York, the King's Regent in France, who is
accompanied by his allies Salisbury and
Warwick, while the King is attended by
his uncles Humphrey, the Lord Protector
of the realm during his minority, and
Cardinal Beaufort, and by the Lancastrians Somerset and Buckingham.

1–52 The formality of the occasion is emphasized by stilted phrasing and sometimes archaic language. Beneath
Suffolk's grandiloquence is the simple
sentence 'As I was instructed to marry
Princess Margaret on your behalf, I did
so, and now deliver her to you'. For
archaisms, see the notes to 'alderliefest'
(l. 28) and 'yclad' (l. 33). The formality is
abruptly shattered when Duke Humphrey
breaks off his reading in mid-word at
l. 52.

1 **by** by order of (*OED prep., adv.* 23). The
King gives Suffolk this order at *1 Henry VI*
5.7.87–93.
    imperial Henry ruled the empire of
England, France, and Ireland.

I had in charge at my depart for France,
As Procurator to your excellence,
To marry Princess Margaret for your grace,
So in the famous ancient city Tours,   5
In presence of the Kings of France and Sicil,
The Dukes of Orléans, Calabre, Bretagne, and Alençon,
Seven earls, twelve barons, and twenty reverend
    bishops,
I have performed my task and was espoused,
And humbly now upon my bended knee,   10
In sight of England and her lordly peers,
Deliver up my title in the Queen
To your most gracious hands, that are the substance
Of that great shadow I did represent:
The happiest gift that ever marquis gave,   15
The fairest queen that ever king received.

KING HENRY

Suffolk, arise. Welcome Queen Margaret.
I can express no kinder sign of love
Than this kind kiss. O Lord that lends me life,

---

2 **had in charge** was commissioned (*OED, charge, sb.* 13b)
    depart departure. For the use of one part of speech for another, see Abbott 451.

3 **Procurator** deputy, representative (*OED sb.* 2a). This word, like other details of Suffolk's speech, comes from Hall's account (see Appendix B, 1.1.1–9).

4 **marry . . . grace** Suffolk married Margaret on Henry's behalf; but this also neatly anticipates their private relationship, dramatically if not historically.

6 **France** Charles VII, who appears in *1 Henry VI* as the Dauphin, or heir-apparent to the French throne.
    Sicil Margaret's father René was King of Sicily, though only in name.

7 **Orléans . . . Alençon** Like René, both appear as allies of Charles in *1 Henry VI*.
    Calabre F's 'Calaber' is an anglicization of 'Calabre', the French version of Calabria, in southern Italy. This Duke was the eldest son of King René of Sicily (see previous line), and therefore Margaret's brother.

9 **espoused** married (by proxy, for the King)

12 **title in** claim to (a legal term: *OED sb.* 6)

13 **that are** you who are

13–14 **substance . . . shadow** A contrast, frequent in Shakespeare, between the reality and the image: in marrying Margaret, Suffolk merely represents the power of the King.

15 **happiest** most fortunate
    marquis An intermediate stage between the earl that Suffolk was in *1 Henry VI* and the duke he becomes at l. 63. See Appendix B, 1.1.1–9.

18 **kinder** more natural

19 **Than . . . life** Henry's response to Margaret is complex. He moves (in mid-line) from his kiss of welcome, usually given on the cheek rather than the lips, to his characteristic gratitude to God, at which most performers of Margaret express amazement, preparing for 1.3.54–65. But later (32–5) he expresses an almost childlike delight in his new wife, much emphasized in recent performances, which prepares for his ready acceptance of her lack of dowry and the surrender of Anjou and Maine (l. 62), which so incenses his court; his personal reaction to Margaret, therefore, is in part responsible for the disasters that follow.

Lend me a heart replete with thankfulness!   20
For thou hast given me in this beauteous face
A world of earthly blessings to my soul,
If sympathy of love unite our thoughts.

QUEEN MARGARET

Great King of England, and my gracious lord,
The mutual conference that my mind hath had—   25
By day, by night; waking, and in my dreams;
In courtly company, or at my beads—
With you, mine alderliefest sovereign,
Makes me the bolder to salute my king
With ruder terms, such as my wit affords,   30
And overjoy of heart doth minister.

KING HENRY

Her sight did ravish, but her grace in speech,
Her words yclad with wisdom's majesty,
Makes me from wond'ring fall to weeping joys,

kind loving (punning on *kinder* in l. 18)
lends grants

20 **replete** filled
23 **sympathy of** mutual
24–31 Margaret has a quite different speech in the Quarto text: see Appendix A, Passage A, and Textual Introduction, p. 90. Here, she picks up Henry's reference to their mutual *thoughts* in his last line, and develops it into an elaborate distinction between the *mutual conference* of their minds, and the *ruder terms*, the *speech*, with which she is now able to express what before only existed in her *mind*.
25 **mutual conference** intimate conversation
27 **In courtly company** among courtiers
   at my beads while saying prayers in private with a rosary, a string of beads to help the user keep a count of the prayers said. As a primarily Roman Catholic devotion, it was criticized as a papist superstition in post-Reformation England (*OED, rosary*, 5a), and may have seemed particularly suitable to a French princess, though Henry also uses *beads* (1.3.57).
28 **mine** my. The two forms are used interchangeably by Shakespeare, but *mine* used before vowels, as here, allows a greater fluency of delivery (Abbott 237).
   alderliefest dearest of all. Although *OED*

(*all*, D.3) says that this 'was a common epithet' in the sixteenth century, it gives few examples, of which this is the last; and McKerrow comments: 'the italics of the Folio suggest that the compositor did not know it and took it for a foreign word.' It may have been meant to sound like the formal utterance of a foreign princess, a verbal equivalent, perhaps, to the French 'r' sound that Peggy Ashcroft used to suggest a foreigner throughout her performance of the part at Stratford-upon-Avon in 1963–4
29 **salute** greet
30 **ruder terms** more unpolished speech
   wit intelligence
31 **overjoy** excess of joy. 'Apparently new as a noun' (McKerrow), this is *OED*'s earliest example.
   minister supply
32 **Her sight** the sight of her
33 **yclad** clothed. The y- prefix derives from Old and Middle English, and is used as an archaism or affectation in Shakespeare's work. Perhaps it is meant to sound stilted here.
34 **Makes** The subject of the sentence is probably *grace*, but could be *grace* and *words*: plural subjects and singular verbs (and vice versa) are common in Elizabethan English (Abbott 333, 336).
   wond'ring admiring

Such is the fullness of my heart's content.   35
Lords, with one cheerful voice, welcome my love.
LORDS (*kneeling*)
Long live Queen Margaret, England's happiness.
QUEEN MARGARET We thank you all.
  Flourish. They all rise
SUFFOLK
My lord Protector, so it please your grace,
Here are the articles of contracted peace   40
Between our sovereign and the French King Charles,
For eighteen months concluded by consent.

DUKE HUMPHREY (*reads*) 'Imprimis: it is agreed between the
French King Charles and William de la Pole, Marquis of
Suffolk, ambassador for Henry, King of England, that the   45
said Henry shall espouse the Lady Margaret, daughter
unto René, King of Naples, Sicilia, and Jerusalem, and
crown her Queen of England, ere the thirtieth of May
next ensuing.

'Item: that the duchy of Anjou and the county of   50
Maine shall be released and delivered to the King her
fa—'
  ⌈*He lets the paper fall*⌉
KING HENRY
Uncle, how now?
DUKE HUMPHREY Pardon me, gracious lord.

---

37 LORDS (*kneeling*)] *All kneel.* F   38.1 *They all rise*] *not in* F   43 DUKE HUMPHREY] This edition
throughout; F *varies between 'Gloster' and 'Humfrey', or abbreviations of these, throughout*
Imprimis] F (Inprimis)   47 René] F (*Reignier*)   52 fa—] Q (fa.); *father.* F   52.1 *He . . . fall*] Q
(*Duke Humphrey lets it fall.*); *not in* F

39 **Lord Protector** Humphrey was Lord
Protector of the realm during Henry's
minority, as he specifically states at
1.3.121; but see Introduction, p. 35.

43 **Imprimis** firstly (the normal Latin opening of an official document including a
list of items)

47 **René** (modernized form of F's 'Reignier')
Naples, Sicilia (one kingdom)

50 **Item: that** Oxford follows the Quarto in
inserting 'it is further agreed between
them', as in Beaufort's reading of the
item at ll. 57–8, on the grounds that 'both
readings of the document should be
identical' (*Textual Companion*, p. 179). Not
necessarily: as Hattaway says, Humphrey

may 'be skimming on to the important
part of the document'. It may be dramatically more effective *not* to repeat phrases
mechanically.
Item likewise (Latin, used to introduce each new article in an official
document)

51 **released** given up

52 **fa–** Duke Humphrey's breaking off here,
and his dropping of the paper, are in the
Quarto but not in the Folio; they are
surely what is intended, and what happened in performance. See the Introduction, pp. 37–8.

53 **how now** What is the matter? (a
common catch-phrase)

Some sudden qualm hath struck me at the heart
And dimmed mine eyes that I can read no further.   55

KING HENRY (*to Cardinal Beaufort*)
Uncle of Winchester, I pray read on.

CARDINAL BEAUFORT (*reads*) 'Item: it is further agreed
between them that the duchies of Anjou and Maine shall
be released and delivered to the King her father, and she
sent over of the King of England's own proper cost and   60
charges, without having any dowry.'

KING HENRY
They please us well. (*To Suffolk*) Lord Marquis, kneel
down.
We here create thee the first Duke of Suffolk,
And gird thee with the sword. Cousin of York,
We here discharge your grace from being regent   65
I'th' parts of France till term of eighteen months
Be full expired. Thanks uncle Winchester,
Gloucester, York, Buckingham, Somerset,
Salisbury, and Warwick.
We thank you all for this great favour done   70

---

58 duchies] F (*Dutchesse*)   59 delivered] CAIRNCROSS; *deliuered ouer* F

---

54 **qualm** This means 'illness'; but for a
discussion of its wider implications, see
the Introduction, p. 38.
55 **that** so that
56 **Uncle** (actually great-uncle)
58 **the duchies . . . Maine** Oxford follows
Cairncross in repeating 'the duchy of
Anjou and the county of Maine' from ll.
50–1 since 'the Cardinal's reading should
be identical with Gloucester's', but this
may be more 'skimming' (see the first
note to l. 50) as it was played in the BBC
'Age of Kings' version. It also begins the
linking of 'Anjou and Maine' which runs
like a refrain through the later part of the
scene (e.g. ll. 109–18, 208–13, 235).
59 **delivered** F's 'delivered over' is probably
an error, influenced by 'sent over' in
the next phrase. Hall, the source, has
'released and delivered' (see Appendix B,
1.1.40–61).
60 **of** at (Abbott 168)
60–1 **own . . . charges** (a legal formula, gen-

erally used in connection with large state
expenses)
60 **own proper own**
64 **gird** invest (as a Duke, by presenting
Suffolk with a ceremonial sword and
sword-belt; *OED, gird, v.*[1] 3). Compare the
King at *I Henry VI* 3.1.175: 'I gird thee
with the valiant sword of York.'
Cousin A term of intimacy from a
monarch to a nobleman (*OED sb.* 5), but
Henry and York were in fact related, both
descended from Edward III, which is to
lead to York's claim to the crown in 2.2.
65 **regent** ruler on behalf of the King
66 **parts** territories (i.e. those ruled by
England)
67 **full** fully
67–9 **uncle . . . Warwick** Not a mere list of
names, but an opportunity to identify
important characters early in the play,
and to emphasize those already identified.
A further opportunity to do this occurs at
ll. 84–5.

In entertainment to my princely Queen.
Come, let us in, and with all speed provide
To see her coronation be performed.

Flourish. Exeunt King Henry, Queen Margaret, and Suffolk.
Duke Humphrey stays all the rest

DUKE HUMPHREY

Brave peers of England, pillars of the state,
To you Duke Humphrey must unload his grief,   75
Your grief, the common grief of all the land.
What, did my brother Henry spend his youth,
His valour, coin, and people in the wars,
Did he so often lodge in open field
In winter's cold and summer's parching heat   80
To conquer France, his true inheritance?
And did my brother Bedford toil his wits
To keep by policy what Henry got?
Have you yourselves, Somerset, Buckingham,
Brave York, Salisbury, and victorious Warwick,   85
Received deep scars in France and Normandy?
Or hath mine uncle Beaufort and myself,
With all the learnèd Council of the realm,

73.1 *Flourish*] not in F   73.2 *Duke Humphrey stays all*] Q; *Manet* F

---

71 **entertainment** welcome
   princely royal
73.1 *Flourish* J. H. Long thinks that the
   absence of this direction in F, though
   customary for royal exits, ironically reflects Henry's lack of true royalty and the
   'humiliating' terms of the marriage
   contract (*Shakespeare's Use of Music: The
   Histories and Tragedies* (Gainsville, Florida,
   1971), 24–5). But as far as the King is concerned the terms 'please us well', and the
   trumpeters' job is to mark his exit. For the
   reverse situation, see 4.9.48–49.1 and
   note.
74 **peers . . . pillars** Perhaps there is a pun on
   'piers', meaning 'pillars'.
   pillars . . . state Proverbial (Dent PP10).
77 **Henry** (Henry V)
   spend waste
79 **lodge** camp
81 **To   conquer . . . true   inheritance**
   England   claimed   the   French   throne

through Isabella, daughter of Philip IV of
France, mother of Edward III. Henry V
secured the title 'heir of France' at the
Treaty of Troyes in 1420. Shakespeare
dramatizes the conquest of France in
Henry V.
82 **Bedford** John, Duke of Bedford was named
   Regent of France by Henry V. His death is
   dramatized at *1 Henry VI* 3.5.69–73.
83 **policy** political skill or strategy. The word
   is used in a complimentary or at least a
   neutral sense here, but increasingly during the play it acquires the overtone of
   political expediency or chicanery. See the
   second note to 3.1.23.
87 **hath** See l. 34 n., 'Makes'.
   uncle (because Beaufort was the half-
   brother of Humphrey's father, Henry IV)
   Beaufort (the Cardinal)
88 **Council** i.e. the Privy Council, the
   'Cabinet' of ministers who advised the
   monarch

Studied so long, sat in the Council House
Early and late, debating to and fro,   90
How France and Frenchmen might be kept in awe,
And had his highness in his infancy
Crownèd in Paris in despite of foes,
And shall these labours and these honours die?
Shall Henry's conquest, Bedford's vigilance,   95
Your deeds of war, and all our counsel die?
O peers of England, shameful is this league,
Fatal this marriage, cancelling your fame,
Blotting your names from books of memory,
Razing the characters of your renown,   100
Defacing monuments of conquered France,
Undoing all, as all had never been!

CARDINAL BEAUFORT
Nephew, what means this passionate discourse,
This peroration with such circumstance?
For France, 'tis ours, and we will keep it still.   105

DUKE HUMPHREY
Ay uncle, we will keep it if we can;
But now it is impossible we should.
Suffolk, the new-made duke that rules the roost,
Hath given the duchy of Anjou and Maine

---

92 had] GRANT WHITE; hath F   108 roost] F (rost); roast Q

90 **to and fro** one way and another, for and
against
91 **kept in awe** restrained or controlled by
fear
92 **had** F's 'hath' is probably an error: 'An
original "hat" (for "had") might easily be
miscorrected to "hath"' (McKerrow).
93 **Crownèd in Paris** This is dramatized at *1
Henry VI* 4.1.1–2.
despite (a) spite (b) defiance
97 **league** alliance
99 **books of memory** history books,
chronicles
100 **Razing the characters** erasing the written records
101 **monuments of** records of (*OED*, *monument, sb.* 2) or memorials to, or both, i.e.
the surrendered Anjou and Maine
102 **as** as though
104 **peroration ... circumstance** long-
winded speech with detail

105 **For** as for
still always
106 **Ay** Yes. *OED* says that 'ay' appeared suddenly about 1575, of unknown origin. It
was usually spelt 'I' (as in the Folio text
here), which indicates the pronunciation.
It survives in English dialects and regional
accents.
108 **new-made duke** This is the first of
several derisive references to Suffolk's
promotion for arranging the Henry/
Margaret marriage (e.g. 1.1.123; 1.2.30,
95, and probably 3.1.98; see note).
rules the roost dominates. Tilley R144
confirms *roast* as an acceptable variant
form of the proverb. *Roost* is more
common nowadays' (*Textual Companion*,
p. 179)—and therefore more appropriate
to a modernized text, especially since the
origin of 'roast' remains obscure (*OED
sb.* 1b).

Unto the poor King René, whose large style   110
Agrees not with the leanness of his purse.

SALISBURY

Now by the death of him that died for all,
These counties were the keys of Normandy;
But wherefore weeps Warwick, my valiant son?

WARWICK

For grief that they are past recovery.   115
For were there hope to conquer them again
My sword should shed hot blood, mine eyes no tears.
Anjou and Maine? Myself did win them both.
Those provinces these arms of mine did conquer—
And are the cities that I got with wounds   120
Delivered up again with peaceful words?
Mort Dieu!

YORK

For Suffolk's Duke, may he be suffocate,
That dims the honour of this warlike isle!
France should have torn and rent my very heart   125
Before I would have yielded to this league.
I never read but England's kings have had
Large sums of gold and dowries with their wives—
And our King Henry gives away his own,
To match with her that brings no vantages.   130

DUKE HUMPHREY

A proper jest, and never heard before,
That Suffolk should demand a whole fifteenth

110–11 **whose large . . . purse** This vivid
phrase is borrowed from Hall: see Appendix B.
110 **large style** grandiose titles. These included Duke of Anjou, Lorraine, and
Barre, Count of Provence and Piedmont,
King of Hungary, Naples, both Sicilies,
Jerusalem, and Aragon (Cairncross). A
similar list of the titles of the English
warrior-hero Lord Talbot is mocked by
Joan of Arc as a 'silly, stately style' (*1
Henry VI* 4.7.72).
112 **him . . . all** i.e. Jesus Christ (an echo of
the New Testament: 2 Corinthians 5: 15)
118 **Myself . . . both** Here Richard Neville,
Earl of Warwick ('the Kingmaker') is
credited with the achievements of his

father-in-law Richard de Beauchamp, the
Warwick of *1 Henry VI*.
Myself I myself (Abbott 20)
122 *Mort Dieu* God's death (a common
French oath)
123 **suffocate** suffocated (a common
Elizabethan form of a past participle of
verbs ending in 't': Abbott 342)
126 **yielded** consented
127 **never read but** have always read that
129 **own** (money and possessions)
130 **match with** marry
vantages profits, dowry
131 **proper** real
132 **fifteenth** a tax of one-fifteenth on all personal property. It recurs at 4.7.20, this
time to accuse the Treasurer, Lord Saye,

For costs and charges in transporting her!
She should have stayed in France and starved in France
Before—   135

CARDINAL BEAUFORT

My lord of Gloucester, now ye grow too hot!
It was the pleasure of my lord the King.

DUKE HUMPHREY

My lord of Winchester, I know your mind.
'Tis not my speeches that you do mislike,
But 'tis my presence that doth trouble ye.   140
Rancour will out, proud prelate, in thy face
I see thy fury. If I longer stay
We shall begin our ancient bickerings.
Lordings, farewell, and say when I am gone,
I prophesied France will be lost ere long.   *Exit*   145

CARDINAL BEAUFORT

So, there goes our Protector in a rage.
'Tis known to you he is mine enemy;
Nay more, an enemy unto you all,
And no great friend, I fear me, to the King.
Consider, lords, he is the next of blood   150
And heir apparent to the English crown.
Had Henry got an empire by his marriage,
And all the wealthy kingdoms of the west,
There's reason he should be displeased at it.
Look to it, lords, let not his smoothing words   155

again in the context of giving up French territory.

134 **starved** The original meaning was 'died' (from Old English *steorfan*), but the modern meaning of *starved* involves dying anyway.

136, 140 **ye** (used interchangeably with 'you' in this play)

136 **hot** angry

143 **ancient bickerings** These long-standing squabbles between Humphrey and the Cardinal are extensively dramatized in *1 Henry VI*.

144 **Lordings** gentlemen. A frequent form of address (*OED sb.* 1); the contemptuous sense, 'as when we say Lording for Lord' (Puttenham, *English Poesie*, cited at *OED sb.* 2), doesn't seem applicable

here, unless Humphrey is allowing his annoyance with the Cardinal to colour his farewell to the other lords.

148 **Nay** Literally 'no', but often used, as here and in most of its occurrences in the play, as an intensifier.

150–1 **he is . . . crown** (because the King is so far childless, and Humphrey the last surviving brother of Henry V)

152 **Had Henry** even if Henry had

153 **wealthy . . . west** Usually glossed as an anachronistic reference to Spanish possessions in America, but may refer to the Kingdoms of Europe (the Occident).

154 **he** (Duke Humphrey)

155 **Look to it** be on your guard (a phrase frequently used by Shakespeare)
smoothing flattering

Bewitch your hearts, be wise and circumspect.
What though the common people favour him,
Calling him 'Humphrey, the good Duke of Gloucester',
Clapping their hands and crying with loud voice
'Jesu maintain your royal excellence!'   160
With 'God preserve the good Duke Humphrey!'
I fear me, lords, for all this flattering gloss,
He will be found a dangerous Protector.

BUCKINGHAM
Why should he then protect our sovereign,
He being of age to govern of himself?   165
Cousin of Somerset, join you with me,
And all together, with the Duke of Suffolk,
We'll quickly hoist Duke Humphrey from his seat.

CARDINAL BEAUFORT
This weighty business will not brook delay;
I'll to the Duke of Suffolk presently.   *Exit*   170

SOMERSET
Cousin of Buckingham, though Humphrey's pride
And greatness of his place be grief to us,
Yet let us watch the haughty Cardinal;
His insolence is more intolerable

---

168 hoist] F (hoyse)

162 **fear me** fear. The *me* is an example of
'ethic dative' in which *me* originally meant
'for me'. By Shakespeare's time, it had
become little more than an intensifier.
　this flattering gloss 'either "speci-
ously fair appearance" (on the part of
Humphrey), or "flattering descriptions"
(on the part of the common people)'
(McKerrow).
164–5 **he . . . He** Humphrey . . . Henry
165 **being . . . himself** Historically, Henry
was twenty-four and Humphrey in fact no
longer Protector; but the play retains him
in that office to emphasize Henry's depen-
dence on him and to intensify the cata-
strophe of Humphrey's fall.
　of for
168 **hoist** lift, remove. Oxford treats *hoist* as a
modernization of F's 'hoise', of which

OED (*hoist, v.*) says that *hoist* was originally a corruption. 'Hoys'd' occurs in F
at *Richard III* 4.4.458 (TLN 3334); all
other (later) examples in F use 'hoist',
which may suggest that that became
Shakespeare's preferred form. In any
case, as *OED*'s example of both 'hoise'
and *hoist* make clear, the forms were used
interchangeably in the period to mean 'lift
up' (originally a sail), so *hoist* seems an
acceptable, and more comprehensible,
modernization.
169 **brook** tolerate
170 **I'll** I'll go
　presently immediately (the standard
Elizabethan usage)
172 **place** position
　grief source of grievance
174 **insolence** arrogance

Than all the princes in the land beside.   175
If Gloucester be displaced, he'll be Protector.

BUCKINGHAM

Or thou or I will be Protector, Somerset,
Despite Duke Humphrey or the Cardinal.

Exeunt Buckingham and Somerset

SALISBURY

Pride went before, ambition follows him.
While these do labour for their own preferment,   180
Behoves it us to labour for the realm.
I never saw but Humphrey Duke of Gloucester
Did bear him like a noble gentleman.
Oft have I seen the haughty Cardinal,
More like a soldier than a man o'th' church,   185
As stout and proud as he were lord of all,
Swear like a ruffian, and demean himself
Unlike the ruler of a common weal.
Warwick my son, the comfort of my age,
Thy deeds, thy plainness, and thy housekeeping   190
Hath won thee greatest favour of the commons,
Excepting none but good Duke Humphrey.

---

177 Or . . . Somerset] This edition; Or thou, or I Somerset will be Protectors F   191 thee] Q;
the F

---

175 **princes . . . beside** other nobles
176 **be displaced** loses his *place*, office
177 F's line limps rhythmically (see collation), and 'Protectors' should obviously
be 'Protector'. I think the two problems
are linked. If the dramatist marked
'Somerset' to be moved, or added, in the
manuscript with an insertion mark and
's', this could have been misread by the
compositor. My rearrangement does not
perhaps produce a perfect six-syllable
line, but it is more speakable than F's.
Or . . . or   either . . . or   (common
Elizabethan usage)
179-203 Throughout the play, Salisbury
is presented as a (perhaps the only)
representative of moderation. He can
distinguish between true loyalty and
self-interest here; he tries to let reason
prevail at 1.3.114-15; he has to be persuaded of York's claim to the crown in
2.2, and sees the need to explain the

breaking of his oath of loyalty to the King
at 5.1.182-90.
179 **Pride . . . ambition** This modifies the
proverb 'Pride goes before and shame
comes after' (Dent P576), applied first to
the Cardinal and then to Somerset and
Buckingham together.
181 **Behoves it** it is necessary for (*OED v.* 2)
182 **never saw but have** always seen that
183 **bear him** conduct himself
186 **stout** arrogant
as as if
187 **demean** behave. Despite the context, it is
unlikely to carry the pejorative sense
'lower himself', of which *OED*'s earliest
example is from 1601.
188 **common weal** commonwealth, state
190 **plainness** honesty
housekeeping hospitality
192 **Excepting none but** except for that they
have shown to

And brother York, thy acts in Ireland,
In bringing them to civil discipline,
Thy late exploits done in the heart of France,   195
When thou wert regent for our sovereign,
Have made thee feared and honoured of the people.
Join we together for the public good,
In what we can to bridle and suppress
The pride of Suffolk and the Cardinal   200
With Somerset's and Buckingham's ambition;
And as we may, cherish Duke Humphrey's deeds
While they do tend the profit of the land.

WARWICK

So God help Warwick, as he loves the land,
And common profit of his country!   205

YORK

And so says York, (*aside*) for he hath greatest cause.

SALISBURY

Then let's away, and look unto the main.

WARWICK

Unto the main? O father, Maine is lost,

197] OXFORD *adds, after* Q: The reverence of mine age and Neville's name | Is of no little force if
I command ; *not in* F   207 let's away] OXFORD; lets make hast away F

---

193 **brother** i.e. brother-in-law. York married
Salisbury's sister Cecily.
   acts in Ireland This anticipates York's
Irish campaign that does not happen until
3.1.
195 **late exploits** recent military
achievements
197 **feared** held in awe (*OED v.* 6)
197–8 Between these lines, Oxford inserts
two lines from Q (see collation), which
'explain why Salisbury . . . is important
for the success of Warwick and York'
although 'they do not echo anything
in F' (*Textual Companion*, p. 179). But
Salisbury's authority is quite clearly
established already, and since the policy
of this edition is only to accept Q passages
which fill lacunae or which correct
errors, they are excluded here.
199 **bridle** restrain
202 **cherish** encourage
203 **tend the profit** serve the welfare
206 *aside* Although this term was in use
from the mid-1590s (*Textual Companion*, p.
80), it is always added editorially in this

edition. It simply indicates that lines are
spoken directly to the audience, not that
they are hurriedly thrown away, as *aside*
came to suggest in nineteenth-century
and subsequent drama.
   greatest cause (because he has a claim to
the crown)
207 **let's away** Oxford omits F's 'make
haste' (see collation), thus creating a
regular iambic line, on the grounds that
F's Compositor 'B' shows signs of stretch-
ing his copy here to fill his page (*Textual
Companion*, p. 179).
   look . . . main see to the most important
matters at stake (a proverbial phrase
derived from the game of hazard (Dent
E235), where *main* is a winning throw)
208–11 **Maine . . . Maine** Johnson said that
a verbal quibble was to Shakespeare a
'fatal Cleopatra for which he lost the
world, and was content to lose it'
(Preface, pp. xxiii–xxiv), but puns are
seldom spelled out so relentlessly as those
on 'Maine' and 'main' here.

That Maine which by main force Warwick did win,
And would have kept so long as breath did last!   210
Main chance, father, you meant, but I meant Maine,
Which I will win from France or else be slain.

                              Exeunt Warwick and Salisbury

YORK

Anjou and Maine are given to the French,
Paris is lost, the state of Normandy
Stands on a tickle point now they are gone;   215
Suffolk concluded on the articles,
The peers agreed, and Henry was well pleased
To change two dukedoms for a duke's fair daughter.
I cannot blame them all, what is't to them?
'Tis thine they give away and not their own.   220
Pirates may make cheap pennyworths of their pillage,
And purchase friends, and give to courtesans,
Still revelling like lords till all be gone,
Whileas the silly owner of the goods
Weeps over them, and wrings his hapless hands,   225
And shakes his head, and trembling stands aloof,
While all is shared and all is borne away,
Ready to starve, and dare not touch his own.
So York must sit and fret and bite his tongue,
While his own lands are bargained for and sold.   230
Methinks the realms of England, France, and Ireland
Bear that proportion to my flesh and blood
As did the fatal brand Althaea burnt

---

209 **main** sheer
211 **Main chance** See second note to l. 207.
213–34 **Anjou ... Calydon** This first half of
York's soliloquy is missing from Q. It was
probably cut in the production that Q
reports. But was it also marked for deletion in the copy for F, and retained by the
compositor by accident, especially since
the opening line is virtually repeated
half-way through, the point at which Q's
speech begins? Perhaps; but the second
half is not simply a repeat of the first,
which recapitulates the action of the
scene from York's viewpoint, while the
second looks forward.
215 **on a tickle point** in an unstable
position
216 **concluded** determined

219 **them all** any of them (Abbott 12)
220 **thine** (York addresses himself)
221 **make cheap pennyworths of** sell at a
loss
223 **Still** continually
224 **Whileas** while (Abbott 116)
    silly helpless (*OED a.* 1b)
225 **hapless** unfortunate
226 **aloof** at a distance
229 **bite** i.e. hold
231 **Methinks** it seems to me
232 **proportion** relation
233–4 **fatal ... Calydon** Meleager, *prince
of Calydon*, died when his mother,
Althaea, in a rage burned a piece of wood
(*brand*) upon which the Fates (hence
fatal) had said his life depended (Ovid,
Metamorphoses 8.451–526).

123

Unto the prince's heart of Calydon.
Anjou and Maine both given unto the French!   235
Cold news for me, for I had hope of France,
Even as I have of fertile England's soil.
A day will come when York shall claim his own,
And therefore I will take the Nevilles' parts,
And make a show of love to proud Duke Humphrey,   240
And when I spy advantage, claim the crown,
For that's the golden mark I seek to hit.
Nor shall proud Lancaster usurp my right,
Nor hold the sceptre in his childish fist,
Nor wear the diadem upon his head   245
Whose church-like humours fits not for a crown.
Then York, be still a while till time do serve.
Watch thou and wake when others be asleep,
To pry into the secrets of the state,
Till Henry surfeit in the joys of love   250
With his new bride and England's dear-bought queen,
And Humphrey with the peers be fall'n at jars.
Then will I raise aloft the milk-white rose,
With whose sweet smell the air shall be perfumed,
And in my standard bear the arms of York,   255

---

250 surfeit in the] HANMER; surfetting in F

---

234 **the . . . Calydon** the heart of the prince
   of Calydon
236 **Cold** chilling, unencouraging (*OED
   a.* 10a)
239 **take the Nevilles' parts** ally myself with
   Salisbury and Warwick
240 **show** appearance
241 **advantage** opportunity
242 **mark** target (as in archery)
243 **Lancaster** i.e. Henry VI, who was also
   Duke of Lancaster
244 **childish** Perhaps this implies simple-
   mindedness as well as youth, as in
   Richard III's hypocritical phrase 'I am too
   childish-foolish for this world' (1.3.142),
   but it is hard to be sure how far
   Shakespeare was aware of the historical Henry's apparent attacks of madness;
   see Introduction, p. 34.
245 **diadem** crown

246 **fits** A singular verb with a plural subject
   is common Elizabethan usage; but
   humours may have been regarded as a
   singular subject, the characteristics that
   make up a man's temperament.
247 **still** silent
248 **Watch** stay awake
250 **surfeit in** become cloyed with.
   Hanmer's emendation of F's 'surfeting'
   is needed, since otherwise a verb is
   lacking.
252 **be fall'n at jars** quarrel
253 **white rose** The emblem of the house of
   York throughout the plays, as the red rose
   is of Lancaster. A fictional motive for their
   adoption is vividly dramatized at *1 Henry
   VI* 2.4.
255 **standard** flag of battle
   arms coat of arms (perhaps setting up
   word-play on *grapple* in the next line)

To grapple with the house of Lancaster;
And force perforce I'll make him yield the crown,
Whose bookish rule hath pulled fair England down.

Exit

I.2   *Enter Duke Humphrey of Gloucester and his*
       wife Eleanor

DUCHESS ELEANOR

Why droops my lord like over-ripened corn,
Hanging the head at Ceres' plenteous load?
Why doth the great Duke Humphrey knit his brows,
As frowning at the favours of the world?
Why are thine eyes fixed to the sullen earth,   5
Gazing on that which seems to dim thy sight?
What seest thou there? King Henry's diadem,
Enchased with all the honours of the world?
If so, gaze on, and grovel on thy face
Until thy head be circled with the same.   10
Put forth thy hand, reach at the glorious gold.
What, is't too short? I'll lengthen it with mine;
And having both together heaved it up,
We'll both together lift our heads to heaven
And never more abase our sight so low   15
As to vouchsafe one glance unto the ground.

DUKE HUMPHREY

O Nell, sweet Nell, if thou dost love thy lord,
Banish the canker of ambitious thoughts.

---

256 **grapple** struggle. This is *OED*'s first
recorded use of the idiom, *v.* 8c; it does
not record Q1's 'graffle', which Gary
Taylor suggests may be an error for
'wrassle' (wrestle) (*Textual Companion*,
p. 179), the compositor misreading
Elizabethan long 's' as 'f'.

257 **force perforce** by compulsion (an
emphatic phrase, elsewhere used at
Dream 3.1.133, *King John* 3.1.68, and *2
Henry IV* 4.1.114 and 4.3.46).

258 **bookish** studious (perhaps specifically
implying religious books, in view of
York's criticism of Henry's *church-like
humours* at l. 246)

I.2.2 **Ceres** Roman goddess of the harvest
plenteous load rich harvest

5 **sullen** gloomy

8 **Enchased** adorned as with gems (*OED*,
enchase, v.[2] 1)

9 **grovel on thy face** Perhaps 'to solicit
supernatural aid' (Cairncross): compare
1.4.11; but the phrase may simply be an
extension of her picture of Humphrey
staring fixedly at the *sullen earth* (ll. 5–6);
if he sees Henry's crown in the earth, let
him get even closer to it by *grovelling*.

12 **is't** is your arm

13 **heaved it up** raised your arm. *Heaved*
gives a sense of the great effort involved,
as often in Shakespeare, for example at
History of Lear 4.3.26–7: 'she heaved the
name of "father" | Pantingly forth as if it
pressed her heart'. Compare 4.10.50.

16 **vouchsafe** grant

18 **canker** spreading sore, ulcer

And may that hour when I imagine ill
Against my king and nephew, virtuous Henry,   20
Be my last breathing in this mortal world.
My troublous dream this night doth make me sad.

DUCHESS ELEANOR
What dreamed my lord? Tell me and I'll requite it
With sweet rehearsal of my morning's dream.

DUKE HUMPHREY
Methought this staff, mine office-badge in court,   25
Was broke in twain—by whom I have forgot,
But as I think, it was by th' Cardinal—
And on the pieces of the broken wand
Were placed the heads of Edmund, Duke of Somerset,
And William de la Pole, first Duke of Suffolk.   30
This was my dream, what it doth bode God knows.

DUCHESS ELEANOR
Tut, this was nothing but an argument
That he that breaks a stick of Gloucester's grove
Shall lose his head for his presumption.
But list to me, my Humphrey, my sweet duke: 35
Methought I sat in seat of majesty
In the cathedral church of Westminster,
And in that chair where kings and queens are crowned,

1.2.19 hour] CAIRNCROSS (*conj.* Vaughan); thought F   22 dream] CAPELL; dreames F
38 are] Q; wer F

---

19 **imagine** contrive, plan
21 **last breathing** final breath of life. *OED*,
   breathing, sb. 1a cites a phrase from 1608,
   'forsake me not . . . in my last breathing',
   which suggests that it may have been a
   standard phrase for 'dying moment'.
22 **troublous** troubled
   dream 'The combination of Q ("troubled
   with a dreame"), the singular verb
   "doth", and the occurrence of "dreame"
   in lines 1.2.31 and 1.2.52 support the
   emendation' of F's 'dreams' (*Textual Companion*, p. 180).
   this i.e. last
23 **requite** repay
24 **rehearsal** recital
   morning's dream i.e. dream which will
   come true. 'In folklore a morning dream
   was considered a favourable prophecy'
   (Sanders)—hence '*sweet* rehearsal'.

25 **Methought** it seemed to me
29 **Edmund . . . Somerset** The play confuses
   (or conflates) John, who was Duke
   of Somerset at this time, with Edmund,
   his younger brother, whose death at St
   Albans is dramatized later in the play
   (5.2.65.3).
30 **first** Duke Humphrey gibes again at
   Suffolk's recent promotion.
31 **bode** foretell
32 **Tut** (an exclamation of impatience)
   argument proof, evidence
34 **presumption** (four syllables: 'i-on')
35 **list** listen
38 **chair** (the coronation throne)
   are 'The unusual spelling "wer" in F1
   (preserved in F2) seems to be due to a
   crowded line and does not suggest a
   misprint; but nevertheless [Q's] "are"
   may be correct' (McKerrow).

Where Henry and Dame Margaret kneeled to me,
And on my head did set the diadem.   40

DUKE HUMPHREY

Nay Eleanor, then must I chide outright.
Presumptuous dame, ill-nurtured Eleanor,
Art thou not second woman in the realm,
And the Protector's wife beloved of him?
Hast thou not worldly pleasure at command   45
Above the reach or compass of thy thought?
And wilt thou still be hammering treachery
To tumble down thy husband and thyself
From top of honour to disgrace's feet?
Away from me, and let me hear no more!   50

DUCHESS ELEANOR

What, what, my lord? Are you so choleric
With Eleanor for telling but her dream?
Next time I'll keep my dreams unto myself
And not be checked.

DUKE HUMPHREY

Nay be not angry, I am pleased again.   55

Enter a Messenger

MESSENGER

My Lord Protector, 'tis his highness' pleasure
You do prepare to ride unto Saint Albans,
Whereas the King and Queen do mean to hawk.

DUKE HUMPHREY

I go. Come Nell, thou wilt ride with us?

DUCHESS ELEANOR

Yes my good lord, I'll follow presently.   60

Exeunt Duke Humphrey and the Messenger

Follow I must; I cannot go before

55.1 *a] not in* F   60.1 *Exeunt . . . Messenger] Ex. Hum* F (*after l.* 59)

42 **ill-nurtured** Humphrey is probably criti-
cizing Eleanor for using her education,
'nurture', to ill ends, rather than remind-
ing her that she was once waiting-woman
to his first wife; but see 1.3.84 and second
note.
46 **compass** range
47 **hammering** devising
51 **choleric** angry

52 **telling but** only telling
54 **checked** rebuked
57 **Saint Albans** (twenty miles north of
London)
58 **Whereas** where
   hawk hunt with hawks
61 **Follow . . . before** This echoes the proverb
'They that cannot go before must come
behind' (Dent G156).

While Gloucester bears this base and humble mind.
Were I a man, a duke, and next of blood,
I would remove these tedious stumbling blocks
And smooth my way upon their headless necks.   65
And being a woman, I will not be slack
To play my part in Fortune's pageant.
(*Calling within*) Where are you there? Sir John! Nay, fear
   not, man,
We are alone, here's none but thee and I.
         Enter Sir John Hum

HUM
   Jesus preserve your royal majesty.   70

DUCHESS ELEANOR
   What sayst thou? 'Majesty'? I am but 'grace'.

HUM
   But by the grace of God and Hum's advice
   Your grace's title shall be multiplied.

DUCHESS ELEANOR
   What sayst thou, man? Hast thou as yet conferred
   With Margery Jourdayne, the cunning witch,   75

69.1 *Sir John*] *not in* F   *Hum*] Q;   *Hume* F (*throughout*)

go before claim precedence (as she could if she were Queen)

62 **base** servile
63 **of blood** in line of succession to the crown
66–7 **being . . . pageant** Eleanor associates herself with fortune, who was personified as a woman.
67 **pageant** spectacular show, probably allegorical, since it is *Fortune's* pageant
68 **Sir** This was a common form of address for priests, as in this case, as well as knights.
69.1 **Hum** The Folio and Foxe's *Acts and Monuments* call this character 'Hume', the Quarto and Hall 'Hum' (Holinshed's 'Hun' is clearly a misreading of Hall, from which Holinshed derives). The strongest evidence that the play followed Hall in calling him 'Hum' comes, ironically, in the Folio scene itself, where ll. 88–9 are surely a couplet, 'mum' rhyming with 'Hum'. Why then does F call him 'Hume'? Perhaps to avoid confusion with the abbreviation 'Hum' for 'Humphrey'

earlier in the scene, in which case both compositors must have discussed it, since the name occurs in the stints of each. Whatever the explanation, Hall, the Quarto, and the virtually certain rhyme all support 'Hum'.

70 **majesty** An anachronism: the Tudors were the first monarchs to be so addressed.
71 **but** only
   grace (the title for a duchess)
73 **Your . . . multiplied** (playing upon the biblical phrase 'Grace and peace be multiplied unto you' (1 Peter 1: 2))
75 **With . . . witch** For the textual implications of F's and Q's versions of this line, see the Textual Introduction, p. 87.
   Jourdayne Oxford argues that 'there seems little to recommend the more usual modernization, "Jourdain" [as in Q]' (*Textual Companion*, p. 180); but the metre requires it. The stress falls on the second syllable, not on the first, as in F's 'Jordan'. I have adopted Hall's spelling, which gives the required pronunciation and helps

With Roger Bolingbroke, the conjuror?
And will they undertake to do me good?

HUM

This they have promisèd to show your highness:
A spirit raised from depth of underground
That shall make answer to such questions   80
As by your grace shall be propounded him.

DUCHESS ELEANOR

It is enough, I'll think upon the questions.
When from Saint Albans we do make return,
We'll see these things effected to the full.
Here Hum (*giving him money*), take this reward. Make
   merry, man,   85
With thy confederates in this weighty cause.   *Exit*

HUM

Hum must make merry with the Duchess' gold;
Marry, and shall; but how now, Sir John Hum?
Seal up your lips, and give no words but mum;
The business asketh silent secrecy.   90
Dame Eleanor gives gold to bring the witch;
Gold cannot come amiss were she a devil.
Yet have I gold flies from another coast:
I dare not say from the rich Cardinal
And from the great and new-made Duke of Suffolk,   95
Yet I do find it so; for to be plain,
They, knowing Dame Eleanor's aspiring humour,
Have hired me to undermine the Duchess,
And buzz these conjurations in her brain.
They say 'A crafty knave does need no broker',   100

---

to avoid any confusion with the French
pronunciation which 'Jourdain' might
encourage.
  cunning skilled in magic

76 **conjuror** magician, one who conjures
spirits
77 **do me good** enable me to prosper
81 **propounded** asked
88 **Marry** A mild oath, originally 'by the
Virgin Mary'.
89 **no . . . mum** Proverbial (Dent W767).
  mum i.e. silence
90 **asketh** requires

93 **coast** quarter
95 **new-made Duke** It is not only the aristocrats who comment on Suffolk's recent
promotion (1.1.108, 1.2.30); the commoners obviously do so too.
97 **aspiring humour** ambitious nature
98 **undermine** work secretly against (a
metaphorical expression, drawn from
warfare, where it meant 'place explosives
underneath a wall')
99 **buzz** implant with whispers
  conjurations incantations
100 **A . . . broker** Proverbial (Dent K122).
  broker agent

Yet am I Suffolk and the Cardinal's broker.
Hum, if you take not heed you shall go near
To call them both a pair of crafty knaves.
Well, so it stands; and thus I fear at last
Hum's knavery will be the Duchess' wrack,   105
And her attainture will be Humphrey's fall.
Sort how it will, I shall have gold for all.   *Exit*

1.3   *Enter Peter, the armourer's man, with three or four*
        other Petitioners

FIRST PETITIONER My masters, let's stand close. My Lord
    Protector will come this way by and by and then we may
    deliver our supplications in the quill.
SECOND PETITIONER Marry, the Lord protect him, for he's a
    good man, Jesu bless him.   5
        Enter the Duke of Suffolk and Queen Margaret
⌈FIRST PETITIONER⌉ Here a comes, methinks, and the Queen
    with him. I'll be the first, sure.
        He goes to meet Suffolk and the Queen

1.3.0.1–2 *Enter . . . Petitioners*] *Enter three or foure Petitioners, the Armorers Man being one.* F
6 FIRST PETITIONER] F4; *Peter.* F1   7.1 *He . . . Queen*] *not in* F

---

105 **wrack** destruction (*OED sb.*[1] 3b)
106 **attainture** conviction for treason
107 **Sort how it will** however it turns out
1.3.0.1 **man** servant (and apprentice)
  1 **stand close** This phrase is very common in
    Shakespeare, and usually means 'stand
    close together' to observe someone or,
    as here, to wait for someone (*OED, close,
    adv.* 1).
  2 **by and by** immediately
  3 **supplications** petitions
    in the quill *OED, quill, sb.*[2] 2 conjectures
    that this means 'in a body; in combina-
    tion'; but since this point has already
    been made in *stand close*, and the origin
    of the phrase is obscure, it seems to me
    likelier simply to mean 'written' (i.e. with
    a quill pen), as Steevens suggested: so
    supplications in the quill are written
    petitions.
  4 **Lord protect him** (a pun on 'Lord Protec-
    tor', as at *Richard III* 4.1.19: 'The Lord
    protect him from that kingly title')
  6 FIRST PETITIONER F gives the speech to

Peter. 'The compositor may have misin-
terpreted manuscript *Pet* (i.e. *Petitioner*) as
Peter' (*Textual Companion*, p. 180); but
since the name 'Peter' has not yet
occurred in the scene—its presence in the
opening stage direction here is editorial—
for Compositor A to confuse with 'Petitioner', the slip may be authorial.
Whoever thrusts himself forward here
must also speak ll. 11–12; and since Q does
not have Peter speak till its equivalent of ll.
27–9, it provides supporting evidence that
this speech is the First Petitioner's.
a he. *OED, he, pers. pron.*, says that
colloquial 'tonelessness' produced *a*,
which 'long prevailed in representations
of familiar speech, as in the dramatists';
compare 4.2.51, 108. It seems, however,
that it was giving way to 'he' even in
Shakespeare's lifetime: most examples of
a in this sense in Q2 of *Hamlet* (1604) are
replaced by 'he' in the Folio (1623); and
the Quarto's version of this line, and of
4.2.108, has 'he'.

SECOND PETITIONER Come back, fool—this is the Duke of
Suffolk and not my Lord Protector.
SUFFOLK (*to the First Petitioner*)
How now, fellow; wouldst anything with me?   10
FIRST PETITIONER I pray my lord, pardon me, I took ye for
my Lord Protector.
QUEEN MARGARET 'To my Lord Protector'—are your suppli-
cations to his lordship?
Let me see them.   15
⌈*She takes the First Petitioner's supplication*⌉
What is thine?
FIRST PETITIONER Mine is, an't please your grace, against
John Goodman, my lord Cardinal's man, for keeping my
house and lands and wife and all from me.
SUFFOLK Thy wife too? That's some wrong indeed. ⌈*To the*   20
Second Petitioner⌉ What's yours?
He takes the supplication
What's here? (*Reads*) 'Against the Duke of Suffolk for
enclosing the commons of Melford'.
How now, sir knave?
SECOND PETITIONER Alas sir, I am but a poor petitioner of   25
our whole township.
PETER ⌈*offering his petition*⌉ Against my master Thomas
Horner, for saying that the Duke of York was rightful
heir to the crown.
QUEEN MARGARET What sayst thou? Did the Duke of York   30
say he was rightful heir to the crown?

15.1 *She ... supplication*] not in F   21.1 *He ... supplication*] not in F   27 *offering his petition*] not
in F

10 **fellow** (a contemptuous address to an
inferior)
13 **To** If Margaret glances at the heading of
the petition, Capell's emendation 'For' is
not needed.
17 **an't** if it
23 **enclosing the commons** fencing-in public
land for private use. Although the chronicles accuse Suffolk of oppressing the poor,
he is not actually accused of enclosure;
but it was a red-hot issue in Elizabethan
England, and Shakespeare himself was
involved in a bitter dispute over land he

owned in Welcombe, near Stratford-
upon-Avon, in 1614: Edward Bond makes
it the subject of his play *Bingo* (1974).
Melford Long Melford in Suffolk (which Q
reads, and which may be correct)
24 **sir knave** 'Suffolk ironically combines
a courtesy title with a term of abuse'
(Hattaway).
28–9 **for saying ... crown** The accusation of
an unnamed armourer by his man comes
from the chronicles; but the connection
with York's claim to the crown is only
made in the play.

PETER That my master was? No, forsooth, my master said
    that he was and that the King was an usurper.
SUFFOLK (*calling within*) Who is there?
        Enter a servant
    Take this fellow in and send for his master with a   35
    pursuivant presently. (*To Peter*) We'll hear more of your
    matter before the King.   *Exit the servant with Peter*
QUEEN MARGARET (*to the Petitioners*)
    And as for you that love to be protected
    Under the wings of our Protector's grace,
    Begin your suits anew and sue to him.   40
      ⌈*She*⌉ *tears the supplication*
    Away, base cullions! Suffolk, let them go.
ALL PETITIONERS Come, let's be gone.   *Exeunt Petitioners*
QUEEN MARGARET
    My lord of Suffolk, say, is this the guise,
    Is this the fashions in the court of England?
    Is this the government of Britain's isle,   45
    And this the royalty of Albion's king?

---

32 master] WARBURTON (*subs.*); Mistresse F   33 usurper.] F ; usurer. | QUEEN MARGARET An
usurper thou wouldst say. | PETER Ay, forsooth—an usurper. OXFORD (*after* Q)   34.1 *a*] *not in* F
37 *Exit . . . Peter*] Exit. F   40.1 ⌈*She*⌉ *tears*] Teare F

---

32 **master** It is likelier that the Folio compositor misread a contraction ('M^r') in the
manuscript, and erroneously expanded it
to 'Mistresse' (see collation), than that
Peter is being presented as a gormless
idiot. He seems to know exactly what he is
accusing his master of, and how serious it
is. See the note to 2.3.75–7.
forsooth in truth (a common oath)
33 **was an usurper** Here Oxford adds, from Q,
word-play on 'usurer' (see collation). This
seems to me exactly the kind of material
that easily gets improvised in performance, and equally easily introduced into
a reported text, so I exclude it.
36 **pursuivant** 'state messenger with power
to execute warrants' (*OED sb.* 2): i.e.
Horner is to be arrested.

38–9 **protected . . . Protector** (continues the
pun from l. 4)
40.1 ⌈*She*⌉ **tears** F's direction '*Tear the
supplication*', though placed within the
Queen's speech, is ambiguous; Q is ex-
plicit that Suffolk tears them, logically
enough since there the petitions are presented in a different order, and the one
accusing Suffolk himself of enclosure
comes last.
41 **base** low-born
cullions rascals, scum (from Italian
coglioni, testicles)
43 **guise** custom
44 **Is . . . fashions** See the first note to 1.1.34.
fashions manners and customs (*OED
sb.* 8b)
46 **Albion's** England's

What, shall King Henry be a pupil still
Under the surly Gloucester's governance?
Am I a queen in title and in style,
And must be made a subject to a duke? 50
I tell thee Pole, when in the city Tours
Thou rann'st a-tilt in honour of my love
And stol'st away the ladies' hearts of France,
I thought King Henry had resembled thee
In courage, courtship, and proportion. 55
But all his mind is bent to holiness,
To number Ave-Maries on his beads.
His champions are the prophets and apostles,
His weapons holy saws of sacred writ,
His study is his tilt-yard, and his loves 60
Are brazen images of canonized saints.
I would the college of the cardinals
Would choose him Pope, and carry him to Rome,
And set the triple crown upon his head;
That were a state fit for his holiness. 65

48 **surly** masterful, arrogant (*OED a.* 2a)
49 **style** form of address
51 **Pole** Suffolk's family name, spelt out in full at 1.1.44.
52 **rann'st a-tilt** took part in a tournament. 'The phrase seems to be to run *at* tilt and not to run *a* tilt. Cf. *OED tilt sb.*[2] 3' (McKerrow).
55 **courtship** (a) courtly behaviour (b) wooing ability
proportion physical shape. Such phrases hint markedly at an affair between Margaret and Suffolk, a suggestion heightened by her contrasting outburst against Henry as a husband in the rest of the speech.
56 **bent** inclined
57 **number . . . beads** count off 'Hail Marys' on his rosary. See the second note to 1.1.27. The prayer most often to be repeated when saying the rosary is the one to the Virgin Mary beginning '*Ave Maria*' or 'Hail Mary'.
58 **His champions . . . apostles** The King's *champion* often represented him at tournaments; but there are also two allusions

to St Paul's Epistle to the Ephesians, a well-known biblical text which Shakespeare also echoes in the near-contemporaneous *Comedy of Errors* 2.1.20–5. In Ephesians 6: 11–17, the Christian is urged to put on the armour of God; and at Ephesians 2: 20 Christianity is 'built upon the foundations of the apostles and prophets'. Margaret of course uses the allusions ironically: she would prefer the King's champion to be a warrior like Suffolk.
59 **saws** sayings
61 **brazen images** bronze statues
canonized Since this means 'made a saint', *canonized saints* is a tautology, used by Margaret for contemptuous emphasis. The word is stressed on the second syllable.
62 **college of the cardinals** (the highest council of the Roman Catholic Church, which elects the Pope from its members)
64 **triple crown** i.e. that of the Pope
65 **his holiness** (punning on (a) Henry's piety and (b) the Pope's official title)

SUFFOLK

Madam, be patient; as I was cause
Your highness came to England, so will I
In England work your grace's full content.

QUEEN MARGARET

Beside the haughty Protector have we Beaufort
The imperious churchman, Somerset, Buckingham,   70
And grumbling York; and not the least of these
But can do more in England than the King.

SUFFOLK

And he of these that can do most of all
Cannot do more in England than the Nevilles:
Salisbury and Warwick are no simple peers.   75

QUEEN MARGARET

Not all these lords do vex me half so much
As that proud dame, the Lord Protector's wife.
She sweeps it through the court with troops of ladies
More like an empress than Duke Humphrey's wife.
Strangers in court do take her for the queen.   80
She bears a duke's revenues on her back,
And in her heart she scorns our poverty.
Shall I not live to be avenged on her?

---

69 haughty] F1; haught F2

---

68 **work** bring about
69–71 **haughty   Protector . . . grumbling
    York** Margaret pins down Humphrey,
    Beaufort, and York in brilliant, one-word
    portraits, especially the last.
69 **haughty** F2's 'haught' makes the line
    more regular, but it is perfectly possible
    to retain *haughty* and still maintain the
    rhythm of the line.
71 **grumbling** discontented
73 **he . . . all** whichever of these is most
    influential
75 **no   simple** not humble (because
    Salisbury was a grandson of John of
    Gaunt, and so related to the royal family);
    but with the additional implication of
    'politically subtle'.
76–7 **Not . . . wife** The Duchess of Gloucester
    was in fact disgraced four years before
    Margaret came to England; the play alters
    the chronicles so as to bring the two
    women into sharp conflict, as expressed

in Margaret's incisive speech here and in
her physical attack at ll. 139–40, and so
that Suffolk's plot against her, outlined in
his next speech, becomes an important
factor in her husband's downfall.
78 **sweeps it** struts proudly
80 **Strangers** foreigners
81 **She . . . back** i.e. she wears extremely
    expensive clothes. This alludes to the
    proverb 'He wears a whole lordship on his
    back' (Dent L452), also used by Marlowe
    in the very similar line in *Edward II*: 'He
    wears a lord's revenue on his back'
    (1.4.406). Whether this play or *2 Henry
    VI* was written first is not known.
    bears carries
    revenues income (stressed on the second
    syllable)
82 **our** The royal plural, but with the addi-
    tional suggestion 'mine and my father's'
    in view of ll. 87–8.

Contemptuous base-born callet as she is,
She vaunted 'mongst her minions t'other day   85
The very train of her worst-wearing gown
Was better worth than all my father's lands,
Till Suffolk gave two dukedoms for his daughter.

SUFFOLK

Madam, myself have limed a bush for her,
And placed a choir of such enticing birds   90
That she will light to listen to their lays,
And never mount to trouble you again.
So let her rest; and madam, list to me,
For I am bold to counsel you in this:
Although we fancy not the Cardinal,   95
Yet must we join with him and with the lords
Till we have brought Duke Humphrey in disgrace.
As for the Duke of York, this late complaint
Will make but little for his benefit.
So one by one we'll weed them all at last,   100
And you yourself shall steer the happy helm.

> *Sound a sennet.* ⌈*Enter King Henry with the Duke of*
> *York and the Duke of Somerset on either side of him*

91 their] ROWE; the F 101 helm.] Helme. *Exit.* F 101.1 *Sound a sennet.*] F 101.1–6 *Enter
... Winchester*] Q (*subs.*) ; *Enter the King, Duke Humfrey, Cardinall, Buckingham, Yorke, Salisbury,
Warwicke, and the Duchesse.* F

84 **Contemptuous** *OED a.* 3 says that
this means 'contemptible', presumably
because of the rest of the line; but it is as
likely to have the normal modern meaning, since the Duchess is contemptuous of
Margaret, as the following lines make
clear.
  base-born callet low-born whore.
Margaret is probably simply being abusive, but this phrase may offer some
support for *ill-nurtured* at 1.2.42.
85 **vaunted** boasted
  minions favourites, fawning attendants
86 **worst-wearing** poorest, most
unfashionable
87 **better worth** worth more
88 **two dukedoms** (Anjou and Maine again)
89 **limed a bush** set a trap. Birds were caught
by smearing birdlime, a white sticky
paste, on branches. This metaphor recurs

at 2.4.55 and 3.3.16, and frequently in
Shakespeare; and it is developed in the
following lines, which suggest that the
Duchess is to be lured by a *choir* of *enticing birds* (i.e. Sir John Hum and his accomplices) to whose tempting *lays* (the
prophecies in the next scene) she will listen, be destroyed, and so no longer *mount*
(fly up) in her pride to annoy the Queen.
90 **enticing birds** decoys
91 **light** alight, perch
  lays songs
93 **let her rest** forget about her
94 **am bold** presume
95 **fancy** love
98 **late** recent (i.e. Peter's complaint against
the armourer)
99 **make ... benefit** do him little good
101 **steer ... helm** guide the ship of state
101.1 *sennet* trumpet-call

> *whispering with him. Also enter Duke Humphrey of*
> *Gloucester, Dame Eleanor the Duchess of Gloucester,*
> *the Duke of Buckingham, the Earls of Salisbury and*
> *Warwick, and Cardinal Beaufort Bishop of Winchester*⌉

KING HENRY
For my part, noble lords, I care not which:
Or Somerset or York, all's one to me.

YORK
If York have ill demeaned himself in France
Then let him be denied the regentship.   105

SOMERSET
If Somerset be unworthy of the place,
Let York be regent, I will yield to him.

WARWICK
Whether your grace be worthy, yea or no,
Dispute not that: York is the worthier.

CARDINAL BEAUFORT
Ambitious Warwick, let thy betters speak.   110

WARWICK
The Cardinal's not my better in the field.

BUCKINGHAM
All in this presence are thy betters, Warwick.

WARWICK
Warwick may live to be the best of all.

---

105 denied] F (denay'd)

101.3 **whispering with him** York and
Somerset are each trying to influence the
King as they enter.
101.4 *Dame Eleanor* Neither Q nor F
mentions ladies-in-waiting, but their
presence or absence is an issue at l. 140.
See the second note to that line.
102 **I care not which** Henry presumably
means to be impartial; but the phrase
suggests dangerous indifference to affairs
of state.
104 **ill demeaned himself** behaved impro-
perly. For *demeaned*, see the note to
1.1.187.
105 **regentship** (i.e. ruler of France in the
King's name)

108–9 **Whether . . . that** don't argue about
whether you are worthy or not
111 **field** battlefield
112 **presence** Either 'presence-chamber',
ceremonial chamber (*OED* 2c), or 'in the
presence of the King' (*OED* 2b).
113 **Warwick . . . all** This is the first hint of
Warwick's own ambition, for which he
came to be known as 'the Kingmaker':
this is much developed in *3 Henry VI*,
where Warwick has the longest part in
the play and is a dominating presence. His
father's rebuke in the next line emphasizes this: Salisbury tries to bring *reason*
and argument to what is degenerating
into a personal squabble.

SALISBURY

Peace, son; and show some reason, Buckingham,
Why Somerset should be preferred in this.   115

QUEEN MARGARET

Because the King, forsooth, will have it so.

DUKE HUMPHREY

Madam, the King is old enough himself
To give his censure. These are no women's matters.

QUEEN MARGARET

If he be old enough, what needs your grace
To be Protector of his excellence?   120

DUKE HUMPHREY

Madam, I am Protector of the realm,
And at his pleasure will resign my place.

SUFFOLK

Resign it then, and leave thine insolence.
Since thou wert king—as who is king but thou?—
The commonwealth hath daily run to wrack,   125
The Dauphin hath prevailed beyond the seas,
And all the peers and nobles of the realm
Have been as bondmen to thy sovereignty.

CARDINAL BEAUFORT

The commons hast thou racked, the clergy's bags
Are lank and lean with thy extortions.   130

114–15 **show . . . preferred** Neither Buckingham nor anyone else has actually advocated Somerset; opposition to York and Warwick is taken to imply it.

116 **have it so** Since this denies what the King said as he entered, the Queen is clearly acting on her own initiative. Her sudden intervention in political affairs can have great impact in performance.

118 **censure** judgement

119–20 **If . . . excellence** Margaret's spiky question releases the first group attack on Duke Humphrey. For their charges against him, see Appendix B, 1.3.119–38.

121 **Protector of the realm** i.e. not merely of the King (answering Margaret's accusation). The line is often delivered brusquely, picking up from the tone of 'These are no women's matters' (l. 118); but in the 2001 Watermill production, Matthew Flynn adopted a tone of reasonableness, taking the trouble to *explain* to Margaret. This subtly suggested a Humphrey who was both attempting to curb his turbulent temper, and courteously deferring to the King in answering his wife.

125 **run to wrack** been ruined (as in the modern phrase 'go to wrack and ruin'; *OED, wrack, sb.*[1] 2b)

126 **Dauphin** (title of the eldest son of a French king, here used of King Charles VII himself, because the English considered the King of England the rightful King of France)

128 **bondmen** slaves

129 **racked** taxed by extortion (as if the *commons* were tortured by being stretched out on the rack)
bags purses

130 **lank** shrunk

SOMERSET
  Thy sumptuous buildings and thy wife's attire
  Have cost a mass of public treasury.
BUCKINGHAM
  Thy cruelty in execution
  Upon offenders hath exceeded law
  And left thee to the mercy of the law.   135
QUEEN MARGARET
  Thy sale of offices and towns in France—
  If they were known, as the suspect is great—
  Would make thee quickly hop without thy head.

                                    Exit Duke Humphrey
      Queen Margaret lets fall her fan
  (*To the Duchess*)
  Give me my fan—what, minion, can ye not?
      She gives the Duchess a box on the ear
  I cry you mercy, madam! Was it you?   140
DUCHESS ELEANOR
  Was't I? Yea, I it was, proud Frenchwoman!
  Could I come near your beauty with my nails,
  I'd set my ten commandments in your face.

---

131 wife's] F (Wiues) 138.2 *Queen . . . fan*] The Queene lets fall her gloue Q; *not in* F
143 I'd] Q; I could F

---

131 **sumptuous   buildings**   Grafton's
  Chronicle praises Duke Humphrey for
  building the Divinity School in Oxford
  (ii. 599). Humphrey donated funds for its
  construction, and the room above it, now
  known as Duke Humphrey's Library,
  houses his collection of books, which he
  left to the University.
132 **treasury** money
133 This is a full verse line: *execution* has
  five syllables ('i-on') in Elizabethan
  usage.
137 **known** confirmed, known for certain
  suspect suspicion (stressed on the second
  syllable, unlike modern usage)
138 **hop . . . head** be beheaded (proverbial:
  Dent HH11). This is the first open threat to
  Humphrey's life; he is overcome with
  rage, and abruptly leaves without a word.
  Margaret is characteristically the catalyst
  of a moment of crisis.

139 **minion** hussy (*OED sb.*[1] 1e (b))
140 **cry you mercy** beg your pardon (a mocking apology)
  Was it you? Whether other ladies-in-
  waiting are present or not (see the note
  to l. 101.4) affects how this moment is
  played, since if the Duchess is the only
  one present, the Queen's question lacks
  even the semblance of plausibility.
143 **I'd** F's 'could' was probably caught from
  the previous line.
  set . . . face scratch your face with my ten
  fingernails. Eleanor gives vent to her fury
  by using proverbial slang (Dent C553),
  which ultimately derives from the biblical point that the ten commandments
  were 'written with the finger of God'
  (Exodus 31: 18). This colloquial phrase is
  also used, for instance, by the heroine in
  the anonymous *Taming of a Shrew* 3.153
  (New Cambridge edition, 1998).

KING HENRY

Sweet aunt, be quiet, 'twas against her will.

DUCHESS ELEANOR

Against her will, good King? Look to't in time,   145
She'll pamper thee and dandle thee like a baby.
Though in this place most master wear no breeches,
She shall not strike Dame Eleanor unrevenged!   *Exit*

BUCKINGHAM (*aside to Cardinal Beaufort*)

Lord Cardinal, I will follow Eleanor
And listen after Humphrey how he proceeds.   150
She's tickled now, her fury needs no spurs,
She'll gallop far enough to her destruction.   *Exit*

Enter Duke Humphrey

DUKE HUMPHREY

Now lords, my choler being overblown
With walking once about the quadrangle,
I come to talk of commonwealth affairs.   155
As for your spiteful false objections,

---

146 pamper] OXFORD (*conj.* McKerrow); hamper F   151 fury] GRANT WHITE (*conj.* Dyce); Fume F

---

144 **quiet** calm
   against her will unintentional
146 **pamper** over-indulge. F's 'hamper' 'appears to have no other sense than the usual one of "fetter", "hinder", and does not seem congruent with the phrase "dandle thee like a baby", which follows' (McKerrow, who compares *Richard III* 2.2.87–8: 'I am your sorrow's nurse, | And I will pamper it with lamentation', spoken by the Duchess of York in a context of weeping for children).
   dandle pet, fondle
147 **most master** the ruler (*OED, most, adj.* 1e), i.e. the Queen
   most . . . breeches A proverbial expression (Dent M727) meaning that women rule the house. Eleanor again uses vigorous colloquialism, perhaps in reaction to the *proud Frenchwoman* (l. 141), perhaps to emphasize the familiarity of aunt and nephew.
149–52 See the note to 1.4.39.2.
150 **listen after** enquire about (*OED, listen, v.* 2c)
   Humphrey . . . proceeds how Humphrey behaves

151 **tickled** irritated (as a horse is by flies, leading to *spurs* and *gallop*; see the next note)
   fury Although F's 'fume' in the sense of 'anger' is supported by *Venus* 316, where another horse is irritated by flies, and 'bites the poor flies in his fume', the line requires a two-syllable word, and 'fume' is an easy misreading for 'furie'.
151–2 **needs . . . destruction** (playing upon the proverbial phrase 'Do not spur a free (willing) horse' (Dent H638))
153–60 **Now . . . hand** Humphrey makes a conscious effort to control his turbulent temper after storming out earlier. In ll. 156–9 his indignation rises again, but he controls it with the matter-of-fact phrase *to the matter that we have in hand*, bringing, as it were, the meeting back to the agenda.
153 **choler** anger
   overblown blown over
154 **quadrangle** courtyard: *OED*'s earliest example of *quadrangle* in this sense (*sb.* 2)
155 **commonwealth affairs** matters of state
156 **objections** accusations

Prove them, and I lie open to the law.
But God in mercy so deal with my soul
As I in duty love my King and country.
But to the matter that we have in hand: 160
I say, my sovereign, York is meetest man
To be your regent in the realm of France.

SUFFOLK
Before we make election, give me leave
To show some reason of no little force
That York is most unmeet of any man.   165

YORK
I'll tell thee, Suffolk, why I am unmeet:
First, for I cannot flatter thee in pride;
Next, if I be appointed for the place,
My lord of Somerset will keep me here
Without discharge, money, or furniture,   170
Till France be won into the Dauphin's hands.
Last time, I danced attendance on his will
Till Paris was besieged, famished, and lost.

WARWICK
That can I witness, and a fouler fact
Did never traitor in the land commit.   175

SUFFOLK   Peace, headstrong Warwick.

WARWICK
Image of pride, why should I hold my peace?
     Enter, guarded, Horner the armourer and Peter his man

177.1 *Enter . . . man*] *Enter Armorer and his Man.* F

---

161 **meetest** fittest
163 **election** a choice
167 **for** because
    thee in pride your pride
170 **discharge** financial settlement (*OED sb.*
    5). This antedates *OED*'s first quotation,
    from *Cymbeline* 5.5.263.
    furniture military supplies
172 **Last time . . . will** This refers to an
    episode, dramatized in *1 Henry VI* 4.3 and
    4.4, in which York and Somerset, refus-
    ing to co-operate because of their feud,
    fail to send the English general Talbot nec-

essary reinforcements, resulting in his
death and the loss of Paris. York blames
Somerset, but he himself was as much to
blame.
    danced attendance was kept waiting (a
    proverbial expression (Dent A392), also
    used by Buckingham at *Richard III* 3.7.56,
    where the tone is 'I'm kept hanging
    around')
174 **fact** crime, evil deed (the commonest
    sense in the sixteenth century (*OED sb.*
    1c))
177 **Image** embodiment (*OED sb.* 4c)

SUFFOLK
Because here is a man accused of treason;
Pray God the Duke of York excuse himself.
YORK
Doth anyone accuse York for a traitor?   180
KING HENRY
What mean'st thou, Suffolk? Tell me, what are these?
SUFFOLK
Please it your majesty, this is the man
        He indicates Peter
That doth accuse his master (*indicating Horner*) of
    high treason.
His words were these: that Richard Duke of York
Was rightful heir unto the English crown,   185
And that your majesty was an usurper.
KING HENRY (*to Horner*) Say, man, were these thy words?
HORNER An't shall please your majesty, I never said nor
    thought any such matter. God is my witness, I am falsely
    accused by the villain.   190
PETER ⌈*raising his hands*⌉ By these ten bones, my lords, he
    did speak them to me in the garret one night as we were
    scouring my lord of York's armour.
YORK
Base dunghill villain and mechanical,
I'll have thy head for this thy traitor's speech!   195
(*To King Henry*) I do beseech your royal majesty,
Let him have all the rigour of the law.
HORNER Alas, my lord, hang me if ever I spake the words.
    My accuser is my prentice, and when I did correct him for
    his fault the other day, he did vow upon his knees he   200
    would be even with me. I have good witness of this;

182.1 *He indicates Peter*] *not in* F   183, 210 *indicating Horner*] *not in* F   191 *raising his hands*] *not in* F

180 **for** as
181 **what** who
182 **Please it** if it please
191 **ten bones** i.e. fingers, a common oath
    (Dent TT7). Peter uses a similar colloquial
    expression to Eleanor's at l. 143.
193 **scouring** cleaning. Armour was cleaned

by rolling it in a barrel of sand, to prevent
it rusting.
194 **mechanical** manual labourer (a con-
    temptuous term, like *dunghill* earlier)
197 **rigour** severity
199 **prentice** apprentice
    correct punish

therefore I beseech your majesty, do not cast away an
honest man for a villain's accusation.

KING HENRY (*to Duke Humphrey*)
Uncle, what shall we say to this in law?

DUKE HUMPHREY
This doom, my lord, if I may judge by case: 205
Let Somerset be regent o'er the French,
Because in York this breeds suspicion.
(*Indicating Horner and Peter*)
And let these have a day appointed them
For single combat in convenient place,
For he (*indicating Horner*) hath witness of his servant's
        malice.   210
This is the law, and this Duke Humphrey's doom.

SOMERSET
I humbly thank your royal majesty.

HORNER
And I accept the combat willingly.

PETER ⌈*to Duke Humphrey*⌉ Alas, my lord, I cannot fight; for
God's sake, pity my case! The spite of man prevaileth   215
against me. O Lord have mercy upon me, I shall never be
able to fight a blow! O Lord, my heart!

---

205 by case] CAIRNCROSS (*after* Q); *not in* F   207.1 *Indicating . . . Peter*] *not in* F   211 doom]
doom. KING HENRY Then be it so. My lord of Somerset, | We make you regent o'er the realm of
France | There to defend our rights 'gainst foreign foes. OXFORD (*after* Q)

202 **cast away** destroy
203 **for** on account of
205 **doom** judgement
  by case according to case law, legal precedent. This phrase, inserted from Q, completes the otherwise incomplete verse line
  and directly answers the King's question
  about the *law*.
207 **breeds suspicion** raises doubts (about his
  loyalty)
209 **convenient** suitable (as at 1 *Henry VI*
  2.4.4, 'The garden here is more convenient' to settle the quarrel which leads to
  the Wars of the Roses (*OED adj.* 4))
211 **This . . . doom** Duke Humphrey is of
  course interpreting the law, as the King
  has asked him to do; but the actual phrasing comes perilously close to equating his
  judgement (*doom*) with the law, some-

thing which Jack Cade is later to do:
'My mouth shall be the Parliament of
England' (4.7.13–14).
212 **I . . . majesty** Since in F the King has said
  nothing for Somerset to thank him for,
  editors sometimes add lines based on Q
  (see collation to l. 211). But as C. J.
  Sisson says, 'Humphrey is speaking as
  the King's mouthpiece, and there is no
  difficulty in Somerset replying to the King
  directly' (*New Readings in Shakespeare*
  (Cambridge, 1956), ii. 76).
215–16 **The spite . . . upon me** This echoes
  several phrases in the Psalms, e.g.
  'Wicked deeds have prevailed against
  me; but thou wilt be merciful unto our
  transgressions' (65: 3).
217 **my heart** (contracted form of 'God bless
  my heart')

DUKE HUMPHREY
Sirrah, or you must fight or else be hanged.

KING HENRY
Away with them to prison, and the day
Of combat shall be the last of the next month.   220
Come Somerset, we'll see thee sent away.

Flourish. Exeunt

1.4   *Enter Margery Jourdayne, a witch; Sir John Hum
and John Southwell, two priests; and Roger
Bolingbroke, a conjuror*

HUM Come my masters, the Duchess I tell you expects performance of your promises.

BOLINGBROKE Master Hum, we are therefor provided. Will
her ladyship behold and hear our exorcisms?

HUM Ay, what else? Fear you not her courage.   5

BOLINGBROKE I have heard her reported to be a woman
of an invincible spirit. But it shall be convenient,
Master Hum, that you be by her aloft, while we be busy
below, and so I pray you, go in God's name and
leave us.   *Exit Hum*   10
Mother Jourdayne, be you prostrate and grovel on the
earth. John Southwell, read you, and let us to our work.
⌈*Enter Duchess Eleanor and Hum aloft*⌉

1.4.0.1-3 *Enter . . . conjuror*] *Enter the Witch, the two Priests, and Bullingbrooke.* F   12.1 *and Hum*] *not in* F

218 **Sirrah** A contemptuous address to an inferior.
1.4 In the chronicles, Eleanor and her accomplices were accused of making a wax image of the King, a device used by witches to cause people harm. This conjuring scene seems to be the dramatist's invention; but is the conjuring genuine or a put-up job by a bunch of charlatans, like the 'conjuror' Pinch in *The Comedy of Errors*? Hum tells us at 1.2.93–107 that he has been paid by Suffolk and the Cardinal to betray the Duchess, and perhaps he and the others simply tell her what she wants to hear. That was suggested at Stratford-upon-Avon in 1963–4, and in the BBC television production, where the spirit does not appear but its prophecies are spoken 'through' Jourdayne. On the

other hand, those prophecies come true. See the next note.

1–2 **performance** This may simply be a neutral phrase ('carrying out'), but it may imply the playing of a part, hinting at a deception from the start.
3 **therefor provided** equipped for that purpose
4 **exorcisms** This properly means clerical expulsion of evil spirits, but it was used more generally for conjuring up spirits, as here (*OED* 1b).
5 **what else** certainly
   Fear doubt
11 **be you prostrate** —in order, suggests the Quarto, to 'talk and whisper with the devils below' (l. 495)
12.1 **aloft** i.e. on the balcony of the Elizabethan playhouse

DUCHESS ELEANOR Well said, my masters, and welcome all.
To this gear the sooner the better.
BOLINGBROKE
Patience, good lady, wizards know their times.   15
Deep night, dark night, the silent of the night,
The time of night when Troy was set on fire,
The time when screech-owls cry and bandogs howl,
And spirits walk, and ghosts break up their graves:
That time best fits the work we have in hand.   20
Madam, sit you, and fear not: whom we raise
We will make fast within a hallowed verge.
> *Here they do the ceremonies belonging, and make the*
> *circle. Southwell reads 'Coniuro te', etc. It thunders*
> *and lightens terribly, then the spirit riseth*
SPIRIT *Adsum.*
WITCH Asmodeus,

22.1 *they*] not in F   22.2 *Southwell*] *Bullingbrooke or Southwell* F   24 Asmodeus] This edition;
Asmath F

---

13 **Well said** (in response to Bolingbroke's *let us to our work* which she hears as she enters)
14 **To . . . better** the quicker we get on with this business the better
15 **wizards . . . times** (i.e. the most appropriate moments for raising spirits)
16–20 **Deep . . . hand** This rather overwritten speech draws on the traditional associations, or clichés, of the supernatural. See note to ll. 18–19.
16 **silent** This might be a misreading of 'silenc' (silence), but Shakespeare often substitutes one part of speech for another; and compare 2 *Henry IV* 5.3.51–2: 'the sweet o'th' night'.
17 **The . . . fire** The destruction of Troy is described in Virgil's *Aeneid*, Book 2.
18–19 **screech-owls . . . graves** These details come from Ovid's description of the prodigies that preceded the murder of Julius Caesar (*Metamorphoses* 15.791–8).
18 **bandogs** fierce, tied-up watchdogs
21 **whom** whichever spirit
22 **hallowed verge** charmed circle
22.1 *ceremonies belonging* rituals proper to raising spirits
22.2 **Southwell** The Folio's permissive direction says 'Bolingbroke or Southwell', but

Bolingbroke asks Southwell to read at l. 12.
Coniuro te I conjure you (the beginning of a Latin invocation)
22.2–3 *thunders and lightens* 'Thunder could be imitated either by the battering of drums or by the rolling of stones or cannonballs down a thunder run. . . . The call for lightning would make its customary demands upon the theatre's pyrotechnics experts' (Stanley Wells, 'Staging Shakespeare's Apparitions and Dream Visions', the first Globe Theatre lecture, Globe Education (1990), pp. 5–6). Such theatrical devices, used to simulate 'real' thunder and lightning, could also be used, of course, by Hum's accomplices to deceive the Duchess. There is more than a hint of this in BBC television's staging of the scene.
22.3 *riseth* (from the trapdoor in the stage floor)
23 *Adsum* I am here (Latin)
24 **Asmodeus** F has 'Asmath', but no devil by this name is known. Cairncross suggests that it is a misprint for 'Asnath', an anagram of 'Sathan'. A simpler explanation is that the manuscript read 'Asmode' or a similar abbreviation of Asmodeus, the

By the eternal God whose name and power   25
Thou tremblest at, answer that I shall ask,
For till thou speak, thou shalt not pass from hence.

SPIRIT

Ask what thou wilt, that I had said and done.

BOLINGBROKE (*reads*)

'First, of the King: what shall of him become?'

SPIRIT

The Duke yet lives that Henry shall depose,   30
But him outlive, and die a violent death.

        As the spirit speaks, ⌈*Southwell*⌉ *writes the answer*

BOLINGBROKE (*reads*)

'What fate awaits the Duke of Suffolk?'

SPIRIT

By water shall he die, and take his end.

BOLINGBROKE (*reads*)

'What shall betide the Duke of Somerset?'

SPIRIT

Let him shun castles. Safer shall he be   35
Upon the sandy plains than where castles mounted
        stand.
Have done, for more I hardly can endure.

31.1 *As . . . answer*] *not in* F   32 fate awaits] Q2–3; fates await F; fate awayt Q1   34 betide]
Q; befall F

'evil spirit' in the (apocryphal) biblical
book of Tobit, 3: 8–17, which was misread
through confusion between 'd' and 'e'
(with final flourish) and cursive 't' and 'h'
ligature, in Elizabethan secretary hand.

25–6 **God . . . at** A biblical allusion: 'the
devils also believe it, and tremble' (James
2: 19).
26 **that** what
28 **that . . . done** The spirit wants to get the
questions and answers over quickly. Spirits were apparently reluctant to answer
questions, as at *Macbeth* 4.1.88: 'Dismiss
me. Enough', perhaps because they were
in agony: compare l. 37.
30–1 **The . . . death** For the ambiguity of this
prophecy, see ll. 58–61 and note.
31.1 *Southwell* This is not specified in F
(Southwell does not appear in the Q version), but someone has to write down the

answers, and this gives Southwell more of
a function in the scene.
32 **fate awaits** L. 63, and Q's version of that
line, confirm that F's 'fates await' is an
error.
34 **betide** F's 'befall' may have arisen from
contamination with 'shall' in this and in
the preceding and following lines; *betide*
agrees with l. 65, and is confirmed by Q.
35–6 For F's lineation, see Appendix C. 'The
metre is rough here, however arranged;
but it is especially unlikely that one irregular verse line stood between two incomplete lines. As rearranged, one regular
line is followed by a hexameter with an
extra syllable after the caesura' (*Textual
Companion*, p. 640).
36 **mounted** situated on mountains
37 **Have done** finish
more . . . endure See the note to l. 28.

BOLINGBROKE

Descend to darkness and the burning lake!

False fiend, avoid!

> *Thunder and lightning. The spirit sinks down again*
> *Enter, breaking in, the Dukes of York and Buckingham*
> *with Sir Humphrey Stafford and their guard*

YORK

Lay hands upon these traitors and their trash.   40

> ⌈*Bolingbroke, Southwell, and Jourdayne are taken*
> *prisoner. Buckingham takes the writings from*
> *Bolingbroke and Southwell*⌉

(*To Jourdayne*) Beldam, I think we watched you at an
   inch.

(*To the Duchess*) What, madam, are you there? The King
   and common weal

Are deeply indebted for this piece of pains.

My lord Protector will, I doubt it not,

See you well guerdoned for these good deserts.   45

---

38 **burning lake** A biblical allusion: 'a lake of fire, burning with brimstone' (Revelation 19: 20).

39 **False** treacherous
   avoid depart (echoing Christ's words 'Avoid Satan' (Matthew 4: 10))

39.2 *Enter . . . York and Buckingham* It is curious that, the trap having been laid by Suffolk and the Cardinal, it should not be sprung by Suffolk. Buckingham is Suffolk's ally (1.1.167) and the Cardinal's (1.3.149-52), and may be acting as their agent, but York is their opponent and does not conspire with Suffolk against Humphrey until 3.1.238 ff. But perhaps it was thought dramatically more important that Suffolk should appear with the Queen in the next scene, and that York should set up his meeting to outline his claim to the crown at ll. 77-8.

39.3 *Sir Humphrey Stafford* Since Buckingham addresses a 'Stafford' at l. 51, this is probably the character who

confronts, and is killed by, Jack Cade in 4.2-3.

40 **trash** i.e. the conjuring paraphernalia

41 **Beldam** witch, hag
   at an inch closely

42 **What . . . there** This feigned surprise—of course he knows whose house it is —echoes Margaret's after striking the Duchess in the previous scene—'Was it you?' (l. 140)—a similarity which makes it the more surprising that the speaker isn't Suffolk (see the note to l. 39.2).

43 **deeply** Oxford emends this to 'deep' because the Folio line 'is metrically unacceptable'; but it is perfectly possible to speak it as it stands and maintain the iambic rhythm, as often in such cases.
   this piece of pains the trouble you have gone to (ironical)

45 **guerdoned** rewarded
   these good deserts what you have well deserved

DUCHESS ELEANOR

Not half so bad as thine to England's king,
Injurious Duke, that threatest where's no cause.

BUCKINGHAM

True, madam, none at all: (*indicating the writings*) what
call you this?
Away with them, let them be clapped up close
And kept asunder. (*To the Duchess*) You, madam, shall
with us.   50
Stafford, take her to thee.

> *Exeunt Stafford ⌈and others⌉ to arrest the Duchess*
> ⌈*and Hum*⌉ *above*

We'll see your trinkets here all forthcoming.
All away!

> *Exeunt below Jourdayne, Southwell, and Bolingbroke,*
> *guarded, and above ⌈Hum and⌉ the Duchess guarded by*
> *Stafford ⌈and others⌉*

YORK

Lord Buckingham, methinks you watched her well.
A pretty plot, well chosen to build upon.   55
Now pray, my lord, let's see the devil's writ.

> ⌈*Buckingham gives him the writings*⌉

What have we here?
(*Reads*) 'The Duke yet lives that Henry shall depose,

---

48 *indicating the writings*] *not in* F   51.1–2 *Exeunt . . . above*] *not in* F   53.1–3 *Exeunt . . .*
others] *Exit.* F   56.1 *Buckingham . . . writings*] *not in* F

---

47 **Injurious** insulting
49 **clapped up close** securely imprisoned
50 **asunder** separate
   shall must go
52 **trinkets** tools of the trade
   forthcoming be kept in safe custody (to be
   produced in evidence); a legal term (*OED*
   ppl. a. 1)
53 **All away** away with them. In the BBC television production, *All* is used specifically
   to refer to Hum: he is to be arrested with
   the others, despite having been used to
   bait the trap.
55 **plot** (a) plan (to trap the Duchess) (b) piece
   of ground (to *build upon*)
   to build upon This may simply mean 'to
   bring down the Lord Protector'; but it
   may also be another suggestion that the

conjuring was a put-up job (see the first
and second notes to this scene).
56 **devil's writ** (as opposed to 'holy writ', a
   traditional phrase for the scriptures)
58–67 For the Quarto's different placing of
   these lines, see Appendix A, Passage
   C, discussed in the Textual Introduction,
   pp. 90–1.
58–61 **'The Duke . . .** *posse* Oracles were tra-
   ditionally ambiguous. *Shall depose* and *die*
   a violent death can refer to York or Henry.
   York is aware of their unreliability, citing
   the ambiguous response of the Pythian
   Apollo to the Greek Pyrrhus when he
   asked if he would conquer Rome: 'O son
   of Aeacus, my prediction is | That you
   the Roman army will defeat' (Cicero, *De*
   Divinatione 2.56.116).

But him outlive, and die a violent death.'
Why this is just   60
Aio Aeacidam Romanos vincere posse.
Well, to the rest.
'Tell me what fate awaits the Duke of Suffolk?
By water shall he die, and take his end.
What shall betide the Duke of Somerset?   65
Let him shun castles. Safer shall he be
Upon the sandy plains than where castles mounted
    stand.'
Come come my lord, these oracles are hard,
Hardly attained and hardly understood.
The King is now in progress towards Saint Albans;   70
With him the husband of this lovely lady.
Thither goes these news as fast as horse can carry them,
A sorry breakfast for my lord Protector.

BUCKINGHAM
Your grace shall give me leave, my lord of York,
To be the post in hope of his reward.   75

YORK
At your pleasure, my good lord.   *Exit Buckingham*
                              Who's within there, ho!
        Enter a servingman
Invite my lords of Salisbury and Warwick
To sup with me tomorrow night. Away.

                              Exeunt severally

---

61 *Aeacidam*] OXFORD (*conj.* J. W. Binns); *Æacida* F *posse*] F2; *posso* F1 68 lord] OXFORD;
Lords F 68–9 are hard, | Hardly attained] This edition (*conj.* G. R. Hibbard); are hardly
attain'd F 76 *Exit Buckingham*] Q; *not in* F 78.1 *severally*] *not in* F

---

60 **just** exactly, precisely
68–9 G. R. Hibbard's rearrangement of the
    Folio lines (see collation) skilfully solves
    the problem of F's irregular first line
    (*N&Q* 210 (1965), p. 332).
69 **Hardly . . . understood** obtained with dif-
    ficulty and barely comprehensible
70 **in progress** making a royal visit. The
    monarch's *progress* to visit different parts

of the kingdom was a favourite habit of
    Queen Elizabeth I.
72 **these news** *News* was often treated as
    plural in the Elizabethan period.
75 **post** messenger
78.1 *severally* separately (a standard
    Elizabethan stage direction, though here
    editorial)

2.1 *Enter King Henry, Queen Margaret with her hawk on her fist, Duke Humphrey of Gloucester, Cardinal Beaufort, and the Duke of Suffolk, with falconers hollering*

QUEEN MARGARET

Believe me, lords, for flying at the brook
I saw not better sport these seven years' day;
Yet by your leave, the wind was very high,
And ten to one, old Joan had not gone out.

KING HENRY (*to Duke Humphrey*)

But what a point, my lord, your falcon made,   5
And what a pitch she flew above the rest!

2.1.0.1–4 Enter . . . hollering] *Enter the King, Queene, Protector, Cardinall, and Suffolke, with Faulkners hallowing.* F   0.1–2 *with her hawk on her fist*] Q

2.1 This scene brings together material from quite different sources. The hawking opening may have been suggested by a passage in Hall (p. 236) describing how in 1457 Margaret took Henry on a progress into Warwickshire 'with hawking and hunting', ostensibly 'for his health and recreation', but in fact as part of an unsuccessful attempt to lure York, Salisbury, and Warwick into a trap at Coventry, while the false miracle episode took place during a different royal progress described by Grafton and Foxe (see the Introduction, p. 31, and Appendix B). Both episodes focus the King's religious feeling (e.g. ll. 7, 18, 34, 64–5, 73, 83–5) and his disappointment when the miracle turns out to be a fake (see the note to l. 111).

0.1–5 *Enter . . . made* The court has been hunting waterfowl along the river's edge (*flying at the brook*), for which short-winged hawks—goshawks and sparrowhawks—were flown from the gloved fist; but Duke Humphrey appears to be using falcons (l. 5), long-winged hawks more usually employed in open country (see T. R. Henn, *The Living Image* (1972), pp. 30–1), so perhaps this hawking party is a composite or idealized one. Its dramatic function is to point up the dissension between the nobles; the parallel is summarized at l. 53.

0.1–2 *with . . . fist* This vivid detail comes from the Quarto stage direction; but was the hawk real, as in some modern performances, or a 'property' one? Either way, the Queen presumably hands it to one of the falconers after l. 4, to avoid being encumbered with it for the rest of the scene.

0.4 *hollering* calling the dogs (*OED*, *hollo, hollow, v.* 1–3) at the end of the day's sport

2 *these seven years' day* Literally 'for seven years', this is a widely-used expression simply meaning 'for a long time' (*OED*, *seven, a.* 1d).

4 *ten . . . out* The odds were against the hawk *old Joan* flying, because of the high wind; hawks were often lost when they flew away in windy weather.
had . . . out would not have flown (with the implication 'but in fact did so', as Q's version of ll. 1–3 makes explicit: 'My lord, how did your grace like this last flight? | But as I cast her off the wind did rise' (553–4)—and the hawk returned, despite the wind, as the Queen has her safely *on her fist*)

5 *point* advantageous position to which the hawk rises to await its prey (*OED sb.*[1] C 4, whose first example is from 1651)

6 *pitch* the highest point to which the hawk flies (frequently used metaphorically in Shakespeare, as at *Richard II* 1.1.109: 'How high a pitch his resolution soars!')

To see how God in all his creatures works!
Yea, man and birds are fain of climbing high.

SUFFOLK

No marvel, an it like your majesty,
My lord Protector's hawks do tower so well;   10
They know their master loves to be aloft,
And bears his thoughts above his falcon's pitch.

DUKE HUMPHREY

My lord, 'tis but a base ignoble mind
That mounts no higher than a bird can soar.

CARDINAL BEAUFORT

I thought as much, he would be above the clouds.   15

DUKE HUMPHREY

Ay my lord Cardinal, how think you by that?
Were it not good your grace could fly to heaven?

KING HENRY

The treasury of everlasting joy.

CARDINAL BEAUFORT (*to Duke Humphrey*)

Thy heaven is on earth, thine eyes and thoughts
Beat on a crown, the treasure of thy heart,   20
Pernicious Protector, dangerous peer,
That smooth'st it so with King and common weal.

DUKE HUMPHREY

What, Cardinal? Is your priesthood grown peremptory?
Tantaene animis caelestibus irae?

---

7 **To ... works** The phrasing echoes several biblical passages, including 1 Corinthians 12:6: 'God ... worketh all in all.'

8 **fain** fond

9 **an it like** if it please

10 **tower** fly in circular spirals until the 'pitch' (see note to l. 6) is reached. The information provided by editors, that Duke Humphrey's badge was a falcon with a maiden's head, is dramatically irrelevant; the parallel between the rising bird and the aspiring Duke emerges naturally out of the dialogue.

11 **aloft** above others (dominating them)

16 **how think you** what do you mean

18, 20 **treasury ... treasure** The King's heartfelt reaction to heaven, echoing St

Matthew's gospel, 6:20, 'lay up treasures for yourselves in heaven', contrasts with the Cardinal's malicious gibe at Humphrey.

20 **Beat on** think, dwell upon (perhaps with a play upon another term from falconry, 'bate', which means 'flutter around, flap the wings impatiently' (*OED, bate, v.*[1] 2). Both words occur together at *Shrew* 4.1.182, describing hawks 'That bate and beat'.)

21 **Pernicious** dangerous
   dangerous threatening

22 **smooth'st it** flatters

23 **peremptory** dictatorial (*OED a.* 5)

24 *Tantaene ... irae* 'Can there be such anger in heavenly souls?' (Virgil, *Aeneid* 1.11)

Churchmen so hot? Good uncle, hide such malice   25
With some holiness—can you do it?

SUFFOLK
No malice, sir, no more than well becomes
So good a quarrel and so bad a peer.

DUKE HUMPHREY
As who, my lord?

SUFFOLK   Why, as you, my lord,
An't like your lordly Lord's Protectorship.   30

DUKE HUMPHREY
Why Suffolk, England knows thine insolence.

QUEEN MARGARET
And thy ambition, Gloucester.

KING HENRY   I prithee peace,
Good Queen, and whet not on these furious peers,
For blessèd are the peacemakers on earth.

CARDINAL BEAUFORT
Let me be blessèd for the peace I make   35
Against this proud Protector with my sword.
⌈*Duke Humphrey and Cardinal Beaufort speak privately
to one another*⌉

DUKE HUMPHREY
Faith, holy uncle, would't were come to that.

CARDINAL BEAUFORT
Marry, when thou dar'st.

DUKE HUMPHREY
Make up no factious numbers for the matter,
In thine own person answer thy abuse.   40

---

26 some] OXFORD; such F   36.1–2 *Duke . . . another*] *not in* F

26 **some** Oxford argues that F's 'such' was
caught from the *such* of the previous line.
But perhaps F's line means: 'Even with
such holiness, can you do it (i.e. hide such
malice)?'
27 **well becomes** is appropriate to
28 **good** just
32 **prithee** pray you
33 **whet not on** don't encourage
34–5 **blessèd . . . blessèd** Another repetition,
as in ll. 18 and 20, contrasting the King's
and the Cardinal's attitude to religious matters. The King characteristically quotes from Christ's Sermon on

the Mount (Matthew 5: 9), the Cardinal
equally characteristically perverts and
derides it. His next line may echo Christ's
more warlike phrase 'I came not to send
peace, but the sword' (Matthew 10: 34).
37 **that** i.e. a sword-fight
38–9 For a discussion of the Quarto lines
which some editions insert between these
lines, and reasons for excluding them, see
the Textual Introduction, p. 89.
39 **Make . . . matter** do not assemble members of your faction for this quarrel (to
support you)
40 **abuse** insult

CARDINAL BEAUFORT
    Ay, where thou dar'st not peep; an if thou dar'st,
    This evening on the east side of the grove.
KING HENRY
    How now, my lords?
CARDINAL BEAUFORT   Believe me, cousin Gloucester,
    Had not your man put up the fowl so suddenly,
    We had had more sport. (*Aside to Duke Humphrey*) Come
      with thy two-hand sword.   45
DUKE HUMPHREY   True, uncle.
    (*Aside to Cardinal Beaufort*)
    Are ye advised? The east side of the grove.
CARDINAL BEAUFORT (*aside to Duke Humphrey*)
    I am with you.
KING HENRY   Why, how now, uncle Gloucester?
DUKE HUMPHREY
    Talking of hawking, nothing else, my lord.
    (*Aside to the Cardinal*)
    Now by God's mother, priest, I'll shave your crown for
      this,   50
    Or all my fence shall fail.
CARDINAL BEAUFORT (*aside to Duke Humphrey*)
                      Medice, teipsum,
    Protector, see to't well, protect yourself.

48 CARDINAL] CAIRNCROSS (*conj.* McKerrow); Cardinall, F

41 **an if** if (an idiom used for emphasis, since the Cardinal has just said that Humphrey dare not appear)
44 **man** i.e. falconer
    put up the fowl roused the game (*OED*, *put*, *v.*[1] 56b). The Cardinal uses another hawking term to show the King that his whispered conversation with Humphrey is merely *Talking of hawking* (l. 49).
45 **two-hand sword** 'A weapon long out of date in Shakespeare's time. There may be a suggestion that Gloucester was somewhat behind the times (though the weapon would have been appropriate to this date) or the Cardinal may have meant to imply that it was to be a fight to the death, and not a fencing-match' (McKerrow).

47 **advised** agreed
48 **CARDINAL** In F, this is part of Duke Humphrey's speech, which editors have often rearranged. Perhaps removing 'Cardinal' from the start of this line to the speech-prefix makes a more regular iambic line, although the verse in this scene is not particularly regular anyway, and is often hard to distinguish from prose (see the note to ll. 75–149).
50 **shave your crown** An allusion to the priest's tonsure, the shaved crown of the head, but with deadlier intention.
51 **fence** swordsmanship
    Medice, teipsum physician, heal thyself (the Geneva Bible's translation of St Luke 4: 23, in the Vulgate version of the Bible, it became proverbial: Dent P267)

KING HENRY

    The winds grow high, so do your stomachs, lords.

    How irksome is this music to my heart!

    When such strings jar, what hope of harmony?   55

    I pray, my lords, let me compound this strife.

        Enter one crying 'a miracle'

DUKE HUMPHREY What means this noise?

    Fellow, what miracle dost thou proclaim?

ONE A miracle, a miracle!

SUFFOLK

    Come to the King and tell him what miracle.   60

ONE (*to King Henry*)

    Forsooth, a blind man at Saint Alban's shrine

    Within this half-hour hath received his sight,

    A man that ne'er saw in his life before.

KING HENRY

    Now God be praised, that to believing souls

    Gives light in darkness, comfort in despair!   65

        Enter the Mayor of Saint Albans and his brethren, with

        music, bearing the man, Simpcox, between two in a

        chair, and Simpcox's Wife with them

CARDINAL BEAUFORT

    Here comes the townsmen on procession

    To present your highness with the man.

65.1–3 *Enter . . . chair*| F (*subs.*)   1–2 *with music*] Q   3 *and . . . with them*] not in F

---

53 **stomachs** i.e. anger

55 **jar** grow discordant

56 **compound** settle

61 **Saint Alban** Allegedly the first Christian martyr in Britain, Alban was executed by the Romans in Verulamium (later renamed St Albans), for harbouring Christian converts.

65 **light in darkness** This echoes the Benedictus for Morning Prayer, 'To give light to them that sit in darkness' (St Luke, 1: 79), in *The Book of Common Prayer* (1559).

65.1 *brethren* i.e. members of the corporation. These should be enough to carry Simpcox on, without requiring extra townspeople.

65.1–2 *with music* This detail, from Q, presumably reflects staging. The sources (see Appendix B) say that a *Te Deum* was sung, but perhaps the procession is merely accompanied by drumbeats.

66 **on** in (an obsolete use)

67 This is a faulty verse line. An adjective of two syllables before 'highness' may be missing (e.g. 'gracious'). Q offers no help here.

KING HENRY
  Great is his comfort in this earthly vale,
  Although by his sight his sin be multiplied.
DUKE HUMPHREY (*to the townsmen*)
  Stand by, my masters, bring him near the King.   70
  His highness' pleasure is to talk with him.
KING HENRY (*to Simpcox*)
  Good fellow, tell us here the circumstance,
  That we for thee may glorify the Lord.
  What, hast thou been long blind and now restored?
SIMPCOX
  . Born blind, an't please your grace.   75
SIMPCOX'S WIFE Ay, indeed, was he.
SUFFOLK What woman is this?
SIMPCOX'S WIFE His wife, an't like your worship.
DUKE HUMPHREY Hadst thou been his mother thou couldst
  have better told.   80
KING HENRY (*to Simpcox*) Where wert thou born?
SIMPCOX At Berwick in the north, an't like your grace.
KING HENRY
  Poor soul, God's goodness hath been great to thee.
  Let never day nor night unhallowed pass,
  But still remember what the Lord hath done.   85
QUEEN MARGARET (*to Simpcox*)
  Tell me, good fellow, cam'st thou here by chance,
  Or of devotion to this holy shrine?

68–9 Great . . . multiplied Again the King's religious character is expressed in verbal echoes: *earthly vale* may recall the *Homily against Disobedience and Wilful Rebellion*, 'this wretched earth and vale of misery', and the second line, St John 9: 41: 'If ye were blind, ye should not have sin: but now ye say "We see": therefore your sin remaineth.'

69 his sin be multiplied i.e. having sight will lure him into temptation

72 circumstance detail

73 glorify the Lord This echoes Matthew 5: 16: 'glorify your Father which is in heaven.'

75–149 It is difficult to distinguish between prose and irregular verse in this episode, and the Folio layout, which does not dif-

ferentiate typographically between prose and half-lines of verse, does not help. The Quartos print Humphrey's speech ll. 123–31 as prose; but since there are clear verse rhythms in it, F (which was probably printed from Q copy here) turns it into indifferent verse. I follow Oxford's relineation, but without much confidence in the verse created there or elsewhere in this episode. It may be that the Quartos are right and that Humphrey's speech works best as markedly rhythmical prose.

79–80 thou couldst . . . told i.e. you would have been in a better position to know

82 Berwick (a fortress town on the Scottish border)

84 unhallowed unblessed

SIMPCOX

God knows, of pure devotion, being called
A hundred times and oftener, in my sleep,
By good Saint Alban, who said, 'Simpcox, come;   90
Come offer at my shrine and I will help thee.'

SIMPCOX'S WIFE

Most true, forsooth, and many a time and oft
Myself have heard a voice to call him so.

CARDINAL BEAUFORT (*to Simpcox*)

What, art thou lame?

SIMPCOX   Ay, God almighty help me.

SUFFOLK

How cam'st thou so?

SIMPCOX   A fall off of a tree.   95

SIMPCOX'S WIFE (*to Suffolk*)

A plum tree, master.

DUKE HUMPHREY   How long hast thou been blind?

SIMPCOX

O born so, master.

DUKE HUMPHREY   What, and wouldst climb a tree?

SIMPCOX

But that in all my life, when I was a youth.

SIMPCOX'S WIFE (*to Duke Humphrey*)

Too true, and bought his climbing very dear.

DUKE HUMPHREY (*to Simpcox*)

Mass, thou loved'st plums well that wouldst venture so.   100

---

90 Simpcox] POPE 1728 (*conj.* Theobald); *Symon* F   92 many a] This edition; many F

90 **Simpcox** The Folio calls him 'Symon' here, 'Saunder Simpcox' at l. 122. McKerrow suggests that the MS may have had 'Sym.' which the printer expanded to 'Simon' instead of 'Simpcox'.
91 **offer** make an offering of money
92 **many a time and oft** Abbott 86 says that F's 'many time' 'seems used as one word adverbially' but gives no other examples; *OED, time, sb.* 18 gives four examples, from 1250, 1375, 1590, and 1622. 'Many a time' seems to have replaced it as the usual form (it occurs at 4.10.10 and 12), and since it is frequent in Shakespeare, especially in the phrase 'many a time and

oft' (e.g. *Merchant* 1.3.105; *1 Henry IV* 1.1.49–50; *Julius Caesar* 1.1.37), I adopt it here.
94 **lame** Simpcox's lameness is an addition to the sources.
96 **plum tree** 'allusive of vagina. . . . climbing the tree indicates copulation. . . . If *plums* are the wife's genitals, . . . *damsons* [l. 101] connote his own' (Williams, pp. 240–1). The joke, such as it is, hardly seems worth the effort, and distracts from the more important point that Simpcox is already beginning to incriminate himself.
98 **But that** i.e. only that once
100 **Mass** by the Mass

SIMPCOX

    Alas, good master, my wife desired some damsons,

    And made me climb with danger of my life.

DUKE HUMPHREY (*aside*)

    A subtle knave, but yet it shall not serve.

    (*To Simpcox*) Let me see thine eyes: wink now, now open

        them.

    In my opinion yet thou seest not well.   105

SIMPCOX

    Yes, master, clear as day, I thank God and Saint Alban.

DUKE HUMPHREY

    Sayst thou me so? (*Pointing*) What colour is this cloak of?

SIMPCOX

    Red, master, red as blood.

DUKE HUMPHREY   Why, that's well said.

    What colour is my gown of?

SIMPCOX   Black, forsooth,

    Coal-black as jet.   110

KING HENRY

    Why then, thou know'st what colour jet is of?

---

106 Alban] F2; *Albones* F1   109–10 What . . . jet] F ; (*Pointing*) And his cloak ? SIMPCOX Why, that's green. GLOUCESTER (*pointing*) And what colour's | His hose ? SIMPCOX Yellow, master ; yellow as gold. | GLOUCESTER And what colour's my gown ? SIMPCOX Black, sir ; coal-black, as jet. OXFORD (*after* Q)

101 **desired some damsons** See the note to l. 96.

103 **subtle** crafty

    shall not serve i.e. he won't get away with it

104 **wink** close

106–10 Simpcox uses three proverbs to emphasize the truth of his answers: *clear as day* (Dent D56), *red as blood* (Dent B455), *black as jet* (Dent J49).

107 **Sayst . . . so** you say that, do you?

    me Another example of the so-called 'ethic dative', used for emphasis. (See the first note to 1.1.162.)

108–9 Between these lines, Oxford inserts some Quarto lines asking Simpcox to identify more colours (see collation), on the grounds that 'Q probably represents the performing text' and the 'allusion to this episode slightly later in the scene [ll. 126–8] requires Q here' (*Textual Com-*

panion, p. 182). But if this edition's view that the Folio text represents a revision of the original reported by Q is correct, Shakespeare may simply have decided that the two colours, red and black, are sufficient to make the point, and revised the passage so that the focus is less upon Simpcox's naming a list of colours than on the King's reaction to what that implies (see the next note).

111 **thou know'st . . . of** The King's realization that the miracle is a sham is a powerful dramatic moment, emphasizing his religious faith even as it tests it. Harold Hobson described how, in David Warner's performance at Stratford-upon-Avon, 'as the fraud is exposed, the King's face is stricken. We see a man's faith, which is all in all to him, momentarily destroyed' (*Sunday Times*, 21 July 1963).

SUFFOLK
  And yet I think jet did he never see.
DUKE HUMPHREY
  But cloaks and gowns before this day, a many.
SIMPCOX'S WIFE
  Never before this day in all his life.
DUKE HUMPHREY Tell me, sirrah, what's my name?   115
SIMPCOX Alas, master, I know not.
DUKE HUMPHREY What's his name?
SIMPCOX I know not.
DUKE HUMPHREY Nor his?
SIMPCOX No indeed, master.   120
DUKE HUMPHREY What's thine own name?
SIMPCOX Sander Simpcox, an if it please you, master.
DUKE HUMPHREY
  Then Sander, sit thou there the lying'st knave
  In Christendom. If thou hadst been born blind,
  Thou mightst as well have known our names as thus   125
  To name the several colours we do wear.
  Sight may distinguish colours, but suddenly
  To nominate them all, it is impossible.

---

119 Nor his] OXFORD *continues, after* Q : SIMPCOX No, truly, sir. | GLOUCESTER (*pointing*) Nor his name? 123 sit thou] HANMER; sit F 125 our] CAIRNCROSS; all our F 127 distinguish] OXFORD (*conj.* Cairncross); distinguish of F

---

113 a many many (a common construction in Shakespeare: Abbott 87)

119–20 Oxford inserts two lines from the Quarto here (see collation), since 'the F omission could easily have resulted from eyeskip' (*Textual Companion*, p. 183)—but equally from authorial deletion.

122–3 **Sander** F calls him 'Simon' at l. 90. Since this passage was probably based on Quarto copy, and since an actor called Sander was a member of Pembroke's Men, from whose production Q probably derives, Scott McMillin suggests that he played Simpcox and that his own name slipped into the text ('Casting for Pembroke's Men', *SQ* 23 (1972), p. 155). For McKerrow's simpler explanation of

the discrepancy, see the note to l. 90. *Sander* is probably an abbreviation of 'Alexander'.

123 **sit thou there** there you are (exposed as)

123–4 **the ... Christendom** A common Elizabethan idiom, also occurring at *Shrew* Induction 2.22–3.

126 **several** different

128 **To ... impossible** This is one of the phrases which Oxford believes requires extra lines about colours to be inserted earlier from Q (see the note to ll. 108–9). But it is worth noting that if *all*, *it* were omitted, a regular iambic line would result (as at l. 125, where Oxford omits 'all' from the QF line 'all our names').

My lords, Saint Alban here hath done a miracle;
And would ye not think his cunning to be great   130
That could restore this cripple to his legs again?
SIMPCOX O master, that you could!
DUKE HUMPHREY
My masters of Saint Albans,
Have you not beadles in your town, and things called
    whips?
MAYOR Yes, my lord, if it please your grace.   135
DUKE HUMPHREY Then send for one presently.
MAYOR Sirrah, go fetch the beadle hither straight.
                              Exit one
DUKE HUMPHREY Now fetch me a stool hither by and by.
          A stool is brought
      (*To Simpcox*) Now sirrah, if you mean to save yourself
from whipping, leap me over this stool and run away.   140
SIMPCOX Alas master, I am not able to stand alone. You go
about to torture me in vain.
          Enter a Beadle with whips
DUKE HUMPHREY Well sir, we must have you find your
legs. Sirrah beadle, whip him till he leap over that same
stool.   145
BEADLE I will, my lord. (*To Simpcox*) Come on sirrah, off
with your doublet quickly.
SIMPCOX Alas master, what shall I do? I am not able
to stand.
          After the Beadle hath hit him once, he leaps over the
          stool and runs away; and they follow and cry, 'A
          miracle!'

---

130 his] Q; it F   137.1 *one*] Q; *not in* F   138.1 *A . . . brought*] *not in* F

Even as the text stands in F, and in this
edition, the references to the colours
make perfect sense in performance.
nominate name

130 **cunning** skill
134 **beadles** Minor parish officials, often
assigned to inflict corporal punishment.
things called whips An emphatic phrase
(does it carry a hint of cruel relish?)

that either was or became a catch-phrase
(Dent W 306.1).
137 **straight** straight away
138 **by and by** immediately. This adverbial
phrase (*OED* 3) is very common in
Shakespeare.
140 **me** The 'ethic dative' again; see the
second note to l. 107.
147 **doublet** jacket

KING HENRY

O God, seest thou this and bear'st so long?   150

QUEEN MARGARET

It made me laugh to see the villain run.

DUKE HUMPHREY ⌈*to the Beadle*⌉

Follow the knave, and take this drab away.

SIMPCOX'S WIFE Alas sir, we did it for pure need.

⌈*Exit the Beadle with the Wife*⌉

DUKE HUMPHREY ⌈*to the Mayor*⌉

Let them be whipped through every market-town

Till they come to Berwick, from whence they came.   155

Exeunt the Mayor and aldermen

CARDINAL BEAUFORT

Duke Humphrey has done a miracle today.

SUFFOLK

True: made the lame to leap and fly away.

DUKE HUMPHREY

But you have done more miracles than I:

You made in a day, my lord, whole towns to fly.

Enter the Duke of Buckingham

KING HENRY

What tidings with our cousin Buckingham?   160

BUCKINGHAM

Such as my heart doth tremble to unfold.

A sort of naughty persons, lewdly bent,

Under the countenance and confederacy

Of Lady Eleanor, the Protector's wife,

The ringleader and head of all this rout,   165

153.1 *Exit . . . Wife*] *not in* F   155.1 *Exeunt . . . aldermen*] *Exit.* F

150–1 The contrasted reactions of the King and Queen emphasize the difference between them, the King's religious attitude shocked by the fraudulent miracle, the Queen simply treating it as a joke.

150 **bear'st** endures, puts up with

152 **drab** slut

153 **pure need** sheer necessity

155 **Berwick** Berwick on the Scottish border is a long way from St Albans, so this is a severe punishment.

157 **made . . . leap** A mocking biblical echo: 'Then shall the lame man leap' (Isaiah 35: 6).

159 **made . . . fly** Another reference to the surrender of Anjou and Maine in Margaret's marriage settlement.

162 **sort** crew, gang (a contemptuous phrase)

naughty . . . lewdly Stronger expressions then than now, implying wickedness or evil.

bent inclined

163 **Under . . . confederacy** with the patronage and complicity

165 **head** leader

rout disorderly mob

Have practised dangerously against your state,
Dealing with witches and with conjurors,
Whom we have apprehended in the fact,
Raising up wicked spirits from under ground,
Demanding of King Henry's life and death,   170
And other of your highness' Privy Council,
As more at large your grace shall understand.

CARDINAL BEAUFORT (*to Duke Humphrey*)
And so, my lord Protector, by this means
Your lady is forthcoming yet at London.
(*Aside to Duke Humphrey*)
This news, I think, hath turned your weapon's edge.   175
'Tis like, my lord, you will not keep your hour.

DUKE HUMPHREY
Ambitious churchman, leave to afflict my heart.
Sorrow and grief have vanquished all my powers,
And vanquished as I am, I yield to thee
Or to the meanest groom.   180

KING HENRY
O God, what mischiefs work the wicked ones,
Heaping confusion on their own heads thereby.

QUEEN MARGARET
Gloucester, see here the tainture of thy nest,
And look thyself be faultless, thou wert best.

DUKE HUMPHREY
Madam, for myself, to heaven I do appeal,   185

---

166 **practised** conspired
168 **in the fact** in the very act, red-handed
170 **Demanding of** asking questions about
171 **other** other members
172 Oxford omits this Folio line and follows the Quarto, which has the spirit's prophecies read out here rather than by York at 1.4.58–67. Q's version is reproduced at Appendix A, passage C.
     at large in full
174 **forthcoming** in custody, awaiting trial. See the second note to 1.4.52.
175 **turned** bent back, and so made blunt (*OED v.* 9b)
176 **like** likely
     keep your hour i.e. turn up for the planned duel
177 **leave to afflict** cease from afflicting
180 **meanest groom** lowest servant. A *groom*

did not necessarily work with horses, though he often did; the word is usually disparaging in Shakespeare, as at 4.1.53 and 4.2.115.
181–4 **O God . . . best** As at ll. 150–1, the King's and Queen's reactions are sharply contrasted: the King quotes from the Bible to comment in general about mankind's wickedness—'His mischief shall return upon his own head' (Psalm 7: 16)—with no specific reference to Humphrey; the Queen typically uses the situation to incriminate him.
183 **tainture** defilement (alluding to the proverb 'It is a foul bird that defiles his own nest': Dent B377).
184 **look . . . best** you had better be sure that you yourself are not involved in her crime

How I have loved my King and common weal;
And for my wife, I know not how it stands.
Sorry I am to hear what I have heard.
Noble she is, but if she have forgot
Honour and virtue and conversed with such   190
As like to pitch, defile nobility,
I banish her my bed and company,
And give her as a prey to law and shame
That hath dishonoured Gloucester's honest name.

KING HENRY

Well, for this night we will repose us here;   195
Tomorrow toward London back again,
To look into this business thoroughly,
And call these foul offenders to their answers,
And poise the cause in Justice' equal scales,
Whose beam stands sure, whose rightful cause prevails.   200

Flourish. Exeunt

2.2 *Enter the Duke of York and the Earls of Salisbury
and Warwick*

YORK

Now, my good lords of Salisbury and Warwick,

187 **And** 'But' might have been expected
here; perhaps, however, Humphrey is
about to say that his wife is innocent too,
but then realizes that he cannot guaran-
tee this, and so changes tack in the second
half of the line.
 how it stands what the facts are
190 **conversed** consorted
191 **like . . . defile** Proverbial: 'He that
touches pitch shall be defiled' (Dent
P358), drawn from the Bible (the apocryphal book of Ecclesiasticus 13: 1).
198 **answers** defence (in court)
199 **poise the cause** weigh the case
200 **beam** bar from which scales are
balanced
 stands sure is perfectly balanced (i.e.
without bias)
2.2 The dramatic function of this scene is the
Duke of York's formal presentation of
his claim to the crown. It also helps to
establish that, despite his soliloquies at

1.1.213–58 and 3.1.331–83, he is not
simply a devious Machiavellian schemer
like his son Richard III, but takes the trouble to argue his case. He does so partly to
convince his two chief allies, and their
contribution to the scene is important:
in the BBC television production, for instance, Warwick is easily persuaded, but
Salisbury, presented throughout the F
text as a figure of moderation and loyalty,
is only persuaded reluctantly. York
presents an elaborate genealogy of his
descent from Edward III, but the crux is
one very simple point: he is descended
from Edward III's *third* son, Henry from
the fourth. The genealogy is a metrified
version of passages from Hall's chronicle:
see Introduction, p. 31. For the important
textual arguments that have been based
on this scene, see the Textual Introduction, pp. 78–9.

Our simple supper ended, give me leave
In this close walk to satisfy myself
In craving your opinion of my title,
Which is infallible, to England's crown.   5
SALISBURY
My lord, I long to hear it out at full.
WARWICK
Sweet York, begin, and if thy claim be good,
The Nevilles are thy subjects to command.
YORK   Then thus:
Edward the Third, my lords, had seven sons: 10
The first, Edward the Black Prince, Prince of Wales;
The second, William of Hatfield; and the third,
Lionel Duke of Clarence; next to whom
Was John of Gaunt, the Duke of Lancaster;
The fifth was Edmund Langley, Duke of York;   15
The sixth was Thomas of Woodstock, Duke of
   Gloucester;
William of Windsor was the seventh and last.
Edward the Black Prince died before his father,
And left behind him Richard, his only son,

2.2.6 it out] OXFORD (*conj.* McKerrow); it F

2 **supper** (to which York invited them at
  1.4.77–8)
3 **close walk** secluded path
3–4 **satisfy myself | In** give myself the
  satisfaction of
9 **Then thus**: The incomplete line suggests a
  pause as York prepares to launch into the
  account of his descent from Edward III.
  Sometimes, as at the Old Vic, London, in
  1957, York unfurls a map of his family
  tree, to help Salisbury and Warwick, and
  (if it is big enough) the audience, to follow
  his argument. The notes that follow only
  provide historical information which the
  text itself does not provide, or gets wrong,
  and which clarifies the situation.
10 **Edward the Third** He reigned for fifty years
  (1327–77). His conquest of France is dramatized in an anonymous play named
  after him, often attributed in part or
  whole to Shakespeare.
11 **the Black Prince** (so called because of the
  colour of his armour at the battle of
  Crécy, a famous victory over the French
  dramatized at *Edward III* 3.4)

13 **Lionel** York claims the crown, through his
  mother, from Lionel.
14 **John of Gaunt** So named after his
  birthplace, Ghent in Flanders; he is a
  major character in Shakespeare's *Richard
  II*.
15 **York** He too plays an important role in
  Richard II, but, although York in this play
  obviously inherits the dukedom from him,
  he has to claim the crown not from him,
  but from his mother's line, which goes
  back to Edward's *third* son, whereas York
  was the fifth.
16 **Woodstock** He is the central character
  of an anonymous Elizabethan play
  untitled but named after him in modern
  editions, which dramatizes events leading
  to his murder, almost certainly on the
  instructions of his nephew, Richard II,
  in 1397. It is this event which sparks
  off the opening quarrel of *Richard II*, leading to Bolingbroke's seizure of the crown
  and Richard's murder, alluded to in ll.
  21–7.
19 **Richard** (i.e. Richard II)

Who after Edward the Third's death, reigned as king   20
Till Henry Bolingbroke, Duke of Lancaster,
The eldest son and heir of John of Gaunt,
Crowned by the name of Henry the Fourth,
Seized on the realm, deposed the rightful king,
Sent his poor queen to France from whence she came,   25
And him to Pomfret; where, as all you know,
Harmless Richard was murdered traitorously.

WARWICK (*to Salisbury*)
Father, the Duke of York hath told the truth;
Thus got the house of Lancaster the crown.

YORK
Which now they hold by force and not by right;   30
For Richard, the first son's heir, being dead,
The issue of the next son should have reigned.

SALISBURY
But William of Hatfield died without an heir.

YORK
The third son, Duke of Clarence, from whose line
I claim the crown, had issue Philippa, a daughter,   35
Who married Edmund Mortimer, Earl of March;
Edmund had issue Roger, Earl of March;
Roger had issue Edmund, Anne, and Eleanor.

SALISBURY
This Edmund, in the reign of Bolingbroke,

---

28 Duke of York] CAIRNCROSS; Duke F   35, 49 Philippa] This edition (*conj*. Collier); *Phillip* F

---

23 **Henry** Probably here given three syllables—'Hen-er-y'—which makes the line
regular.
26 **Pomfret** Pontefract Castle in Yorkshire.
F's spelling, 'Pumfret', probably indicates
the Elizabethan pronunciation.
   all Oxford emends to 'well'; but 'all',
referring to only two people, seems to
have been Elizabethan idiom: it occurs,
for instance, at *2 Henry IV* 3.1.34. Q's
'both' supports F's sense rather than
Oxford's.
28 **of York** Cairncross inserts these words,
which regularize the metre, arguing that
'the printer's eye has jumped from du*ke* to
York*e*'; on the other hand, a pause may be

intended: perhaps Salisbury is lost in
thought or non-committal, so that
Warwick has to urge York's case.
35, 49 **Philippa** Oxford modernizes F's
'Phillip' as 'Phillipe', leaving the line
irregular. Collier's conjecture 'Philippa'
makes the line marginally more
speakable.
38 **Edmund** Fifth Earl of March, he was
declared heir presumptive by Richard II in
1398.
39–42 **This Edmund . . . died** Like Hall
and Holinshed, Shakespeare confuses
Edmund Mortimer, the fifth Earl (see the
previous note) with Sir Edmund
Mortimer, brother of the fourth Earl, who

As I have read, laid claim unto the crown,   40
And but for Owen Glendower, had been king,
Who kept him in captivity till he died.
But to the rest.

YORK   His eldest sister, Anne,
My mother, being heir unto the crown,
Married Richard, Earl of Cambridge, who was son   45
To Edmund Langley, Edward the Third's fifth son.
By her I claim the kingdom: she was heir
To Roger, Earl of March, who was the son
Of Edmund Mortimer, who married Philippa,
Sole daughter unto Lionel, Duke of Clarence.   50
So, if the issue of the elder son
Succeed before the younger, I am king.

WARWICK
What plain proceedings is more plain than this?
Henry doth claim the crown from John of Gaunt,
The fourth son, York claims it from the third: 55

---

45 was son] ROWE; was F   46 son] THEOBALD; Sonnes Sonne F

---

was held captive by Glendower (see the next note). He repeats the mistake when the latter character appears in *1 Henry IV*.

41 **Owen Glendower** A Welsh rebel against Henry IV, he makes a powerful single appearance in *1 Henry IV*, 3.1. In both plays, Oxford follows its policy of representing Shakespeare's anglicizations of foreign names with their modern equivalents: hence 'Owain Glyndŵr'. I retain Shakespeare's anglicization as I think it is easier for actors to pronounce and audiences to understand, except perhaps for Welsh-speaking ones.

42 **Who** (Glendower)

kept . . . died Hall uses this phrase of another prisoner of Glendower's, Lord Grey of Ruthin, also married to one of his daughters, and mentioned just before Glendower's capture of Mortimer (p. 23). Shakespeare either confuses or conflates the two, as he does the two Mortimers (see note to ll. 39–42).

45 **Richard . . . Cambridge** Executed for attempting to assassinate Henry V,

an attempt dramatized at 2.2 of Shakespeare's play.

47–52 **By her . . . king** After giving his allies (and the audience) an elaborate genealogy, York summarizes the crucial point in these lines, especially in the trenchant final two, reinforced by Warwick at ll. 54–5.

53 **What . . . this** As in the Archbishop of Canterbury's exposition of Henry V's claim to the French Crown (*Henry V* 1.2.35–86), a complicated genealogy is followed by an anti-climactic comment, which the Archbishop provides himself: 'as clear as is the summer's sun'. Shakespeare characteristically uses humour to help the actors, and the audience, through tricky, detailed narrative, without necessarily using that humour to cheapen or undercut the claim being made.

proceedings pedigree, line of descent. McKerrow conjectures that this plural phrase looks like a reference 'to some customary phrase, perhaps legal', though *OED* does not provide any supporting evidence.

Till Lionel's issue fails, Gaunt's should not reign.
It fails not yet, but flourishes in thee
And in thy sons, fair slips of such a stock.
Then father Salisbury, kneel we together,
And in this private plot be we the first   60
That shall salute our rightful sovereign
With honour of his birthright to the crown.

SALISBURY *and* WARWICK

Long live our sovereign Richard, England's king!

YORK

We thank you, lords; but I am not your king
Till I be crowned, and that my sword be stained   65
With heart-blood of the house of Lancaster;
And that's not suddenly to be performed,
But with advice and silent secrecy.
Do you as I do in these dangerous days,
Wink at the Duke of Suffolk's insolence,   70
At Beaufort's pride, at Somerset's ambition,
At Buckingham, and all the crew of them,
Till they have snared the shepherd of the flock,
That virtuous prince, the good Duke Humphrey.
'Tis that they seek, and they, in seeking that,   75
Shall find their deaths, if York can prophesy.

SALISBURY

My lord, break off; we know your mind at full.

---

56 Gaunt's] This edition (*conj.* Oxford), John's OXFORD; his F   77 off] CAPELL; we off F

---

56 **Gaunt's** Oxford reads 'John's' for F's 'his', but conjectures 'Gaunt's' which I think is clearer.

58 **slips . . . stock** cuttings from such a tree (punning on 'family tree')

60 **private plot** secluded piece of ground (the *close walk* of l. 3)

62 **birthright** right by birth, inheritance, 'specifically used of the special rights of the first-born' (*OED* 1)

64 **We . . . I** His case made, York starts to use the royal plural, but then reverts to 'I' to stress that he is not yet king.

67 **suddenly** immediately

68 **advice** mature consideration

70 **Wink at** close your eyes to, ignore

73 **shepherd of the flock** This phrase echoes

Hall's praise of Henry V, 'a shepherd whom his flock loved' (p. 112), and probably also the biblical description of Christ the good shepherd in St John 10; 11–12; and, as Cairncross says, it makes a striking tribute to Humphrey, spoken by his enemies.

77 **break off** don't say any more. It is possible that Salisbury dislikes York's approval of snaring Duke Humphrey, as in the BBC production; but perhaps he simply means that nothing more needs to be said. F's 'break we off' results in an irregular and less effective line: 'we' is probably an error, influenced by the second 'we' in the line.

WARWICK

My heart assures me that the Earl of Warwick
Shall one day make the Duke of York a king.

YORK

And Neville, this I do assure myself: 80
Richard shall live to make the Earl of Warwick
The greatest man in England but the King.

Exeunt

2.3   *Sound trumpets. Enter King Henry and state, with
guard, to banish the Duchess: King Henry and Queen
Margaret, Duke Humphrey of Gloucester, the Duke of
Suffolk ⌈and the Duke of Buckingham, Cardinal
Beaufort⌉, and, led with officers, Dame Eleanor
Cobham the Duchess, Margery Jourdayne the witch,
John Southwell and Sir John Hum the two priests, and
Roger Bolingbroke the conjuror; ⌈and then enter to
them⌉ the Duke of York and the Earls of Salisbury ⌈and
Warwick⌉*

KING HENRY

Stand forth Dame Eleanor Cobham, Gloucester's wife.

She comes forward

In sight of God and us your guilt is great;
Receive the sentence of the law for sins
Such as by God's book are adjudged to death.
(*To the Witch, Southwell, Hum, and Bolingbroke*)

2.3.0.1–2 *Sound . . . Duchess*] F (*subs.*)   0.2–10 *King Henry . . . Warwick*] Q (*subs.*)   0.6–8
Margery . . . conjuror] not in F, Q   1.1 *She comes forward*] not in F   3 sins] THEOBALD; sinne F

---

82 **but** except for. Is York warning Warwick
against overreaching himself? That was
certainly suggested by Jack May in the
BBC 'Age of Kings' version and by
Donald Sinden at Stratford-upon-Avon in
1963–4.

2.3.0.1–10 This direction conflates those of F
and Q (see collation). F's is characteristically curt, quickly specifying the business
in hand, Q's characteristically detailed.
Neither mentions the Duchess's accomplices, though they are addressed at l. 5. Q
directs Buckingham, the Cardinal, and

Warwick to enter, though none of them
speaks: perhaps they are needed, the
Cardinal especially, to give a sense of
judgement being passed before a formal
assembly, or *state* (o.1). Q brings on York,
Salisbury, and Warwick last and separately, in accordance with the convention
that characters who have just left the
stage do not immediately re-enter.

4 **adjudged** deemed worthy of (*OED ppl.
a.* 2)—in, for example, Exodus 22: 18:
'Thou shalt not suffer a witch to live'.

You four, from hence to prison back again;   5
From thence, unto the place of execution.
The witch in Smithfield shall be burned to ashes,
And you three shall be strangled on the gallows.
⌈*Exeunt Witch, Southwell, Hum, and Bolingbroke, guarded*⌉
(*To the Duchess*)
You, madam, for you are more nobly born,
Despoilèd of your honour in your life,   10
Shall, after three days' open penance done,
Live in your country here in banishment
With Sir John Stanley in the Isle of Man.

DUCHESS ELEANOR
Welcome is banishment, welcome were my death.

DUKE HUMPHREY
Eleanor, the law thou seest hath judgèd thee;   15
I cannot justify whom the law condemns.
⌈*Exit the Duchess, guarded*⌉
Mine eyes are full of tears, my heart of grief.
Ah Humphrey, this dishonour in thine age
Will bring thy head with sorrow to the grave.
I beseech your majesty, give me leave to go.   20
Sorrow would solace, and mine age would ease.

KING HENRY
Stay, Humphrey Duke of Gloucester. Ere thou go,
Give up thy staff. Henry will to himself
Protector be; and God shall be my hope,

8.1 *Exeunt . . . guarded*] *not in* F   16.1 *Exit . . . guarded*] *not in* F   19 grave] CAIRNCROSS;
ground F

---

7 **Smithfield** The usual place in London
where victims were burnt at the stake,
usually for religious reasons.

8 **you three** Hum is sentenced to hang
with the others, despite the fact that he
arranged the betrayal of the Duchess; in
the chronicles he is pardoned, so the play
makes a deliberate change, presumably to
suggest that Suffolk and the Cardinal are
getting rid of someone who might talk too
much.

9 **for** because

10 **Despoiled . . . life** deprived of your reputation for the rest of your life

11 **open** public

13 **With** in the custody of

14 **were** would be

16 **justify** exonerate

19 **grave** Cairncross amends F's 'ground'
because of the biblical echo 'ye shall bring
my gray head with sorrow unto the grave'
(Genesis 42: 38), and a similar (presumed) error at *Hamlet* 4.5.38, where F
and Q1 read 'grave', Q2 'ground'.

21 **would** would have

22 **Stay** wait

23 **staff** (the symbol of his protectorship)

24–5 **God . . . feet** Henry characteristically
draws on various texts from the Psalms:
'thou, O Lord God, . . . art my hope'

My stay, my guide, and lantern to my feet.   25
And go in peace, Humphrey, no less beloved
Than when thou wert Protector to thy King.

QUEEN MARGARET

I see no reason why a king of years
Should be to be protected like a child.
God and King Henry govern England's helm.   30
Give up your staff, sir, and the King his realm.

DUKE HUMPHREY

My staff? Here, noble Henry, is my staff.
As willingly do I the same resign
As erst thy father Henry made it mine;
And even as willing at thy feet I leave it   35
As others would ambitiously receive it.
    He lays the staff at King Henry's feet
Farewell good King. When I am dead and gone,
May honourable peace attend thy throne.   *Exit*

QUEEN MARGARET

Why now is Henry King and Margaret Queen,
And Humphrey Duke of Gloucester scarce himself,   40

---

30 helm] STEEVENS–REED (*conj.* Johnson); Realme F   34 erst] Q; ere F   35 willing] Q; willingly F   36.1 *He . . . feet*] *not in* F

(71: 5); 'O Lord, thou art my guide and
stay' (42: 9, in Sternhold and Hopkins's
metrified version, 1583); 'Thy word is a
lantern unto my feet' (119: 105).

28 **of years** who is of age, no longer a minor
29 **be to be** If the first *be* is not a misprint, it is
probably the *be* 'of necessity, obligation,
. . . in which sense *have* is now commonly
substituted' (*OED v.* 16); but I suspect
that Compositor A substituted *be* for some
other word (perhaps 'need', which gives
the required sense), influenced by the
second *be* in the phrase, as in the next line
he substituted 'realm' for 'helm', his eye
catching the rhyme word in l. 31. Since *be
to be* will be meaningless to a modern
audience, 'need to be' makes a simple and
comprehensible alternative, and may in
any case be correct.
30 **govern** steer
31 **King his** This is sometimes interpreted

by editors as an Elizabethan possessive,
'King's' (Abbott 217), but surely the
whole line means 'Give up your staff and
give the King his realm'.
34 **erst** in the first place (*OED adv.* B2).
Although F's 'ere' makes sense, meaning
'on a former occasion' (*OED adv.* A4),
Oxford assumes that F was contaminated
by Q3 copy here. Erst 'occurs once elsewhere in this play (2.4.14): Compositor
A, who set this line, also set that one, so it
is doubtful that he altered the spelling
here' (*Textual Companion*, p. 184).
    thy father . . . mine Hall reports the
dying Henry V as saying 'I would my
brother Humphrey should be Protector
of England during the minority of my
child' (p. 112).
35 **willing** F's 'willingly' was probably
caught by the compositor from l. 33. See
note to l. 29 for probable similar slips.

That bears so shrewd a maim; two pulls at once:
His lady banished and a limb lopped off.
        She picks up the staff, and gives it to King Henry
This staff of honour raught, there let it stand
Where it best fits to be, in Henry's hand.

SUFFOLK

Thus droops this lofty pine and hangs his sprays;   45
Thus Eleanor's pride dies in her youngest days.

YORK

Lords, let him go. Please it your majesty,
This is the day appointed for the combat,
And ready are the appellant and defendant,
The armourer and his man, to enter the lists,   50
So please your highness to behold the fight.

QUEEN MARGARET

Ay, good my lord, for purposely therefor
Left I the court to see this quarrel tried.

KING HENRY

A God's name, see the lists and all things fit;
Here let them end it, and God defend the right.   55

YORK

I never saw a fellow worse bestead,
Or more afraid to fight, than is the appellant,
The servant of this armourer, my lords.

42.1 *She . . . Henry*] *not in* F

---

41 **bears . . . maim** endures so severe a
   mutilation
   two pulls at once two things torn from
   him at the same time (his wife and
   his staff of office). It is characteristic of
   Margaret that she should exult in
   Humphrey's double misfortune: this is
   kicking a man when he is down.
43 **raught** seized, torn (from him by us)
   (*OED, reach, v.*[1] 4c), as at *Antony* 4.10.29:
   'The hand of death hath raught him.'
45 **lofty pine** Perhaps a reference to the badge
   of Henry IV, Humphrey's father; but the
   idea of the pine drooping is frequent in
   Shakespeare, for example at *Cymbeline*
   4.2.175–7, where the wind makes 'the
   mountain pine . . . stoop to th' vale'.
   sprays branches

46 **in . . . days** in its greatest vigour. *Her*
   refers to *pride*, not to Eleanor, who isn't
   young.
47 **let him go** forget about him. York is anxious to get on with the combat, and to
   clear his name from the imputation of
   treason (or appear to do so).
49 **appellant and defendant** challenger and
   defender
50 **lists** combat area
51 **So please** if it please
52 **Ay** i.e. do so
   therefor for that reason (*OED* 1b)
53 **tried** resolved by combat
54 **A** in (a worn-down form of Old English
   preposition *an, on: OED prep.*[1] 10)
   fit properly arranged
56 **bestead** prepared

Enter at one door Horner the armourer and his
Neighbours, drinking to him so much that he is drunk;
and he enters with a drummer before him and
⌈*carrying*⌉ *his staff with a sandbag fastened to it. Enter*
at the other door Peter his man, also with a drummer
and a staff with sandbag, and Prentices drinking to him

FIRST NEIGHBOUR (*offering drink to Horner*) Here, neighbour
Horner, I drink to you in a cup of sack, and fear not,   60
neighbour, you shall do well enough.

SECOND NEIGHBOUR (*offering drink to Horner*) And here,
neighbour, here's a cup of charneco.

THIRD NEIGHBOUR (*offering drink to Horner*) And here's a pot
of good double beer, neighbour: drink, and fear not your   65
man.

HORNER ⌈*accepting the offers of drink*⌉ Let it come, i' faith, and
I'll pledge you all, and a fig for Peter.

FIRST PRENTICE (*offering drink to Peter*) Here, Peter, I drink to
thee, and be not afraid.   70

SECOND PRENTICE (*offering drink to Peter*) Be merry, Peter, and
fear not thy master. Fight for credit of the prentices!

PETER ⌈*refusing the offers of drink*⌉ I thank you all. Drink and
pray for me, I pray you, for I think I have taken my last
draught in this world. Here, Robin, an if I die, I give thee   75

58.1–6 *Enter . . . to him*] F (*subs.*)   59, 62, 64 *offering . . . Horner*] *not in* F   67 *accepting . . .*
drink] *not in* F   69, 71 *offering . . . Peter*] *not in* F   73 *refusing . . . drink*] *not in* F

58.2 **drinking to** pledging, 'toasting'
58.4 **staff . . . it** A *sandbag* was not a
mock-weapon, as *OED sb.* 2c makes clear;
this is a real duel, not a parody one. The
crude weapon may have been used by
people of inferior rank, but a blow from a
bag crammed hard with sand could be
lethal, as events in this scene prove; and
in the source for *Othello*, the equivalents
of Othello and Iago batter the wife to
death with stockings filled with sand.
60 **sack** The general name for a class of white
wine imported from Spain and the
Canary Islands; it is a favourite drink of
Falstaff's in *Henry IV*.
63 **charneco** Sweet wine, perhaps named
after a village near Lisbon (*OED obs.*).
65 **double** strong
67 **Let it come** let the glass go round (a drink-

ing expression, as at *2 Henry IV* 5.3.54)
68 **fig** Obscene slang, from Italian *fica*
(vagina), usually accompanied by a
gesture of thrusting the thumb between
two closed fingers or into the mouth.
70–1 Between these lines, Q inserts two more
in which the apprentices encourage Peter
to drink. Oxford includes them, supposing them to be added in rehearsal;
but, as Oxford also says, there is 'nothing
in these lines beyond the power of a
reporter or an actor to invent' (*Textual*
Companion, p. 184), so I omit them.
72 **credit** reputation
75–7 **Here . . . have** The pathos of this
moment, as Peter, thinking he is about to
die, makes an impromptu will, is further
evidence that he is not a gormless idiot;
see the note to 1.3.32. He also has the

my apron; and Will, thou shalt have my hammer; and here, Tom, take all the money that I have. O Lord bless me, I pray God, for I am never able to deal with my master, he hath learned so much fence already.

SALISBURY Come, leave your drinking, and fall to blows. (*To* 80
Peter) Sirrah, what's thy name?

PETER Peter, forsooth.

SALISBURY Peter? What more?

PETER Thump.

SALISBURY Thump! Then see thou thump thy master well. 85

HORNER Masters, I am come hither, as it were, upon my man's instigation, to prove him a knave and myself an honest man; and touching the Duke of York, I will take my death I never meant him any ill, nor the King, nor the Queen; and therefore Peter, have at thee with a 90
downright blow.

YORK
Dispatch; this knave's tongue begins to double.
Sound trumpets, alarum to the combatants.

Flourish. They fight and Peter strikes Horner down

HORNER Hold, Peter, hold—I confess, I confess treason.

He dies

93.1 *Flourish*] *not in* F   *Horner*] *him* F   94.1 *He dies*] Q; *not in* F

good sense not to go into a mortal combat drunk.

79 **fence** fencing skill

81–5 **Sirrah . . . well** This exchange, with its final line punning on Peter's surname, anticipates a similar exchange at *Measure* 2.1.203–10, on the name 'Pompey Bum'.

88–9 **take my death** take my oath on pain of death

90 **have at thee** let me get at you (a standard phrase for launching a fight)

91 **downright** forthright, forcible (literally, 'perpendicular', downwards). Q's version of the speech continues 'as Bevis of Southampton fell upon Askapart' (879); and since 'Bevis' at F TLN 2319 / 4.2.0.1 (see the note) is assumed by most commentators to be an actor's name, an actor called Bevis has been constructed for whose existence there is no shred of corroborating evidence, and this phrase is said to be his self-advertising 'gag'. In

fact, the reference is to a well-known Middle English romance, *Sir Bevis of Hampton*, featuring a folklore hero who killed the giant Ascopard; and since Shakespeare echoes *Bevis* at *History of Lear* (see Stanley Wells's note to Sc. 11.124–5 in his edition of *King Lear* in this series), he may well have written the Quarto's line; if he did, he cut it in the process of revision suggested in the Textual Introduction.

92 **Dispatch** get on with it
double be slurred with drink, but with the overtone, conscious or otherwise, of speaking deceitfully (*OED v.* 11): Horner is defending a false case in denying that he said York was heir to the crown; his deceit mirrors York's.

93 **Sound . . . combatants** Give the signal, trumpeters, for the combat to begin. As this line is not in Q, Oxford treats it as a stage direction.

YORK (*to an attendant, pointing to Horner*) Take away his 95
weapon. (*To Peter*) Fellow, thank God and the good wine
in thy master's wame.

PETER O God, have I overcome mine enemy in this presence?
O Peter, thou hast prevailed in right.

KING HENRY (*to attendants, pointing to Horner*)
Go, take hence that traitor from our sight, 100
For by his death we do perceive his guilt.
And God in justice hath revealed to us
The truth and innocence of this poor fellow,
Which he had thought to have murdered wrongfully.
(*To Peter*) Come fellow, follow us for thy reward. 105
        Sound a flourish. Exeunt, some carrying Horner's body

2.4 *Enter Duke Humphrey of Gloucester and his men in mourning cloaks*

DUKE HUMPHREY
Thus sometimes hath the brightest day a cloud;
And after summer evermore succeeds
Barren winter, with his wrathful nipping cold;

95, 100 *pointing to Horner*] not in F   97 wame] OXFORD; way F   98 enemy] F2; Enemies F1
105.1 *Exeunt . . . body*] Exeunt. F

---

97 **wame** belly. This is Oxford's emendation of F's 'way'. 'OED records *wame* to have been a current northern term for *belly* in the sixteenth century, one which by the seventeenth century had been adopted in southern use as a jocular substitute for *belly*' (*Textual Companion*, p. 185). York's joke—that Peter won because Horner was drunk, not necessarily because he was a traitor—has its darker side: if Horner is a traitor, so is York.
100 **hence** away from here
104 **Which** whom
2.4.0.2 *mourning cloaks* Long black cloaks with hoods, worn at funerals.
1–4 **Thus . . . fleet** Shakespeare frequently compares human joys and sorrows to the changing weather and to the changing seasons. See the following notes.
 1 **Thus . . . cloud** 'No day so clear but has dark clouds' is proverbial (Dent D92),

but the expression is a Shakespearian favourite: compare the probably contemporaneous *Two Gentlemen* 1.3.84–7: 'O, how this spring of love resembleth | The uncertain glory of an April day, | Which now shows all the beauty of the sun, | And by and by a cloud takes all away'; and Sonnets 33 and 34, where Shakespeare expresses the changing relationship between his lover and himself in terms of a 'glorious morning' being overcast with clouds.
2–3 **after . . . cold** Compare Sonnet 5, 5–6: 'never-resting time leads summer on | To hideous winter, and confounds him there', and Sonnet 13, 11–12: 'the stormy gusts of winter's day, | And barren rage of death's eternal cold'.
 2 **succeeds** follows
 3 **nipping** biting (as at *Hamlet* 1.4.2: 'It is a nipping and an eager air')

So cares and joys abound as seasons fleet.
Sirs, what's a clock?   5
SERVANT Ten, my lord.

DUKE HUMPHREY

Ten is the hour that was appointed me
To watch the coming of my punished Duchess;
Uneath may she endure the flinty streets,
To tread them with her tender-feeling feet.   10
Sweet Nell, ill can thy noble mind abrook
The abject people gazing on thy face
With envious looks, laughing at thy shame,
That erst did follow thy proud chariot wheels
When thou didst ride in triumph through the streets.   15
But soft, I think she comes, and I'll prepare
My tear-stained eyes to see her miseries.

> *Enter the Duchess, Dame Eleanor Cobham, barefoot,*
> *with a white sheet about her, written verses pinned on*
> *her back, and a wax taper burning in her hand, with the*
> *Sheriff of London, and Sir John Stanley, and officers*
> *with bills and halberds*

2.4.17.1–5 *Enter . . . halberds*] Q (subs.) ; *Enter the Duchesse in a white Sheet, and a Taper burn-ing in her hand, with the Sherife and Officers.* F

4 **cares . . . fleet** Compare Sonnet 19's address to time: 'Make glad and sorry seasons as thou fleet'st' (l. 5).
  fleet rapidly pass by
9 **Uneath** scarcely, hardly. It was in very common use from *c.*1300 to *c.*1600: *OED adv.* 1 gives numerous examples; but it does not occur elsewhere in Shakespeare.
11 **abrook** brook, endure. The Old English prefix 'a-' originally added intensity to verbs (*OED, a-, prefix.* 1), and is probably used here for emphasis, perhaps coined for the purpose, since this is *OED*'s only example of *abrook*.
12 **abject** low, common (*OED ppl. a.* 2)
13, 36 **envious** spiteful, malicious. The use of *envy, envious,* and *envies* in this play is usually stronger than in modern usage ('feel jealous of'), implying 'active evil, harm, mischief' (*OED, envy, sb.* 2).
14–15 **follow . . . streets** These lines echo two passages in Marlowe's *Tamburlaine*: the repeated 'And ride in triumph through Persepolis' (Part 1, 2.5.49–54), and 'as thou ridest in triumph through the streets, | The pavement underneath thy

chariot wheels | With Turkey carpets shall be coverèd' (Part 2, 1.2.41–3).
16 **soft** stay, wait a moment
17.1–3 **Enter . . . hand** Standing *barefoot* and wearing a *white sheet* was a form of public penance in Shakespeare's day as well as Henry VI's. The *written verses* presumably specified her crimes. F's *taper* and Q's 'wax candle' are the same thing; in fact the King calls it a 'wax taper' when pronouncing sentence at Q l. 811 (the equivalent of 2.3.11).
17.4 **Sheriff** Q has two sheriffs; Oxford points out that two 'appear to have been the rule' (*Textual Companion*, p. 185) and introduce a second sheriff into their text; but if the textual hypothesis of this edition is correct (see Textual Introduction, p. 88), Shakespeare may have deleted a superfluous character when revising the manuscript used for F.
17.5 **bills** long-handled weapons with a hook-shaped blade
  halberds six-foot long weapons with an axe-shaped blade and a spike at the top

SERVANT (*to Duke Humphrey*)
  So please your grace, we'll take her from the sheriff.
DUKE HUMPHREY
  No, stir not for your lives, let her pass by.
DUCHESS ELEANOR
  Come you, my lord, to see my open shame?   20
  Now thou dost penance too. Look how they gaze,
  See how the giddy multitude do point
  And nod their heads, and throw their eyes on thee.
  Ah Gloucester, hide thee from their hateful looks,
  And in thy closet pent up, rue my shame,   25
  And ban thine enemies, both mine and thine.
DUKE HUMPHREY
  Be patient, gentle Nell, forget this grief.
DUCHESS ELEANOR
  Ah Gloucester, teach me to forget myself;
  For whilst I think I am thy married wife,
  And thou a prince, Protector of this land,   30
  Methinks I should not thus be led along,
  Mailed up in shame, with papers on my back,
  And followed with a rabble that rejoice
  To see my tears and hear my deep-fet groans.
  The ruthless flint doth cut my tender feet,   35
  And when I start, the envious people laugh,
  And bid me be advisèd how I tread.

---

19 **for your lives** i.e. on pain of death
20 **open shame** public humiliation
21 **how they gaze** Unless the *giddy multitude* of the next line enters with the Duchess, which neither Q nor F direct, *they* may be imagined as amongst the audience.
22 **giddy** inconstant, frivolous
23 **nod their heads** (perhaps knowingly, as if anticipating that Eleanor's disgrace will lead to Humphrey's fall)
  throw their eyes on stare at. For the idiom, compare *Cymbeline* 5.6.395–6, where Innogen 'throws her eye | On', gazes steadily at, her husband.
24 **hateful** filled with hate, malignant (*OED a.* 1). This conflicts with the attitude of the commons to Humphrey elsewhere (1.1.157–61, 1.3.4–5, 3.1.240, 3.2.250, 4.1.76, etc.), so Eleanor may be reading

their animosity to her into their reactions to her husband.
25 **closet** private room
  pent up confined
  rue grieve for
26 **ban** curse (*OED v.* 2a)
32 **Mailed** wrapped (a term from falconry, which means to cover a hawk with linen cloth, either to help tame it, or keep it quiet during an operation: *OED v.*³ 2)
  papers (detailing her offences)
33 **with** by
34 **my deep-fet** fetched from deep within my being. *OED, fet, v. obs.* says that after the Old English period, the verb *fet* was chiefly used, as here, as a past participle: compare 'far-fet' at 3.1.293.
36 **start** flinch
37 **be advisèd** consider, be careful

Ah Humphrey, can I bear this shameful yoke?
Trow'st thou that e'er I'll look upon the world,
Or count them happy that enjoys the sun?   40
No, dark shall be my light, and night my day;
To think upon my pomp shall be my hell.
Sometime I'll say I am Duke Humphrey's wife,
And he a prince and ruler of the land;
Yet so he ruled, and such a prince he was,   45
As he stood by whilst I, his forlorn Duchess,
Was made a wonder and a pointing stock
To every idle rascal follower.
But be thou mild and blush not at my shame,
Nor stir at nothing till the axe of death   50
Hang over thee, as sure it shortly will.
For Suffolk, he that can do all in all
With her that hateth thee and hates us all,
And York, and impious Beaufort that false priest,
Have all limed bushes to betray thy wings,   55
And fly thou how thou canst, they'll tangle thee.
But fear not thou until thy foot be snared,
Nor never seek prevention of thy foes.

DUKE HUMPHREY
Ah Nell, forbear; thou aimest all awry.
I must offend before I be attainted,   60
And had I twenty times so many foes,
And each of them had twenty times their power,
All these could not procure me any scathe

39 **Trow'st thou** do you believe
43 **Sometime** from time to time
46 **As that** (Abbott 109)
  forlorn abandoned
47 **wonder** spectacle, something to be gawped at. See the first note to l. 70.
  pointing stock something to be pointed at in mockery
48 **rascal** good-for-nothing
  follower pursuer (in order to mock her)
50 **Nor . . . nothing** (an Elizabethan double negative, used for emphasis: Abbott 406)
52 **all in all** everything
53 **her** i.e. Margaret
55 **limed . . . wings** This repeats the image of trapping birds with birdlime from 1.3.89 (see note): it is developed in *tangle* and *snared* in the following lines.

56 **fly . . . canst** no matter how you try to escape
58 **seek prevention of** try to forestall
59 **forbear** stop
  aimest . . . awry your speculations are wide of the mark
60–4 **I must . . . crimeless** Because he himself is just and has faith in the due process of the law, Humphrey seriously underestimates the power of those who do not. Despite his long reign as Protector, he has remained a political innocent, as his wife realizes. In this respect, as in others, he has something in common with his nephew the King.
60 **attainted** condemned for treason
63 **scathe** harm

So long as I am loyal, true, and crimeless.
Wouldst have me rescue thee from this reproach?   65
Why, yet thy scandal were not wiped away,
But I in danger for the breach of law.
Thy greatest help is quiet, gentle Nell.
I pray thee sort thy heart to patience.
These few days' wonder will be quickly worn.   70
            Enter a Herald
HERALD I summon your grace to his majesty's parliament,
    holden at Bury the first of this next month.
DUKE HUMPHREY
    And my consent ne'er asked herein before?
    This is close dealing. Well, I will be there.   *Exit Herald*
    My Nell, I take my leave; and, Master Sheriff,   75
    Let not her penance exceed the King's commission.
SHERIFF
    An't please your grace, here my commission stays,
    And Sir John Stanley is appointed now
    To take her with him to the Isle of Man.
DUKE HUMPHREY
    Must you, Sir John, protect my lady here?   80
STANLEY
    So am I given in charge, may't please your grace.

---

74 *Exit Herald*] *not in* F

66 **were not** would not be
68 **Thy . . . quiet** Humphrey's advice to his
    wife may have been suggested by Hall's
    phrase about Humphrey's own reaction
    to his wife's sentence: he 'took all these
    things patiently, and said little': see
    Appendix B, 2.3.9–16.
69 **sort** adapt
70 **few days' wonder** a spectacle that will
    only last for a short time (alluding to the
    proverb 'A wonder lasts but nine days':
    Dent W728)
    worn worn out, and so forgotten
72 **holden** to be held. 'In the sixteenth cen-
    tury, *holden* began to be displaced by *held*
    . . . but preserved . . . in legal and formal
    language' (*OED*, hold, *v.*), which is per-
    haps why it is chosen for the Herald's

speech of summons; it does not occur
elsewhere in Shakespeare.
Bury Bury St Edmunds, in Suffolk
73 **my . . . before** my agreement about it not
    asked in advance
74 **close dealing** secret plotting. Even
    Humphrey (see the note to ll. 60–4)
    recognizes the political manoeuvre here.
    He is right: historically, the Parliament
    was called at Bury specifically to trap him,
    away from his supporters in London:
    he was arrested on the second day, and
    murdered that night, as dramatized in
    the next two scenes.
76 **commission** warrant
77 **stays** ends
80 **protect** act as custodian of
81 **given in charge** ordered

DUKE HUMPHREY

Entreat her not the worse in that I pray
You use her well. The world may laugh again,
And I may live to do you kindness if
You do it her. And so, Sir John, farewell.   85
  ⌈*Duke Humphrey begins to leave*⌉

DUCHESS ELEANOR

What, gone, my lord, and bid me not farewell?

DUKE HUMPHREY

Witness my tears, I cannot stay to speak.
                        Exeunt Duke Humphrey and his men

DUCHESS ELEANOR

Art thou gone too? All comfort go with thee,
For none abides with me. My joy is death;
Death, at whose name I oft have been afeard,   90
Because I wished this world eternity.
Stanley, I prithee go and take me hence.
I care not whither, for I beg no favour,
Only convey me where thou art commanded.

STANLEY

Why madam, that is to the Isle of Man,   95
There to be used according to your state.

DUCHESS ELEANOR

That's bad enough, for I am but reproach;
And shall I then be used reproachfully?

85.1 *Duke . . . leave*] *not in* F   87.1 *Exeunt . . . men*] *Exit Gloster.* F   91 world] *This edition*;
Worlds F

82 **Entreat** treat
   in that because
83 **The . . . again** i.e. I may once more be in a
   position of influence
88 **gone too** *Too* is odd, since there is no one
   else who has left in the scene. One might
   suspect that F's spelling 'to' represents a
   misreading of 'so' (compare Juliet's 'Art
   thou gone so' (*Romeo* 3.5.43), in another
   scene of abrupt parting), did not Q support *too*. Hattaway's gloss 'alas' does not
   find support in *OED*, as he claims, for *too*
   used absolutely. Perhaps Eleanor simply
   feels alone, with no one she knows to turn
   to.

91 **this world eternity** This world to be
   eternity, to enjoy eternity in this world.
   Editors offer this gloss, or a similar one,
   of F's phrase 'this Worlds eternitie',
   modernizing 'Worlds' as 'world's', but
   'world's' does not make very good sense,
   and I suspect that this is an example of an
   intrusive 's', common in F printing (see
   the note to 3.1.78).
93 **whither** where
96 **state** rank (which Eleanor punningly
   turns to mean 'condition' in the next
   line)
97 **but reproach** in complete disgrace

STANLEY

Like to a duchess and Duke Humphrey's lady,
According to that state you shall be used.   100

DUCHESS ELEANOR

Sheriff farewell, and better than I fare,
Although thou hast been conduct of my shame.

SHERIFF

It is my office, and madam, pardon me.

DUCHESS ELEANOR

Ay ay, farewell, thy office is discharged.   ⌈*Exit Sheriff*⌉
Come Stanley, shall we go?   105

STANLEY

Madam, your penance done, throw off this sheet,
And go we to attire you for our journey.

DUCHESS ELEANOR

My shame will not be shifted with my sheet;
No, it will hang upon my richest robes
And show itself, attire me how I can.   110
Go lead the way, I long to see my prison.   *Exeunt*

3.1   *Sound a sennet. Enter to the parliament: two heralds
        before, then the Dukes of Buckingham and Suffolk, and
        then the Duke of York and Cardinal Beaufort, and then
        King Henry and Queen Margaret, and then the Earls of
        Salisbury and Warwick, ⌈with attendants⌉*

KING HENRY

I muse my lord of Gloucester is not come.

---

104 *Exit Sheriff*] not in F
   3.1.0.1 *Sound a sennet*] F   0.1–5 *Enter . . . attendants*] Q (subs.) ; *Enter King, Queene, Cardinall, Suffolke, Yorke, Buckingham, Salisbury, and Warwicke, to the Parliament.* F

101 **better than I fare** may you prosper
    better than I
102 **conduct** conductor, guide
103 **pardon me** (as the executioner asks for-
    giveness of his victim)
104 **is discharged** has been carried out
108 **shifted** removed (with a pun on 'shift',
    undergarment)
110 **attire . . . can** no matter what I wear
3.1.0.1–5 *Enter to . . . Warwick* The details
    of this ceremonial assembly of the

Parliament (held, historically, at Bury
St Edmunds in 1447, to trap Duke
Humphrey: see Appendix B, 3.1.97–138)
are from Q, and probably reflect stage
practice. Neither F or Q specify *attendants*,
but for such a grand entry they were
almost certainly included, and besides
they are needed at l. 188; but see the first
note to that line.
1 **muse** am surprised that

'Tis not his wont to be the hindmost man,
Whate'er occasion keeps him from us now.

QUEEN MARGARET

Can you not see, or will ye not observe,
The strangeness of his altered countenance?   5
With what a majesty he bears himself,
How insolent of late he is become,
How proud, how peremptory, and unlike himself?
We know the time since he was mild and affable,
And if we did but glance a far-off look,   10
Immediately he was upon his knee,
That all the court admired him for submission.
But meet him now, and be it in the morn
When everyone will give the time of day,
He knits his brow, and shows an angry eye,   15
And passeth by with stiff unbowèd knee,
Disdaining duty that to us belongs.
Small curs are not regarded when they grin,
But great men tremble when the lion roars,
And Humphrey is no little man in England.   20

2 **wont** habit
  hindmost last to arrive
3 **Whate'er** whatever
  occasion cause, reason (as frequently in
  Shakespeare)
4 **see . . . observe** These appear to be mere
  synonyms; but Margaret may be drawing
  a distinction between what Henry physically *sees* and what he chooses to notice
  (*observe*), implying that he is wilfully
  ignoring what is obvious to everyone else,
  a distinction about seeing similar to the
  one Falstaff makes about hearing at *2
  Henry IV* 1.2.122–4, when he differentiates between not hearing and not
  listening.
5 **strangeness** remoteness, aloofness. For
  the implication of *strange* here, compare *1
  Henry IV* 1.3.284: 'make us strangers to
  his looks of love.'
6 **With . . . himself** An echo of Marlowe's
  Tamburlaine, Part 1, 1.2.164: 'With what a
  majesty he rears his looks!', though the
  use to which it is put is interestingly different. In Marlowe, it is an uncomplicated
  expression of admiration, here subtly
  twisted to reflect Margaret's criticism of
  Humphrey.

7–8 **insolent . . . peremptory** Margaret uses
  against Humphrey terms that he himself
  had applied to his opponents at 2.1.23,
  31.
9 **We . . . since** we remember when
10–12 **And . . . submission** Margaret must be
  making this up, as part of her fabricated
  case against Duke Humphrey, since it is
  impossible to imagine the Humphrey we
  see in the play ever behaving in so servile
  a manner.
10 **far-off** from a distance (perhaps with the
  implication 'remote, critical')
12 **admired** was amazed by (the most
  frequent use in Shakespeare, though
  the modern sense, also present in
  Shakespeare, would make as good,
  perhaps better, sense)
14 **give . . . day** greet, say 'good morning'.
  This antedates *OED*'s three earliest examples (*time, sb.* 28b), all from Shakespeare.
17 **Disdaining duty** refusing to show respect
  to us belongs is our due
18 **Small curs** little dogs
  grin bare their teeth
20 **And . . . England** A nice piece of under-
  statement on Margaret's part.

First note that he is near you in descent,
And should you fall, he is the next will mount.
Meseemeth then it is no policy,
Respecting what a rancorous mind he bears
And his advantage following your decease,   25
That he should come about your royal person,
Or be admitted to your highness' Council.
By flattery hath he won the commons' hearts,
And when he please to make commotion,
'Tis to be feared they all will follow him.   30
Now 'tis the spring, and weeds are shallow-rooted;
Suffer them now, and they'll o'ergrow the garden,
And choke the herbs for want of husbandry.
The reverent care I bear unto my lord
Made me collect these dangers in the Duke.   35
If it be fond, call it a woman's fear;
Which fear if better reasons can supplant,
I will subscribe and say I wronged the Duke.
My lord of Suffolk, Buckingham, and York,
Reprove my allegation if you can,   40

---

22 **mount** (the throne)
23 **Meseemeth** it appears to me
   no policy not politically wise, expedient.
   Policy increasingly takes on its frequent
   critical overtone of 'political expediency'
   as the net closes around Duke Humphrey
   (3.1.235, 238, 293, 341). It is associated
   with Machiavelli's *The Prince* (first published 1532) which coolly argues that
   politicians should follow the stratagems
   that will enable them to win, regardless of
   moral considerations. The word occurs
   more frequently in this than in any other
   Shakespeare play.
24 **Respecting** considering
   rancorous spiteful
25 **advantage . . . decease** what he will gain
   at your death (i.e. the crown, to which he
   is the heir: see 1.1.150–1 and note)
26 **come about** be in contact with
28 **By . . . hearts** Humphrey is popular with
   the common people (compare 1.1.157–61
   and 1.3.4–5); Margaret characteristically
   attributes this popularity to *flattery*.
29 **make commotion** raise a rebellion (four
   syllables: this 'spreading' of the word at
   the end of the line emphasizes it)
31–3 **weeds . . . husbandry** For the com-

parison of a misgoverned state to an
overgrown garden, compare *Richard II*
3.4.30–67.
31 **shallow-rooted** (and so easier to pull out)
32 **Suffer** tolerate, allow to flourish
33 **husbandry** care, good gardening
34 **reverent** devoted, respectful. The phrase
   reverent care also occurs at *Shrew* 4.1.190
   ('all is done in reverent care of her').
35 **collect** gather (information about)
   (Onions)
36 **fond** foolish
37 **supplant** uproot (continuing the gardening expressions from ll. 31–3)
38 **subscribe** 'agree, from the sense of
   signing at the foot of an agreement'
   (Cairncross), but with the implication
   'admit error', as at *I Henry VI* 2.4.44: 'I
   subscribe in silence.'
39 **and York** Peggy Ashcroft at Stratford-
   upon-Avon in 1963–4 paused slightly
   before this phrase, subtly seeking the
   approval of someone who was not an ally,
   and demonstrating that lists of names
   in Shakespeare can yield more dramatic
   point than might at first appear.
40 **Reprove** disprove, refute

Or else conclude my words effectual.

SUFFOLK

Well hath your highness seen into this Duke,
And had I first been put to speak my mind,
I think I should have told your grace's tale.
The Duchess by his subornation,   45
Upon my life, began her devilish practices;
Or if he were not privy to those faults,
Yet by reputing of his high descent,
As next the King he was successive heir,
And such high vaunts of his nobility,   50
Did instigate the bedlam brainsick Duchess
By wicked means to frame our sovereign's fall.
Smooth runs the water where the brook is deep,
And in his simple show he harbours treason.
The fox barks not when he would steal the lamb.   55
(*To King Henry*)
No, no, my sovereign, Gloucester is a man
Unsounded yet, and full of deep deceit.

CARDINAL BEAUFORT (*to King Henry*)

Did he not, contrary to form of law,
Devise strange deaths for small offences done?

YORK (*to King Henry*)

And did he not, in his Protectorship,   60

---

41 **effectual** to the point
42–65 Once again, Margaret acts as a catalyst for an outbreak of violence (see note
to 1.3.138); led by her, the rest of the pack
turn on Duke Humphrey, first in his
absence, and then to his face (ll. 95–
138). The exceptions are Salisbury and
Warwick: although both F and Q include
them in the opening stage direction, they
have nothing to say; perhaps they provide
a mute perspective on the behaviour of
the others, presumably a disapproving
one in Salisbury's case in view of
1.1.182–3.
45 **subornation** instigation (*OED* 1), from the
more specific sense of procuring (suborn-
ing) a witness to commit perjury (*OED* 2),
in which sense Humphrey uses it at l. 145.
46 **practices** plots
47 **privy to** familiar with
   faults crimes

48 **reputing of** priding himself upon
49 **next . . . heir** he was next in line of succession to the throne
50 **vaunts** boasts
51 **bedlam** lunatic (a shortened form of the
'Bethlehem' Hospital for the insane in
London; the hospital itself is mentioned
at 5.1.131)
52 **frame** contrive
53 **Smooth . . . deep** Proverbial: 'Water runs
smoothest where it is deepest' (Dent
W123).
54 **simple show** honest appearance
55 **The fox . . . lamb** This sounds proverbial,
but is not recorded.
57 **Unsounded** unfathomed (picking up
the metaphor from l. 53), i.e. 'we do
not yet know the depth of his deceit'
(Montgomery)
59, 122 **strange** unusual, exceptionally cruel
60–3 **And did . . . revolted** This accusation

Levy great sums of money through the realm
For soldiers' pay in France, and never sent it,
By means whereof the towns each day revolted?
BUCKINGHAM (*to King Henry*)
Tut, these are petty faults to faults unknown,
Which time will bring to light in smooth Duke
    Humphrey.   65
KING HENRY
My lords at once: the care you have of us
To mow down thorns that would annoy our foot
Is worthy praise; but shall I speak my conscience,
Our kinsman Gloucester is as innocent
From meaning treason to our royal person   70
As is the sucking lamb or harmless dove.
The Duke is virtuous, mild, and too well given
To dream on evil or to work my downfall.
QUEEN MARGARET
Ah, what's more dangerous than this fond affiance?
Seems he a dove? His feathers are but borrowed,   75
For he's disposèd as the hateful raven.
Is he a lamb? His skin is surely lent him,
For he's inclined as is the ravenous wolf.

78 wolf] ROWE; Wolues F

may have been suggested by a phrase
from Hall's account of Somerset's surrender of France, about the rumour that 'the
Duke of Somerset, for his own peculiar
profit, kept not half his number of soldiers, and put their wages in his purse' (p.
216), especially since Somerset is about to
enter with the news of the loss of France
(ll. 82–5).

64 **petty** trivial
   to compared to
65 **smooth** plausible
66 **at once** to answer you all together. The
   other possible glosses, 'once and for all' or
   'without further discussion', seem less
   appropriate to the King's unassertive
   character.
67 **mow . . . foot** The King picks up
   Margaret's gardening metaphors from
   ll. 31–3.
   annoy wound

68 **shall . . . conscience** if I am to speak
   according to my conscience
71 **sucking lamb, harmless dove** Traditional
   images of innocence, derived from the
   Bible: 'Samuel took a sucking lamb, and
   offered it' (1 Samuel 7: 9); 'harmless as
   the doves' (Matthew 10: 16, Bishops'
   Bible).
72 **given** disposed
74 **fond affiance** Editors concur that this
   means 'foolish confidence' (*OED, affiance,*
   2); but I think that another obsolete sense
   given at *OED* 4—'intimate relationship,
   affinity'—is closer and that the Queen is
   accusing Henry of partiality towards
   Humphrey to the point of foolishness.
76 **disposèd** has the disposition of
78 **wolf** F's 'wolves' is probably an example of
   the common printing error of substitut-
   ing a plural for a singular; but since ll.
   77–8 echo Christ's Sermon on the Mount,
   'Beware of false prophets, which come to

Who cannot steal a shape that means deceit?
Take heed, my lord, the welfare of us all   80
Hangs on the cutting short that fraudful man.
   Enter the Duke of Somerset

SOMERSET

All health unto my gracious sovereign.

KING HENRY

Welcome Lord Somerset. What news from France?

SOMERSET

That all your interest in those territories
Is utterly bereft you: all is lost.   85

KING HENRY

Cold news, Lord Somerset; but God's will be done.

YORK (*aside*)

Cold news for me, for I had hope of France,
As firmly as I hope for fertile England.
Thus are my blossoms blasted in the bud,
And caterpillars eat my leaves away.   90
But I will remedy this gear ere long,
Or sell my title for a glorious grave.
   Enter Duke Humphrey of Gloucester

DUKE HUMPHREY

All happiness unto my lord the King.
Pardon, my liege, that I have stayed so long.

SUFFOLK

Nay Gloucester, know that thou art come too soon   95
Unless thou wert more loyal than thou art.
I do arrest thee of high treason here.

---

you in sheep's clothing, but inwardly they
are ravening wolves' (Matthew 7: 15),
'wolves' may be correct.

79 **Who . . . deceit** what man who wishes to
deceive cannot assume a false role
81 **cutting short** Perhaps specifically
'beheading', as at *Richard II* 3.3.13–14:
'to shorten you . . . your whole head's
length', and in the proverb 'shorten by
the head' (Dent SS10).
   fraudful treacherous (compare *full of deep
deceit* at l. 57)
86 **God's will be done** Henry characteristi-

cally echoes the Lord's Prayer, 'Thy will
be done'.
89 **Thus . . . bud** Proverbial: 'To nip in the
bud' (Dent B702).
90 **caterpillars . . . away** Compare *Venus*
797–8, where lust is said to destroy beauty
'As caterpillars do the tender leaves'.
91 **gear** business
92 **sell . . . grave** York repeats the idea at *3
Henry VI* 1.4.17, when he reports that his
son Richard urged him: 'A crown or else a
glorious tomb!'
94 **liege** lord
   stayed stayed away, delayed

DUKE HUMPHREY

Well, Suffolk's Duke, thou shalt not see me blush,
Nor change my countenance for this arrest.
A heart unspotted is not easily daunted.   100
The purest spring is not so free from mud
As I am clear from treason to my sovereign.
Who can accuse me? Wherein am I guilty?

YORK

'Tis thought, my lord, that you took bribes of France,
And being Protector, stayed the soldiers' pay,   105
By means whereof his highness hath lost France.

DUKE HUMPHREY

Is it but thought so? What are they that think it?
I never robbed the soldiers of their pay,
Nor ever had one penny bribe from France.
So help me God, as I have watched the night,   110
Ay, night by night, in studying good for England,
That doit that e'er I wrested from the King,
Or any groat I hoarded to my use,
Be brought against me at my trial day.
No: many a pound of mine own proper store,   115

---

98 Suffolk's Duke] Q; *Suffolke* F   114 my trial] F; the iudgement Q

---

98 **Suffolk's Duke** Q's phrase is likelier to be correct than F's 'Suffolk', in view of the repeated mockery of Suffolk's elevation to a dukedom (1.1.108, 123; 1.2.30, 95); it also makes the verse line regular. But F's irregularity can be turned to dramatic advantage, as by Paul Hardwick at Stratford-upon-Avon in 1964, who followed his aggressive delivery of 'Suffolk' with an emphatic pause, equivalent to one beat of the five-stress line.

99 **change my countenance** distort my features as a result of emotion (*OED sb.* 4b)—i.e. show any embarrassment. The phrase is interesting as a statement of Humphrey's innocence, since he elsewhere shows emotion so passionately and easily (1.1.52–5, 1.3.138.1, 153): he is unfazed by his arrest.
for as a result of

100 **A heart unspotted** a pure heart, an image of innocence. It is ironic under the

circumstances that Margaret herself uses the same phrase when she sends 'a pure unspotted heart' to Henry as a token of her love at *I Henry VI* 5.5.138–9.

104 **of** from (as frequently in Shakespeare: Abbott 166)

105 **stayed** withheld

107 **Is . . . think it** Humphrey's vigorous response swiftly exposes the feebleness ('*Tis thought*) of the trumped-up charge.
What who

110 **watched** remained awake throughout

112–13 **That doit . . . groat** even coins of such little value

114 **my trial day** The phrase is misleading, since the context of arrest might suggest that he means the day on which he is put on trial; but it refers to the Day of Judgement, as Q's reading confirms (see collation).

115 **proper** personal
store fortune

Because I would not tax the needy commons,
Have I dispursèd to the garrisons,
And never asked for restitution.

CARDINAL BEAUFORT
It serves you well, my lord, to say so much.

DUKE HUMPHREY
I say no more than truth, so help me God.   120

YORK
In your Protectorship you did devise
Strange tortures for offenders, never heard of,
That England was defamed by tyranny.

DUKE HUMPHREY
Why, 'tis well known that whiles I was Protector
Pity was all the fault that was in me,   125
For I should melt at an offender's tears,
And lowly words were ransom for their fault.
Unless it were a bloody murderer,
Or foul felonious thief that fleeced poor passengers,
I never gave them condign punishment.   130
Murder indeed, that bloody sin, I tortured
Above the felon or what trespass else.

SUFFOLK
My lord, these faults are easy, quickly answerèd,
But mightier crimes are laid unto your charge
Whereof you cannot easily purge yourself.   135
I do arrest you in his highness' name,
And here commit you to my good lord Cardinal
To keep until your further time of trial.

137 my good] Q; my F

117 **dispursèd** paid out
118 **restitution** reimbursement
123 **defamed by** infamous for
124 **whiles** An older form of 'while' (Abbott 137).
126 **should** would
127 **lowly ... fault** (i.e. he would be moved to pardon those who spoke humbly, repented their faults)
129 **felonious** wicked
      fleeced plundered

passengers wayfarers
130 **condign** deserved
132 **Above ... else** Sanders glosses: 'more than the man convicted of a felony or any other kind of crime'; but in view of the balance between *felon* and *trespass* in the line, *felon* is as likely to mean 'felony', in the obsolete sense recorded at *OED sb.*[1] 4.
133 **easy** slight, insignificant
138 **keep** (under arrest)

KING HENRY

My lord of Gloucester, 'tis my special hope
That you will clear yourself from all suspect.   140
My conscience tells me you are innocent.

DUKE HUMPHREY

Ah gracious lord, these days are dangerous.
Virtue is choked with foul ambition,
And charity chased hence by rancour's hand.
Foul subornation is predominant,   145
And equity exiled your highness' land.
I know their complot is to have my life,
And if my death might make this island happy
And prove the period of their tyranny,
I would expend it with all willingness.   150
But mine is made the prologue to their play,
For thousands more that yet suspect no peril
Will not conclude their plotted tragedy.
Beaufort's red sparkling eyes blab his heart's malice,

---

140 suspect] CAPELL; suspence F

---

140 **suspect** Of F's 'suspense' McKerrow says
'This perhaps *may* mean doubt or suspicion, but examples of its use in this sense
are few'. Two, in fact, apart from this
line: *OED, suspense, sb.* 3d gives
an example from Nashe's *Unfortunate
Traveller* (1594), Cairncross another from
Gabriel Harvey's *A New Letter* (1593). This
evidence does not seem to me decisive
enough to support 'suspense', whereas
suspect as a noun meaning 'suspicion'
occurs elsewhere in the play (1.3.137,
3.2.139), is stressed on the second syllable, as here, and above all makes much
clearer sense.

143 **choked . . . ambition** Ambition is also
represented as choking twice in *1 Henry
VI*: 'be choked with thy ambition' (Suffolk
to York at 2.4.112), 'Choked with ambition of the meaner sort' (York on his
uncle Mortimer, who has just died, at
2.5.123). *Choked* also of course anticipates Humphrey's own end.

145 **subornation** instigation to perjury (or
perhaps to crime in general)

predominant in the ascendant (an astro-
logical term)

146 **equity . . . land** The phrase was probably
suggested by Hall's account of the year
1453: 'justice and equity was
clearly exiled' (p. 231); it also echoes
Ovid, *Metamorphoses* 1.150, 'Astraea
[justice] abandoned the earth', quoted at
Titus 4.3.4.

equity justice

exiled exiled from (stressed on the first syllable, unlike modern prose usage)

147 **complot** conspiracy (as at *Richard III*
3.1.197: 'We may digest our complots in
some form'); stressed on the first syllable.

149 **period** end

150 **expend** spend (i.e. give up)

153 **conclude . . . tragedy** bring their conspiracy to its fatal end

154–60 **Beaufort's . . . life** Humphrey pins
down each of his enemies in a series
of brief portraits, as Margaret had done
at 1.3.69–71, though, as Emrys Jones
remarks, he spares Margaret herself 'the
humiliation of having her likeness

And Suffolk's cloudy brow his stormy hate;   155
Sharp Buckingham unburdens with his tongue
The envious load that lies upon his heart;
And doggèd York that reaches at the moon,
Whose overweening arm I have plucked back,
By false accuse doth level at my life.   160
(*To Queen Margaret*)
And you, my sovereign lady, with the rest,
Causeless have laid disgraces on my head,
And with your best endeavour have stirred up
My liefest liege to be mine enemy.
Ay, all of you have laid your heads together—   165
Myself had notice of your conventicles—
And all to make away my guiltless life.
I shall not want false witness to condemn me,
Nor store of treasons to augment my guilt.
The ancient proverb will be well effected: 170
'A staff is quickly found to beat a dog.'
CARDINAL BEAUFORT
My liege, his railing is intolerable.
If those that care to keep your royal person
From treason's secret knife and traitor's rage
Be thus upbraided, chid, and rated at,   175
And the offender granted scope of speech,
'Twill make them cool in zeal unto your grace.

caught' (*Origins*, p. 45), but not of being
sharply criticized.

155 **cloudy** clouded, frowning
157 **envious** malicious. See the note to
2.4.13, 36.
158 **doggèd** (a) determined (b) dog-like,
currish
reaches at the moon Proverbial for
extreme actions: 'He casts beyond the
moon' (Dent M1114).
159 **overweening** overreaching
160 **accuse** accusation
level aim
162 **Causeless** causelessly. Adjectives were
often used as adverbs (Abbott 1).
164 **liefest** dearest (the only example in

Shakespeare, though *alderliefest* occurs at
1.1.28)
166 **conventicles** secret meetings (*OED* 3).
The word was probably suggested by a
passage in Hall, where the Yorkists 'had
knowledge of [these] secret conventicles'
(p. 242); it does not occur elsewhere in
Shakespeare's work in this sense, since
even if he wrote *Edward III* 2.1.63, *conven-
ticle* there means 'meeting-place'.
167 **make away** put an end to
168 **want** lack
169 **store** plenty
170 **proverb** (Dent T138)
effected proved
175 **rated at** berated, scolded
176 **scope** licence

SUFFOLK

Hath he not twit our sovereign lady here
With ignominious words, though clerkly couched,
As if she had subornèd some to swear   180
False allegations to o'erthrow his state?

QUEEN MARGARET

But I can give the loser leave to chide.

DUKE HUMPHREY

Far truer spoke than meant. I lose indeed;
Beshrew the winners, for they played me false.
And well such losers may have leave to speak.   185

BUCKINGHAM

He'll wrest the sense, and hold us here all day.
Lord Cardinal, he is your prisoner.

CARDINAL BEAUFORT (*to some of his attendants*)

Sirs, take away the Duke and guard him sure.

DUKE HUMPHREY

Ah, thus King Henry throws away his crutch
Before his legs be firm to bear his body.   190
Thus is the shepherd beaten from thy side,
And wolves are gnarling who shall gnaw thee first.

178 **twit** twitted, taunted. The final 'ed' was
often omitted after 't' or 'd' in Elizabethan
usage.
179 **ignominious** shameful (a stronger term
then than now)
clerkly couched skilfully phrased (as if by
a *clerk* or scholar)
180 **subornèd** instigated. The idea runs
through the scene: compare ll. 45 and
145.
181 **state** high position
182 **But . . . chide** Proverbial: 'Give losers
leave to speak' (Dent L458).
183 **spoke** Elizabethan English often used
spoke where we would use 'spoken'
(Abbott 343). Compare ll. 266, 268, 280.
184 **Beshrew** curse
played me false betrayed me
185 **well . . . speak** Humphrey develops the
proverb cited by Margaret at l. 182, as
Titus Andronicus does at *Titus* 3.1.231–2,
a scene in which Titus' enemies pile a
series of blows upon him as Humphrey's
enemies pile a series of accusations upon

him: 'losers will have leave | To ease their
stomachs with their bitter tongues.'
186 **wrest** distort, quibble on
188 **Sirs . . . sure** The Quarto has a different
version of this moment: the Cardinal calls
offstage for his attendants, who have not,
apparently, entered at the start of the
scene (see the note to the opening stage
direction).
sure securely
191–2 **Thus . . . first** These lines echo at least
two biblical passages: 'I will smite the
shepherd, and the sheep of the flock shall
be scattered' (Matthew 26: 31); and 'the
good shepherd giveth his life for his sheep.
But an hireling . . . seeth the wolf coming, and he leaveth the sheep, and fleeth,
and the wolf catcheth them' (John 10:
1–16). York has already likened
Humphrey to the good shepherd at
2.2.73–4.
192 **gnarling** Were it not for the alliteration
with *gnaw*, it would be tempting to emend
to 'snarling', which is what it means, or

Ah that my fear were false, ah that it were!
For good King Henry, thy decay I fear.

Exit Duke Humphrey, guarded by the Cardinal's men

KING HENRY

My lords, what to your wisdoms seemeth best   195
Do or undo, as if ourself were here.

QUEEN MARGARET

What, will your highness leave the Parliament?

KING HENRY

Ay Margaret, my heart is drowned with grief,
Whose flood begins to flow within mine eyes,
My body round engirt with misery,   200
For what's more miserable than discontent?
Ah uncle Humphrey, in thy face I see
The map of honour, truth, and loyalty;
And yet, good Humphrey, is the hour to come
That e'er I proved thee false, or feared thy faith. 205
What louring star now envies thy estate,
That these great lords and Margaret our Queen
Do seek subversion of thy harmless life?
Thou never didst them wrong, nor no man wrong.
And as the butcher takes away the calf,   210
And binds the wretch, and beats it when it strains,

194.1 *Exit . . . men*] *Exit Gloster.* F   211 strains] CAIRNCROSS (*conj.* Vaughan); strayes F; strives THEOBALD

to Q's 'snarring', which means the same and which seems to be the commoner word, to judge from the relative number of examples in *OED*.

194 **decay** ruin

194.1 Perhaps responding to Hall's information that Humphrey was arrested by the 'High Constable of England, accompanied by the Duke of Buckingham and other' (see Appendix B, 3.1.97–138); the BBC television production has Buckingham escort Humphrey off here. This neatly turns to dramatic use the fact that Buckingham has nothing to do in the rest of the scene, at least in F; but see the note to 222.1.

198–222 **Ay Margaret . . . none** This is the King's longest and most eloquent speech so far, and it unmistakably expresses where his most intense commitment lies,

after his devotion to God: not to his wife, but to his uncle. For further discussion, see the Introduction, p. 41.

200 **engirt** surrounded (as if with a girdle: *OED v. Obs.* 2, here figurative)

203 **map** image. This figurative use of *map* to reveal a person's nature also occurs at *Richard II* 5.1.12 ('map of honour') and *Titus* 3.2.12 ('map of woe').

206 **louring** ominous
envies thy estate 'shows malice towards your position' (Sanders), or perhaps more generally, 'towards you' (*OED, estate, sb.* 1a)

208 **subversion** destruction (as at *1 Henry VI* 2.3.65: 'Razeth your cities and subverts your towns')

211 **strains** This emendation of F's 'strayes' (where the manuscript probably read 'strayes') is supported by an apparently identical error by the same compositor

Bearing it to the bloody slaughterhouse,
Even so remorseless have they borne him hence;
And as the dam runs lowing up and down,
Looking the way her harmless young one went,   215
And can do naught but wail her darling's loss,
Even so myself bewails good Gloucester's case
With sad unhelpful tears, and with dimmed eyes
Look after him, and cannot do him good,
So mighty are his vowèd enemies.   220
His fortunes I will weep, and 'twixt each groan,
Say 'Who's a traitor? Gloucester, he is none'.
                            Exit ⌈with Salisbury and Warwick⌉

QUEEN MARGARET
Free lords, cold snow melts with the sun's hot beams.
Henry my lord is cold in great affairs,
Too full of foolish pity; and·Gloucester's show   225
Beguiles him as the mournful crocodile ·

222.1 *Exit . . . Warwick*] Q (*subs.*); *Exit.* F

at *Henry V* 3.1.32; and, in terms of sense,
by the (almost certainly authorial) stage
direction at *Errors* 4.4.106.2, where
servants '*offer to bind him. He strives*'
(which supports Theobald's emendation
'strives'). On the other hand, Sanders,
who retains 'strays', says that '*binds* may
mean "pens in" rather than "ties up"',
though this sense is not recorded in *OED*.
The straying calf, watched helplessly by
its mother, has arguably greater pathos
as an image of the deserted Humphrey
and the weakly helpless Henry than the
straining one.

214 **dam** mother
219 **do him good** help him
222.1 *Exit . . . Warwick* No trumpet 'flourish' accompanies the King's exit, emphasizing that it is an unscheduled departure
that disrupts the ceremony of the scene.
Q has Salisbury and Warwick leave with
him, so that they do not hear the plot
to murder Humphrey. Riverside remove
Buckingham as well here, but there is no
reason why he should not overhear the
conspiracy; if he leaves, only Somerset is
left, other than the conspirators, which is
awkward unless they are pointedly ignoring him until York's derisive reference at
l. 290. Q has a different version of the

scene from this point, which involves
Buckingham: see Appendix A, Passage D;
but the local problem reflects a general
awkwardness in the play's handling of
both Buckingham and Somerset. If any
attendants have been left on stage after
the arrest of Humphrey, they could leave
here or at l. 330; but the conspiracy suggests that what was a very public scene
now contracts to an intimate one.
223 **Free** noble (*OED a.* 3, adding that in Middle English it was a 'stock epithet' as it
may be here; but if it carries, as editors
suggest, the implication 'generous,
magnanimous' (*OED a.* 4a), it is deeply
ironic—but unconscious, of course, on
the Queen's part—in view of what these
free lords have done, and are about to do.)
cold . . . beams Proverbial: 'To melt like
snow before the sun' (Dent S593.1).
224 **cold . . . affairs** indifferent to matters of
state
225 **show** outward appearance
226, 228 **crocodile, snake** These may have
been suggested by a phrase about deception in Hall that combines them: 'This
cankered crocodile and subtle serpent'
(p. 239).
226 **mournful crocodile** The crocodile was
supposed to make sobbing noises to lure
sympathetic victims; compare 'crocodile

With sorrow snares relenting passengers,
Or as the snake rolled in a flow'ring bank
With shining chequered slough doth sting a child
That for the beauty thinks it excellent.   230
Believe me, lords, were none more wise than I—
And yet herein I judge mine own wit good—
This Gloucester should be quickly rid the world
To rid us from the fear we have of him.

CARDINAL BEAUFORT
That he should die is worthy policy;   235
But yet we want a colour for his death.
'Tis meet he be condemned by course of law.

SUFFOLK
But in my mind that were no policy.
The King will labour still to save his life,
The commons haply rise to save his life;   240
And yet we have but trivial argument,
More than mistrust, that shows him worthy death.

YORK
So that, by this, you would not have him die?

SUFFOLK
Ah York, no man alive so fain as I.

YORK (*aside*)
'Tis York that hath more reason for his death.—   245

tears', and *Othello* 4.1.246: 'Each drop
she falls would prove a crocodile.'

227 **relenting** pitying (the crocodile tears)
228 **snake . . . bank** This is the first of a
series of expressions featuring a treacherous snake or serpent (see 3.1.343–4;
3.2.47, 261–2, 268, 330). The 'snake in
the grass' is proverbial (Dent S585).
rolled curled up (see the next note)
229 **chequered slough** patterned skin. The
snake lying curled up occurs at *Titus*
2.3.13–15, where *chequered* is also used,
this time to apply to the shadow cast by
the sun through the leaves, rather than
the snake's skin. *OED, slough, sb.*² records
a dialect form 'sluff' which indicates the
pronunciation.
233 **rid** removed from (i.e. killed)
234 **rid** free (quibbling on the other sense
from the previous line)

235, 238 **policy** See the second note to l. 23.
236 **colour** pretext. There are several quib-
bles here: *colour* also (a) has its usual
meaning, for a pun on 'dye' and 'die' (in
the previous line) and 'death' in this one;
and (b) means noose or 'collar'. All these
associations cluster around Shallow's line
to Falstaff at *2 Henry IV* 5.5.85: 'A colour
I fear that you will die in'.
237 **meet** fitting
    course due process
240 **haply** perhaps
241 **but trivial argument** only skimpy
    evidence
242 **More than mistrust** other than
    suspicion
243 **by** according to
244 **fain** eager (*OED a.* 3)
245 **more reason** (because, while Humphrey
lives, he will try to defend the King against
York (ll. 158–9); and because Humphrey

But my lord Cardinal, and you my lord of Suffolk,
Say as you think, and speak it from your souls.
Were't not all one an empty eagle were set
To guard the chicken from a hungry kite,
As place Duke Humphrey for the King's Protector?   250

QUEEN MARGARET
So the poor chicken should be sure of death.

SUFFOLK
Madam, 'tis true; and were't not madness then
To make the fox surveyor of the fold,
Who being accused a crafty murderer,
His guilt should be but idly posted over   255
Because his purpose is not executed?
No, let him die in that he is a fox,
By nature proved an enemy to the flock,
Before his chops be stained with crimson blood,
As Humphrey, proved by reasons, to my liege.   260
And do not stand on quillets how to slay him:
Be it by gins, by snares, by subtlety,
Sleeping or waking, 'tis no matter how,

---

259 chops] F (Chaps)

---

is next in line of succession to the throne:
see the last lines of the scene)

247 **Say . . . souls** Proverbial (Dent S725).
York is asking them to be absolutely candid: *speak it from your souls* has something of the gravity of Warwick's oath at 3.2.153–7. What they are to *speak from* their *souls*, of course, is a decision to commit murder.

248 **all one** the same thing (if)
empty hungry. Compare *Venus* 55–6: 'Even as an empty eagle, sharp by fast, | Tires with her beak on feathers, flesh, and bone', and *3 Henry VI* 1.1.269–70, where Henry says that York will, 'like an empty eagle, | Tire on the flesh of me and of my son'.

249 **kite** (scavenging bird of prey, very common in Elizabethan London)

252–3 **were't . . . fold** Proverbial: 'Give not the wolf (fox) the wether (sheep) to keep' (Dent W602).

253 **surveyor** guardian
fold sheepfold

255 **but . . . posted over** only foolishly ignored, passed quickly over. For *posted over*, compare *2 Henry IV* 1.2.151–2: 'your quiet o'erposting that action'.

256 **Because . . . executed** simply because his plan was not carried out

259 **chops** jaws. F's 'chaps' is a variant spelling since *chops* is 'now more usual' (*OED*, *chap*, *sb.*²) and so seems the appropriate modernization, especially as Shakespeare elsewhere uses 'chops' and 'chaps' indifferently.

260 **Humphrey . . . liege** Humphrey is proved an enemy to the King for the reasons we have outlined (as the fox is an enemy to the sheep in ll. 257–8).

261 **stand on quillets** insist on legal niceties, subtleties. In *1 Henry VI* 2.4.17, Warwick refers to 'these nice sharp quillets of the law'.

262 **gins** traps

So he be dead; for that is good deceit
Which mates him first that first intends deceit.   265

QUEEN MARGARET
Thrice-noble Suffolk, 'tis resolutely spoke.

SUFFOLK
Not resolute, except so much were done;
For things are often spoke and seldom meant;
But that my heart accordeth with my tongue,
Seeing the deed is meritorious,   270
And to preserve my sovereign from his foe,
Say but the word and I will be his priest.

CARDINAL BEAUFORT
But I would have him dead, my lord of Suffolk,
Ere you can take due orders for a priest.
Say you consent and censure well the deed,   275
And I'll provide his executioner;
I tender so the safety of my liege.

SUFFOLK
Here is my hand; the deed is worthy doing.

QUEEN MARGARET And so say I.

---

264 deceit] F; conceit OXFORD (*conj*. Delius)

---

264 **So** so long as
264–5 **deceit . . . deceit** This probably draws on the proverb 'To deceive the deceiver is no deceit' (Dent D182), although Suffolk seems to be taking the more Machiavellian view that it is satisfying to checkmate (*mate*) a deceiver by using a similar deceit. Oxford adopts Delius's conjecture 'conceit' for the first *deceit*, on the grounds that it 'could easily have been caught from the following line' (*Textual Companion*, p. 185), and F's Compositor A makes similar slips elsewhere: see the note to 2.3.29. 'Conceit' also makes good sense: it is a good idea to deal with your opponent's treachery in advance.
267 **except** unless
269 **that** to show that
  my . . . tongue Proverbial: 'what the heart thinks the tongue speaks' (Dent H334).

accordeth with corresponds to
270 **meritorious** As a theological term, this meant an action especially deserving reward from God (*OED a.* 1); Suffolk's use of it in this context is deeply cynical.
272 **be his priest** (and so give him the last rites, i.e. be his killer; proverbial: Dent P587)
274 **Ere** before
  take due orders prepare yourself for holy orders (to become a priest): this from the Cardinal is even more cynical than Suffolk's *meritorious* at l. 270. He cuts through Suffolk's metaphor at l. 272, and offers to provide him with an assassin (*executioner*, l. 276).
275 **censure well** approve
276 **executioner** assassin, as at *Richard III* 1.3.337, where Richard calls the murderers of Clarence 'my executioners'.
277 **tender so** am so concerned for

YORK

And I. And now we three have spoke it,   280
It skills not greatly who impugns our doom.
    Enter a Post

POST

Great lords, from Ireland am I come amain
To signify that rebels there are up
And put the Englishmen unto the sword.
Send succours, lords, and stop the rage betime,   285
Before the wound do grow uncurable;
For being green, there is great hope of help.   ⌐Exit⌐

CARDINAL BEAUFORT

A breach that craves a quick expedient stop!
What counsel give you in this weighty cause?

YORK

That Somerset be sent as regent thither.   290
'Tis meet that lucky ruler be employed,
Witness the fortune he hath had in France.

---

287 Exit] _not in_ F

281 **it . . . doom** Is this a jibe at the present
but silent Somerset and Buckingham, or
more general?
  skills not greatly doesn't matter much.
OED says that the idiom _skills not_ was
'extremely common from _c._ 1525 to _c._
1670' (_OED_, _skill_, _v._[1] 2b), occurring, for
example, at _Twelfth Night_ 5.1.286: 'it
skills not much when they are delivered.'
  impugns questions
  doom judgement, sentence
281.1 _Post_ messenger (from the sixteenth-
century custom of stationing horsemen
along the post-roads to carry messages as
swiftly as possible, in relays (_OED_ _sb._[2]
1, 2))
282 **amain** at full speed. Formed in the sixteenth century from _a_ (at) and _main_ (from
Old English 'maegn' power (_OED_ _adv._ 2),
it is common in Shakespeare, especially
in the earlier plays.
283 **signify** report
  up (in arms)
285 **succours** assistance. _Succours_ and _suc-
cour_ (more usual in Shakespeare) were
used identically in the period (_OED_ _sb._),
but perhaps the plural is used here to
emphasize the need for reinforcements.

rage Hattaway thinks that this means
'rabies' (seeing the Irish as mad dogs?),
drawing upon an obsolete sense in _OED_
(_sb._ 1c), Sanders 'outrage'; but doesn't it
just mean the furious attack by the Irish
on the English?
  betime in time (_OED adv. Obs._)
286–7 **Before . . . help** Proverbial: 'A green
wound is soon healed' (Dent W927).
287 **green** fresh
288 **breach** break-up, fracture (of relations,
i.e. rebellion: _OED sb._ 1, 3)
  expedient hasty, 'expeditious' (_OED_ 1).
This is the usual sense in Shakespeare,
rather than the modern 'advantageous',
though that sense occurs at _Much Ado_
5.2.75–6, 'most expedient for the wise',
which might be the sense here; but it is
likelier that _expedient_ merely intensifies
'quick'.
  stop remedy
291 **meet** fitting
  lucky fortunate. York's mockery of
Somerset's loss of France, recently reported (ll. 82–6), serves to prevent their
feud disappearing from view, and to bring
Somerset back into the scene.

SOMERSET

    If York, with all his far-fet policy,
    Had been the regent there instead of me,
    He never would have stayed in France so long.   295

YORK

    No, not to lose it all as thou hast done.
    I rather would have lost my life betimes
    Than bring a burden of dishonour home
    By staying there so long till all were lost.
    Show me one scar charactered on thy skin;   300
    Men's flesh preserved so whole do seldom win.

QUEEN MARGARET

    Nay then, this spark will prove a raging fire
    If wind and fuel be brought to feed it with.
    No more, good York; sweet Somerset, be still.
    Thy fortune, York, hadst thou been regent there,   305
    Might happily have proved far worse than his.

YORK

    What, worse than naught? Nay, then a shame take all!

SOMERSET

    And in the number, thee, that wishest shame.

CARDINAL BEAUFORT

    My lord of York, try what your fortune is.
    Th'uncivil kerns of Ireland are in arms   310
    And temper clay with blood of Englishmen.

---

293 **far-fet** cunningly devised, devious. For *fet*, see the note to 2.4.34. The Quarto text at this point has 'far fetcht', which may imply that the modern form (though not the modern meaning 'improbable') was gaining ground at this time, and was more familiar to the reporter.

297 **betimes** early, before my time (*OED adv.* 1)

300 **charactered** inscribed (i.e. written in alphabetical characters); stressed on the second syllable.

301 **so whole** unwounded

302 **Nay then** A good example of *nay* used less as a negative than as an intensifier or exclamation (see the note to 1.1.148). The Queen urges unity rather than, as elsewhere, acting as a catalyst for strife, perhaps because she shrewdly understands how this quarrel, which has already lost

France, could imperil her power and her husband's, perhaps because she is keen to keep the nobles united until Humphrey has been eliminated. She still manages, in the following lines, to criticize York.

this . . . fire Proverbial: 'of a little spark a great fire' (Dent S714).

304 **still** quiet

306 **happily** haply, perhaps

307 **a shame take all** (an exclamation of disapproval: *OED, shame, sb.* 16a)

308 **in the number** among them (*all*): Somerset takes York's catch-phrase and applies it literally.

310 **uncivil** barbarous

    kerns lightly armed Irish foot-soldiers (but often used contemptuously for the Irish in general)

311 **temper clay** moisten the ground

To Ireland will you lead a band of men
Collected choicely, from each county some,
And try your hap against the Irishmen?

YORK
I will, my lord, so please his majesty.   315

SUFFOLK
Why, our authority is his consent,
And what we do establish he confirms.
Then, noble York, take thou this task in hand.

YORK
I am content. Provide me soldiers, lords,
Whiles I take order for mine own affairs.   320

SUFFOLK
A charge, Lord York, that I will see performed.
But now return we to the false Duke Humphrey.

CARDINAL BEAUFORT
No more of him; for I will deal with him
That henceforth he shall trouble us no more.
And so break off; the day is almost spent.   325
Lord Suffolk, you and I must talk of that event.

YORK
My lord of Suffolk, within fourteen days
At Bristol I expect my soldiers;
From there I'll ship them all for Ireland.

SUFFOLK
I'll see it truly done, my lord of York.   330

                           Exeunt all but York

YORK
Now, York, or never, steel thy fearful thoughts,
And change misdoubt to resolution.

---

329 From] This edition (*conj.* Oxford); For F

---

313 **Collected . . . some** some chosen from
   every county
314 **hap** luck
320 **take order** make arrangement
321 **charge** duty
324 **henceforth** from now on
325 **spent** over
329 **From** Oxford's conjecture makes much
   better sense than F's 'For'. Perhaps
   Compositor A misread a manuscript

'Frö', or his eye caught *for* later in the line,
the kind of slip he seems to have made
elsewhere: see the note to 2.3.29. Oxford
notes several other examples of the
for/from error (*Textual Companion*, p. 185).
331 **Now . . . or never** Proverbial (Dent
   N351).
   steel harden, stiffen
   fearful full of fear
332 **misdoubt** *OED* says that this means 'mis-

Be that thou hop'st to be, or what thou art
Resign to death; it is not worth th'enjoying.
Let pale-faced fear keep with the mean-born man   335
And find no harbour in a royal heart.
Faster than springtime showers comes thought on
   thought,
And not a thought but thinks on dignity.
My brain, more busy than the labouring spider,
Weaves tedious snares to trap mine enemies.   340
Well, nobles, well: 'tis politicly done
To send me packing with an host of men.
I fear me you but warm the starvèd snake,
Who cherished in your breasts will sting your hearts.
'Twas men I lacked, and you will give them me.   345
I take it kindly; yet be well assured
You put sharp weapons in a madman's hands.
Whiles I in Ireland nurse a mighty band,
I will stir up in England some black storm
Shall blow ten thousand souls to heaven or hell,   350

---

348 nurse] F (nourish)

---

trust, suspicion', but perhaps it is simply
an emphatic way of saying 'doubt', York
nerving himself to seize his opportunity,
as *steel* in the previous line implies.

333 **Be . . . art** For the rhythm and phrasing,
compare Olivia's 'Be that thou know'st
thou art, and then thou art | As great as
that thou fear'st' (*Twelfth Night*
5.1.147–8), where she urges Viola to steel
herself and take courage, as York urges
himself here.
that what
what thou art i.e. the life you are living
334 **it . . . th'enjoying** For the rhythm and
phrasing, compare another line about
resigning life, Cleopatra's 'It is not worth
leave-taking' (*Antony* 5.2.293).
335 **pale-faced fear** Fear is also associated
with paleness at *Macbeth* 4.1.101: 'pale-
hearted fear'.
keep dwell
mean-born lowly-born
336 **harbour** refuge
338 **dignity** high rank (kingship)

340 **tedious** laboriously intricate
341 **politicly** skilfully (with the overtone of
'policy' in l. 23; see note)
342 **host** army
343–4 **you . . . hearts** Proverbial: 'To nourish a viper (snake) in one's bosom' (Dent
V68); York picks up Margaret's comparison from ll. 228–30, but applies it to himself rather than to Duke Humphrey.
343 **starvèd** stiff with cold (*OED* ppl. a. 4).
The *starvèd snake* also occurs at *Titus*
3.1.250, a scene that has other connections with this one (see note to l. 185).
347 **You . . . hands** Proverbial: 'put not a
naked sword in a madman's hand' (Dent
P669).
348 **nurse** '*OED* records a variety of forms—
nourish, nourice, nursh, nurse—all
having the same meaning, differing only
in the extent to which they have been
reduced in pronunciation. Metrically a
monosyllable is required here, as at *Titus*
5.1.84', where F has 'nourish', as it does
here (*Textual Companion*, p. 185).
350 **Shall** which shall

And this fell tempest shall not cease to rage
Until the golden circuit on my head
Like to the glorious sun's transparent beams
Do calm the fury of this mad-bred flaw.
And for a minister of my intent   355
I have seduced a headstrong Kentishman,
John Cade of Ashford,
To make commotion, as full well he can,
Under the title of John Mortimer.
In Ireland have I seen this stubborn Cade   360
Oppose himself against a troop of kerns,
And fought so long till that his thighs with darts
Were almost like a sharp-quilled porcupine;
And in the end being rescued, I have seen
Him caper upright like a wild Morisco,   365
Shaking the bloody darts as he his bells.
Full often like a shag-haired crafty kern
Hath he conversèd with the enemy,
And undiscovered, come to me again
And given me notice of their villainies.   370

363 porcupine] F (Porpentine)

351 **fell** ferocious
352 **circuit** crown
354 **mad-bred** created by the *madman* of
l. 347, York himself
flaw squall (of the *tempest*, l. 351), as in
the storm scene in *Pericles*, when Pericles
replies to the sailor's 'What, courage,
sir!', with 'Courage enough, I do not fear
the flaw' (Sc. 11.38–9).
355 **minister** agent
356–7 **I have seduced . . . Cade** The collusion
between York and Cade has no apparent
historical basis. It was probably derived
from Hall (Appendix B, 3.1.355–78), so
that Cade's rebellion leads with dramatic
inevitability to York's return to claim the
crown.
357 **Ashford** (a town in east Kent)
358 **make commotion** lead an uprising. York
echoes the phrase that Margaret uses to
slander Humphrey at l. 29.
359, 372 **John Mortimer** At 1 *Henry VI* 2.5,
the dramatist follows the chronicles in
confusing this character, who was imprisoned in the Tower until he was exe-

cuted in 1424, with his cousin Edmund
Mortimer whom Richard II named heir
to the crown in 1398. It is from the
Mortimers' line that York claims the
crown (see 2.2.34–52), and it is to test
the acceptability of this claim to the
country in general that he is using Cade.
360 **stubborn** untameable, fierce (*OED a.* 1).
Q applies the word not to Cade but
to the Irish themselves (Appendix A,
Passage D, l. 30).
362 **till that** until
darts arrows
365 **caper** perform rhythmic jumps into the
air, as in Morris dancing
Morisco morris-dancer (derived from the
Spanish word for 'Moor' (*OED sb.* 4),
perhaps because Morris dancers used to
blacken their faces, making them look like
Moors (Cecil Sharp and A. P. Oppé, *The
Dance* (1924), p. 5))
366 **as he his bells** as the morris-dancer
would shake the bells attached to his leg
367 **shag-haired** rough-haired, shaggy
370 **notice** information

This devil here shall be my substitute,
For that John Mortimer, which now is dead,
In face, in gait, in speech, he doth resemble.
By this I shall perceive the commons' mind,
How they affect the house and claim of York.   375
Say he be taken, racked, and torturèd;
I know no pain they can inflict upon him
Will make him say I moved him to those arms.
Say that he thrive, as 'tis great like he will,
Why then from Ireland come I with my strength   380
And reap the harvest which that coistrel sowed.
For Humphrey being dead, as he shall be,
And Henry put apart, the next for me.   *Exit*

3.2   *Enter two or three, running over the stage from the*
        murder of Duke Humphrey

FIRST MURDERER
    Run to my lord of Suffolk; let him know
    We have dispatched the Duke as he commanded.

---

381 coistrel] Q; Rascall F

---

371 **substitute** deputy
372 **For that** because
375 **affect** favour
376 **racked** tortured (by having the body
     stretched and dislocated on a *rack* or metal
     frame)
378 **moved . . . arms** instigated him to take
     up arms (against the King)
379 **great like** very likely
380 **strength** army
381 **coistrel** Oxford adopts this reading from
     Q, rather than F's 'rascal', noting that
     'Either word could easily be misread as
     the other; but whereas *rascal* is very com-
     mon, *coistrel* is a rare word; . . . most of
     [OED's] examples cluster in the period
     1577–1601' (*Textual Companion*, p. 186);
     and Shakespeare uses it twice elsewhere:
     at *Twelfth Night* 1.3.38, spoken by Sir
     Toby, and of the brothel customers
     at *Pericles* Sc. 19.190. OED's examples
     do not include those from *Pericles* or from
     Q.
383 **put apart** set aside (as at *Winter's Tale*
     2.2.15). This sounds like a euphemism for

'deposed'. That was certainly suggested
by the sinister edge given to the phrase by
Donald Sinden at Stratford-upon-Avon
in 1963–4, and by the still more sinister suggestion made by Emrys James there in
1977; see the Introduction, p. 14.
3.2.0.1–2 The opening of the scene requires
     different stagings in F and Q. Q shows the
     murder of Humphrey, F does not, perhaps
     to focus on the consequences of the mur-
     der, rather than the murder itself. This
     edition prints F's version in the text, Q's in
     Appendix A, Passage D.
2 **dispatched** killed (*OED v.* 4, where the first
     citation (1530) is, interestingly, a
     reference to the historical murder of
     Duke Humphrey). At l. 6 *dispatched*
     means 'carried out' (*OED v.* 5), but both
     senses essentially derive from the same
     sixteenth-century meaning, summarized
     by Florio in his Italian/English dictionary
     A World of Words, glossing *dispacciare*: 'to
     dispatch, to hasten, to speed, to rid away
     any work', cited by OED.

SECOND MURDERER

   O that it were to do! What have we done?

   Didst ever hear a man so penitent?

     Enter the Duke of Suffolk

FIRST MURDERER Here comes my lord.   5

SUFFOLK

   Now sirs, have you dispatched this thing?

FIRST MURDERER Ay my good lord, he's dead.

SUFFOLK

   Why, that's well said. Go, get you to my house.

   I will reward you for this venturous deed.

   The King and all the peers are here at hand.   10

   Have you laid fair the bed? Is all things well,

   According as I gave directions?

FIRST MURDERER 'Tis, my good lord.

SUFFOLK

   Away, be gone!   *Exeunt the Murderers*

     Sound trumpets. Enter King Henry and Queen

     Margaret, Cardinal Beaufort, the Duke of Somerset,

     and attendants

KING HENRY ⌈*to Suffolk*⌉

   Go call our uncle to our presence straight.   15

   Say we intend to try his grace today

   If he be guilty, as 'tis publishèd.

3.2.14–14.0.3 *Exeunt . . . attendants*] Exeunt. | *Sound Trumpets. Enter the King, the Queene,*
Cardinall, Suffolke, Somerset, with Attendants. F   15 *to Suffolk*] *after* Q (My Lord of Suffolke)

as he commanded There is no contradiction here with 3.1.276: the Cardinal provided the assassin, Suffolk briefed him.

3 **were to do** were still to be done (i.e. that we had not done it)

4 **penitent** repentant (for his sins) as one is supposed to be before death: Humphrey made a 'good end', in marked contrast to the Cardinal's 'bad' one, much emphasized at 3.3.5–6, 30.)

9 **venturous** daring, as at *Dream* 4.1.34–5, where Titania's 'venturous' fairy will raid the squirrel's hoard to fetch nuts for Bottom.

11 **laid fair** rearranged (to remove suspicious traces of struggle—not very efficiently according to ll. 172–8)

14–14.3 *Exeunt . . . attendants* Q specifies that the murderers leave; Suffolk remains, to be addressed by the King as he enters, the staging that is followed in this edition. But F merely has an '*Exeunt*', and directs Suffolk to enter with the King and the court. This is probably an error; compare the unambiguously erroneous exit provided by F for Suffolk at 1.3.101 (see collation). But it is just possible that F is correct, and that Suffolk leaves with the murderers and then slips on again during the court's general entry, in order to dissociate himself from any involvement with the dead body that he is about to 'discover'.

17 **If** whether
publishèd publicly proclaimed

SUFFOLK

I'll call him presently, my noble lord.   *Exit*

KING HENRY

Lords, take your places; and I pray you all

Proceed no straiter 'gainst our uncle Gloucester   20

Than from true evidence, of good esteem,

He be approved in practice culpable.

QUEEN MARGARET

God forbid any malice should prevail

That faultless may condemn a noble man;

Pray God he may acquit him of suspicion.   25

KING HENRY

I thank thee Meg, these words content me much.

Enter Suffolk

How now? Why look'st thou pale? Why tremblest
thou?

Where is our uncle? What's the matter, Suffolk?

SUFFOLK

Dead in his bed, my lord: Gloucester is dead.

QUEEN MARGARET Marry, God forfend!   30

CARDINAL BEAUFORT

God's secret judgement: I did dream tonight

The Duke was dumb and could not speak a word.

King Henry swoons

QUEEN MARGARET

How fares my lord? Help, lords, the King is dead.

---

26 Meg] CAPELL; *Nell* F

---

20 **straiter** with more severity
21 **of good esteem** worthy to be believed
22 **approved** proven
   in practice culpable guilty of 'practices',
   treason
24 **faultless . . . man** may condemn a good
   and innocent man. F prints *noble man* as
   two words, making it clear that Margaret
   uses the phrase in deference to Henry's
   view of Humphrey as a good man (*OED*,
   noble, a. 5a), not necessarily an aristocrat
   ('nobleman').
25 **him** himself
26 **Meg** F's '*Nell*' is Duke Humphrey's pet
   name for his wife (1.2.17, etc.); at l. 79 F

has 'Dame Elianor' for *Queen Margaret*,
and *Elianor* or *Elinor* for *Margaret* again at
ll. 100 and 120. These errors must surely
be authorial, prompted by the context of
the destruction of Duke Humphrey, with
which the disgrace of his wife was so
closely associated. For the textual implications, see the Textual Introduction, p. 99.
30 **forfend** forbid
31 **God's secret judgement** The near-
   blasphemous hypocrisy here blackens the
   Cardinal even more than usual, anticipating his shocking end in the next scene; see
   also the note to l. 185.1.
   tonight last night

SOMERSET

Rear up his body, wring him by the nose.

QUEEN MARGARET

Run, go, help, help! O Henry, ope thine eyes.   35

SUFFOLK

He doth revive again. Madam, be patient.

KING HENRY

O heavenly God!

QUEEN MARGARET   How fares my gracious lord?

SUFFOLK

Comfort, my sovereign; gracious Henry, comfort.

KING HENRY

What, doth my lord of Suffolk comfort me?

Came he right now to sing a raven's note   40

Whose dismal tune bereft my vital powers;

And thinks he that the chirping of a wren,

By crying comfort from a hollow breast,

Can chase away the first-conceivèd sound?

Hide not thy poison with such sugared words.   45

Lay not thy hands on me; forbear, I say.

---

34 **Rear** raise

wring . . . nose Presumably an attempt to restore circulation and so consciousness, as Adonis attempts to revive Venus (*Venus* 475).

35 **Run . . . help** Presumably there is a general bustle of servants here, and in the confusion Somerset and the Cardinal, who have nothing more to say in the scene, could leave. For another possibility, see the note to l. 185.1.

39 **my lord . . . me** It is interesting that, as the King revives, he instantly rejects Suffolk; he seems not to need any proof that Suffolk had Humphrey murdered, but knows it instinctively. Presumably neither Suffolk nor Margaret had anticipated this (hence, perhaps, in part, the extremity of Margaret's reaction in ll. 73–121)—but the consequences of Humphrey's murder are swift: by l. 301 Suffolk is banished; by the end of the scene Suffolk and Margaret have parted for ever; in the following scene Beaufort dies; by 4.1.142 Suffolk is dead.

40 **right now** just now

raven's note The raven was proverbially a bird of ill omen: 'the croaking raven

bodes misfortune' (Dent R33).

41 **bereft** robbed me of

vital powers faculties necessary to sustain life

42 **chirping . . . wren** Although the wren is a small bird, it has an astonishingly loud song; this disproportion is used to suggest the emptiness of Suffolk's comfort, as the next lines make clear.

43 **hollow** deceitful

44 **first-conceivèd** previously perceived

46–55 Much of the language here (*baleful messenger* (48), *murderous tyranny* (49), *thine eyes are wounding* (51), *come, basilisk* (52)) suggests at the very least intensity of feeling, but perhaps more than that—hysteria, near-madness even. This impression is intensified by ll. 51–3, where Henry first commands Suffolk not to look at him, then changes his mind and asks Suffolk to kill him with his look. They may imply that the King is losing control at the shock of Humphrey's death, and even hint at the periods of madness from which the historical Henry suffered. For further discussion, see Introduction, pp. 34 and 44.

46 **forbear** stop (i.e. don't touch me)

Their touch affrights me as a serpent's sting.
Thou baleful messenger, out of my sight!
Upon thy eyeballs murderous tyranny
Sits in grim majesty to fright the world.   50
Look not upon me, for thine eyes are wounding;
Yet do not go away; come, basilisk,
And kill the innocent gazer with thy sight.
For in the shade of death I shall find joy;
In life, but double death, now Gloucester's dead.   55

QUEEN MARGARET
Why do you rate my lord of Suffolk thus?
Although the Duke was enemy to him,
Yet he most Christian-like laments his death.
And for myself, foe as he was to me,
Might liquid tears, or heart-offending groans,   60
Or blood-consuming sighs recall his life,
I would be blind with weeping, sick with groans,
Look pale as primrose with blood-drinking sighs,
And all to have the noble Duke alive.
What know I how the world may deem of me,   65
For it is known we were but hollow friends;

47 **serpent's sting** This picks up the allusions to treacherous snakes and serpents that are frequent in this section of the play (e.g. 3.1.228–30, 343–4); more examples follow at ll. 261–71 and 330.

48 **baleful** deadly

49 **murderous tyranny** the tyranny of murder

52 **basilisk** A mythical serpent that killed anyone who looked at it with its glance.

54 **shade** shadow. The phrase 'shadow of death' was proverbial (Dent 885), deriving from the Bible: 'the valley of the shadow of death' (Psalm 23: 4). It is likely that the devout Henry makes the reference deliberately: only in death will he *find joy*.

55 **double death** The phrase captures the depth of Henry's emotional bond with his uncle.

56 **rate** berate, chide

58 **most Christian-like** because Christians are supposed to love their enemies (Matthew 5: 44), although nothing that Suffolk has said implies that, even on the surface, he *laments his death*. The Queen is perhaps becoming desperate in the face of

the King's reaction, as the extravagance of her following lines suggests. See the notes.

59 **for** as for

60 **liquid tears** floods of tears

60–3 **heart-offending, blood-consuming, blood-drinking** These compound adjectives suggest a deliberately heightened, 'written-up' style: the Queen is either over-doing her grief for Humphrey in an attempt to disguise her and Suffolk's complicity in his murder, or is becoming genuinely hysterical. Sighs and groans were thought to draw drops of blood from the heart, as at *Dream* 3.2.97: 'sighs of love that costs the fresh blood dear.'

63 **pale as primrose** John Gerard in his *Herbal* (1597), refers to 'the common white field primrose' (p. 637). Shakespeare also associates their paleness with the pallor of death at *Cymbeline* 4.2.222 and *Winter's Tale* 4.4.122–3.

65 **deem** of judge

66 **hollow** faint (another of Margaret's understatements, as at 3.1.20)

It may be judged I made the Duke away.
So shall my name with slander's tongue be wounded
And princes' courts be filled with my reproach.
This get I by his death. Ay me unhappy,   70
To be a queen, and crowned with infamy.

KING HENRY
Ah, woe is me for Gloucester, wretched man!

QUEEN MARGARET
Be woe for me, more wretched than he is.
What, dost thou turn away and hide thy face?
I am no loathsome leper, look on me.   75
What, art thou like the adder waxen deaf?
Be poisonous too and kill thy forlorn queen.
Is all thy comfort shut in Gloucester's tomb?
Why then Queen Margaret was ne'er thy joy.
Erect his statua and worship it,   80
And make my image but an alehouse sign.
Was I for this nigh wrecked upon the sea,
And twice by awkward winds from England's bank
Drove back again unto my native clime?
What boded this, but well forewarning winds   85
Did seem to say, 'Seek not a scorpion's nest,

---

79 Queen Margaret] OXFORD; Dame *Elianor* F; Dame Margaret ROWE   80 statua] F (Statue)
83, 85 winds] Q; winde F

---

67 **judged** thought that
69 **reproach** condemnation
72 **woe is me** A very common phrase used to express grief (*OED, woe, int.* 3b); in the next line, Margaret picks it up and turns it into a plea for sympathy for herself.
73–121 **Be . . . long** This is the longest and most problematic speech in the play. For a discussion of it, see the Introduction, pp. 42–4.
73 **Be woe for me** express grief for me (rather than for Humphrey)
76–7 **like . . . too** This alludes to the belief that the adder resisted the snake charmer by stopping one ear with its tail and pressing the other on the ground. Both this and the Queen's following phrase derive from Psalm 58: 4–5: 'As the poison of a serpent: even like the deaf adder that stoppeth her ears, which refuseth to hear the voice of the charmer.'

76 **waxen** grown
77 **forlorn** abandoned, deserted
79 **ne'er** never
80 **statua** As Hattaway says, 'the metre demands the three-syllable form' of 'statue'.
81 **alehouse sign** crudely-painted image; at 5.2.67 such a sign is called 'paltry'.
82 **nigh** nearly
83 **awkward** adverse
83, 85 **winds** F has 'wind', but 'Compositor B . . . is known to be guilty of addition or deletion of -s once every two Folio pages' (*Textual Companion*, p. 186).
83 **bank** sea-coast (*OED sb.*[1] 9)
84 **Drove** driven (Abbott 343)
   clime country
85 **What boded this** what did this foretell
   but but that
   well forewarning predicting truthfully
86 **scorpion's nest** The sting of the scorpion

Nor set no footing on this unkind shore'?
What did I then, but cursed the gentle gusts
And he that loosed them forth their brazen caves,
And bid them blow towards England's blessèd shore,   90
Or turn our stern upon a dreadful rock?
Yet Aeolus would not be a murderer,
But left that hateful office unto thee.
The pretty vaulting sea refused to drown me,
Knowing that thou wouldst have me drowned on shore   95
With tears as salt as sea through thy unkindness.
The splitting rocks cow'red in the sinking sands,
And would not dash me with their ragged sides,
Because thy flinty heart, more hard than they,
Might in thy palace perish Margaret.   100
As far as I could ken thy chalky cliffs,
When from thy shore the tempest beat us back,
I stood upon the hatches in the storm,
And when the dusky sky began to rob
My earnest-gaping sight of thy land's view,   105
I took a costly jewel from my neck—
A heart it was, bound in with diamonds—

100 Margaret] ROWE; *Elianor* F

is very painful. The reference connects
with those to serpents and other stinging
creatures that run through the scene.

89 **he** Aeolus, classical god of the winds
(anticipating the specific reference at
l. 92)
loosed them forth released them
(from the *caves* in which he kept them
imprisoned)
brazen caves In Homer's *Odyssey* 10.3–4,
the island of Aeolus was surrounded by
walls of brass, but the only reference to
caves of brass seems to be in Nashe's *Summer's Last Will and Testament* (?1592)
1793–4: 'imprison him . . . with the
winds in bellowing caves of brass' (*Works*,
iii. 289). Compare *Pericles* Sc. 11.2–3:
'thou that hast | Upon the winds com-
mand, bind them in brass'.
94 **pretty** attractively
vaulting leaping (the waves rising and
falling)
97 **splitting** i.e. which split ships
sinking i.e. which cause ships to sink

99 **Because** so that
flinty . . . they Proverbial· 'A heart as
hard as a flint' (Dent H311).
100 **perish** destroy (cause to *perish*)
101 **ken** discern (a nautical term: *OED v.*[1] 6)
chalky cliffs This phrase, describing the
south coast of England, seems to have
been as common then as now, since
it is the basis of a joke in *Errors*, about
the teeth of a kitchen-maid: 'Where
England?—I looked for the chalky cliffs,
but I could find no whiteness in them'
(3.2.128–30).
103 **hatches** deck. At *Richard III* 1.4.13,
Clarence describes a dream in which he
and Richard walked 'Upon the hatches'
and 'looked toward England', as Margaret
does here.
104, 112 **dusky** darkened (as if it were
dusk)
105 **earnest-gaping** eagerly peering
107 **heart . . . diamonds** Compare *Love's
Labour's Lost* 5.2.3: 'A lady walled about
with diamonds'.

And threw it towards thy land. The sea received it,
And so I wished thy body might my heart.
And even with this I lost fair England's view,   110
And bid mine eyes be packing with my heart,
And called them blind and dusky spectacles
For losing ken of Albion's wishèd coast.
How often have I tempted Suffolk's tongue—
The agent of thy foul inconstancy—   115
To sit and witch me, as Ascanius did,
When he to madding Dido would unfold
His father's acts, commenced in burning Troy!
Am I not witched like her? Or thou not false like him?
Ay me, I can no more. Die Margaret,   120
For Henry weeps that thou dost live so long.
        Noise within. Enter the Earls of Warwick and
        Salisbury with many commons

WARWICK
    It is reported, mighty sovereign,
    That good Duke Humphrey traitorously is murdered
    By Suffolk and the Cardinal Beaufort's means.
    The commons, like an angry hive of bees   125

---

116 witch] THEOBALD; watch F   120 Margaret] ROWE; *Elinor* F   121.1–2 *and Salisbury*] Q;
not in F

111 **be packing** be gone
    heart (i.e. the jewel of l. 107)
112 **spectacles** instruments of sight. For the
    transferred use of *spectacles* from some-
    thing that assists the eyes to mean the
    eyes themselves, compare *Cymbeline*
    1.6.38: 'spectacles so precious'.
113 **ken** sight. Compare *Lucrece* 1114: ''Tis
    double death to drown in ken of shore.'
    wishèd longed-for
114 **tempted** induced
115 **agent** (because he arranged the mar-
    riage and represented the King at the
    ceremony)
116 **witch** bewitch
116–18 **Ascanius . . . Troy** In Virgil's *Aeneid*
    1.658 ff., Venus gives her son Cupid, god
    of love, the shape of Aeneas' son
    Ascanius, so that he can simultaneously
    tell Dido of his father's feats during the
    siege of Troy, and make Dido fall in love
    with Aeneas. The latter incident is vividly

dramatized in Marlowe's (and Nashe's?)
Dido Queen of Carthage, 3.1.
117 **madding** driven mad by love
119 **false** (because, at the gods' command,
    Aeneas deserted Dido in order to fulfil his
    destiny of founding Rome)
120 **I can no more** I am capable of no more
    (i.e. 'my strength fails me' (Schmidt), a
    phrase also used by the dying Laertes
    (*Hamlet* 5.2.273) and Antony (*Antony*
    4.16.61))
121.2 **Salisbury with many commons** F does
    not bring Salisbury on here, though he is
    obviously needed at ll. 134–5; Q does.
    Conversely, Q does not introduce the com-
    mon people, while F does. F's unspecific
    phrase '*many commons*' is typical of
    authorial 'permissive' directions, the
    writer imaging the *commons* swarming on
    to the stage. Both F and Q keep the *com-
    mons* offstage (*within*) for the rest of the
    scene.

That want their leader, scatter up and down
And care not who they sting in his revenge.
Myself have calmed their spleenful mutiny,
Until they hear the order of his death.

KING HENRY

That he is dead, good Warwick, 'tis too true.   130
But how he died God knows, not Henry.
Enter his chamber, view his breathless corpse,
And comment then upon his sudden death.

WARWICK

That shall I do, my liege.—Stay, Salisbury,
With the rude multitude till I return.   135

⌜*Exeunt Warwick at one door, Salisbury*
and commons at another⌝

KING HENRY

O thou that judgest all things, stay my thoughts,
My thoughts that labour to persuade my soul
Some violent hands were laid on Humphrey's life.

135.1–2 *Exeunt . . . another*] *Exet Salbury.* Q; *not in* F   137 My thoughts that . . . soul] F; That
. . . grievèd soul OXFORD *conj.*

---

126 **want** lack
127 **care . . . revenge** No sooner is Duke
  Humphrey dead than the disorder which
  he has so far held in check breaks out.
  This point is developed in the Lieutenant's
  speech at 4.1.76, 91–103, and in the brutal violence of that scene and especially of
  the Jack Cade scenes, 4.2–7.
  his revenge revenge for his death
128 **spleenful mutiny** angry uprising. The
  spleen was 'viewed as the seat of emotions and passions' (Onions).
129 **order** manner (how he died)
131 **God knows, not Henry**—although he
  suspects Suffolk, as ll. 39–55 make clear.
  'God he knows, not I' is proverbial (Dent
  G189.1), but Henry never refers to God in
  a casual way, so it is more than a catch-
  phrase here.
132 **breathless** lacking breath, lifeless
133 **comment . . . upon** explain
135 **rude** uncivilized
135.1–2 *Exeunt . . . another* F provides no
  exit here, Q one for Salisbury. It is sometimes suggested that Salisbury and the
  commons do not leave, but retire to
  another part of the stage; but since both

texts provide an entry for Salisbury at
l. 243.1, and refer to the commons as
'within', Oxford's direction seems appropriate: 'Warwick exits through whichever
door the bed is later thrust out of . . . ,
while Salisbury and those Commons who
entered with him exit through another'
(*Textual Companion*, p. 186). See the note
to ll. 146.1–2.
136 **thou . . . things** Henry's prayer to God
  echoes Genesis 18: 25: 'the judge of all
  the world'.
  stay restrain
136–7 **my thoughts, | My thoughts**
  Stanley Wells thinks the repetition un-
  Shakespearian, citing Sonnet 146, 1–2,
  'where the repetition is generally agreed
  to be accidental' (*Textual Companion*, p.
  186); for his emendation, see collation.
  On the other hand, *The Comedy of Errors*,
  a play probably near to this one in date,
  has 'I am pressed down with conceit: |
  Conceit, my comfort and my injury'
  (4.2.64–5), where the repetition is for
  emphasis, as probably here: Henry does-
  n't want his suspicion that Humphrey
  was murdered to prove true.

If my suspect be false, forgive me God,
For judgement only doth belong to thee.   140
Fain would I go to chafe his paly lips
With twenty thousand kisses, and to drain
Upon his face an ocean of salt tears,
To tell my love unto his dumb, deaf trunk,
And with my fingers feel his hand unfeeling.   145
But all in vain are these mean obsequies,

⌈*Enter Warwick who draws apart the curtains and*
shows Duke Humphrey dead in his bed.⌉ *Bed put forth*

And to survey his dead and earthy image,
What were it but to make my sorrow greater?

WARWICK
Come hither, gracious sovereign, view this body.

KING HENRY
That is to see how deep my grave is made: 150
For with his soul fled all my worldly solace,
For seeing him I see my life in death.

WARWICK
As surely as my soul intends to live
With that dread King that took our state upon him

146.1–2 *Enter . . . forth*] *Warwicke* drawes the curtaines and showes Duke *Humphrey* in his bed.
Q; *Bed put forth.* F

---

139 **suspect** suspicion (stressed on the second
 syllable)
140 **judgement . . . thee** For God's pre-
 rogative of judgement, compare e.g.
 Psalm 94: 1: 'O Lord God to whom
 vengeance belongeth', and Matthew 7: 1:
 'Judge not, that ye be not judged', also
 echoed by the King at 3.3.31.
141–5 **Fain . . . unfeeling** The extreme
 expressions in these lines may suggest
 hysteria or near-madness; see the note to
 ll. 46–55.
141 **Fain** gladly
 chafe warm (by rubbing: *OED v.* 3)
 paly pale
142 **drain** rain, let fall. This is *OED*'s only
 example of *drain* in this sense: *v.* 2b.
143 **ocean . . . tears** Proverbial (Dent T82.1).
144 **trunk** body
145 **unfeeling** empty of feeling
146 **mean obsequies** inadequate funeral
 rites. Compare the 'maimèd rites' for
 Ophelia at *Hamlet* 5.1.214.

146.1–2 **Enter . . . forth** Since Q omits the
 whole of Henry's speech, ll. 136–48,
 Warwick in that version does not exit at
 l. 135, but goes straight to the 'discovery
 space' or to one of the doors at the back of
 the stage and 'draws the curtains and
 shows Duke Humphrey in his bed' (Q,
 1246–7). F has the terse '*Bed put forth*' at
 this point. But the two directions comple-
 ment each other, as McKerrow shows:
 the curtains of an upstage entrance 'are
 drawn, discovering Gloucester dead in his
 bed (in his room). The bed is then (according to the Folio) pushed out on to the
 main stage, as was normally done in such
 scenes where it was necessary for several
 persons to gather round'.
147 **earthy** (made only of earth, now that the
 life has gone from it)
152 **my life in death** an image of my own
 death
154–5 **that dread . . . curse** Christ (who took
 on human form (*our state*) to redeem

To free us from his father's wrathful curse,   155
I do believe that violent hands were laid
Upon the life of this thrice-famèd Duke.

SUFFOLK

A dreadful oath, sworn with a solemn tongue!
What instance gives Lord Warwick for his vow?

WARWICK

See how the blood is settled in his face.   160
Oft have I seen a timely-parted ghost
Of ashy semblance, meagre, pale, and bloodless,
Being all descended to the labouring heart,
Who in the conflict that it holds with death
Attracts the same for aidance 'gainst the enemy,   165
Which with the heart there cools, and ne'er returneth
To blush and beautify the check again.
But see, his face is black and full of blood;
His eyeballs further out than when he lived,
Staring full ghastly like a strangled man;   170
His hair upreared, his nostrils stretched with struggling,
His hands abroad displayed, as one that grasped

mankind from the *curse* resulting from the 'Original Sin' of Adam and Eve). The gravity of Warwick's oath, and of its phrasing, justifies Suffolk's reaction at l. 158.

154 **that . . . him** This echoes the collect for Christmas Day in *The Book of Common Prayer* (1559): 'thy only begotten son, to take our nature upon him'.

155 **To . . . curse** This echoes a biblical phrase about Man's Fall and redemption: 'Christ hath redeemed us from the curse of the law' (Galatians 3: 13).

157 **thrice-famèd** i.e. very famous

158 **dreadful** awesome, full of dread

159 **instance** evidence, proof

160 **settled** not flowing, coagulated (*OED ppl. a.* 6, whose earliest example is from *2 Henry IV* 4.2.99–100: 'the warming of the blood, . . . before cold and settled')

161 **timely-parted** i.e. that died a natural, timely death
    ghost corpse (*OED sb.* 9), or perhaps person (*OED sb.* 4)

162 **ashy . . . pale** The words are combined at *Venus* 76 and *Lucrece* 1512, and imply pale grey, like ashes.

semblance appearance
meagre emaciated (*OED a.* 1)

163 **Being all descended to** (the blood) having all drained into
    labouring The heart is working overtime to keep the body alive.

164 **Who** (the heart)

165 **the same** (the blood)
    aidance aid

166 **Which** (the blood)

167 **blush** bring colour to
    beautify make beautiful. Although Polonius criticizes 'beautified' as 'a vile phrase' at *Hamlet* 2.2.111, *beautify* does not seem to be used for critical effect in any of its other occurrences in the Shakespeare canon; but it is interesting that at *Lucrece* 404–6 it also occurs in a context of life and death, though there these are figurative.

170 **full** very
    ghastly Both the 'early uses' cited at *OED a.* 1a seem relevant: Humphrey is staring in terror, 'suggestive of the kind of horror evoked by the sight of death' (his own).

171 **upreared** standing on end

172 **abroad displayed** spread wide apart

And tugged for life and was by strength subdued.
Look on the sheets: his hair, you see, is sticking;
His well-proportioned beard made rough and rugged,   175
Like to the summer's corn by tempest lodged.
It cannot be but he was murdered here.
The least of all these signs were probable.

SUFFOLK
Why Warwick, who should do the Duke to death?
Myself and Beaufort had him in protection,   180
And we I hope, sir, are no murderers.

WARWICK
But both of you were vowed Duke Humphrey's foes,
(*To Cardinal Beaufort*)
And you, forsooth, had the good Duke to keep.
'Tis like you would not feast him like a friend;
And 'tis well seen he found an enemy.   185
⌈*Exit Cardinal Beaufort assisted by Somerset*⌉

QUEEN MARGARET
Then you belike suspect these noblemen
As guilty of Duke Humphrey's timeless death?

WARWICK
Who finds the heifer dead and bleeding fresh,

185.1 *Exit . . . Somerset*] OXFORD (*after l. 202, following Q's 'Exet Cardinall'*); *not in* F

---

173 **strength** force, violence
174 **sticking** (with sweat?)
175 **well-proportioned** neatly shaped, trimmed
     rugged shaggy
176 **lodged** flattened. *OED, lay, v.*[1] 1c says that 'lay', meaning 'beat down crops', was often spelt 'ledge' in the sixteenth and seventeenth centuries, which may have led to this use of 'lodge', *OED*'s first example of which is *Richard II* 3.3.161: 'lodge the summer corn' (*lodge, v.* 5).
180 **protection** custody
183 **keep** guard
184 **'Tis like** it is likely
185 **well seen** very obvious
185.1 *Exit . . . Somerset* F provides no exit for either the Cardinal or Somerset; Q gives the Cardinal an exit at l. 202, Somerset no exit at all. They might leave in the flurry at l. 35 (see note), but, as McKerrow suggests, the Cardinal

'may have been represented as becoming ill in the course of the scene and as being . . . helped out', Oxford suggests by Somerset. He dies in the next scene, tormented by guilt-ridden images of the dead Humphrey. But as McKerrow admits, the placing of his exit in Q is at 'an unlikely point', seriously distracting from the argument between Suffolk and Warwick; so I have taken a hint from Oxford's direction that ll. 183–5 be addressed specifically (and accusingly) to the Cardinal, and suggested he leave here: he cannot leave with the King and Warwick at l. 303.1, since Margaret at l. 307 refers to 'two of you', and her contrasting references to Suffolk and Beaufort at ll. 195–6 may imply that the Cardinal is no longer on stage.
186 **belike** perhaps
187 **timeless** untimely

And sees fast by a butcher with an axe,
But will suspect 'twas he that made the slaughter?   190
Who finds the partridge in the puttock's nest
But may imagine how the bird was dead,
Although the kite soar with unbloodied beak?
Even so suspicious is this tragedy.

QUEEN MARGARET
Are you the butcher, Suffolk? Where's your knife?   195
Is Beaufort termed a kite? Where are his talons?

SUFFOLK
I wear no knife to slaughter sleeping men,
But here's a vengeful sword, rusted with ease,
That shall be scourèd in his rancorous heart
That slanders me with murder's crimson badge.   200
Say, if thou dar'st, proud Lord of Warwickshire,
That I am faulty in Duke Humphrey's death.

WARWICK
What dares not Warwick, if false Suffolk dare him?

QUEEN MARGARET
He dares not calm his contumelious spirit,
Nor cease to be an arrogant controller,   205
Though Suffolk dare him twenty thousand times.

WARWICK
Madam be still, with reverence may I say,
For every word you speak in his behalf
Is slander to your royal dignity.

189 **fast** close
191 **puttock** kite, a scavenging bird of prey referred to at 3.1.249. Kites also stole sheets left out to dry, and spread the plague. In *Shakespeare's Imagination* (revised edn., 1963), E. A. Armstrong shows how groups of words and images recur in Shakespeare's work: the occurrence of one will suggest the others. So the reference to *sheets* at l. 174 leads to the appearance of the kite, in a context of death (pp. 11–17).
192 **was dead** came to be killed
198 **ease** disuse
199 **scourèd** cleaned
200 **badge** (worn by a servant to identify who his master was; so a *crimson* one will metaphorically identify Suffolk as a murderer)

202 **faulty in** guilty of. Q reads 'guilty' here.
204 **contumelious** slanderous
205 **controller** critic, detractor
207 **Madam ... say** Brewster Mason at Stratford-upon-Avon in 1963–4 brought out the variety of this line, modulating from a snapped *be still* ('shut up!') to a delivery of *with reverence* (i.e. with respect) that exposed the perfunctoriness of Warwick's courtesy; by contrast, Geff Francis at Stratford in 2000 spoke the line with smiling courtesy, conscious of his moral superiority. For the force of *with reverence*, compare the sixteenth-century 'save (one's) reverence' (*OED, reverence, sb.* 5a), and the modern idiom 'with respect', used to preface disagreement or criticism.

SUFFOLK

Blunt-witted lord, ignoble in demeanour,   210
If ever lady wronged her lord so much,
Thy mother took into her blameful bed
Some stern untutored churl, and noble stock
Was graffed with crabtree slip, whose fruit thou art,
And never of the Nevilles' noble race.   215

WARWICK

But that the guilt of murder bucklers thee
And I should rob the deathsman of his fee,
Quitting thee thereby of ten thousand shames,
And that my sovereign's presence makes me mild,
I would, false murd'rous coward, on thy knee   220
Make thee beg pardon for thy passèd speech,
And say it was thy mother that thou meant'st,
That thou thyself wast born in bastardy;
And after all this fearful homage done,
Give thee thy hire and send thy soul to hell,   225
Pernicious bloodsucker of sleeping men!

SUFFOLK

Thou shalt be waking while I shed thy blood,
If from this presence thou dar'st go with me.

210–23 **Blunt-witted . . . bastardy** The dialogue degenerates from accusations of Duke Humphrey's murder to a slanging-match, Suffolk and Warwick accusing each other (literally) of being a bastard.

210 **ignoble in demeanour** looking and behaving like a commoner, not a nobleman

212 **blameful** guilty

213 **stern** cruel (*OED a.* 3)
 untutored untaught
 churl peasant (contemptuous)

213–14 **noble stock . . . slip** a cutting (slip) of the wild apple (*crabtree*), which has inferior, harsh-tasting fruit, was grafted on to a worthier tree-trunk (*noble stock*), thus contaminating it. The metaphor refers to a common horticultural practice, which normally allows a variety bearing superior fruit to use the vigour of a stronger, inferior-tasting one. From this grafting, inferior *fruit* (Warwick) resulted. There is probably a pun on 'slip' meaning 'moral lapse'.

216 **But that** were it not for the fact that
 bucklers protects. A *buckler* was a shield; Shakespeare characteristically uses one part of speech for another.

217 **deathsman** executioner
 of his fee (for executing Suffolk for the murder of Humphrey)

218 **Quitting** clearing, freeing
 shames (of a public execution)

221 **passèd** uttered

224 **fearful homage** cowardly submission

225 **Give . . . hire** Proverbial: 'To give one his hire' i.e. kill him (Dent H474.1).
 hire payment

226 **Pernicious** destructive
 bloodsucker bloodthirsty person, one who sheds another's blood (*OED* 2), as at *Richard III* 3.3.5: 'A knot you are of damnèd bloodsuckers.' This extremely insulting line leads to a further intensification of the scene: see the second note to l. 229.

228 **presence** royal presence

WARWICK
　　Away even now, or I will drag thee hence.
　　Unworthy though thou art, I'll cope with thee,   230
　　And do some service to Duke Humphrey's ghost.
　　　　　　　　　　　Exeunt Suffolk and Warwick

KING HENRY
　　What stronger breastplate than a heart untainted?
　　Thrice is he armed that hath his quarrel just;
　　And he but naked, though locked up in steel,
　　Whose conscience with injustice is corrupted.   235
COMMONS (*within*) Down with Suffolk! Down with Suffolk!
QUEEN MARGARET What noise is this?
　　　　Enter Suffolk and Warwick with their weapons drawn
KING HENRY
　　Why how now, lords? Your wrathful weapons drawn
　　Here in our presence? Dare you be so bold?
　　Why, what tumultuous clamour have we here?   240
SUFFOLK
　　The trait'rous Warwick with the men of Bury
　　Set all upon me, mighty sovereign.
COMMONS (*within*) Down with Suffolk! Down with Suffolk!
　　　　Enter from the commons the Earl of Salisbury
SALISBURY (*to the commons, within*)
　　Sirs, stand apart, the King shall know your mind.
　　(*To King Henry*)
　　Dread lord, the commons send you word by me   245

231.1 *Exeunt . . . Warwick*] Warwicke puls him out. | *Exet Warwicke and Suffolke* Q; *Exeunt.* F
236 COMMONS . . . Suffolk!] OXFORD (*after* Q); *A noyse within.* F   243 COMMONS . . . Suffolk!]
OXFORD (*after* Q); *not in* F   243.1 *Enter . . . Salisbury*] OXFORD (*after* Q); *Enter Salisbury.* F

229　even now at once
　　I . . . hence (as Q instructs him to do: see
　　collation to 231.1)
230　cope come to blows (*OED v.*² 2)
232　What . . . untainted Proverbial: 'Inno-
　　cence bears its defence with it' (Dent I81),
　　deriving from various biblical references,
　　including Ephesians 6: 14: 'Having on
　　the breastplate of righteousness.'
　　untainted innocent, uncorrupted
234　naked unprotected by armour, as at
　　Othello 5.2.265: 'naked as I am, I will
　　assault thee.'
　　locked . . . steel wearing a complete suit
　　of armour

236, 243　Down . . . Suffolk Q specifies what
　　F's '*noise within*' might be. The Folio's
　　vagueness of direction is characteristic of
　　'foul papers' copy.
238–9　Your . . . bold It was a serious offence
　　to draw a weapon in the presence of the
　　King.
244　stand apart stand aside (i.e. wait
　　outside)
245–71　Dread . . . life Emrys Jones calls this
　　long speech 'formally eloquent; it has as a
　　kind of refrain the words "They say". . . .
　　Salisbury speaks as the cultured voice
　　of the rude commons. It is the moment
　　. . . when the precarious harmony

Unless Lord Suffolk straight be done to death,
Or banishèd fair England's territories,
They will by violence tear him from your palace
And torture him with grievous ling'ring death.
They say by him the good Duke Humphrey died;   250
They say in him they fear your highness' death;
And mere instinct of love and loyalty,
Free from a stubborn opposite intent,
As being thought to contradict your liking,
Makes them thus forward in his banishment.   255
They say, in care of your most royal person,
That if your highness should intend to sleep,
And charge that no man should disturb your rest
In pain of your dislike, or pain of death,
Yet notwithstanding such a strait edict,   260
Were there a serpent seen with forkèd tongue,
That slily glided towards your majesty,
It were but necessary you were waked,
Lest being suffered in that harmful slumber,
The mortal worm might make the sleep eternal.   265
And therefore do they cry, though you forbid,

of Humphrey's commonwealth is over-
turned' (*Origins*, p. 167). Suffolk sneers at
its formality in ll. 274–80.
245 **Dread** revered, held in awe (*OED ppl. a.*
2): alluding to the awesome power of a
King, though perhaps tinged with irony
in the present circumstances, as 'mighty
sovereign' (l. 122) also may be.

246 **done** put
252 **mere** pure
    instinct impulse (stressed on the second
    syllable)
253 **opposite intent** antagonistic purpose.
    The commons are making it clear that
    they are not rebelling against the King's
    wishes, a point reinforced in the next line.
254 **As being** which might be
    contradict your liking oppose your wishes
255 **forward in** insist upon
258 **charge** order
259 **In** on
260 **edict** (stressed on the second syllable,
    unlike modern prose usage)
261 **forkèd** two-pronged (popularly supposed

to be the sting of the snake, as at *Measure*
3.1.16–17: 'the soft and tender fork | Of a
poor worm')
263 **but** only (i.e. although you commanded
us not to wake you, there was no alternative to disobeying you, in order to save
your life)
264 **Lest** in case
    suffered allowed to remain
    harmful dangerous
265 **mortal worm** deadly snake. *Worm*
(from Old English *wyrm*) is often used in
Shakespeare for 'snake', most memorably
in the conversation between Cleopatra
and the countryman who brings her the
asp with which to kill herself; as she does
so, she calls it 'mortal wretch' (*Antony*
5.2.238–74, 298). Compare also the lines
from *Measure* cited in the note to l. 261.
    sleep eternal Death is also seen as an *eter-
nal sleep* at *Titus* 1.1.155, 2.4.15; the
phrase derives from the *eternal*, everlasting, quality associated with God (*OED,
eternal, a.* 3a).

That they will guard you, whe'er you will or no,
From such fell serpents as false Suffolk is,
With whose envenomèd and fatal sting
Your loving uncle, twenty times his worth,   270
They say, is shamefully bereft of life.

COMMONS (*within*) An answer from the King, my lord of
Salisbury!

SUFFOLK
'Tis like the commons, rude unpolished hinds,
Could send such message to their sovereign.   275
But you, my lord, were glad to be employed,
To show how quaint an orator you are.
But all the honour Salisbury hath won
Is that he was the Lord Ambassador
Sent from a sort of tinkers to the King.   280

COMMONS (*within*) An answer from the King, or we will all
break in!

KING HENRY
Go Salisbury, and tell them all from me
I thank them for their tender loving care,
And had I not been 'cited so by them,   285
Yet did I purpose as they do entreat;
For sure my thoughts do hourly prophesy
Mischance unto my state by Suffolk's means.
And therefore by his majesty I swear,
Whose far unworthy deputy I am,   290

---

267 whe'er] F (where)   281 COMMONS] CAPELL; *not in* F

---

267 **whe'er . . . no** whether you want them
to or not. 'Whether one will or no' is a
common catch-phrase (Dent W400.1).
268 **fell** cruel
270 **his worth** worth more than he
271 **bereft** deprived
274 **like** likely that. For the ironic tone, compare the modern idiom 'a likely story'.
rude barbarous
hinds peasants
275 **Could send** were capable of sending
277 **quaint** skilful (a common sixteenth-
century use, as at *Shrew* 3.3.20: 'quaint
musician')

280 **sort of tinkers** gang of vagabonds. An
abusive phrase: for the critical sense of
sort, see *OED sb.*² 17a, and compare
2.1.162; *tinkers*, though technically wandering craftsmen who mended household
utensils, were held in such low repute
that *tinker* was virtually synonymous
with 'vagrant' (*OED sb.* 1a).
285 **'cited** incited, urged
286 **purpose** intend to do
288 **Mischance** disaster
289–90 **by his . . . I am** That the king was
God's deputy on earth was an Elizabethan
commonplace.

He shall not breathe infection in this air
But three days longer, on the pain of death.

⌐*Exit Salisbury*⌐

QUEEN MARGARET
O Henry, let me plead for gentle Suffolk.

KING HENRY
Ungentle Queen, to call him gentle Suffolk.
No more, I say! If thou dost plead for him   295
Thou wilt but add increase unto my wrath.
Had I but said, I would have kept my word;
But when I swear, it is irrevocable.
(*To Suffolk*) If after three days' space thou here beest
    found
On any ground that I am ruler of,   300
The world shall not be ransom for thy life.
Come Warwick, come good Warwick, go with me.
I have great matters to impart to thee.

Exeunt King Henry and Warwick with attendants
⌐*who remove the bed and draw the curtains as they leave*⌐

QUEEN MARGARET
Mischance and sorrow go along with you!
Heart's discontent and sour affliction   305
Be playfellows to keep you company!
There's two of you, the devil make a third,
And threefold vengeance tend upon your steps!

292.1 *Exit Salisbury*] Q; *not in* F   303.1 *Exeunt . . . Warwick*] Q; *Exit.* F   303.1–2 *with . . . leave*] *not in* F

---

291 **breathe . . . in** pollute
292 **But** (i.e. more than)
293–4 **gentle . . . Ungentle** Margaret prob-
     ably intends both meanings of *gentle*
     ('noble' and 'kind'); Henry seizes upon
     the second in his reply.
296 **add increase unto** increase
297 **Had . . . said** if I had only pronounced
     (the sentence)
303.2 **who remove the bed** The bed was 'put
     forth' at l. 146.2; this is the obvious place
     for it to be removed. It is needed again for
     the death of Cardinal Beaufort in the next
     scene.
304–416 For a discussion of this emotionally

powerful scene, see the Introduction, pp.
45–7.
304 **Mischance** In her fury with the King,
     Margaret picks up and turns against him
     the word he used at l. 288 to apply to
     Suffolk's malign influence.
307 **the devil . . . third** Alluding to the
     proverb 'There cannot lightly come a
     worse except the devil come himself'
     (Dent W910), also used at *Merchant*
     3.1.72–3: 'A third cannot be matched
     unless the devil himself turn Jew.'
308 **tend upon** attend upon, serve (i.e.
     follow)

SUFFOLK

Cease, gentle Queen, these execrations,

And let thy Suffolk take his heavy leave.   310

QUEEN MARGARET

Fie coward woman and soft-hearted wretch!

Hast thou not spirit to curse thine enemies?

SUFFOLK

A plague upon them! Wherefore should I curse them?

Could curses kill, as doth the mandrake's groan,

I would invent as bitter searching terms,   315

As curst, as harsh, and horrible to hear,

Delivered strongly through my fixèd teeth,

With full as many signs of deadly hate,

As lean-faced envy in her loathsome cave.

My tongue should stumble in mine earnest words;   320

Mine eyes should sparkle like the beaten flint;

---

312 enemies] Q; enemy F   314 Could] Q; Would F

---

309 **execrations** curses

310 **heavy** sorrowful, 'weighed down' with grief (*OED a.*[1] 27a), as at *Errors* 5.1.45: 'he hath been heavy, sour, sad'.

312 **enemies** Q's reading is supported by 'them' in the next line (in both F and Q).

313–32 At Stratford-upon-Avon in 2000, Richard Dillane began quietly (implying 'What is the point of cursing? What will it achieve?'), only gradually building to the outbursts in the later part of the speech, an excellent demonstration of the way in which long speeches in Shakespeare are often graded so that the actor can build gradually through them, without needing to release the full intensity of passion all at once. This is especially important in cursing speeches, as here. Many of Suffolk's curses draw upon clichés—the *mandrake's groan*, *fixèd teeth*, *envy* in her cave, *poison*, *cypress trees*, *basilisks*, *serpent's hiss*, *screech-owls*, etc. (see the notes)—to such an extent that Margaret intervenes to stop him at l. 333. But having got all this out of his system, his language develops during the scene, moving to an expression of *desolation* (l. 368) and finally to the utter simplicity of 412 and 416, lines shared between the two of them as they part.

314 **mandrake's groan** The root of the poisonous *mandrake* was shaped like a human body; the popular superstition was that it shrieked when pulled out of the ground, causing the hearer to die or go mad.

315 **searching** piercing (as in probing a wound to examine it)

316 **curst** malignant

317 **fixèd** clenched

319 **lean-faced . . . cave** In Ovid's *Metamorphoses* 2.760–82, envy is personified as an emaciated old woman living in a cave filthy with blackened blood.

320 **My tongue . . . words** Suffolk would be so eager to utter his curses that his words would *stumble* over each other. Shakespeare elsewhere uses *stumble* to convey rapid speech: at *Love's Labour's Lost* 2.1.238–9: 'His tongue . . . Did stumble with haste'; and *Winter's Tale* 2.3.51–2: 'I let her run, | But she'll not stumble.'

earnest impassioned, violent (*OED a.* 1)

321 **like . . . flint** as flint when struck gives out a spark (as at *Two Noble Kinsmen* 5.6.61–3: 'what envious flint . . . darted a spark', when a horse's hooves strike the pavement)

My hair be fixed on end, as one distraught;
Ay, every joint should seem to curse and ban,
And even now my burdened heart would break
Should I not curse them. Poison be their drink!   325
Gall, worse than gall, the daintiest that they taste!
Their sweetest shade a grove of cypress trees!
Their chiefest prospect murd'ring basilisks!
Their softest touch as smart as lizards' stings!
Their music frightful as the serpent's hiss,   330
And boding screech-owls make the consort full!
All the foul terrors in dark-seated hell—

QUEEN MARGARET
Enough sweet Suffolk, thou torment'st thyself,
And these dread curses, like the sun 'gainst glass,
Or like an overchargèd gun, recoil   335
And turns the force of them upon thyself.

SUFFOLK
You bade me ban, and will you bid me leave?
Now by the ground that I am banished from,
Well could I curse away a winter's night,
Though standing naked on a mountain top,   340

---

322 My] Q; Mine F   on] F (an)   distraught] F (distract)

---

322 **My hair** Oxford gives several examples
of this phrase in Shakespeare, but F's
'*mine hair* occurs only here' (*Textual
Companion* p. 187).
fixed on end standing on end. Compare
modern 'hair-raising'.
distraught mentally deranged
323 **ban** Since *ban* means 'curse', it merely
reinforces *curse* earlier in the line. The
specifically religious meaning 'excommu-
nicate' (Cairncross) doesn't seem relevant
here or at l. 337.
326 **Gall . . . gall** Gall is a bitter fluid, the
secretion of the liver (*OED sb.*[1] 1), but it
was also used to mean 'poison' (*OED sb.*[1]
5), so the phrase probably means 'Poison,
more bitter even than bile'.
daintiest most delicious
327 **cypress trees** (because cypresses are
associated with graveyards, and so with
death, as at *Twelfth Night* 2 4.50–1: 'come
away death, | And in sad cypress let me
be laid')
328 **prospect** view (because when you look at

the *basilisk*, its stare kills you; see the note
to l. 52)
329 **smart** stinging, smarting
lizards' stings (thought to be poisonous,
since lizards were confused with snakes)
331 **boding** ominous, prophesying death
screech-owls Their screeching was considered ominous; compare *Dream* 5.2.6–
8: 'the screech-owl, screeching loud, |
Puts the wretch that lies in woe | In
remembrance of a shroud.'
make the consort full complete the group
of musicians
332 **dark-seated** situated in the dark
334 **like . . . glass** as if the sun were reflected
in a mirror, so dazzling the beholder.
The comparison is used again for the
heroine in *Cymbeline*: 'She shines
not upon fools lest the reflection should
hurt her' (1.2.31–2).
335 **overchargèd** overloaded. Elizabethan
firearms were notoriously unreliable, as
likely to injure their owners as the enemy.
337 **leave** leave off, cease

Where biting cold would never let grass grow,
And think it but a minute spent in sport.

QUEEN MARGARET

O let me entreat thee cease. Give me thy hand,
That I may dew it with my mournful tears;
Nor let the rain of heaven wet this place   345
To wash away my woeful monuments.

⌈*She kisses his palm*⌉

O could this kiss be printed in thy hand
That thou mightst think upon these lips by the seal,
Through whom a thousand sighs are breathed for thee!
So get thee gone, that I may know my grief.   350
'Tis but surmised whiles thou art standing by,
As one that surfeits thinking on a want.
I will repeal thee, or be well assured,
Adventure to be banishèd myself.
And banishèd I am, if but from thee.   355
Go, speak not to me; even now be gone.
O go not yet. Even thus two friends condemned
Embrace, and kiss, and take ten thousand leaves,

346.1 *She ... palm*] *not in* F   348 these lips] OXFORD; these F

343–416 Cairncross suggests that some of the language here may have been influenced by Ovid's account of his parting from his wife to go into exile, and his imagining his death there without her (*Tristia* 1.3, 3.3); Emrys Jones (*Origins*, p. 24) that the style was derived 'with impressionistic freedom' from another Ovid work, *Heroides*, a series of imaginary letters written by classical heroines parted from their lovers, a line from which is quoted at 3 *Henry VI* 1.3.48. The phrasing also looks forward to the other end of Shakespeare's career and another pair of lovers separated by a king, Posthumus and Innogen in *Cymbeline*. See the notes to ll. 356–7 and 413.

345 **rain of heaven** (as opposed to the rain from her eyes, tears). For the phrasing, compare Portia's 'gentle rain from heaven' at *Merchant* 4.1.182.

346 **woeful monuments** memorials of grief (i.e. her tear-stains). Tears are described as 'Poor wasting monuments' at *Lucrece* 797–8.

348–9 **thou ... thee** you might think about my lips which left their imprint (*seal*) on your hand, and through which a thousand sighs for you have passed. (By adding *lips* to F's line at 348, Oxford makes the sense clearer.)

350 **know** fully experience

351 **but surmised** only imagined, guessed at

352 **surfeits** overeats
    want lack of food

353 **repeal thee** have your banishment repealed

354 **Adventure to be** risk being

356–7 **be gone.** | **O go not yet** Margaret's contradicting herself, unable to bear letting Suffolk go, is a desperate reversal of the volte-face at their first meeting, when Suffolk, having captured her, magnanimously says 'Go, and be free', only to stop her: 'O stay! (*Aside*) I have no power to let her pass' (1 *Henry VI* 5.5.15–16). Her technique here anticipates that of Innogen in *Cymbeline* as she is forced to part from her husband Posthumus (1.1.109–12).

Loather a hundred times to part than die.
Yet now farewell, and farewell life with thee.   360
SUFFOLK
Thus is poor Suffolk ten times banishèd,
Once by the King, and three times thrice by thee.
'Tis not the land I care for, wert thou thence;
A wilderness is populous enough,
So Suffolk had thy heavenly company.   365
For where thou art, there is the world itself,
With every several pleasure in the world;
And where thou art not, desolation.
I can no more. Live thou to joy thy life;
Myself no joy in naught but that thou liv'st.   370
        Enter Vaux
QUEEN MARGARET
Whither goes Vaux so fast? What news, I prithee?
VAUX
To signify unto his majesty
That Cardinal Beaufort is at point of death.
For suddenly a grievous sickness took him
That makes him gasp, and stare, and catch the air,   375
Blaspheming God and cursing men on earth.
Sometime he talks as if Duke Humphrey's ghost
Were by his side; sometime he calls the King,
And whispers to his pillow, as to him,
The secrets of his overchargèd soul;   380
And I am sent to tell his majesty
That even now he cries aloud for him.

---

363 **wert thou thence** if you were not there
365 **So** provided that
367 **several** individual
369 **I can no more** See the note to l. 120.
    joy enjoy
370 **no . . . naught** An Elizabethan double negative, used for emphasis (Abbott 406).
371 **Vaux** Perhaps Sir William Vaux, a Lancastrian killed at the battle of Tewkesbury in 1471, though Shakespeare's chronicle sources do not mention him. Q's spelling 'Vawse' indicates the pronunciation (i.e. not as in French).
372 **signify** make known

373 **That . . . death** Retribution is catching up swiftly with those who engineered Duke Humphrey's death. See the next note.
375 **gasp . . . air** These details echo Warwick's conjectural description of how Duke Humphrey died (ll. 170–3).
377–8 **Sometime . . . sometime** from time to time
379–80 **whispers . . . soul** Compare *Macbeth* 5.1.69–70. 'Infected minds | To their deaf pillows will discharge their secrets.'
380 **overchargèd** overburdened. Compare *Macbeth* 5.1.51: 'The heart is sorely charged.'

QUEEN MARGARET

   Go tell this heavy message to the King.   *Exit Vaux*

   Ay me! What is this world? What news are these?

   But wherefore grieve I at an hour's poor loss,   385

   Omitting Suffolk's exile, my soul's treasure?

   Why only, Suffolk, mourn I not for thee,

   And with the southern clouds contend in tears—

   Theirs for the earth's increase, mine for my sorrow's?

   Now get thee hence. The King, thou know'st, is coming.   390

   If thou be found by me, thou art but dead.

SUFFOLK

   If I depart from thee, I cannot live.

   And in thy sight to die, what were it else

   But like a pleasant slumber in thy lap?

   Here could I breathe my soul into the air,   395

   As mild and gentle as the cradle babe

   Dying with mother's dug between it lips;

   Where, from thy sight, I should be raging mad,

   And cry out for thee to close up mine eyes,

   To have thee with thy lips to stop my mouth,   400

   So shouldst thou either turn my flying soul

397 it] This edition; it's F; his Q

384 **Ay me . . . these** As one piece of bad news follows another, Margaret's momentary sense of disorientation, and the rhythm that expresses it, anticipate the revived Thaisa at *Pericles* Sc. 12.103: 'Where am I? Where's my lord? What world is this?'

385 **an hour's poor loss** (because the elderly Cardinal would not have had much more life than that in him anyway; Lord Talbot makes a similar point at *1 Henry VI* 4.6.36–7: 'By me they nothing gain, and if I stay | 'Tis but the short'ning of my life one day.')

386 **Omitting** forgetting

387 **Why . . . thee** Why do I not mourn for you alone, Suffolk?

388 **southern clouds** (which were supposed to bring rain)
    contend compete

389 **increase** crops

391 **by me** at my side
    art but are as good as

393, 404 **die** As well as the usual sense, *die* in Elizabethan English could also mean 'experience orgasm', as at *Much Ado* 5.2.92, 'die in thy lap', where *lap* also has a sexual connotation.

397 **dug** nipple
    it Arguing that 'its' as a possessive does not appear in Shakespeare's work earlier than *Winter's Tale* 1.2.159, Oxford replace F's 'its' with Q's 'his'. But I think F is a misreading of 'it', an early form of the genitive 'its', which Shakespeare often uses in contexts involving children, for example in Hermione's reference to her baby, the 'innocent milk in it most innocent mouth' (*Winter's Tale* 3.2.99). It would not be surprising if the Q reporter substituted the more familiar 'his'.

398 **Where** whereas
    from out of

401 **turn my flying soul** i.e. stop my soul from escaping out of my mouth, back into my body (and so prevent me dying)

Or I should breathe it, so, into thy body—
⌈*He kisseth her*⌉
And then it lived in sweet Elysium.
To die by thee were but to die in jest;
From thee to die were torture more than death.   405
O let me stay, befall what may befall!

QUEEN MARGARET
Away. Though parting be a fretful corrosive,
It is applièd to a deathful wound.
To France, sweet Suffolk. Let me hear from thee.
For wheresoe'er thou art in this world's globe   410
I'll have an Iris that shall find thee out.

SUFFOLK
I go.

QUEEN MARGARET And take my heart with thee.
⌈*She kisseth him*⌉

SUFFOLK
A jewel, locked into the woefull'st cask
That ever did contain a thing of worth.

402.1 *He kisseth her*] *not in* F   412.1 *She kisseth him*] Q; *not in* F

402 **Or . . . body** For the idea of a kiss
drawing a soul from one lover to another,
compare Marlowe's *Faustus*, speaking of
Helen of Troy: 'Her lips sucks forth my
soul' (A-text, 5.1.94).
403 **lived** would live
Elysium (the heaven of classical
mythology)
404 **but . . . jest** i.e. not to die at all
405 **From** away from
torture more a greater torture
406 **befall . . . befall** whatever may happen.
Proverbial: 'Come (befall) what come
(befall) may' (Dent C529), also used at
Titus 5.1.57 and *Love's Labour's Lost*
5.2.856.
407 **fretful corrosive** physically irritating
remedy (*OED, corrosive, sb.* 2b). *Corrosive*
is also used by Joan of Arc at *1 Henry
VI* 3.7.3, though there in the sense of
'destroying, eating away' (*OED a.* 1).
These are the only occurrences of *corrosive* in Shakespeare, and may have been
suggested by a phrase in Holinshed
describing the grief of Edward IV's queen

Elizabeth as 'a corrosive to a noble mind'
(iii. 300). In the plays, it is stressed on the
first rather than the second syllable.
408 **deathful** deadly
411 **Iris** The classical goddess of the rainbow,
and the messenger of Juno, queen of the
gods.
412 **take . . . thee** With this line, Margaret
cuts herself off from Henry and from
tender feelings: from now on, her heart
is hardened.
413 **A jewel** i.e. her heart. Compare
Innogen's lines about her husband at
Cymbeline 1.1.91–3 as she is forced to part
from him: she is 'not comforted to live |
But that there is this jewel in the world |
That I may see again'. Shakespeare expresses the intensity and desperation
of two enforced partings in similar
language. See the note to l. 356–7.
into in (Abbott 159)
cask casket, i.e. his body. 'Apparently
the only occurrence of this form in
Shakespeare, though he uses "casket"
frequently' (McKerrow).

Even as a splitted barque, so sunder we: 415
This way fall I to death.
QUEEN MARGARET   This way for me.

Exeunt severally

3.3   *Enter King Henry and the Earls of Salisbury and
Warwick. Then the curtains be drawn and Cardinal
Beaufort is discovered in his bed raving and staring as if
he were mad.* ⌈*Bed put forth*⌉

KING HENRY
How fares my lord? Speak, Beaufort, to thy sovereign.
CARDINAL BEAUFORT
If thou beest death, I'll give thee England's treasure
Enough to purchase such another island,
So thou wilt let me live and feel no pain.
KING HENRY
Ah, what a sign it is of evil life   5
Where death's approach is seen so terrible.
WARWICK
Beaufort, it is thy sovereign speaks to thee.
CARDINAL BEAUFORT
Bring me unto my trial when you will.
Died he not in his bed? Where should he die?
Can I make men live whe'er they will or no?   10
O torture me no more, I will confess.

416.1 *severally*] not in F
  3.3.0.1–2 *Enter . . . Warwick*] *Enter the King, Salisbury, and Warwicke, to the Cardinal in bed.* F
0.2–4 *Then . . . mad*] Q (subs.)   0.4 *Bed put forth*] not in F, Q

---

415 **splitted barque** ship split in two
   sunder part
3.3.0.1–4 *Enter . . . forth* This stage direction is largely from Q (see collation). The
   curtains are presumably those of a 'discovery space' in the back wall of the
   stage, or across one of the two doors set
   into that wall on either side. Neither F nor
   Q has the bed '*put forth*', as Humphrey's is
   in F at 3.2.146.2, but it seems inconceivable that a scene as important as this
   should take place in a restricted space
   as far as possible from the majority of the
   audience (and actually invisible from

those at the sides). So I assume that after
the *curtains be drawn*, the Cardinal's bed is
put forth by the servants who draw the
curtains (see McKerrow's note cited at the
Commentary to 3.2.146.1–2). It might be
thought clumsy for Duke Humphrey's bed
to be *put forth*, removed, and then exactly
the same happen to the Cardinal's—but
this in fact emphasizes the dramatic irony
that Humphrey's death leads directly to
that of one of those who contrived it.
4 **So if**
9 **he** i.e. Humphrey
10 **whe'er . . . no** See the note to 3.2.267.

Alive again? Then show me where he is.
I'll give a thousand pound to look upon him.
He hath no eyes! The dust hath blinded them.
Comb down his hair—look, look, it stands upright,   15
Like lime twigs set to catch my wingèd sou..
Give me some drink, and bid the apothecary
Bring the strong poison that I bought of him.

KING HENRY

O thou eternal mover of the heavens,
Look with a gentle eye upon this wretch.   20
O beat away the busy meddling fiend
That lays strong siege unto this wretch's soul,
And from his bosom purge this black despair.

WARWICK

See how the pangs of death do make him grin.

SALISBURY

Disturb him not, let him pass peaceably.   25

KING HENRY

Peace to his soul, if God's good pleasure be.
Lord Card'nal, if thou think'st on heaven's bliss,

---

13 **a thousand pound** A much larger sum then than now, but in any case it is a common phrase simply meaning 'a great deal of money' (Dent T248.1), and is frequently so used in Shakespeare, e.g. *Merry Wives* 3.3.115–16: 'I had rather than a thousand pound he were out of the house.'

14 **He hath no eyes** The horrific eyeless spectre of Humphrey resembles that of Banquo at *Macbeth* 3.4.94: 'Thou hast no speculation [sight] in those eyes'. Perhaps the hint came from the eyeless socket of a skull.

  dust Perhaps the dust to which man returns at death (Hattaway).

15 **upright** on end (as Warwick points out that it does at 3.2.171)

16 **Like . . . soul** This repeats the bird-catching image from 1.3.89 (see the note) and 2.4.54–5 (where Humphrey's wife specifically warns him against the Cardinal: now the Cardinal suffers the same fate as his victim).

  wingèd (because the soul was thought to

fly out from the body in which it had been imprisoned at death; compare *flying soul* at 3.2.401)

17–18 **bid . . . him** What does the Cardinal want the poison for? Hardly to kill himself, since he finds the approach of death so terrible (ll. 2–6); perhaps in his delirium he hopes to dispose of Humphrey's ghost that way; or perhaps the lines are simply there to emphasize that the Cardinal is the kind of man who uses strong poisons (i.e. is a murderer).

18 **of** from

19 **mover** In medieval astronomy, God was seen as the '*primum mobile*', or first mover, of the universe (*OED, mover*[1], 2a).

21 **meddling** interfering (with men's souls)

22 **lays strong siege** (as if attacking a castle)

24 **pangs of death** The phrase is biblical: 2 Samuel 22: 5.

  grin bare his teeth (as at 3.1.18—another link between the Cardinal's dying agony and the baiting of Humphrey)

25 **pass** die

Hold up thy hand, make signal of thy hope.
Cardinal Beaufort dies
He dies and makes no sign. O God forgive him.

KING HENRY

WARWICK

So bad a death argues a monstrous life.   30

KING HENRY

Forbear to judge, for we are sinners all.
Close up his eyes and draw the curtain close,
And let us all to meditation.
            Exeunt. ⌜*The bed is removed and*⌝ *the curtains drawn*

4.1   *Alarums within, and the chambers be discharged like as*
        it were a fight at sea. And then enter the Lieutenant, the
        Master, the Master's Mate, Walter Whitmore, ⌜*and*
        others⌝. *With them, as their prisoners, the Duke of*
        Suffolk, disguised, and two gentlemen

LIEUTENANT

The gaudy, blabbing, and remorseful day

28.1 *Cardinal . . . dies*] Q (*subs.*); *not in* F   33.1 *The bed . . . drawn*] *not in* F
    4.1.0.1–2 *Alarums . . . sea*] Q; *Alarum. Fight at Sea. Ordnance goes off.* F   0.2–5 *And then . . .*
gentlemen] Q (*subs., but with* 'Captaine of the ship' *for* 'Lieutenant') ; *Enter Lieutenant, Suffolke,*
and others. F   1 LIEUTENANT] F; *Cap<tain>.* Q (*throughout scene*)

28 **Hold up thy hand** (to make a solemn declaration, as when undertaking to tell the
truth in a modern law-court)
    make signal give a sign. Henry tries to
make it easier for the dying man by not
asking him to speak.
    hope (of salvation)
30 **argues** gives evidence of
31 **Forbear to judge** Henry echoes the biblical
prohibition 'Judge not, that ye be not
judged' (Matthew 7: 1). He might appear
to contradict his own lines 5–6; or perhaps he is rebuking himself for what he
said then as much as reproving Warwick.
The phrase gives a good idea of the range
of interpretation of which the role is
capable: for David Warner at Stratford-
upon-Avon in 1963–4 it was full of quiet
humility; but for Alan Howard there in
1977 it was an intense rebuke to
Warwick, unleashed with tremendous
vocal power.
    for . . . all Another biblical echo: 'for all
have sinned' (Romans 3: 23).
32 **Close . . . eyes** (the traditional last office of
respect for the dead)

33 **meditation** prayer
4.1 For a discussion of this scene as a transition between the court world and that of
Cade's rebellion, see the Introduction,
pp. 50–1.
0.1–5 *Alarums . . . gentlemen* This stage
direction substantially follows Q. F's
'*Alarum. Fight at Sea. Ordnance* [cannon]
goes off' is a characteristically authorial
one, the dramatist impressionistically
dashing down the sound effects needed
before the characters enter; when they
do, Q specifies all the characters needed as
F does not. Q mentions Walter Whitmore
last, perhaps implying that he follows the
prisoners, guarding them.
0.1 *Alarums* A standard term in stage
directions for sounds of trumpets and/or
drums to indicate an attack.
    chambers small cannons used to fire
salutes
    discharged fired
0.2 *Lieutenant* He is called 'Captain' in Q,
the chronicles, and even in F's version of
the scene at l. 66. For further discussion,
see Textual Introduction, pp. 91–2.

Is crept into the bosom of the sea;
And now loud-howling wolves arouse the jades
That drag the tragic melancholy night;
Who with their drowsy, slow, and flagging wings   5
Clip dead men's graves, and from their misty jaws
Breathe foul contagious darkness in the air.
Therefore bring forth the soldiers of our prize,

6 Clip] F (Cleape)

0.3 *Walter Whitmore* Both this character
and the prophecy he was created to ful-
fil (1.4.32–3) are the invention of the
dramatist. The name 'Walter' was often
pronounced 'Water' in Shakespeare's
day; it is spelt like that throughout Q's
scene and even in F at ll. 115 and 139.1,
and 'it is quite possible that the [F] MS
spelt "Water" throughout' (McKerrow)
but was sophisticated by Compositor B,
who did the same thing when setting
Richard III 5.8.14 (*Textual Companion*,
p. 187).

1–7 Shakespeare's authorship of these lines
has been questioned; but G. R. Hibbard
shows how they anticipate *Lucrece*
764–812 and *Macbeth* 3.2.37–57 (*The
Making of Shakespeare's Dramatic Poetry*
(Toronto, 1981), pp. 24–9, 32–51); other
connections are noted below.

1 **gaudy** excessively bright. Adonis needs to
wear a hat to protect himself from the
'gaudy sun' at *Venus* 1088.
  blabbing tell-tale (revealing the secrets of
the dark, as at *Lucrece* 747, where 'day . . .
night's scapes doth open lay')
  remorseful conscience-stricken (presumably for revealing the secrets of the night)

2 **Is crept . . . sea** i.e. has set. 'He will creep
into your bosom' is proverbial (Dent
B546) and is used at *1 Henry IV* 1.3.262;
the idiom 'creep into' is frequent in
Shakespeare, and recurs at l. 102.
Richard III refers to 'the deep bosom of
the ocean' at the start of his play (1.1.4).

3 **loud-howling wolves** Howling wolves are
associated with night, as at *Dream* 5.2.2:
'the wolf behowls the moon'. Presumably
the wolves need to *arouse* the *jades* (see
next note) because they are *flagging* and
so not drawing night's chariot quickly
enough.
  jades This is usually a contemptuous
reference to horses, but here it must refer

to the dragons (presumably with similar
contempt) that drew the chariot of night,
as *flagging wings* at l. 5 makes clear. Compare *Dream* 3.2.380: 'night's swift dragons cut the clouds full fast'. The origin of
both passages is Ovid's *Metamorphoses*
7.179–237, where the sorceress Medea is
transported in a dragon-drawn chariot
sent by Night, a passage which also forms
the basis of Prospero's renunciation of
his magic at *Tempest* 5.1.41–50.

5 **flagging** drooping (presumably because
they are tired from drawing the chariot)

6 **Clip** embrace, encircle (*OED v.*[1] 1 and 2):
as the huge, beating wings droop downwards, they hover over the gravestones
and seem to embrace them. But Dover
Wilson conjectures that F's 'cleape'
may represent an obsolete verb 'clepe',
meaning summon (*OED v.* 2), glossing
'Night summons the dead from their
graves, which already begin to yawn'.
This would certainly fit another detail in
the passage from *Metamorphoses* from
which these lines partly derive, Medea's
admission that she has called the dead
from their graves (7.206), and with
Hamlet 3.2.378–9: 'churchyards yawn,
and hell itself breathes out | Contagion to
this world', a passage which, like this one,
seems deliberately over-written. In this
interpretation, the *misty jaws* spreading
contagion would be those of the dead, not
of the dragons, as the next note assumes.
  misty The smoke from the dragons' fiery
mouths looks like mist.

7 **contagious** causing diseases. At *Dream*
2.1.89–90 Titania speaks of 'contagious
fogs' which have been 'sucked up from
the sea'.

8 **soldiers of our prize** those captured from
the vessel we have taken. But *soldiers*
seems odd here; does it mean 'those who
stood up to us'? There is another unusual
use of *soldiers* at l. 133; see the note.

For whilst our pinnace anchors in the downs
Here shall they make their ransom on the sand,   10
Or with their blood stain this discoloured shore.
Master, (*pointing to the First Gentleman*) this prisoner
    freely give I thee,
(*To the Mate*) And thou that art his mate, make boot of
    this.
        He points to the Second Gentleman
    (*To Walter Whitmore*)
The other (*pointing to Suffolk*), Walter Whitmore, is thy
    share.
FIRST GENTLEMAN (*to the Master*)
What is my ransom, Master, let me know.   15
MASTER
A thousand crowns, or else lay down your head.
MATE (*to the Second Gentleman*)
And so much shall you give, or off goes yours.
LIEUTENANT (*to both the Gentlemen*)
What, think you much to pay two thousand crowns,
And bear the name and port of gentlemen?
⌈WHITMORE⌉
Cut both the villains' throats, ⌈*to prisoners*⌉ for die you
    shall.   20
The lives of those which we have lost in fight
⌈   ⌉
Be counterpoised with such a petty sum.

12 *pointing . . . Gentleman*] *not in* F   13.1 *He . . . Gentleman*] *not in* F   14 *pointing to Suffolk*] *not in* F   20 WHITMORE Cut] OXFORD (*conj.* Malone 1821); Cut F

9 **pinnace** a small, light boat. At first this appears a surprising vessel to use; in the chronicles a warship attacked Suffolk's ship. But *pinnace* may be intended to suggest a *pirate* ship. According to *The Naval Tracts of Sir William Monson*, drawn up between 1585 and 1603, pirates 'first cut down their half decks, and all other weighty things overhead [so that] no ship is able to equal them in going' (cited by A. F. Falconer, *Shakespeare and the Sea* (1964), p. 52)—i.e. it can move very fast.
downs (an anchorage off the coast of Kent, sheltered by the Goodwin Sands)
11 **stain this discoloured shore** discolour this shore (with their blood)

13 **boot of** profit from
16 **crowns** (coins worth five shillings each)
19 **port** life-style
20–3 These lines are part of the previous speech in F; but Malone's suggestion that Whitmore intervenes is probably right: the Lieutenant urges 'Be not so rash, take ransom, let him live' at l. 29, so these lines seem inappropriate to him, but very apt to Whitmore, in view of l. 28. Malone also suggested that a line was missing, hence the lacuna marked in this edition. Ll. 21–3 do not make sense as they stand: something along the lines of 'will not adequately' is needed.
23 **counterpoised** compensated

FIRST GENTLEMAN (*to the Master*)
    I'll give it, sir, and therefore spare my life.
SECOND GENTLEMAN (*to the Mate*)
    And so will I, and write home for it straight.   25
WHITMORE (*to Suffolk*)
    I lost mine eye in laying the prize aboard,
    And therefore to revenge it, shalt thou die,
    And so should these, if I might have my will.
LIEUTENANT
    Be not so rash, take ransom, let him live.
SUFFOLK
    Look on my George; I am a gentleman.   30
    Rate me at what thou wilt, thou shalt be paid.
WHITMORE
    And so am I; my name is Walter Whitmore.
        Suffolk starteth
    How now? Why starts thou? What doth thee affright?
SUFFOLK
    Thy name affrights me, in whose sound is death.
    A cunning man did calculate my birth,   35
    And told me that by water I should die.
    Yet let not this make thee be bloody-minded;
    Thy name is Gualtier, being rightly sounded.
WHITMORE
    Gualtier or Walter, which it is I care not.
    Never yet did base dishonour blur our name   40

32.1 *Suffolk starteth*] Q (He starteth.); *not in* F   33 thee] CAIRNCROSS (*conj.* Vaughan); death F

---

25 **straight** immediately
26 **laying . . . aboard** boarding the captured ship (by bringing his own ship alongside it): *OED, aboard, adv.* 2c.
30 **George** A badge showing St George, 'the principal jewel of the insignia of the Order of the Garter' (McKerrow).
31 **Rate** value
33 **starts** 'In verbs ending with -*t*, -*test* . . . the second person singular often becomes -*ts* for euphony' (Abbott 340).
    What . . . affright? F's phrase, punctuated to read 'what, doth death affright?' makes sense, but lessens the impact of the next line: *Thy name affrights me* is a natural reply to *What doth thee affright?*,

and it is likely that the compositor's eye was caught by *death* in the next line.
35 **cunning** skilful (i.e. an astrologer)
    calculate my birth cast my horoscope
36 **And . . . die** Although the audience will naturally relate this to the spirit's prophecy at 1.4.32–3, Suffolk alludes to a quite different kind of prophecy, which is an argument against the Quarto's repositioning of the reading of the spirit's prophecy to 2.1.172, where Suffolk can hear and comment on it. See the Textual Introduction, p. 90.
38 **Gualtier** (the French form of 'Walter')
    sounded pronounced
40–4 **Never . . . world** Whitmore claims to be

But with our sword we wiped away the blot.
Therefore, when merchant-like I sell revenge,
Broke be my sword, my arms torn and defaced,
And I proclaimed a coward through the world.

SUFFOLK

Stay, Whitmore, for thy prisoner is a prince,   45
The Duke of Suffolk, William de la Pole.

WHITMORE

The Duke of Suffolk muffled up in rags?

SUFFOLK

Ay, but these rags are no part of the Duke.
Jove sometime went disguised, and why not I?

LIEUTENANT

But Jove was never slain as thou shalt be.   50

SUFFOLK

Obscure and lousy swain, King Henry's blood,
The honourable blood of Lancaster,
Must not be shed by such a jady groom.

49 Jove . . . I] Q; *not in* F   51 SUFFOLK] Q; *not in* F   52 The] Q; *Suf<folke>*. The F   53 jady] Q
(Iadie); iaded F

a gentleman, who is bound by the aristocratic code to take revenge for the loss of
his eye, unlike a merchant who would
agree to a ransom for financial gain, an
attitude Whitmore despises.

43 **arms** coat of arms (a sign of a gentleman)
torn and defaced obliterated (a heraldic
way of disgracing a gentleman, as at
Richard II 3.1.24–7: 'torn my household
coat, . . . leaving me no sign . . . To show
the world I am a gentleman')

49–51 **Jove . . . blood** There is confusion in
the Folio text here: l. 49, present in the
Quarto, is omitted, obviously by accident,
as it is required by l. 50; then the first line
of Suffolk's next speech (l. 51) is tacked on
to the end of the Lieutenant's. A possible
explanation is offered in the Textual Introduction, p. 92.

49 **Jove . . . disguised** Jove (Jupiter, the King
of the Roman gods) frequently assumed
the shape of mortals or animals, usually
to seduce mortal women (summarized in
Ovid's *Metamorphoses* 6.103–14).

50 At first sight this seems inconsistent with
his attitude at l. 29; but he presumably

changes his mind when he realizes that
his prisoner is Suffolk, in whose service he
seems to have been employed (ll. 54–65).

51 **lousy** Literally 'infested with lice', the
word was then as now a common term of
abuse (*OED a.* 2).
swain peasant
King Henry's blood Suffolk's mother was
a distant relative of Henry VI; he is claiming royal blood in order to intensify the
distance between himself and the *swain*
he is addressing.

53 **jady** Oxford adopts Q's '*jady*', meaning
'tricky' (*OED a.*) rather than F's 'jaded',
meaning 'worn out' (*OED ppl. a.* 1, 3).
Both make sense; both are derived from
'jade', a contemptuous word for a horse,
and so fit well with *groom*; perhaps *jady*
emphasizes Suffolk's contempt. Oxford
comments: 'Q repeats "Iadie" at 4.1.[129]
. . . , in place of F's "Vulgar"; Q thus
gives double warrant for a form not otherwise recorded until 1873. F's word, by
contrast, is common. We have accepted
Q as the rarer reading, of which F
might easily be a corruption' (*Textual
Companion*, p. 187).

Hast thou not kissed thy hand and held my stirrup,
Bare-headed plodded by my foot-cloth mule   55
And thought thee happy when I shook my head?
How often hast thou waited at my cup,
Fed from my trencher, kneeled down at the board
When I have feasted with Queen Margaret?
Remember it, and let it make thee crestfall'n,   60
Ay, and allay this thy abortive pride,
How in our voiding lobby hast thou stood
And duly waited for my coming forth.
This hand of mine hath writ in thy behalf,
And therefore shall it charm thy riotous tongue.   65

WHITMORE
Speak Captain, shall I stab the forlorn swain?

LIEUTENANT
First let my words stab him as he hath me.

SUFFOLK
Base slave, thy words are blunt and so art thou.

LIEUTENANT
Convey him hence, and on our longboat's side
Strike off his head.

SUFFOLK   Thou dar'st not for thy own.   70

---

54 **kissed thy hand** (a gesture of servility). At
    Love's Labour's Lost 5.2.324, a courtier is
    said to have 'kissed his hand away in
    courtesy'.
55 **Bare-headed** (a gesture of respect)
    foot-cloth ornamental draperies worn by
    horses, stretching to the ground
56 **happy** fortunate
    shook nodded (i.e. gave the slightest sign
    of recognition)
58 **trencher** dinner plate
    board dining table
60 **crestfall'n** humble (mockingly punning
    on 'deprived of a crest', a coat-of-arms)
61 **allay** moderate, lessen
    abortive fruitless, useless (*OED a.* 2)
62 **How** (i.e. remember how)
    voiding lobby waiting room (where
    petitioners waited for a lord as he was
    voiding—leaving—the main chamber)

63 **duly** dutifully
64 **writ in thy behalf** written references for
    you
65 **charm** silence
    riotous unrestrained
66 **forlorn** wretched
    swain Is Whitmore turning Suffolk's own
    insult (l. 51) back on him? Or, if *forlorn
    swain* carries its other sense of 'lover', as
    at *Two Gentlemen* 5.4.12, is he gibing
    at Suffolk's affair with Margaret, as the
    Lieutenant does at l. 75?
68 **blunt** harmless (because lacking edge)
69 **Convey . . . hence** take him away
    longboat 'The largest boat belonging to a
    sailing vessel' (*OED*): presumably the boat
    in which they have come ashore from the
    pinnace of l. 9.
70 **for thy own** because you risk losing your
    own head in reprisal

LIEUTENANT
  Pole—
⌈SUFFOLK⌉ Pole?
LIEUTENANT   Ay, kennel, puddle, sink, whose filth and dirt
  Troubles the silver spring where England drinks,
  Now will I dam up this thy yawning mouth
  For swallowing the treasure of the realm.
  Thy lips that kissed the Queen shall sweep the ground,   75
  And thou that smiled'st at good Duke Humphrey's death
  Against the senseless winds shall grin in vain,
  Who in contempt shall hiss at thee again.
  And wedded be thou to the hags of hell,
  For daring to affy a mighty lord   80
  Unto the daughter of a worthless king,
  Having neither subject, wealth, nor diadem.
  By devilish policy art thou grown great,
  And like ambitious Sulla, overgorged
  With gobbets of thy mother's bleeding heart.   85
  By thee Anjou and Maine were sold to France.
  The false revolting Normans, thorough thee,

---

71 LIEUTENANT . . . LIEUTENANT] ALEXANDER (*conj.* McKerrow); *Lieu. Poole*, *Sir Poole?* Lord, F
84 Sulla] F (Sylla)   85 mother's bleeding] ROWE; Mother-bleeding F

---

71 **Pole . . . kennel** F muddles this exchange (see collation), but is easily corrected, as McKerrow and Alexander independently did (see the Textual Introduction, p. 91). The Lieutenant responds to Suffolk's insults by calling Suffolk by his family name, rather than according to his rank; Suffolk is outraged: 'Pole?'; then, since 'Pole' was pronounced 'pool', the Lieutenant's punning insults follow. Since this correction of F is so simple and satisfactory, there is no need to complicate the issue by drafting in material from Q, as some editors do, especially since a passage of invective like this lends itself to embroidering in the performing and/or reporting.
    kennel street gutter, used as an open drain (*OED sb.*²). Q reverses *kennel* and *puddle* in this line, and, since this meaning of *kennel* is no longer current, it might be

helpful in modern performance to follow Q's order, thus instantly establishing the punning on 'pool'.
    sink cesspit, sewer
72 **Troubles** muddies
73 **yawning** devouring (*OED ppl. a.* 1)
77 **senseless** unfeeling
78 **at thee again** back at you
79 **hags of hell** the classical Furies
80 **affy** betroth, affiance
82 **diadem** crown
83 **policy** See the second note to 3.1.23.
84 **Sulla** Lucius Cornelius Sulla (138–78 BC) was notorious for the ruthless slaughter of his political opponents.
    overgorged overfed
85 **gobbets** chunks of flesh
    mother's country's: i.e. England's in Suffolk's case, Rome in Sulla's
87 **revolting** rebellious
    thorough through, because of

Disdain to call us lord, and Picardy
Hath slain their governors, surprised our forts,
And sent the ragged soldiers wounded home.   90
The princely Warwick and the Nevilles all,
Whose dreadful swords were never drawn in vain,
As hating thee, are rising up in arms;
And now the house of York, thrust from the crown
By shameful murder of a guiltless king   95
And lofty, proud, encroaching tyranny,
Burns with revenging fire, whose hopeful colours
Advance our half-faced sun, striving to shine,
Under the which is writ, '*Invitis nubibus*'.
The commons here in Kent are up in arms,   100
And to conclude, reproach and beggary
Is crept into the palace of our King,
And all by thee. (*To Whitmore*) Away, convey him hence.

SUFFOLK

O that I were a god, to shoot forth thunder
Upon these paltry, servile, abject drudges.   105
Small things make base men proud. This villain here,
Being captain of a pinnace, threatens more
Than Bardulis, the strong Illyrian pirate.

---

93 are] ROWE; *and* F   108 Bardulis . . . pirate] F (*Bargulus*); mightie Abradas, | The great Masadonian Pyrate Q

88–9 **Picardy . . . forts** This appears to be
the dramatist's invention, as there is no
account of a rebellion in Picardy in the
chronicles.
95 **guiltless King** Richard II
96 **encroaching tyranny** i.e. Bolingbroke's,
in usurping Richard's throne. See
2.2.19–27.
97 **colours** banners
98 **Advance** raise, display
   our half-faced sun The emblem of Edward
III and Richard II showed the sun's rays
emerging from a cloud. As Oxford says,
our is odd (*Textual Companion*, p. 187),
unless the Lieutenant is asserting that he
is a Yorkist.
99 *Invitis nubibus* 'In spite of clouds.' This
Latin phrase has not been identified.
100 **The commons . . . arms** This prepares
for Jack Cade's rebellion in the following
scenes, where the Lieutenant's reflection

of popular indignation, for example at the
loss of France, is greatly reinforced.
104 **a god** Jupiter, king of the gods, who
hurled thunderbolts
105 **abject drudges** contemptible slaves
107 **Being** i.e. being merely
108 **Bardulis . . . pirate** Bardulis was a notorious pirate who defied the power
of Rome, as this 'pirate' defies Suffolk:
he is mentioned in Cicero's *De Officiis*
2.11.40, a standard textbook in
Elizabethan schools. Oxford suggests that
F's phrase derives from Cicero's juxtaposition of '*archipirata*' with '*Bardulis Illyrius
Iatro*' (*Textual Companion*, p. 188). F's
spelling 'Bargulus' derives from transla-
tions using Renaissance Latin editions,
and should not be retained in a modernized edition. For a discussion of Q's
alternative version, see the Textual
Introduction, pp. 92–3.

Drones suck not eagles' blood, but rob beehives.
It is impossible that I should die   110
By such a lowly vassal as thyself.
Thy words move rage, and not remorse in me.
I go of message from the Queen to France:
I charge thee, waft me safely cross the Channel.

LIEUTENANT Walter—   115

WHITMORE
Come Suffolk, I must waft thee to thy death.

SUFFOLK
Paene gelidus timor occupat artus—
It is thee I fear.

WHITMORE
Thou shalt have cause to fear before I leave thee.
What, are ye daunted now? Now will ye stoop?   120

FIRST GENTLEMAN (*to Suffolk*)
My gracious lord, entreat him, speak him fair.

---

115 16 Walter—| WHITMORE Come] F (Water : W. Come)   117 *Paene*] MALONE; *Pine* F

109 **Drones . . . beehives** Both the beliefs
mentioned here, that the drone beetle
sucks the eagle's blood and that the drone
(male) bee eats the honey of the hives, are
from folklore rather than natural history.
Suffolk distinguishes between the beetle,
one of the lowest forms of life, and the
eagle, one of the highest, to imply that the
Lieutenant (the drone) has no power to
spill his blood (the eagle's), as the next
lines emphasize.
111 **By** by the hand of
vassal base or abject person; slave.
Knowles points out that the first occurrence of this pejorative sense recorded
by *OED* (*sb.* and *a.* 3) is from Greene's
Menaphon (1589), where it occurs shortly
before the phrase echoed in Q's version
of line 108. *Menaphon* seems to be in
Shakespeare's mind during the early
1590s, since he gives the name to the
Duke's uncle at *Errors* 5.1.370.
112 **remorse** compunction of conscience
(Schmidt). Suffolk is replying to the
Lieutenant's accusations: he is not sorry
for anything that he has done.
112–13 Between these lines, several editors
interpolate a version of Q's line, 'Ay,
but my deeds shall stay thy fury soon'

(l. 1521); but the policy of this edition is
not to insert readings from Q unless there
is a problem with F (as at l. 49), which
is not the case here. Moreover, the reporting of this scene so rearranges the sequence that this line may well be an insert
intended to hold a shakily-remembered
scene together.
113 **of** on (often interchanged in Elizabethan
usage: Abbott 175)
114, 116 **waft** convey across water (*OED v.*[1]
2); Whitmore turns the word to a more
sinister sense (*OED, waftage*, 2b), as he
seems to take on something of the linea-
ments of the classical boatman Charon
who ferried the dead across the river Styx
to Hades; perhaps he assumes the semi-
mythical status hinted at for this one-eyed
bringer of death throughout the scene.
115 **Walter** The Lieutenant seems to be in-
structing Whitmore to deal with Suffolk:
no further detail is needed.
117 **Paene . . . artus** cold fear almost over-
powers my limbs. This seems a conflation,
or confusion, of two classical quotations:
'*subitus tremor occupat artus*' (Virgil,
Aeneid 7.446) and '*gelidos pavor occupat
artus*' (Lucan, *Pharsalia* 1.246).
121 **fair** politely

SUFFOLK

   Suffolk's imperial tongue is stern and rough,
   Used to command, untaught to plead for favour.
   Far be it we should honour such as these
   With humble suit. No, rather let my head   125
   Stoop to the block than these knees bow to any
   Save to the God of heaven and to my king;
   And sooner dance upon a bloody pole
   Than stand uncovered to the vulgar groom.
   True nobility is exempt from fear;   130
   More can I bear than you dare execute.

LIEUTENANT

   Hale him away, and let him talk no more.

SUFFOLK

   Come soldiers, show what cruelty ye can,
   That this my death may never be forgot.
   Great men oft die by vile Bezonians;   135
   A Roman sworder and banditto slave

133 SUFFOLK Come] HANMER; Come F   134 That] HANMER; *Suf.* That F

122–39 **Suffolk's . . . pirates** Suffolk's climactic speeches underline an interesting aspect of his behaviour in this scene. On the one hand, he 'starts' at Whitmore's name, and says that he fears him; on the other, he seems to do everything he can to provoke Whitmore and the Lieutenant. It is as if he simultaneously fears his fate and wills it to happen. As his death approaches, he takes on the stature of a tragic hero like Coriolanus, whose magnificently scornful 'You common cry of curs . . . *I* banish *you*' (3.3.124–7) Suffolk's speeches anticipate. Whatever else Suffolk may be accused of, he is never mealy-mouthed, as his reference to his *imperial tongue* at l. 122 emphasizes.

124–5 **Far . . . suit** never let it be said that we (Suffolk uses the royal or imperial *we*) should stoop to honour people as low as this by pleading with them

128 **pole** (1) Another pun on Suffolk's family name; (2) traitor's heads were displayed on poles; (3) this anticipates Jack Cade's butchery at 4.7.122–5.

129 **uncovered** bareheaded (as a mark of respect)
    vulgar groom low-born servant

(contemptuous)

132 **Hale** drag

133 **Come soldiers . . . can** F's Compositor B seems to have misplaced a speech-prefix, making this line the end of the previous speech rather than the start of Suffolk's. But it is just possible that F is right: the Lieutenant orders the others to torment Suffolk, who then cuts in and turns it to his advantage. This might, too, lessen the awkwardness of Suffolk calling his piratical assailants *soldiers*, an awkwardness Oxford acknowledges by placing it in quotation marks.

135–9 **Great men . . . Great** Suffolk reworks various myths about the murders of great men to argue his case.

135 **Bezonians** beggars, base rogues (from the Italian *bisogno* or Spanish *bisoño*, meaning a raw recruit: *OED obs.* b).

136–7 **Tully** (Cicero) was murdered by a centurion and a tribune, on Mark Antony's orders. *Sworder* probably means 'cutthroat', or simply 'one who kills another with a sword' (*OED* 1): at *Antony* 3.13.30 it is used of Antony himself, challenging Octavius Caesar to single combat; *slave* may refer to a story recorded by Nashe that 'Tully by one of his own slaves was

SECOND REBEL I see them, I see them! There's Best's son, the
tanner of Wingham.

FIRST REBEL He shall have the skins of our enemies to make
dog's leather of.

SECOND REBEL And Dick the butcher.   25

FIRST REBEL Then is sin struck down like an ox, and
iniquity's throat cut like a calf.

SECOND REBEL And Smith the weaver.

FIRST REBEL Argo, their thread of life is spun.

SECOND REBEL Come, come, let's fall in with them.   30

> *Enter Jack Cade, Dick the Butcher, Smith the Weaver, a*
> *sawyer, and a drummer, with infinite numbers, ⌈all*
> *with long staves⌉*

CADE We, John Cade, so termed of our supposed father—

BUTCHER Or rather of stealing a cade of herrings.

CADE For our enemies shall fall before us, inspired with the
spirit of putting down kings and princes—command
silence.   35

BUTCHER Silence.

30.1–2 *Enter . . . numbers*] F (*subs.*)   2–3 *all with long staves*] Q (*subs.*)   33 fall] F4; faile F1

21–2 **Best's son, the tanner** the son of Best
the tanner
22 **Wingham** A village near Canterbury in
Kent.
24 **dog's leather** (inferior leather, used for
making gloves)
29 **Argo** A corruption, or an Elizabethan
pronunciation, of Latin *ergo*, meaning
'therefore', which also occurs at *Sir
Thomas More*, Add. II.D, another insur-
rection scene attributed to Shakespeare,
where it is followed by a reference to halfpenny loaves (ll. 7–10); compare ll. 60–1
of this scene.
thread . . . spun A proverbial phrase
(Dent T249), alluding to Clotho, the Fate
who spun the threads of human life in
Greek mythology.
30 **fall in with** join
30.2 *sawyer* one who saws timber (*OED* 1)
infinite numbers This indefinite, and
optimistic, phrase is typical of authorial
manuscripts, the dramatist imagining as
large a number as possible swarming on
to the stage.
31 **We, John Cade** As Cade begins his
oration he uses the correct form of his
Christian name (rather than the familiar

'Jack' later adopted), which is also used
by York at 3.1.357 and by the chroniclers;
and like York at 2.2.64, he uses the royal
We.
so termed of thus named after
32 For a discussion of whether this and the
following comments about Cade from his
followers are spoken *aside* or not, see the
Introduction, p. 52.
cade of barrel containing five hundred
33 **For** because. The phrasing is probably
intended to give a grand, even biblical
resonance (see the next note), but the
sentence is unfinished; Cade interrupts
himself to order his unruly followers to be
quiet.
our enemies . . . us F's 'faile' is almost
certainly a misprint for 'falle', as F4 clearly thought. If so, 'Cade may be borrowing
Scriptural language to give color to his
rebellion. Compare Leviticus 26 : 8: "Your
enemies shall fall before you." But this
may also be a pun on his name: Latin
cado, I fall' (Shaheen, p. 316). And the
next phrase, *inspired with the spirit*, may
also allude to heavenly inspiration and
the Holy Spirit.

CADE My father was a Mortimer—

BUTCHER He was an honest man and a good bricklayer.

CADE My mother a Plantagenet—

BUTCHER I knew her well, she was a midwife.   40

CADE My wife descended of the Lacys—

BUTCHER She was indeed a pedlar's daughter and sold many
laces.

WEAVER But now of late, not able to travel with her furred
pack, she washes bucks here at home.   45

CADE Therefore am I of an honourable house.

BUTCHER Ay, by my faith, the field is honourable, and there
was he born, under a hedge; for his father had never a
house but the cage.

CADE Valiant I am—   50

WEAVER A must needs, for beggary is valiant.

CADE I am able to endure much—

BUTCHER No question of that, for I have seen him whipped
three market days together.

CADE I fear neither sword nor fire.   55

---

37 **Mortimer** Cade is carrying out York's plan at 3.1.359.

38 **bricklayer** (punning on 'mortarer' (builder) and Mortimer)

39–40 **Plantagenet . . . midwife** The name *Plantagenet* derives from *planta genista* or 'broom plant', the badge of Henry II and his successors. It was revived by the historical York after it had fallen into disuse to emphasize his royal ancestry. In view of the plethora of puns in this passage, there is probably a pun on *Plantagenet*/jennet (a young female horse often used as a symbol of breeding and sexuality, suggesting *midwife*, often a euphemism for 'bawd' (Williams, pp. 173, 206)).

41 **Lacys** The name of a family related by marriage to the Mortimers invites the inevitable pun on *laces* at l. 43.

44–5 **travel with her furred pack** A pun on 'travel' and 'travail' (labour sexually) leads to another on *furred pack*: (a) pedlar's bag made of animal fur; (b) vagina edged by pubic hair. Q's version, 'occupy her furred pack' (l. 1577), spells out the obscene sense, since 'occupy' means 'possess sexually' (Williams, p. 221). See the next note.

45 **washes bucks** 'buckwashes', i.e. does laundry. 'Buck' is the usual, singular form (as repeatedly in *Merry Wives* e.g. 3.3.150–1), so that one might suspect that F's Compositor B had carelessly and characteristically added the 's', were it not for the obscene sense 'massages men' (Williams, pp. 56, 332; *OED, buck, sb.*[1] 2a), which Q's version 'She washeth bucks up and down the country' (l. 1578), with the usual pun on 'cunt' and 'country', again spells out.

46 **honourable** noble

47 **field** (with a pun on heraldic field, the background of a coat-of-arms)

48 **under a hedge** Proverbial for the lowly born (Dent H361.1). The Butcher reverses Talbot's contrast between the 'honourable' order of Knights of the Garter and 'a hedge-born swain' (*1 Henry VI*, 4.1.41–3).

49 **cage** A small prison, often in a market-place.

51 **A must needs** he must be
valiant sturdy. It was illegal to give alms to able-bodied beggars.

53 **whipped** (the usual punishment for vagabonds, as at 2.1.154–5)

WEAVER He need not fear the sword, for his coat is of proof.

BUTCHER But methinks he should stand in fear of fire, being
burned i'th' hand for stealing of sheep.

CADE Be brave then, for your captain is brave and vows
reformation. There shall be in England seven halfpenny   60
loaves sold for a penny, the three-hooped pot shall have
ten hoops, and I will make it felony to drink small beer.
All the realm shall be in common, and in Cheapside shall
my palfrey go to grass; and when I am king, as king I will
be—   65

ALL CADE'S FOLLOWERS God save your majesty!

CADE I thank you good people—there shall be no money, all
shall eat and drink on my score, and I will apparel them
all in one livery that they may agree like brothers, and
worship me their lord.   70

BUTCHER The first thing we do, let's kill all the lawyers.

CADE Nay, that I mean to do. Is not this a lamentable thing,
that of the skin of an innocent lamb should be made
parchment; that parchment, being scribbled o'er, should
undo a man? Some say the bee stings, but I say 'tis the   75
bee's wax; for I did but seal once to a thing, and I was
never mine own man since. How now? Who's there?

Enter some with the Clerk of Chatham

66, 98, 143, 162 ALL CADE'S FOLLOWERS] OXFORD; *All.* F   77.1 *Enter . . . Chatham*] Q (*subs.*);
Enter a Clearke. F

56 **proof** proof armour (*OED sb.* 10b). Dover
  Wilson cites a passage from Nashe's
  Unfortunate Traveller (*Works*, ii. 233–4)
  that explains this: 'As sailors do pitch [i.e.
  put pitch on] their apparel to make it
  storm-proof, so had most of them pitched
  their patched clothes to make them
  impierceable: a nearer way than to be at
  the charges of armour by half.'
58 **burned i'th' hand** (with a 'T' for 'thief')
61–2 **the three-hooped . . . hoops** 'A wooden
  drinking-cup holding a quart was bound
  by three equidistantly placed hoops; so
  that Cade's reform will make it three-and-
  a-half times as large as it is' (Sanders).
62 **small** weak, diluted
63 **All . . . common** At the time of the
  Peasants' Revolt in 1381, this was a
  slogan of the priest John Wall or Ball (see
  Appendix B).

in common shared communally
63–4 **in Cheapside . . . grass** The chief market area of Elizabethan London, west of St
  Paul's Churchyard, will be turned into a
  field for Cade's horse to graze upon.
64 **palfrey** A small horse for easy riding,
  rather than a war-horse.
68 **on my score** at my expense, 'on my
  account'
69 **livery** (standard uniform worn by all the
  servants of a particular household)
71 **kill all the lawyers** See Appendix B.
75 **undo** ruin
76 **bee's wax** i.e. the wax sealing legal
  documents
  I did . . . thing I only signed and sealed a
  document once
77 **mine own man** i.e. my own master
77.1 *Clerk* The parish clerk often also served
  as the village schoolmaster: see l. 81.

WEAVER The Clerk of Chatham: he can write and read and
cast account.

CADE O monstrous!   80

WEAVER We took him setting of boys' copies.

CADE Here's a villain.

WEAVER He's a book in his pocket with red letters in't.

CADE Zounds, then he is a conjuror!

BUTCHER Nay, he can make obligations and write court   85
hand.

CADE I am sorry for't. The man is a proper man, of mine
honour. Unless I find him guilty, he shall not die. Come
hither, sirrah, I must examine thee. What is thy name?

CLERK Emmanuel.   90

BUTCHER They use to write that on the top of letters. 'Twill
go hard with you.

CADE Let me alone. (*To the Clerk*) Dost thou use to write thy
name? Or hast thou a mark to thyself like an honest
plain-dealing man?   95

---

78 Chatham] Q; Chartam F   83 He's] F (Ha's)   84 Zounds] Q; Nay F   91 that] Q; it F
94 an] F2; a F1

---

78 **Chatham** F has 'Chartham', which is
a village near Canterbury, but Q's
'Chatham' (near Rochester) is much likelier to be correct. As the Oxford editors
point out, Cade and his army have passed
through Wingham (l. 22) and Ashford,
from which Cade himself and Dick the
Butcher come (4.3.1) on their way to
London, so if they are near Chartham,
they must have *retreated*, whereas
Chatham would be on their direct route.
In fact the chronicles relate that Cade did
retreat strategically, to lure the Staffords
into a trap, but the play omits this detail:
Cade simply confronts the Staffords later
in this scene and kills them in battle
offstage.
write and read An attack on literacy was
also a major aspect of the Peasants'
Revolt of 1381 (see Appendix B)—as of
some modern 'revolutions' (see the Introduction, p. 52).

79 **cast account** do arithmetic

81 **setting of boys' copies** preparing
writing exercises

83 **red letters** (in some textbooks and al-
manacs, capital letters were printed in red)

84 **Zounds** A strong oath, literally 'by God's
wounds'. F has 'Nay', but since the next
speech also begins with 'Nay', the repetition is suspicious, and since Q has
'Zounds' at the start of Cade's speech, the
F line was probably censored; as Oxford
remarks, 'This oath is often removed editorially from the Folio; it only occurs once
in the entire volume' (*King John* 2.1.467)
(*Textual Companion*, p. 189).
conjuror i.e. one who consults alman-
acs; see the note to l. 83. Dr Pinch in *The
Comedy of Errors* is both a schoolmaster
and a conjuror.

85 **make obligations** draw up legal bonds

85–6 **court hand** (handwriting used in legal
documents, as opposed to secretary hand,
used in private letters)

87 **proper** decent-looking
of on

90–1 **Emmanuel . . . letters** (in order to give
an impression of piety: *Emmanuel* means
'God with us')

94 **mark** i.e. a personal mark, rather than a
signature (to show he is illiterate)
an honest 'The collocation *an honest*
occurs in Shakespeare at least 62 times;

CLERK Sir, I thank God I have been so well brought up that I
can write my name.

ALL CADE'S FOLLOWERS He hath confessed—away with him!
He's a villain and a traitor.

CADE Away with him, I say. Hang him with his pen and   100
inkhorn about his neck.   *Exit one with the Clerk*
        Enter a Rebel

REBEL Where's our general?

CADE Here I am, thou particular fellow.

REBEL Fly, fly, fly! Sir Humphrey Stafford and his brother
are hard by with the King's forces.   105

CADE Stand, villain, stand, or I'll fell thee down. He shall be
encountered with a man as good as himself. He is but a
knight, is a?

REBEL No.

CADE To equal him I will make myself a knight presently.   110
        He kneels and knights himself

Rise up, Sir John Mortimer.
        He rises

Now have at him!
        *Enter Sir Humphrey Stafford and his brother, with a
        herald, a drummer and soldiers*

STAFFORD
Rebellious hinds, the filth and scum of Kent,
Marked for the gallows, lay your weapons down;
Home to your cottages, forsake this groom.   115
The King is merciful, if you revolt.

101.1 *a Rebel*] This edition; *Michael* F 102, 104, 109 REBEL] This edition; *Mich<ael>*. F
110.1 *He . . . himself*] not in F 111.1 *He rises*] not in F 112.1–2 *a herald*] not in F

[F's] *a honest* only here' (*Textual Companion*, p. 188).

101 **inkhorn** portable inkwell/stand made of
horn
103 **particular** (a punning contrast to *general*
in the previous line)
108 **a** he (which Q reads). See the second
note to 1.3.6.
109 **No** i.e. nothing but a knight
112 **have at** let me get at
112.1 *Sir Humphrey Stafford and his*

brother Humphrey and William Stafford
'were descendants of one of William
the Conqueror's favourite captains'
(Sanders), and presumably sent against
Cade by Queen Margaret (as Hall reports;
see Appendix B, 4.2.112–4.3.0.1) because
they were seasoned soldiers.
113 **hinds** peasants
115 **groom** base fellow. See the note to
2.1.180.
116 **revolt** (i.e. from Cade)

STAFFORD'S BROTHER
But angry, wrathful, and inclined to blood,
If you go forward; therefore yield or die.

CADE
As for these silken-coated slaves, I pass not.
It is to you, good people, that I speak,   120
Over whom, in time to come, I hope to reign,
For I am rightful heir unto the crown.

STAFFORD
Villain, thy father was a plasterer,
And thou thyself a shearman, art thou not?

CADE
And Adam was a gardener.

STAFFORD'S BROTHER   And what of that?   125

CADE
Marry, this: Edmund Mortimer, Earl of March,
Married the Duke of Clarence' daughter, did he not?

STAFFORD Ay, sir.

CADE
By her he had two children at one birth.

STAFFORD'S BROTHER That's false.   130

CADE
Ay, there's the question; but I say 'tis true.
The elder of them, being put to nurse,
Was by a beggar-woman stol'n away,
And ignorant of his birth and parentage,
Became a bricklayer when he came to age.   135
His son am I, deny it if you can.

---

126 this : Edmund] this *Edmund* F

---

119 **silken-coated** This may simply be a gibe
at the expensive clothes of aristocrats, but
silken could be literal: the surcoats that
knights wore over their armour originated in the Crusades, when the silk was used
to reduce the heat of the metal in the
fierce sun of the Middle East.
pass care

124 **shearman** One who cut the excess nap
from the cloth during manufacture: this
recalls references to *clothier* and *nap* at ll.
4–5.

125 **And . . . gardener** Cade quickly retorts to
Stafford's insult to his lowly trade with a
biblical reference: 'The Lord God took the
man, and put him into the garden of
Eden, that he might dress it and keep it'
(Genesis 2: 15). In the Peasants' Revolt of
1381, John Ball made the same point; see
Appendix B.

125–6 **And what . . . this** When Cade's point
about Adam is dismissed, he tries another
tack, attempting to prove his noble
ancestry.

BUTCHER

Nay, 'tis too true, therefore he shall be king.

WEAVER Sir, he made a chimney in my father's house, and
the bricks are alive at this day to testify it. Therefore deny
it not.   140

STAFFORD (*to Cade's followers*)

And will you credit this base drudge's words

That speaks he knows not what?

ALL CADE'S FOLLOWERS

Ay, marry will we, therefore get ye gone.

STAFFORD'S BROTHER

Jack Cade, the Duke of York hath taught you this.

CADE (*aside*)

He lies, for I invented it myself.—   145

Go to, sirrah, tell the King from me that for his father's
sake, Henry the Fifth, in whose time boys went to span-
counter for French crowns, I am content he shall reign,
but I'll be Protector over him.

BUTCHER And furthermore, we'll have the Lord Saye's head   150
for selling the dukedom of Maine.

CADE And good reason, for thereby is England maimed, and
fain to go with a staff, but that my puissance holds it up.
Fellow-kings, I tell you that that Lord Saye hath gelded
the commonwealth, and made it an eunuch, and more   155

---

152 maimed] F (main'd), Q (maimde)

---

141 **drudge** base fellow

145 **He . . . myself** An awkward line, since
York did in fact teach him *this*. Perhaps
Cade is becoming carried away by his own
self-importance; but if this aside is more
than a quick throwaway and is addressed
to his followers, his abandonment of all
pretence that his claim is genuine supports this edition's treatment of his followers' earlier remarks about him as overt
statements, not asides: i.e. they don't
believe it either. See Introduction, p. 52.

146 **Go to** An expression of impatience (like
modern 'come, come').

147–8 **span-counter** A game in which the
object was to throw a *counter* near (within
a *span* of nine inches) an opponent.

148 **French crowns** (a) coins (b) kingdoms (c)

the baldness caused by venereal disease
(all references to Henry V's French wars)

150 **Lord Saye** The Treasurer of England; he
first appears in 4.4.

152 **maimed** crippled. Modernization is difficult. F's 'mained' brings out the pun on
'Maine', but in itself it is meaningless for a
modern audience; Q's 'maimed' blunts
the pun but is comprehensible.

153 **fain to go with** obliged to use
puissance power

154 **Fellow-kings** Cade's mock-heroic phrase
echoes Marlowe's *Tamburlaine*, where the
hero calls his allies 'loving friends and fellow kings' (*2 Tamburlaine* 1.3.151).

154–5 **gelded the commonwealth** This
phrase may have been suggested by
Cicero, *De Oratore* 3.41.165, quoted in

than that, he can speak French, and therefore he is a
traitor.

STAFFORD
O gross and miserable ignorance!

CADE Nay, answer if you can. The Frenchmen are our
enemies; go to, then, I ask but this: can he that speaks   160
with the tongue of an enemy be a good counsellor or no?

ALL CADE'S FOLLOWERS No, no, and therefore we'll have his
head!

STAFFORD'S BROTHER (*to Stafford*)
Well, seeing gentle words will not prevail,
Assail them with the army of the King.   165

STAFFORD
Herald away, and throughout every town
Proclaim them traitors that are up with Cade,
That those which fly before the battle ends
May even in their wives' and children's sight
Be hanged up for example at their doors;   170
And you that be the King's friends, follow me!
    Exeunt ⌈the Staffords, the herald and their soldiers⌉

CADE
And you that love the commons, follow me!
Now show yourselves men, 'tis for liberty.
We will not leave one lord, one gentleman:
Spare none but such as go in clouted shoon,   175
For they are thrifty honest men, and such
As would, but that they dare not, take our parts.

BUTCHER They are all in order, and march toward us.

CADE But then are we in order when we are most out of
order. Come, march forward!   ⌈*Exeunt*⌉   180

171.1 *Exeunt . . . soldiers*] *Exit.* F   180 *Exeunt*] *not in* F

Talaeus' *Rhetorica*, a textbook used
in sixteenth-century schools (Wilson).

174 **leave** spare (another aim of the 1381
    rebels)

175 **clouted   shoon** hobnailed boots.
    'Clout-shoe' became a type-phrase for

a country bumpkin (*OED obs.* 2), and
'clubs and clouted shoon' a catch-phrase
for revolt in the sixteenth century
(Hattaway).

176 **thrifty** worthy (*OED a.* 2a)

178 **in order** in battle formation

179–80 **out of order** in disorder, rebellion

4.3   *Alarums to the fight, wherein both the Staffords are*
         slain. Enter Jack Cade, Dick the Butcher, and the rest

CADE Where's Dick, the butcher of Ashford?

BUTCHER Here, sir.

CADE They fell before thee like sheep and oxen, and thou
    behaved'st thyself as if thou hadst been in thine own
    slaughterhouse. Therefore thus will I reward thee—the   5
    Lent shall be as long again as it is, and thou shalt have a
    licence to kill for a hundred, lacking one.

BUTCHER I desire no more.

CADE And to speak truth, thou deserv'st no less.
        ⌜*He apparels himself in Stafford's armour*⌝
    This monument of the victory will I bear, and the bodies   10
    shall be dragged at my horse heels till I do come to
    London, where we will have the Mayor's sword borne
    before us.

BUTCHER If we mean to thrive and do good, break open the
    jails and let out the prisoners.   15

CADE Fear not that, I warrant thee. Come, let's march
    towards London.
                Exeunt, ⌜*dragging the Staffords' bodies*⌝

4.4   *Enter King Henry* ⌜*reading*⌝ *a supplication, and Queen*
         Margaret with Suffolk's head, the Duke of
         Buckingham, and the Lord Saye, ⌜*with others*⌝

QUEEN MARGARET
    Oft have I heard that grief softens the mind,

4.3.0.2 *Dick the Butcher*] *not in* F   9.1 *He . . . armour*] *not in* F   17.1 *dragging . . . bodies*]
not in F
    4.4.0.1 *reading*] Q; *with* F   0.3 *with others*] Q; *not in* F

4.3.0.1–2 **Alarums . . . rest** The battle is off-
    stage, as Cade's entry makes clear.
5–7 **the Lent . . . one** Butchers were not
    allowed to slaughter meat during Lent
    (the forty days of preparation for Easter, a
    penitential period when Christians were
    encouraged to eat fish rather than meat),
    except by special licence. Dick is being
    rewarded with such a *licence*, and his
    privileges are extended by doubling the
    period of Lent.
7 **for a hundred, lacking one** A standard
    term for a 99-year lease.
10 **monument** memorial

12–13 **the Mayor's . . . us** (as it was on
    ceremonial occasions)
14 **do good** prosper
14–15 **break . . . prisoners** (as the rebels did
    in both 1381 and 1450, as well as in more
    recent 'revolutions'; see Introduction,
    p. 53)
16 **Fear not that** do not doubt that we will do
    so
    I warrant thee A common colloquial
    expression of strong belief: 'I'll be bound'
    (*OED v.* 4a).
4.4 There are two main strands in this
    scene: Margaret's obsession with

And makes it fearful and degenerate;
Think therefore on revenge, and cease to weep.
But who can cease to weep and look on this?
Here may his head lie on my throbbing breast,   5
But where's the body that I should embrace?

BUCKINGHAM (*to King Henry*)
What answer makes your grace to the rebels'
    supplication?

KING HENRY
I'll send some holy bishop to entreat,
For God forbid so many simple souls
Should perish by the sword. And I myself,   10
Rather than bloody war shall cut them short,
Will parley with Jack Cade their general.
But stay, I'll read it over once again.

QUEEN MARGARET
Ah barbarous villains! Hath this lovely face

Suffolk's death (boldly dramatized by
her carrying his severed head) to the
exclusion of everything else; and
Buckingham's attempt to get the King to
focus on the urgency of the political
situation.

0.1 **supplication** petition (the list of the
    rebels' demands)
1–6 In a dramatic device almost as bold
    as the severed head, Margaret begins the
    scene by sharing her thoughts with
    the audience and ignoring the other
    characters, developing and intensifying
    the sense of desolation at being separated
    from Suffolk that she expressed when we
    last saw her at the end of 3.2.

2 **fearful** full of terror
  degenerate Although this basically carries the modern meaning 'unworthy', the
  context also implies the original sense of
  'fallen from the virtue of the ancestors'
  (Schmidt), as when it is used against King
  Henry for disinheriting his son at the
  start of 3 *Henry VI* (1.1.184); this stronger
  implication leads into Margaret's turning
  her thoughts to *revenge* in the next line.

3 **revenge** This becomes her main motivation in the rest of the play and accounts
  for the ferocity of her behaviour in 3
  Henry VI.

5 **throbbing** (with grief)
7 **what . . . supplication** It is not clear from
  F's layout whether this apparently irregular line is verse or prose; but 'the rest of
  the scene is verse, and this line is an
  acceptable hexameter, if . . . "to the" is
  elided' (*Textual Companion*, p. 641).
8–12 This speech is characteristic of Henry.
  It emphasizes his positive qualities in his
  choice of a *bishop* to *entreat* (negotiate), in
  his concern for his subjects, and in the
  echo of the Bible in his phrasing (see the
  note to l. 10); but also his impractical
  unworldliness, in his belief that it will
  be possible (or safe) for him to *parley* in
  person with the Cade whom the audience
  has just seen. Suggestions for this
  speech come from Hall's account: in an
  episode not dramatized, the King sent
  the Archbishop of Canterbury and
  Buckingham to meet Cade (they brought
  back the supplication which the King is
  reading: see Appendix B). Another hint
  may have come from the Peasants' Revolt
  of 1381, when the young Richard II
  courageously met the rebels in person.
10 **perish by the sword** Henry echoes Christ's
  words when he is arrested: 'all that take
  the sword shall perish with the sword'
  (Matthew 26: 52).
11 **cut them short** destroy them

Ruled like a wandering planet over me, 15
And could it not enforce them to relent,
That were unworthy to behold the same?

KING HENRY
Lord Saye, Jack Cade hath sworn to have thy head.

SAYE
Ay, but I hope your highness shall have his.

KING HENRY (*to Queen Margaret*)
How now, madam? 20
Still lamenting and mourning Suffolk's death?
I fear me, love, if that I had been dead,
Thou wouldest not have mourned so much for me.

QUEEN MARGARET
No my love, I should not mourn, but die for thee.
Enter a Messenger

KING HENRY
How now? What news? Why com'st thou in such haste? 25

MESSENGER
The rebels are in Southwark. Fly, my lord!
Jack Cade proclaims himself Lord Mortimer,
Descended from the Duke of Clarence' house,
And calls your grace usurper openly,
And vows to crown himself in Westminster. 30
His army is a ragged multitude
Of hinds and peasants, rude and merciless.

---

21 mourning] POPE; mourning for F   23 wouldest] THEOBALD; would'st F

---

15 **Ruled . . . planet** It was a popular belief
that the stars influenced the fate of those
born under them.
16 **enforce** compel
them (the murderers of Suffolk)
20 **How now, madam?** For *How now*, see the
note to 1.1.53. Incomplete verse lines usually suggest a pause either before or after
the phrase spoken; perhaps Henry pauses
to draw attention to Margaret's grief, and
his reaction to it (see the note to ll. 22–4).
21 **Still . . . death** By omitting F's 'for' (see
collation), Oxford creates a regular verse
line, but then sacrifices it again by tacking
l. 21 on to F's incomplete l. 20 and printing it as prose. *Lamenting* is stressed on the
first syllable.
22–4 **I fear . . . for thee** Even Henry is
moved to make a mild comment about
Margaret's obsession with Suffolk; she
caps it with spiky irony, as Peggy Ashcroft
made clear at Stratford-upon-Avon in
1963–4. The split between them is now
overt.
26 **Southwark** On the south bank of the
Thames, Southwark was in Henry's
(and Shakespeare's) time a suburb of
London, outside the city's jurisdiction
(and therefore a site used for Elizabethan
theatres).
28 **Duke of Clarence** See 2.2.13, and York's
claims in that scene.

Sir Humphrey Stafford and his brother's death
Hath given them heart and courage to proceed.
All scholars, lawyers, courtiers, gentlemen, 35
They call false caterpillars and intend their death.

KING HENRY
O graceless men, they know not what they do.

BUCKINGHAM
My gracious lord, retire to Kenilworth
Until a power be raised to put them down.

QUEEN MARGARET
Ah, were the Duke of Suffolk now alive 40
These Kentish rebels would be soon appeased!

KING HENRY
Lord Saye, the traitors hateth thee,
Therefore away with us to Kenilworth.

SAYE
So might your grace's person be in danger.
The sight of me is odious in their eyes, 45
And therefore in this city will I stay
And live alone as secret as I may.

Enter another Messenger

SECOND MESSENGER (*to King Henry*)
Jack Cade hath almost gotten London Bridge;
The citizens fly and forsake their houses;
The rascal people, thirsting after prey, 50

38, 43 Kenilworth] F (Killingworth)   48 almost] Q; *not in* F

---

36 **caterpillars** parasites (on the garden of
the state), as at *Richard II* 2.3.165, where
Bolingbroke calls Richard's advisers 'The
caterpillars of the commonwealth'. Compare 3.1.90, and note.

37 **graceless** i.e. deprived of divine grace
they … do A striking biblical echo,
typical of Henry, of Christ on the cross:
'Father, forgive them: for they know not
what they do' (Luke 23: 34).

38 **Kenilworth** Kenilworth Castle, in
Warwickshire, is one hundred miles
north of London. The King fled there
for security because the main support
for Cade was in the south, because
Kenilworth Castle was never taken by
direct attack throughout its history, and

because it was Margaret's property, at the
heart of the Midlands area with which
Margaret had been endowed in 1446
(Griffiths, p. 259).

39 **a power** an army

41 **appeased** made peaceful

42 An eight-syllable line, but these are common in Shakespeare, and emendation is
unnecessary.
traitors hateth Third-person plurals
ending in '-th' were acceptable in
Elizabethan grammar (Abbott 334).

48 **almost** This insert from Q creates a regular verse line.

50 **rascal people** rabble (the phrase is from
Hall)

Join with the traitor, and they jointly swear
To spoil the city and your royal court.

BUCKINGHAM

Then linger not, my lord, away, take horse!

KING HENRY

Come Margaret, God our hope will succour us.

QUEEN MARGARET

My hope is gone, now Suffolk is deceased.   55

KING HENRY (*to Saye*)

Farewell my lord, trust not the Kentish rebels.

BUCKINGHAM (*to Saye*)

Trust nobody, for fear you be betrayed.

SAYE

The trust I have is in mine innocence,
And therefore am I bold and resolute.

        Exeunt | Saye at one door, the rest at another⌉

4.5   *Enter Lord Scales ⌈and Matthew Gough⌉ upon the*
       Tower, walking. Then enters two or three Citizens
       below

SCALES How now? Is Jack Cade slain?

FIRST CITIZEN No, my lord, nor likely to be slain, for they
have won the bridge, killing all those that withstand

---

57 be betrayed] F2; betraid F1   59.1 *Saye . . . another*] *not in* F
    4.5.0.1 *and Matthew Gough*] This edition (*conj.* Oxford); *not in* F

52 **spoil** plunder
54 **God our hope** This echoes various biblical
passages, e.g. Psalm 71: 5, 39: 7.
55 **My . . . deceased** Margaret's final line in
this scene underlines her despair: only
revenge (l. 3) now remains. Her line contrasts markedly with the hope of the
King's preceding one.
58 **The . . . innocence** Proverbial: 'Innocence is bold' (Dent I82).
4.5.0.1–2 **Lord Scales . . . the Tower** Scales
was not the Lieutenant of the Tower of
London, but was left in charge of it when
the King fled to Kenilworth Castle (see
4.4.38). Since the texts (and even the layout) of F and Q3 are almost identical at
this point, F was probably set from Q3
here (see Textual Introduction, pp. 99–
I00); neither mentions Scales by name.
The reporter of Q may have omitted a line
or phrase identifying Scales, or he may

simply have known who Scales was
through rehearsal discussion, while the
audience may not even have needed to
know his name: his essential dramatic
function is to be an authority figure
defending the Tower.
0.1 **Matthew Gough** Acting on a suggestion
by Gary Taylor (*Textual Companion*, p.
I89), this edition introduces Gough here,
so that he can be identified at l. I0 (see the
note).
0.1–2 **upon the Tower** The balcony above the
Elizabethan stage would have been used
to suggest the walls of the Tower.
3 **won** taken
   withstand Oxford says that 'the tense
. . . seems wrong' (*Textual Companion*, p.
I89), but it may be a 'vivid' present,
reflecting the citizen's sense of excitement
and urgency.

them. The Lord Mayor craves aid of your honour from the
Tower to defend the city from the rebels.   5
SCALES
Such aid as I can spare you shall command,
But I am troubled here with them myself.
The rebels have essayed to win the Tower.
But get you to Smithfield, and gather head,
And thither I will send you Matthew Gough.   10
Fight for your king, your country, and your lives!
And so farewell, for I must hence again.
          Exeunt Scales ⌈and Gough⌉ above, the Citizens below

4.6   *Enter Jack Cade and the rest. Cade strikes his staff on
          London Stone*
CADE Now is Mortimer lord of this city. And here sitting
upon London Stone, I charge and command, that of the
city's cost the Pissing Conduit run nothing but claret
wine this first year of our reign. And now henceforward
it shall be treason for any that calls me other than Lord   5
Mortimer.
          Enter a Soldier, running
SOLDIER Jack Cade, Jack Cade!

12.1 *Exeunt . . . below*] *Exeunt* F

---

8 **essayed** attempted
9 **Smithfield** An open space outside the city
walls. It is not connected with Cade in the
chronicles, but it was where the leader of
the Peasants' Revolt of 1381, Wat Tyler,
was murdered.
   gather head raise forces
10 **I will send you Matthew Gough** Gough is
frequently mentioned by Hall as a very
experienced soldier, which is why Scales
proposes to send him to the citizens' aid.
But this, as it turns out, is no great help,
since the opening stage direction of 4.7
has Matthew Gough enter, to be immediately slain. The only way in which an
audience could grasp this ironic reversal
would be for Scales to identify Gough with
a gesture here. Perhaps Gough was killed
offstage, like the Staffords at 4.3.0.1–2;
but in that case why take the trouble to

specify him here and in the opening direction of 4.7?
4.6.0.1 **staff** Q (like the chronicles) gives
Cade a sword; but then at 4.8.59 incon-
sistently and irritatingly replaces F's
'sword' with a 'staff'. In the face of such
inconsistency, this edition observes its
textual policy and follows F in both cases.
0.2 **London Stone** An ancient landmark
which stood in Shakespeare's day in
Canwick (now Cannon) Street.
2–3 **of the city's cost** at the city's expense
3 **the Pissing Conduit** The popular name
of Little Conduit in Cheapside, a water
supply.
3–4 **run . . . wine** 'A parody . . . of Henry
VI's return to London after his Paris coronation [in 1431] when the conduits of
Cheapside ran with wine', as reported in
Fabyan's chronicle (Hattaway).

CADE Knock him down there.

　　　They kill him

⌈WEAVER⌉ If this fellow be wise, he'll never call ye Jack Cade
　　more; I think he hath a very fair warning.   10

　　　⌈*Enter Dick the Butcher*⌉

BUTCHER My lord, there's an army gathered together in
　　Smithfield.

CADE Come then, let's go fight with them; but first, go and
　　set London Bridge on fire, and if you can, burn down the
　　Tower too. Come, let's away.   *Exeunt*   15

4.7   *Alarums.* ⌈*Excursions, wherein*⌉ *Matthew Gough is*
　　　　slain, and all the rest of his men with him. Then enter
　　　　Jack Cade with his company, among them Dick the
　　　　Butcher, Smith the Weaver, and John, a rebel

CADE So, sirs, now go some and pull down the Savoy;
　　others to th' Inns of Court, down with them all.

BUTCHER I have a suit unto your lordship.

CADE Be it a lordship, thou shalt have it for that word.

BUTCHER Only that the laws of England may come out of   5
　　your mouth.

JOHN (*aside to his fellows*) Mass, 'twill be sore law then, for

---

4.6.9 WEAVER] ROWE; *But<cher>.* F   10.1 *Enter . . . Butcher*] *not in* F
　　4.7.1.0 *Excursions, wherein*] *not in* F   0.2 *of . . . him*] *not in* F   0.3–4 *among . . . rebel*] *not*
in F

9–11 WEAVER . . . BUTCHER These speeches
are given in F to '*But<cher>*' and '*Dicke*'
respectively; but Dick *is* the Butcher, so
something has gone wrong. Q agrees with
F that the second speech is Dick's, so the
simplest course is to give the first one to
the Weaver, as here. This helps to solve
another problem: how do they know the
messenger's news, since they've just
killed him? Presumably an entry for Dick
is missing, supplied here.

4.7.0.1–2 *Alarums . . . with him* See the
note to 4.5.10.

0.1 *Excursions* A standard term in
Elizabethan stage directions to suggest a
physical skirmish, here added editorially
to suggest that Gough is killed on stage.

1–13 **pull down . . . realm** The historical
details come, not from the chronicle

accounts of Cade's rebellion, but from
those of Wat Tyler's in 1381 (see Appendix B, 4.7.1–2). The *Savoy* was the London
palace of Richard II's powerful uncle,
John of Gaunt, whom the rebels particularly hated: they burnt it down.

2 **Inns of Court** (centre of the legal profes-
sion in London)

4 **lordship** a lord's domain

7 JOHN This may be the 'John Holland', perhaps an actor, whom F introduces at
4.2.0.1 (see the note), where this edition,
following Oxford, designates his character simply as a 'rebel'. Oxford is also
followed here: 'We treat John . . . as a
miscellaneous rebel, and retain his name
only because he is addressed by it' at l. 10
(*Textual Companion*, p. 190).

he was thrust in the mouth with a spear, and 'tis not
whole yet.

WEAVER Nay, John, it will be stinking law, for his breath   10
stinks with eating toasted cheese.

CADE I have thought upon it, it shall be so. Away, burn
all the records of the realm. My mouth shall be the
Parliament of England.

JOHN (*aside*) Then we are like to have biting statutes unless   15
his teeth be pulled out.

CADE And henceforward all things shall be in common.

  Enter a Messenger

MESSENGER My lord, a prize, a prize! Here's the Lord Saye
which sold the towns in France. He that made us pay
one-and-twenty fifteens and one shilling to the pound,   20
the last subsidy.

  Enter a rebel with the Lord Saye

CADE Well, he shall be beheaded for it ten times. (*To Saye*)
Ah thou say, thou serge, nay, thou buckram lord, now
art thou within point-blank of our jurisdiction regal.
What canst thou answer to my majesty for giving up of   25
Normandy unto Mounsieur Buss-my-cue, the Dolphin of

21.1 *a rebel*] George F 26 *Buss-my-cue*] Q (bus mine cue); *Basimecu* F

---

9 **whole** healed
15 **biting** severe (with a pun on *biting* teeth)
17 **in common** See the notes to 4.2.63.
19–21 **sold . . . subsidy** Lord Saye, the Treasurer of England, was associated with
 Suffolk in giving up Anjou and Maine to
 Margaret's father; but it seems that the
 issue of the taxation is at least as great a
 cause of resentment for the rebels. See the
 next note.
20 **one-and-twenty . . . pound** i.e. very high
 tax on personal property (see the note to
 1.1.132): twenty-one fifteens (140 per
 cent)—plus a shilling—is a humorous, or
 grotesque, exaggeration.
 shilling A small silver coin widely used in
 England before the introduction of deci-
 mal currency in 1971 replaced it with the
 five (new) pence coin.
21 **the . . . subsidy** in the last tax assessment
23 **say** A cloth of fine texture.
 serge A durable woollen fabric, often
 worn by the poorer classes.
 buckram A coarse linen cloth stiffened

with glue, used to make stage properties,
so a *buckram lord* is a 'stuffed lord'
(Sanders).
24 **within point-blank** (range)
26 **Mounsieur** (mocking anglicization of
 French *monsieur*, Mr)
 Buss-my-cue Q's anglicization of F's
 'Basimecu', a derisive reference to a
 Frenchman: *baise mon cue* means 'kiss my
 arse' (which is sometimes substituted in
 performance). 'Buss' is used for 'kiss' elsewhere in Shakespeare, as when Falstaff
 says to the prostitute Doll Tearsheet 'Thou
 dost give me flattering busses' (*2 Henry
 IV* 2.4.270), and 'cue' can mean 'tail',
 though OED's first citation is from 1867
 (*sb.*[3] 3).
 Dolphin Properly modernized to
 'Dauphin' (see *OED, dauphin, Fr. Hist.*),
 F is retained here because the word
 was often used in a derisive way which
 drew attention to its other meaning
 (the porpoise-like mammal), as it is in *1
 Henry VI*, where Talbot derides Joan of Arc

France? Be it known unto thee by these presence, even
the presence of Lord Mortimer, that I am the besom that
must sweep the court clean of such filth as thou art. Thou
hast most traitorously corrupted the youth of the realm   30
in erecting a grammar school; and whereas before, our
forefathers had no other books but the score and the
tally, thou hast caused printing to be used, and contrary
to the King his crown and dignity, thou hast built a
paper-mill. It will be proved to thy face that thou hast   35
men about thee that usually talk of a noun and a verb
and such abominable words as no Christian ear can
endure to hear. Thou hast appointed justices of peace to
call poor men before them about matters they were not
able to answer. Moreover, thou hast put them in prison,   40
and because they could not read, thou hast hanged them,
when indeed only for that cause they have been most
worthy to live. Thou dost ride on a foot-cloth, dost thou
not?

SAYE What of that?   45

CADE Marry, thou ought'st not to let thy horse wear a
cloak when honester men than thou go in their hose and
doublets.

BUTCHER And work in their shirts too; as myself, for example, that am a butcher.   50

---

43 on] Q; in F   49 shirts] OXFORD; shirt F

(Joan la Pucelle) and the Dauphin as '*Puzel*
or *Pussel*, Dolphin or Dog-fish' (Folio TLN
581; 1.6.85). That pronunciation seems
appropriate to Cade here, especially after
he has just called the Dauphin 'Mounsieur
Buss-my-cue' (see previous note).

27–8 **by . . . Mortimer** Cade confuses 'these
presents', a legal term meaning 'the present document' and which begins many
legal writings, with being in 'the presence' of the King.

28 **besom** broom

29–38 **Thou hast . . . hear** Another attack
on literacy: see 4.2.78 and note.

32–3 **score . . . tally** A *score* was a notch cut
in a stick (*tally*), used to mark numbers, a
primitive form of account-keeping.

33 **printing** Anachronistic: Caxton set up the
first press in England in 1476.
used practised

34 **the King . . . dignity** (another standard
legal formula)
King his King's (i.e. Cade's)

35 **paper-mill** The first record of a paper-mill
in England dates from 1495.

41–3 **because . . . live** If a criminal could
demonstrate that he could read Latin,
he could claim 'benefit of clergy' and so
escape hanging. Cade typically inverts
established values, and argues that *only
for that cause* (for that reason alone)—i.e.
an inability to read) they deserved to live.

43 **on a foot-cloth** on a horse wearing a sur-
coat. Q's *on*, the correct idiom, suggests
that F's 'in' is a misprint rather than an
example of Cade's ignorance.

47 **go in** wear only (i.e. without a cloak)

47–8 **hose and doublets** 'Doublet and hose'
(jacket and tights) was the standard
Elizabethan wear for men.

SAYE　You men of Kent—

BUTCHER　What say you of Kent?

SAYE

　Nothing but this: 'tis *bona terra, mala gens.*

CADE　Away with him, away with him, he speaks Latin.

SAYE　Hear me but speak, and bear me where you will.　　　55

　Kent, in the commentaries Caesar writ,

　Is termed the civil'st place of all this isle;

　Sweet is the country, because full of riches;

　The people liberal, valiant, active, wealthy;

　Which makes me hope you are not void of pity.　　　60

　I sold not Maine, I lost not Normandy;

　Yet to recover them would lose my life.

　Justice with favour have I always done,

　Prayers and tears have moved me, gifts could never.

　When have I aught exacted at your hands,　　　65

　But to maintain the King, the realm, and you?

　Large gifts have I bestowed on learnèd clerks

　Because my book preferred me to the King,

　And seeing ignorance is the curse of God,

　Knowledge the wing wherewith we fly to heaven.　　　70

　Unless you be possessed with devilish spirits

　You cannot but forbear to murder me.

　This tongue hath parleyed unto foreign kings

　For your behoof—

54 Away . . . Latin] F ; *Bonum terrum*—zounds, what's that ? | BUTCHER He speaks French. |
⌐FIRST REBEL⌐ No, 'tis Dutch. | ⌐SECOND REBEL⌐ No, 'tis Out-talian, I know it well enough. OXFORD
(*after* Q)　66 But] RANN (*conj.* Johnson); Kent F

53 *bona terra, mala gens* 'a good land, a bad
　people' (apparently an Italian catch-
　phrase of unknown origin applied to the
　English). It is tactless of Lord Saye to use a
　foreign language here, as Cade's reply
　emphasizes, especially if anyone knew
　what it meant.
54 Oxford replaces this speech with four lines
　from Q (see collation) on the grounds that
　they give the other rebels something to
　say. By the same token, they could easily
　be small-part actors' interjections, and
　are not included here.
55 **Hear me but** just give me the chance to
56 **the commentaries Caesar writ** In Arthur
　Golding's translation of Caesar's *Com-
　mentarii de Bello Gallico*, which describe

his campaigns from 58 to 52 BC (5.14), the
people of Kent are called the 'civilest', a
word that occurs in the next line
(Steevens).
59 **liberal** refined, like gentlemen (Onions)
60 **void** devoid
63 **favour** leniency, mercy
65 **aught . . . hands** taken anything from
　you in taxes
66 **But** except
67 **clerks** scholars
68 **book** learning
　preferred recommended
72 **forbear** refrain from murdering
73 **parleyed unto** negotiated with
74 **behoof** advantage

CADE Tut, when struck'st thou one blow in the field?   75
SAYE

Great men have reaching hands. Oft have I struck
Those that I never saw, and struck them dead.

REBEL O monstrous coward! What, to come behind folks?
SAYE

These cheeks are pale with watching for your good—

CADE Give him a box o'th' ear, and that will make 'em red   80
again.

> ⌈*One of the rebels strikes Saye*⌉

SAYE

Long sitting to determine poor men's causes
Hath made me full of sickness and diseases.

CADE Ye shall have a hempen caudle, then, and the help of
hatchet.   85

BUTCHER (*to Saye*) Why dost thou quiver, man?
SAYE

The palsy, and not fear, provokes me.

CADE Nay, he nods at us as who should say 'I'll be even with
you'. I'll see if his head will stand steadier on a pole or no.
Take him away, and behead him.   90

SAYE

Tell me wherein have I offended most?
Have I affected wealth or honour? Speak.

---

78 REBEL] OXFORD; *Geo<rge>*. F   79 with] F2; for F1   81.1 *One . . . Saye*] *not in* F   84
caudle] F4; Candle F1   help of] F; health o'th' OXFORD

---

75 **the field** (of battle)
76 **Great . . . hands** Proverbial: 'Kings have
long arms' (Dent K87), originally a line
from Ovid, *Heroides* 17.166.
79 **with** Oxford defends F's 'for': 'G. L. Brook,
The Language of Shakespeare (1976), 94,
shows that *for* can mean "because
of"' (*Textual Companion*, p. 190); but the
compositor could have been misled by the
second 'for' in the line, and F2's *with*
seems much clearer.
watching staying awake (working)
82 **sitting** i.e. as a judge
determine decide
causes law-suits
84 **hempen caudle** This was a euphemism for
the hangman's noose.

caudle warm gruel (for the sick)
help Oxford emends to *health*, citing a similar presumed slip at *Errors* 1.1.151, and
arguing that *health* works better after *caudle* (see note). But as Oxford also says, F
makes sense: Saye is to be hanged first
(with the *hempen caudle*; see first note to
this line), then his head cut off, to be stuck
on a pole—which is what happens later in
the scene.
85 **hatchet** executioner's axe
86 **quiver** tremble
87 **palsy** (an illness that causes the hands to
shake)
provokes causes (to tremble)
88 **as who** like one who
92 **affected** loved

Are my chests filled up with extorted gold?
Is my apparel sumptuous to behold?
Whom have I injured, that ye seek my death?   95
These hands are free from guiltless bloodshedding,
This breast from harbouring foul deceitful thoughts.
O let me live!

CADE I feel remorse in myself with his words, but I'll bridle
it. He shall die an it be but for pleading so well for his life.   100
Away with him, he has a familiar under his tongue; he
speaks not a God's name. Go, take him away, I say, and
strike off his head presently; and then break into his son-
in-law's house, Sir James Cromer, and strike off his head,
and bring them both upon two poles hither.   105

ALL CADE'S FOLLOWERS It shall be done.

SAYE

Ah countrymen, if when you make your prayers,
God should be so obdurate as yourselves,
How would it fare with your departed souls?
And therefore yet relent and save my life.   110

CADE Away with him, and do as I command ye.

Exeunt one or two with the Lord Saye

The proudest peer in the realm shall not wear a head on
his shoulders unless he pay me tribute. There shall not a
maid be married but she shall pay to me her maidenhead
ere they have it. Married men shall hold of me *in capite*.   115
And we charge and command that their wives be as free

---

102 away, I say] OXFORD *adds* (*after* Q) to the Standard in Cheapside   103 and then] OXFORD
adds (*after* Q) go to Mile End Green   106, 121 ALL CADE'S FOLLOWERS] OXFORD; *All*. F   111.1
Exeunt . . . Saye] Q; *not in* F   115 Married] Q; *not in* F

---

96 **guiltless bloodshedding** the shedding of
innocent blood
99 **remorse** pity
100 **an it be but** if only
101 **familiar** demoniac attendant of a witch
102 **a** See note to 2.3.54.
102–3 Oxford inserts two localizing details
from Q (see collation). For their textual
significance, and therefore their omission, see the Textual Introduction, pp.
88–9.
108 **obdurate** stubborn, merciless (stressed
on the second syllable, unlike modern
prose usage)

109 **it fare . . . souls** your souls be treated
when you have died
114 **she . . . maidenhead** Cade alludes to the
droit de seigneur, the feudal lord's right to
spend the wedding night with the bride of
any of his vassals.
115 **hold . . . capite** have their property as
a direct gift from the King (with a
pun on Latin *caput*, head, also slang for
'maidenhead' (Williams, p. 154)); i.e.
they shall have their property, their
wives, directly from me (after I have had
them)
116 **free** sexually available

as heart can wish or tongue can tell.

BUTCHER My lord, when shall we go to Cheapside and take
up commodities upon our bills?

CADE Marry, presently. 120

ALL CADE'S FOLLOWERS O brave!

> *Enter two with the Lord Saye's head and Sir James*
> *Cromer's upon two poles*

CADE But is not this braver? Let them kiss one another, for
they loved well when they were alive.

> ⌈*The two heads are made to kiss*⌉

Now part them again, lest they consult about the giving
up of some more towns in France. Soldiers, defer the spoil 125
of the city until night. For with these borne before us
instead of maces will we ride through the streets, and at
every corner have them kiss. Away!

> *Exeunt carrying the heads*

121.1–2 *Enter . . . poles*] Q; *Enter one with the heads.* F 123.1 *The . . . kiss*] *not in* F 128.1
Exeunt . . . heads] *Exit* F

117 **as heart . . . can tell** as much as you
could want or ask for. Proverbial (Dent
H300.1).

117–18 Between these two lines, Oxford
inserts a longish passage from Q (Appendix A, Passage F), discussed in the Textual
Introduction, p. 96.

118–19 **take up . . . bills** obtain goods on
credit. There are two possible puns, one
brutal ('raise the decapitated heads upon
our weapons (*bills*)'), one sexual ('hoist
women onto our penises (*bills*)'), a quibble expanded by Q: 'he that will lustily
stand to it shall go with me and take up
these commodities following—item, a
gown, a kirtle, a petticoat, and a smock'
(1783–5). Oxford includes these lines in
the text.

121 **brave** splendid

125 **spoil** sack, destruction

127 **maces** (symbols of public office)

128.1–4.8.0.1 There is a serious difficulty
with the Folio stage directions at this
point. Cade has an exit after his *Away!*
Then F has '*Alarum, and Retreat*', standard directions for an offstage battle.
But as Oxford points out, Cade has no
one to fight against: the battle with
Matthew Gough takes place at 4.7.0.1–2;

Buckingham and Clifford have yet to
arrive. Nor is Cade in *Retreat*, since when
he arrives he orders his followers to kill
the citizens, that is, to begin the *spoil of
the city* which he deferred *until night* at
4.7.125–6. And that is the fatal objection
to Oxford's solution: they replace F's
direction with an interrupted exit—see
collation to 4.8.0.1—and continue Scene
7. But this means that no sooner has Cade
said he will defer the spoil than he orders
it. That, presumably, is the point of F's
exit and re-entry for Cade. *Alarum, and
retreat* cannot be correct; F's direction
was probably meant to cue offstage music
to suggest Cade parading round the
streets bearing the severed heads *instead of
maces* (4.7.127) before him; he and his
rabble probably left through one of the
doors in the back wall of the Elizabethan
stage, and, after a short pause covered by
the music to suggest the passage of time,
re-entered through the other door to
begin the spoil of the city. Since there
probably *is* a slight pause, with the stage
cleared, this edition follows most others
rather than Oxford, and begins a new
scene.

4.8   ⌐*Long flourish.*⌐ *Enter again Cade and all his*
         rabblement

CADE Up Fish Street! Down Saint Magnus' Corner! Kill and
      knock down! Throw them into Thames!
         Sound a parley
      What noise is this I hear? Dare any be so bold to sound
      retreat or parley when I command them kill?
         Enter the Duke of Buckingham and old Lord Clifford
         with soldiers

BUCKINGHAM
      Ay, here they be that dare and will disturb thee!   5
      Know, Cade, we come ambassadors from the King
      Unto the commons, whom thou hast misled,
      And here pronounce free pardon to them all
      That will forsake thee and go home in peace.

CLIFFORD
      What say ye, countrymen, will ye relent   10
      And yield to mercy whilst 'tis offered you,
      Or let a rebel lead you to your deaths?
      Who loves the King and will embrace his pardon,
      Fling up his cap and say 'God save his majesty'.
      Who hateth him and honours not his father,   15
      Henry the Fifth, that made all France to quake,
      Shake he his weapon at us, and pass by.
         They forsake Cade

ALL CADE'S FOLLOWERS God save the King! God save the
      King!

CADE What, Buckingham and Clifford, are ye so brave?   20

4.8.0.1 *Long flourish*] This edition ; *Alarum, and Retreat.* F ; *Exeunt two with the heads. The others begin to follow* OXFORD (*continuing* 4.7) 4.2 *with soldiers*] *not in* F 12 rebel] SINGER (*after* Q); rabble F 17.1, 54.1 *They forsake Cade*] Q; *not in* F 18, 32, 53 ALL CADE'S FOLLOWERS] OXFORD; *All.* F

4.8.0.1 *Long flourish* This direction was suggested by one in the Folio text of *Richard II*
(TLN 420; 1.3.122.1), also used to cover a
passage of time (while Richard consults
his council).

1 Fish Street . . . Saint Magnus Corner 'Fish
Street was on the north side of the
Thames, across London Bridge from
Southwark; and at the end of the street
nearest the bridge stood St Magnus'
Church' (Sanders).

4 parley (trumpet call to request a
conference)
8 free generous
12 rebel F's 'rabble' was probably a misreading of the spelling 'rebell'.
13, 15 Who whoever
13 embrace accept
17 Shake . . . weapon (as a sign of
defiance)
20 brave audacious

And you, base peasants, do ye believe him? Will you
needs be hanged with your pardons about your necks?
Hath my sword therefore broke through London gates
that you should leave me at the White Hart in Southwark? I thought ye would never have given out these   25
arms till you had recovered your ancient freedom. But
you are all recreants and dastards, and delight to live in
slavery to the nobility. Let them break your backs with
burdens, take your houses over your heads, ravish your
wives and daughters before your faces. For me, I will   30
make shift for one, and so God's curse light upon you all.

ALL CADE'S FOLLOWERS We'll follow Cade! We'll follow
Cade!

    They run to Cade again

CLIFFORD

Is Cade the son of Henry the Fifth
That thus you do exclaim you'll go with him?   35
Will he conduct you through the heart of France
And make the meanest of you earls and dukes?
Alas, he hath no home, no place to fly to,
Nor knows he how to live but by the spoil,
Unless by robbing of your friends and us.   40
Were't not a shame that whilst you live at jar,
The fearful French, whom you late vanquishèd,
Should make a start o'er seas and vanquish you?
Methinks already in this civil broil

33.1 *They run to Cade again*] Q; *not in* F

22 **hanged . . . necks** i.e. your pardons will
be worthless
24–5 **White Hart in Southwark** See Appendix B.
25 **given out** abandoned (*OED, give, v.* 62e)
26 **ancient** historical
27 **recreants** traitors
  dastards cowards
28–9 **Let them . . . burdens** Compare
Shylock's gibe at the Venetians' slaves:
'Why sweat they under burdens?'
(*Merchant* 4.1.94).
31 **make shift for one** i.e. look after myself
(proverbial, Dent S334.1)
34 **the son of Henry the Fifth** This is a dangerous argument for Clifford to use, since

the actual son of Henry the Fifth, the
King, has signally failed to conduct
anyone *through the heart of France* (l. 36),
and has indeed lost it. But of course
Clifford is making a jingoistic appeal, and
indeed responding to Cade's earlier apparent concern for the loss of Anjou and
Maine.
  Henry probably has three syllables:
'Hen-er-y'.
37 **meanest** lowest-born
39 **the spoil** looting
41 **jar** odds
42 **fearful** cowardly
43 **start** sudden invasion (*OED sb.*[2] 2c)
44 **broil** conflict

I see them lording it in London streets,   45
Crying '*Villiago!*' unto all they meet.
Better ten thousand base-born Cades miscarry
Than you should stoop unto a Frenchman's mercy.
To France, to France, and get what you have lost!
Spare England, for it is your native coast.   50
Henry hath money; you are strong and manly;
God on our side, doubt not of victory.

ALL CADE'S FOLLOWERS A Clifford! A Clifford! We'll follow
the King and Clifford!

    They forsake Cade

CADE (*aside*) Was ever feather so lightly blown to and fro as   55
this multitude? The name of Henry the Fifth hales them
to an hundred mischiefs, and makes them leave me
desolate. I see them lay their heads together to surprise
me. My sword make way for me, for here is no staying.—
In despite of the devils and hell, have through the very   60
midst of you, and heavens and honour be witness that
no want of resolution in me, but only my followers' base
and ignominious treasons, makes me betake me to my
heels.

    He runs through them with his staff, and flies away

BUCKINGHAM
What, is he fled? Go some, and follow him,   65
And he that brings his head unto the King
Shall have a thousand crowns for his reward.

    Exeunt some of them after Cade

---

61 midst] F (middest)   64.1 *He . . . away*] Q; *Exit* F   67.1 *after Cade*] not in F

---

46 *Villiago* coward. In his English/Italian
dictionary *A World of Words* (1598), John
Florio glosses *vigliacco* 'a rascal, a villain';
but it seems strange that the French
should be imagined using an Italian
expression, and McKerrow suggests that
'Jacquot' or 'Jacot', 'a current diminutive
of "Jacques"' was used 'in a depreciatory
sense', and that 'it would seem more
likely that a Frenchman would call an
Englishman "vil Jacquot" than by an Italian term of abuse'.
47 **miscarry** die prematurely

52 **God** with God
53 **A Clifford!** 'A', representing French 'à' (=
to), was often prefixed to a general's name
as a rallying-cry, a practice perhaps originating in the French campaigns.
56 **hales** drags
58 **lay . . . together** conspire (proverbial:
Dent H280)
    surprise capture
60 **despite** spite
64.1 *He . . . away* This stage direction, from
Q, specifies how Cade escapes.
67 **a thousand crowns** (a substantial sum)

(*To the remaining rebels*)
Follow me, soldiers, we'll devise a mean
To reconcile you all unto the King.   *Exeunt*

4.9   *Sound trumpets. Enter King Henry, Queen Margaret,*
        and the Duke of Somerset on the terrace

KING HENRY
Was ever king that joyed an earthly throne
And could command no more content than I?
No sooner was I crept out of my cradle
But I was made a king at nine months old.
Was never subject longed to be a king   5
As I do long and wish to be a subject.
        Enter the Duke of Buckingham and Lord Clifford
BUCKINGHAM (*to King Henry*)
Health and glad tidings to your majesty.

---

68 **mean** way

4.9.0.1–2 This short scene raises several difficulties. (1) F brings the King out *on the Tarras*. There is some evidence that *Tarras* was a technical term referring to the balcony above the Elizabethan stage (George F. Reynolds, 'Was there a "Tarras" in Shakespeare's Globe?', *SS 4* (1951), 97–100), and the King obviously enters on the balcony, suggesting castle walls. *OED* regards *tarras* as a variant spelling of *terrace*, hence the modernization here—at the risk of being misleading, since *terrace* now implies a ground-level rather than an upper area. (2) The natural deduction is that the walls are those of Kenilworth Castle, to which the King fled at the end of 4.4: but it seems a long way to escort *multitudes* of prisoners (l. 9.1) from London; Hall says that the King 'came into Kent' to pass his merciful judgement; and Q's very truncated scene is located at Windsor Castle (l. 1885). On the unlocalized Elizabethan stage, the dramatic situation is that the King appears safely protected on castle walls, and the prisoners are brought to him for judgement at ground level. (3) F begins the scene with '*Sound trumpets*', the usual accompaniment for royal entries; yet the King has a very personal, intimate opening speech, which he has to deliver from the balcony, where scenes 'lose their psychological immediacy' (Reynolds, p. 99). Perhaps that is the point: Henry's introspective personality is set against the standard pomp attending a king. There is a similar juxtaposition at the end of the scene: see l. 49.1 and note.

0.1 *Queen Margaret* She is uncharacteristically silent throughout the scene, but her silence may be eloquent, inviting the performer to suggest alienation from the crisis and the King, or absorption in her own grief for Suffolk, or both. Q gives her a version of 4.4.40–1, which may be a deliberate attempt to break the silence, rather than a reporter's misremembering.

1 **joyed** enjoyed

3 **crept . . . cradle** able to crawl

4 **at nine months old** Henry was born on 6 December 1421; Henry V died on 31 August 1422.

6.1 *Enter . . . Clifford* Oxford suggests that they enter *on the terrace* (i.e. to the King on the balcony), but surely they enter on the same (ground) level as the prisoners they are escorting, as Q implies by bringing Buckingham, Clifford, and the rebel prisoners on at the same time. Calling up to the King helps to emphasize the distance between the ground and (the safe protection of) the castle battlements.

KING HENRY
Why, Buckingham, is the traitor Cade surprised?
Or is he but retired to make him strong?
Enter multitudes with halters about their necks
CLIFFORD
He is fled, my lord, and all his powers do yield,   10
And humbly thus with halters on their necks
Expect your highness' doom of life or death.
KING HENRY
Then heaven, set ope thy everlasting gates
To entertain my vows of thanks and praise.
(*To the multitudes below*)
Soldiers, this day have you redeemed your lives,   15
And showed how well you love your prince and country.
Continue still in this so good a mind,
And Henry, though he be infortunate,
Assure yourselves will never be unkind.
And so with thanks and pardon to you all,   20
I do dismiss you to your several countries.
ALL CADE'S FORMER FOLLOWERS God save the King! God save
the King!   *Exeunt*
Enter a Messenger
MESSENGER (*to King Henry*)
Please it your grace to be advertisèd
The Duke of York is newly come from Ireland,   25
And with a puissant and a mighty power

4.9.22 ALL . . . FOLLOWERS] OXFORD; *All.* F   23 *Exeunt*] not in F

8 **surprised** taken
9 **him** himself
9.1 **multitudes** A typically authorial phrase,
    to indicate as many actors as can be
    spared.
    halters nooses (i.e. ready to be hanged, if
    that is what the King decides)
10 **powers** forces
12 **Expect** await
    doom sentence
13–14 **Then . . . praise** Henry echoes Psalm
    24: 7–9 in Sternhold and Hopkins's ver-
    sion: 'open your gates, stand open, | the
    everlasting gate'.
14 **entertain** receive
18 **infortunate** unfortunate
21 **several countries** different regions

23.1 *Enter a Messenger* Again (see the note
    to 6.1), Oxford puts this entry to the King
    on the terrace. This is possible (and might
    help to avoid a traffic-jam with the depart-
    ing multitudes below); but on the other
    hand, this important information might
    be even more effective called up to the
    King from stage level, and the Messenger
    being amongst the departing rebels might
    help to point up Henry's lines 32–6.
24 **Please it . . . advertisèd** may it please your
    grace to be informed (*advertisèd* is stressed
    on the second syllable, as always in
    Shakespeare)
25 **The Duke . . . Ireland** See Appendix B. He
    makes a ceremonial entry at 5.1.0.1.
26 **puissant . . . power** powerful army

Of galloglasses and stout Irish kerns
Is marching hitherward in proud array,
And still proclaimeth, as he comes along,
His arms are only to remove from thee   30
The Duke of Somerset, whom he terms a traitor.

KING HENRY
Thus stands my state 'twixt Cade and York distressed,
Like to a ship that having scaped a tempest,
Is straightway calmed and boarded with a pirate.
But now is Cade driven back, his men dispersed,   35
And now is York in arms to second him.
I pray thee Buckingham, go and meet him,
And ask him what's the reason of these arms.
Tell him I'll send Duke Edmund to the Tower;
And Somerset, we will commit thee thither,   40
Until his army be dismissed from him.

SOMERSET
My lord, I'll yield myself to prison willingly,
Or unto death, to do my country good.

KING HENRY (*to Buckingham*)
In any case, be not too rough in terms,
For he is fierce and cannot brook hard language.   45

BUCKINGHAM
I will, my lord, and doubt not so to deal
As all things shall redound unto your good.

---

27 stout Irish] COLLIER (*conj.* Mitford); stout F   34 calmed] F4; calme F1

27 **galloglasses** Irish cavalry armed with axes (*kerns* were less well-armed infantry)
stout strong
Irish Collier's insertion creates a regular, more flowing line.
28 **hitherward** in this direction
proud array military formation
30 **arms are** army is
32 **state** Editors gloss 'condition'; but doesn't Henry mean his kingdom, caught between one rebellion and another?
33 **scaped** An aphetic variant of 'escape', common until the end of the seventeenth century (*OED v.*[1] 1).
34 **calmed** becalmed

35 **But now** just now
36 **second** reinforce (which was, of course, York's plan all along: see 3.1.379–81)
37, 40 **Buckingham, Somerset** There is no awkwardness in Henry calling down a command to Buckingham on the stage and then turning to address Somerset beside him on the balcony.
38 **of** for
39 **Duke Edmund** i.e. Somerset
44 **be . . . terms** avoid aggressive language
45 **brook** endure
46 **deal** negotiate
47 **redound unto** turn out for

KING HENRY
    Come wife, let's in and learn to govern better,
    For yet may England curse my wretched reign.

                                    ⌈*Flourish.*⌉ *Exeunt*

4.10   *Enter Jack Cade*

CADE Fie on ambitions; fie on myself that have a sword
    and yet am ready to famish. These five days have I hid
    me in these woods and durst not peep out, for all the
    country is laid for me. But now am I so hungry that if
    I might have a lease of my life for a thousand years,   5
    I could stay no longer. Wherefore o'er a brick wall have I
    climbed into this garden to see if I can eat grass or pick
    a sallet another while, which is not amiss to cool a
    man's stomach this hot weather. And I think this word
    'sallet' was born to do me good; for many a time, but for   10
    a sallet, my brain-pan had been cleft with a brown bill;
    and many a time when I have been dry, and bravely
    marching, it hath served me instead of a quart pot to
    drink in; and now the word 'sallet' must serve me to feed
    on.   15
        Enter Alexander Iden

4.10.6 o'er] HANMER; on F

48–49.1 **Come . . . Flourish** It is awkward
that these lines must be belted out from
the balcony, to be followed by a flourish of
trumpets (see note to 4.9.0.1–2 (3)). They
are surely very personal and intimate,
Henry admitting his failure as a king,
and what is more an ignominious—
wretched—failure, and perhaps, too, trying to draw Margaret out of her state
of grief and/or alienation (see note to
4.9.0.1).
4.10.1 **Fie** An exclamation of reproach.
3 **woods** (surrounding the *garden* into
which Cade says he has *climbed* at l. 7)
durst dared
4 **laid** set with ambushes (*OED*, *lay*, *v.*[1] 18b)
5 **have a lease of my life** i.e. live (proverbial:
'No man has a lease of his life' (Dent
M327))
6 **stay** (in hiding)
o'er F's 'on' makes sense, but it is
probably a slip for *o'er*, spelt 'or' in the

manuscript.
8, 10, 11 **sallet** (a) salad (leaf), herb (b) light
helmet (French *salade*)
8 **while** time
8–9 **cool a man's stomach** (a) satisfy a man's
hunger (b) pacify a man's anger
9–10 **this word 'sallet'** As well as the pun on
sallet (see note to ll. 8, 10, 11), there may
be another on *word* and 'wort', meaning
herb.
10 **but** were it not
11 **cleft** split in two
brown bill 'A long-handled weapon with
an axe-like blade. The brown colour is
from blood or varnish' (Norton).
15.1 **Enter Alexander Iden** Q begins the scene
here, with a simultaneous entry for Cade
and Iden. For further discussion, see Textual Introduction, p. 95.
Iden For a discussion of the divergent
reactions provoked by this character, see
Introduction, pp. 55–6.

IDEN

Lord, who would live turmoilèd in the court
And may enjoy such quiet walks as these?
This small inheritance my father left me
Contenteth me, and worth a monarchy.
I seek not to wax great by others' waning,   20
Or gather wealth I care not with what envy;
Sufficeth that I have maintains my state,
And sends the poor well pleasèd from my gate.

CADE (*aside*) Zounds, here's the lord of the soil come to seize
   me for a stray for entering his fee-simple without leave.   25
   (*To Iden*) Ah villain, thou wilt betray me and get a thousand crowns of the king by carrying my head to him; but
   I'll make thee eat iron like an ostrich and swallow my
   sword like a great pin, ere thou and I part.

IDEN

Why, rude companion, whatsoe'er thou be,   30
I know thee not, why then should I betray thee?
Is't not enough to break into my garden,
And like a thief to come to rob my grounds,
Climbing my walls in spite of me the owner,
But thou wilt brave me with these saucy terms?   35

20 waning] ROWE 1714; warning F   24 Zounds] Q; *not in* F   26 Ah] F (A)

16–17 **who would ... these** Behind these
   lines lies the classical tradition that the life
   of contemplation is superior to that of
   action, as expressed in the Odes of Horace
   and recreated in English seventeenth-
   century poetry in Marvell's *The Garden*
   and *Horatian Ode* (see J. B. Leishman,
   Translating Horace (Oxford, 1956),
   pp. 22–5, 98–100).
16 **turmoilèd** harassed
17 **quiet walks** Compare 2.2.3. It is interesting that both the loyal subject and the
   traitor choose to use secluded paths for
   very different purposes.
19 **and** and is
20 **wax** become
21 **I care ... what** regardless of others'
   envy malice
22–3 **Sufficeth ... gate** This was perhaps
   suggested by a biblical passage: 'If I have
   seen any ... poor without covering ...
   when I saw that I might help him in the

gate' (Job 31 : 19–21).
22 **Sufficeth that** it is enough that what
   maintains my state supports my way of
   life
23 **pleasèd** contented
24 **Zounds** See the first note to 4.2.84.
24–5 **lord of the soil ... stray ...
   fee-simple** These are all legal terms.
   A landowner had the freehold right to
   seize any *stray* animal on his property
   (*fee-simple*).
28 **eat ... like an ostrich** Proverbial (Dent
   I97), based on the belief that ostriches ate
   iron for their digestion. Cade means he
   will force his sword down Iden's throat
   (and so extend it like an ostrich's).
30 **rude companion** base fellow
   whatsoe'er whoever
35 **brave** taunt, insult
   saucy insolent
   terms language

CADE Brave thee? Ay, by the best blood that ever was
broached, and beard thee too! Look on me well: I have eat
no meat these five days, yet come thou and thy five men,
and if I do not leave you all as dead as a doornail I pray
God I may never eat grass more.   40

IDEN
Nay, it shall ne'er be said while England stands
That Alexander Iden, an esquire of Kent,
Took odds to combat a poor famished man.
Oppose thy steadfast gazing eyes to mine;
See if thou canst outface me with thy looks.   45
Set limb to limb, and thou art far the lesser:
Thy hand is but a finger to my fist,
Thy leg a stick comparèd with this truncheon.
My foot shall fight with all the strength thou hast,
And if mine arm be heavèd in the air,   50
Thy grave is digged already in the earth.
As for words, whose greatness answers's words,
Let this my sword report what speech forbears.

CADE By my valour, the most complete champion that ever
I heard. (*To his sword*) Steel, if thou turn the edge or cut   55
not out the burly-boned clown in chines of beef ere thou

36 **best** noblest
37 **broached** caused to flow (as if released
from a wine-cask); *OED ppl. a.*, whose
earliest example is from Ford's *The Broken
Heart* (1633?) 5.2.125: 'It [the blood]
sparkles like a lusty wine new broached'.
beard thee defy you to your face (perhaps
originating from the deadly insult of
plucking a man by the beard)
37 **eat** eaten
38 **thy five men** Perhaps taking its cue from
this phrase, Q introduces servants with
Iden at his entrance, but, as McKerrow
says, there is 'no indication in F that he is
not alone, and the whole tone of the
scene [especially the opening soliloquy]
suggests that he is. The "five men" may be
no more than a vague number suggested
by Cade's five days' fast' (l. 2—which may
itself be a vague term, simply suggesting
'a long time'): Cade may be defying Iden
to bring 'all the men you have'.
39 **as dead ... doornail** Proverbial (Dent

D567).
40 **eat grass** (live to) eat
43 **odds** advantage
44 **Oppose ... mine** look me in the eye
45 **outface ... looks** stare me down
46 **Set** compare
48 **truncheon** thick staff (i.e. Iden's leg)
50 **heavèd** raised
52-3 **As for ... forbears** 'The general sense
seems to be "As for words—my sword
(not my tongue) shall show whose greatness answers his words". [F's] "answer's"
presumably stands for "answers his"'
(McKerrow).
52 **answer's** matches his
53 **forbears** declines (to answer)
54 **complete** accomplished
55 **turn the edge** fail to cut
56 **burly-boned** hulking
clown countryman
in chines into joints
ere before

sleep in thy sheath, I beseech God on my knees thou
mayst be turned to hobnails.

Here they fight, and Cade falls

O I am slain! Famine and no other hath slain me. Let ten
thousand devils come against me, and give me but the ten   60
meals I have lost, and I'd defy them all. Wither, garden,
and be henceforth a burying place to all that do dwell
in this house, because the unconquered soul of Cade is
fled.

IDEN
Is't Cade that I have slain, that monstrous traitor?   65
Sword, I will hallow thee for this thy deed
And hang thee o'er my tomb when I am dead.
Ne'er shall this blood be wipèd from thy point
But thou shalt wear it as a herald's coat
To emblaze the honour that thy master got.   70

CADE Iden farewell, and be proud of thy victory. Tell Kent
from me she hath lost her best man, and exhort all the
world to be cowards. For I, that never feared any, am
vanquished by famine, not by valour.   *He dies*

IDEN
How much thou wrong'st me, heaven be my judge.   75
Die damnèd wretch, the curse of her that bare thee!
And as I thrust thy body in with my sword, ⌜*stabbing
him again*⌝
So wish I I might thrust thy soul to hell.

---

57 God] Q; Ioue F   58.1 *and Cade falls*] Q (*subs.*); *not in* F

---

57 **God** Q's reading makes it almost certain
that F's 'Jove' was a substitution in
response to the law of 1606 against blasphemy in plays; but if so the censorship
was partial, since 'God' occurs frequently
during the play.

58 **turned to hobnails** The steel of the sword
will be used for the nails of boots (proverbial: Dent H480.1).

65 **monstrous** unnatural (as well, perhaps,
as the more usual modern meaning)

66 **hallow** consecrate

67 **hang ... dead** Weapons were often used
as part of the memorial on a tomb.

69 **thou ... coat** The blood on the sword will
act as a heraldic device.

70 **emblaze** proclaim (as a device in
heraldry does its owner)

76 **bare** bore, carried (the usual past tense of
'to bear' until after 1600: OED, *bear, v.*[1])

77–8 Iden's stabbing of Cade's corpse anticipates Richard of Gloucester's stabbing of
King Henry's at 3 *Henry VI* 5.6.66–7: 'If
any spark of life be yet remaining, |
Down, down to hell, and say I sent thee
thither'.

77 **thrust ... in** pierce

Hence will I drag thee headlong by the heels
Unto a dunghill, which shall be thy grave,   80
And there cut off thy most ungracious head,
Which I will bear in triumph to the King,
Leaving thy trunk for crows to feed upon.
                                        Exit with the body

5.1   *Enter the Duke of York and his army of Irish with a*
           drummer and soldiers bearing colours

YORK
From Ireland thus comes York to claim his right
And pluck the crown from feeble Henry's head.
Ring bells aloud, burn bonfires clear and bright,
To entertain great England's lawful king.
Ah *sancta maiestas*! Who would not buy thee dear?   5
Let them obey that knows not how to rule;
This hand was made to handle naught but gold.
I cannot give due action to my words,
Except a sword or sceptre balance it.
A sceptre shall it have, have I a sword,   10
On which I'll toss the fleur-de-lis of France.
    Enter the Duke of Buckingham

83.1 *with the body*] *not in* F
    5.1.0.1–2 *a drummer ... colours*] *Drum and Colours.* F   10 sword] CAIRNCROSS (*conj.*
Johnson); soule F

---

79 **headlong** head downwards
81 **ungracious** wicked (lacking grace)
5.1–3 Act 5 dramatizes the outbreak of the
    Wars of the Roses, condensing chronicle
    material from York's return from Ireland
    in 1451 to the first battle of St Albans in
    1455: see Appendix B, 4.9.25–31, 5.1, 5.2.
5.1.0.1 *army of Irish* the *galloglasses* and
    kerns referred to at 4.9.27: see the note.
    Perhaps they were recognizable by dis-
    tinctive costumes or props—e.g. the *gallo-
    glasses* by their axes; but since this phrase
    only occurs in F, it may simply be an
    authorial identification, rather than a cue
    for staging.
0.2 *soldiers   bearing   colours*
    standard-bearers
  3 **Ring   bells ... burn   bonfires** (in
    celebration)

4 **entertain** welcome
5 *sancta maiestas* sacred majesty (from
    Ovid's *Ars Amatoria* 3.407, where it refers
    to the renown of poets)
7 **gold** (the gold regalia of kingship)
8–9 York's attitude here is cruelly mocked by
    Queen Margaret when she slaughters him
    in *3 Henry VI*: 'York cannot speak unless
    he wear a crown' (1.4.94)—so she gives
    him a paper one.
8 **due** appropriate
9 **Except** unless
10 **have I a sword** as surely as I have a
    sword. This emendation of F's 'soul' is
    necessary, because of the next line: a
    weapon is needed to *toss the fleur-de-lis*.
11 **toss** impale and display (as if on a pike)
    fleur-de-lis lily or iris (the national
    emblem of France)

Whom have we here? Buckingham to disturb me?
The King hath sent him sure; I must dissemble.

BUCKINGHAM
York, if thou meanest well, I greet thee well.

YORK
Humphrey of Buckingham, I accept thy greeting. 15
Art thou a messenger, or come of pleasure?

BUCKINGHAM
A messenger from Henry, our dread liege,
To know the reason of these arms in peace;
Or why thou, being a subject as I am,
Against thy oath and true allegiance sworn, 20
Should raise so great a power without his leave,
Or dare to bring thy force so near the court?

YORK (*aside*)
Scarce can I speak, my choler is so great.
O I could hew up rocks and fight with flint,
I am so angry at these abject terms; 25
And now, like Ajax Telamonius,
On sheep or oxen could I spend my fury.
I am far better born than is the King,
More like a king, more kingly in my thoughts;
But I must make fair weather yet a while, 30
Till Henry be more weak and I more strong.—
Buckingham, I prithee pardon me,
That I have given no answer all this while;
My mind was troubled with deep melancholy.
The cause why I have brought this army hither 35

---

13 **sure** for certain
16 **of pleasure** on your own initiative
18 **of . . . peace** for these armed forces in peacetime
23 Q prefaces its shorter version of York's angry speech with the indignant exclamation 'A subject as he is!' (l. 1981), quoting Buckingham's words at l. 19; it perhaps launches York's speech more effectively, and might be incorporated in modern performance.
choler anger
24 **hew up** This literally means 'cut up by the root' (*OED, hew, v.* 4b), but is here a graphically impressionistic phrase,

'wrench out of the ground'.
with flint (rather than with weapons)
25 **abject terms** insulting words
26–7 **like Ajax . . . fury** During the Trojan Wars, Ajax, son of Telamon, was so incensed that the armour of the dead hero Achilles was given to Ulysses instead of to himself that he slaughtered a flock of sheep in insane rage. This Ajax is a different one from the Ajax who appears in *Troilus and Cressida*.
27 **spend** vent
30 **make fair weather** pretend to be friendly (proverbial: Dent W221)

Is to remove proud Somerset from the King,
Seditious to his grace and to the state.
BUCKINGHAM
That is too much presumption on thy part;
But if thy arms be to no other end,
The King hath yielded unto thy demand: 40
The Duke of Somerset is in the Tower.
YORK
Upon thine honour, is he prisoner?
BUCKINGHAM
Upon mine honour, he is prisoner.
YORK
Then Buckingham, I do dismiss my powers.
Soldiers, I thank you all; disperse yourselves;   45
Meet me tomorrow in Saint George's field.
You shall have pay and everything you wish.
⌈*Exeunt soldiers*⌉
(*To Buckingham*) And let my sovereign, virtuous Henry,
Command my eldest son, nay all my sons,
As pledges of my fealty and love,   50
I'll send them all as willing as I live.
Lands, goods, horse, armour, anything I have
Is his to use, so Somerset may die.
BUCKINGHAM
York, I commend this kind submission.
We twain will go into his highness' tent.   55
  Enter King Henry and attendants

47.1 *Exeunt soldiers*] Q; *not in* F

37 **Seditious** a traitor
43 **Upon . . . prisoner** Buckingham's oath is
   given in good faith; he is compromised by
   the Queen (ll. 85–6).
46 **Saint George's field** An open space
   between Southwark and Lambeth, used
   as a training ground for the London
   militia.
47.1 Although York's commands seem to
   justify Q's stage direction (absent from F),
   it is possible that some soldiers remain,
   to be referred to by the King at l. 60, and
   perhaps by York at l. 109; but see the note
   to ll. 109–10.
49 **Command** i.e. demand (as hostages)
   my eldest . . . sons This prepares for

the introduction of Edward (the future
Edward IV) and Richard (the future
Richard III) at l. 121.1. In some productions (especially when the plays are
performed as a trilogy) the third son,
George of Clarence, also appears here,
although he is not introduced in F until *3
Henry VI*.
50 **fealty** loyalty
53 **so** provided that
54 **kind** natural, loyal
55 **twain** two
   into . . . tent As he does in Hall (see
   Appendix B, 5.1.12–55); there is no need
   to assume that a tent was used in performance, since in the next line, Henry

KING HENRY

    Buckingham, doth York intend no harm to us,

    That thus he marcheth with thee arm in arm?

YORK

    In all submission and humility

    York doth present himself unto your highness.

KING HENRY

    Then what intends these forces thou dost bring? 60

YORK

    To heave the traitor Somerset from hence,

    And fight against that monstrous rebel Cade,

    Who since I heard to be discomfited.

       Enter Iden with Cade's head

IDEN

    If one so rude and of so mean condition

    May pass into the presence of a king, 65

    Lo, I present your grace a traitor's head,

    The head of Cade, whom I in combat slew.

KING HENRY

    The head of Cade? Great God, how just art thou!

    O let me view his visage, being dead,

    That living wrought me such exceeding trouble. 70

    Tell me, my friend, art thou the man that slew him?

IDEN

    Iwis, an't like your majesty.

KING HENRY

    How art thou called? And what is thy degree?

IDEN

    Alexander Iden, that's my name,

    A poor esquire of Kent that loves his king. 75

---

72 Iwis] OXFORD (*conj.* Wilson); I was F

comes to meet them, a point emphasized
by Q's line 'But see, his grace is coming to
meet with us' (2002).

60 **intends** is the purpose of (Onions)
63 **discomfited** defeated
64 **rude** rustic, unpolished
    mean condition low rank
72 **Iwis** yes indeed, certainly (*OED adv.*). F's 'I

was' gives the wrong tense, and Dover
Wilson's emendation is simple and
persuasive. For further discussion, see
Textual Companion, p. 192.
    an't like if it please
73 **How art thou called** what is your name
    degree rank
75 **esquire** (a gentleman below the rank of
    knight)

BUCKINGHAM (*to King Henry*)
>So please it you, my lord, 'twere not amiss
>He were created knight for his good service.

KING HENRY
>Iden, kneel down. Rise up a knight.
>We give thee for reward a thousand marks,
>And will that thou henceforth attend on us.   80

IDEN
>May Iden live to merit such a bounty,
>And never live but true unto his liege.   ⌈*Exit*⌉
>>*Enter Queen Margaret and the Duke of Somerset*

KING HENRY
>See, Buckingham, Somerset comes wi'th' Queen.
>Go bid her hide him quickly from the Duke.

QUEEN MARGARET
>For thousand Yorks he shall not hide his head,   85
>But boldly stand and front him to his face.

YORK
>How now? Is Somerset at liberty?
>Then York, unloose thy long imprisoned thoughts,
>And let thy tongue be equal with thy heart.
>Shall I endure the sight of Somerset?   90
>False King, why hast thou broken faith with me,
>Knowing how hardly I can brook abuse?
>'King' did I call thee? No, thou art not king,
>Not fit to govern and rule multitudes,
>Which dar'st not—no, nor canst not—rule a traitor.   95
>That head of thine doth not become a crown;
>Thy hand is made to grasp a palmer's staff,
>And not to grace an aweful princely sceptre.

---

82 *Exit*] Q; *not in* F   83 wi'th'] OXFORD; with th' F

---

79 **marks** 'These were worth each about two thirds of a pound, although there were no specific coins of this denomination' (Sanders).
80 **will** command
82 Q gives Iden an exit here, which may be right. But the King has just commanded him to *attend on us*; for further discussion, see Introduction, p. 56.

86 **front** confront
89 **be equal with** say precisely what is in
92 **how hardly** with what difficulty
95 **Which** who
96 **doth not become** is not worthy of
97 **palmer's staff** (the staff that was the sign of a pilgrimage made to the Holy Land)
98 **awful** awe-inspiring

That gold must round engird these brows of mine,
Whose smile and frown, like to Achilles' spear,   100
Is able with the change to kill and cure.
Here is a hand to hold a sceptre up,
And with the same to act controlling laws.
Give place! By heaven, thou shalt rule no more
O'er him whom heaven created for thy ruler.   105

SOMERSET

O monstrous traitor! I arrest thee, York,
Of capital treason 'gainst the King and crown.
Obey, audacious traitor, kneel for grace.

YORK

Wouldst have me kneel? First let me ask of these
If they can brook I bow a knee to man.   110
(*To an attendant*)
Sirrah, call in my sons to be my bail.   *Exit attendant*

---

109 these] THEOBALD; thee F   111 sons] Q; sonne F   *Exit attendant*] *not in* F

99 **gold** i.e. the crown
   engird encircle, surround
100 **like to Achilles' spear** The spear of Achilles, the greatest Greek hero in the Trojan War, was reputed to strike a mortal wound and then heal the wound with its rust. The source of the line is probably Ovid's *Metamorphoses* 13.171–2, where Ulysses mentions the spear's double power in the course of a debate over Achilles' arms with the Ajax Telamonius already mentioned by York at l. 26; but the spear's qualities became a proverbial commonplace (Dent S731).
101 **the change** i.e. from smiles to frowns, and back again
103 **act** enact
107 **capital** punishable by death
109–10 **Wouldst . . . man** In l. 109, Theobald emended F's *thee*, which does not make sense, to *these*. The Oxford editors claim that the lines still do not make sense 'since there is no one on stage to whom "these" and "they" (in the second line) can refer. Probably these two lines represent a first thought, abandoned [but inadequately cancelled in the manuscript] when the author realized that York's sons are not

yet on stage' (*Textual Companion*, p. 192), and so omit them from their text. But *someone* must still be on stage for York to send off to fetch his sons in the next line; the simplest explanation is that not all of York's soldiers left at l. 47.1, made likelier by the King's reference to *these forces* at l. 60. Alternatively, as Caincross says, York's 'sons may be assumed to be just off-stage, but within sight'; and he compares l. 147, 'where Warwick and Salisbury are similarly called, and enter immediately'; so York's reference to *my sons* at l. 111 would be a clarification of *these* whom he has already mentioned. There may be other theatrical explanations (at Stratford-upon-Avon in 2000, for example, York's sons ran on to rescue him from Somerset's arrest), and since the lines do not appear irredeemably corrupt, they are retained here.
110 **bow . . . man** kneel to anyone
111 **sons** Historically, Edward was only thirteen at the time of the first battle of St Albans, and Richard three; but dramatic considerations take precedence over historical ones, as they do throughout the play.

I know, ere they will have me go to ward,
They'll pawn their swords for my enfranchisement.

QUEEN MARGARET ⌈*to Buckingham*⌉
Call hither Clifford, bid him come amain,
To say if that the bastard boys of York   115
Shall be the surety for their traitor father.

                         Exit ⌈*Buckingham*⌉

YORK

O blood-bespotted Neapolitan,
Outcast of Naples, England's bloody scourge!
The sons of York, thy betters in their birth,
Shall be their father's bail, and bane to those   120
That for my surety will refuse the boys.

      Enter ⌈*at one door*⌉ *York's sons Edward and Richard*
      ⌈*with a drummer and soldiers*⌉
See where they come, I'll warrant they'll make it good.
      Enter ⌈*at the other door*⌉ *Clifford and his son,* ⌈*with a*
      drummer and soldiers⌉

QUEEN MARGARET
And here comes Clifford to deny their bail.

---

113 for] F2; of F1   116.1 *Exit Buckingham*] CAPELL; *not in* F   121.1–2 *Enter . . . soldiers*] Q
(*subs.*); *Enter Edward and Richard.* F   122.1–2 *Enter . . . soldiers*] Q (*subs.*); *Enter Clifford.* F

---

112 **to ward** into custody
113 **pawn** pledge
     enfranchisement freedom
114, 116.1 **Buckingham** Since he is obviously
not on stage at l. 192, when the King calls
for him, an exit must be found for him,
and this seems the most likely place,
as McKerrow notes. He adds 'it is
strange that he does not return with
Clifford, or indeed later in the scene'.
The problem may have arisen at the
rehearsals for early performances, since Q
moves its version of ll. 192–4 to follow l.
147, so that Buckingham enters to confront Salisbury and Warwick as they
enter. In F's version, there is no obvious
opportunity for Buckingham to reappear.
And see the note to 5.2.71.1–2.
114 **amain** quickly. See the note to 3.1.282.
116 **be the surety** stand bail for
117–18 **blood-bespotted . . . bloody** Not yet:
the dramatist is anticipating Margaret's
contribution to the blood-letting, perhaps
thinking ahead particularly to the scene

where she will ultimately slaughter York
himself (*3 Henry VI* 1.4).
118 **Outcast of Naples** A derisive reference to
Margaret's father being titular King of
Naples.
     scourge whip. Joan of Arc calls herself
'the English scourge' at *1 Henry VI*
1.3.108. 'In this respect Margaret is her
true successor' (Cairncross).
120 **bane** destruction
121.2 **with . . . soldiers** This direction comes
from Q, as do all the entries for soldiers in
the rest of the scene. F brings on the principals alone; this may simply be authorial
shorthand, taking for granted that the
various combatants would need military
support, as in Q; but see the Introduction,
pp. 58–9.
122.1 *Clifford and his son* The Cliffords
were loyal Lancastrians, implacably
opposed to the house of York. Young
Clifford is given an entrance here only in
Q, but he must be present since he speaks
at ll. 211–15.

CLIFFORD (*kneeling before King Henry*)
    Health and all happiness to my lord the King.
        He rises
YORK
    I thank thee, Clifford. Say, what news with thee?   125
    Nay, do not fright us with an angry look;
    We are thy sovereign, Clifford, kneel again.
    For thy mistaking so, we pardon thee.
CLIFFORD
    This is my king, York, I do not mistake.
    But thou mistakes me much to think I do.   130
    (*To King Henry*)
    To Bedlam with him, is the man grown mad?
KING HENRY
    Ay Clifford, a bedlam and ambitious humour
    Makes him oppose himself against his king.
CLIFFORD
    He is a traitor, let him to the Tower,
    And chop away that factious pate of his.   135
QUEEN MARGARET
    He is arrested, but will not obey.
    His sons, he says, shall give their words for him.
YORK (*to Edward and Richard*) Will you not, sons?
EDWARD
    Ay noble father, if our words will serve.
RICHARD
    And if words will not, then our weapons shall.   140
CLIFFORD
    Why, what a brood of traitors have we here!
YORK
    Look in a glass, and call thy image so.

---

124 kneeling . . . Henry] *Clifford kneeles to Henry* Q; *not in* F   124.1 *He rises*] *not in* F

124 Clifford's kneeling, specified in Q but not
     in F, is clearly required by York's *kneel
     again* at l. 127.
130 **thou mistakes** For the idiom *mistakes*,
     rather than '*mistakest*', see the first note
     to 4.1.33.
131, 2 **Bedlam . . . bedlam** The shortened
     form of the 'Bethlehem' Hospital for the
     insane in London is then used by the King
     as an adjective to describe York's mad
     ambition.
132 **humour** disposition
135 **factious pate** rebellious head
139 This is Edward's only line in the Folio
     text, though Q gives him two more at the
     end (see the note to 5.3.0.2). He becomes
     a major character in *3 Henry VI*.
142 **glass** mirror

I am thy king, and thou a false-heart traitor.
Call hither to the stake my two brave bears,
That with the very shaking of their chains   145
They may astonish these fell-lurking curs.
Bid Salisbury and Warwick come to me.

Enter the Earls of Warwick and Salisbury ⌈with a
drummer and soldiers⌉

CLIFFORD
Are these thy bears? We'll bait thy bears to death,
And manacle the bearherd in their chains,
If thou dar'st bring them to the baiting place.   150

RICHARD
Oft have I seen a hot o'erweening cur
Run back and bite, because he was withheld;
Who being suffered with the bear's fell paw,
Hath clapped his tail between his legs and cried;
And such a piece of service will you do,   155
If you oppose yourselves to match Lord Warwick.

CLIFFORD
Hence, heap of wrath, foul indigested lump,
As crooked in thy manners as thy shape!

147.1–2 with . . . soldiers] Q (subs.); not in F   149 bearherd] F (Berard)

---

143 **false-heart** false-hearted, treacherous
144 **Call . . . bears** This reference to Salisbury and Warwick initiates a series of references to bears and bear-baiting (ll. 145–56, 202–10; 5.2.2). Warwick's emblem, a bear and ragged staff (see the note to ll. 202–3). In bear-baiting, the bear was chained to a stake, and set upon by dogs.
146 **astonish** terrify
    fell-lurking savagely waiting (describing the treacherous dogs looking for their moment to attack the chained bear)
149 **manacle** chain up
    bearherd bear-keeper (i.e. York). 'OED assigns Shakespeare's three uses of "berard", etc., to *bearherd* rather than to *bearward*, chiefly because he elsewhere uses *bearherd*, but not *bearward*' (*Textual Companion*, pp. 192–3).
150 **baiting place** bear-baiting pit
151–2 **a hot . . . withheld** The basic idea seems to be that the dog, *withheld* either because restrained by the bear-keeper or because he was watching the moment

to pounce (see l. 146 and second note), became the keener (*o'erweening*) to *run back and bite* the bear, only to be savaged by the bear's paw: this will happen to Clifford if he opposes Warwick.
151 **hot** angry
    o'erweening ambitious
153 **suffered** injured
    with by
156 **oppose yourselves** undertake
157–8 Perhaps these lines should be re-assigned to Young Clifford, as Capell does, thus bringing him into the dialogue sooner, and anticipating his later spat with Richard (ll. 211–16).
    Hence . . . shape This alludes to the view of the Tudor chroniclers (and the plays) that Richard was deformed. *Heap of wrath* suggests a shapeless body consisting entirely of destructive rage: the phrase may be a combination of Arthur Golding's 1567 translation of Ovid's *Metamorphoses* 1.7–8, where chaos is called 'a huge rude heap . . . A heavy lump', with Ovid's *indigestaque*.

YORK

Nay, we shall heat you thoroughly anon.

CLIFFORD

Take heed, lest by your heat you burn yourselves. 160

KING HENRY

Why, Warwick, hath thy knee forgot to bow?
Old Salisbury, shame to thy silver hair,
Thou mad misleader of thy brainsick son!
What, wilt thou on thy deathbed play the ruffian,
And seek for sorrow with thy spectacles? 165
O where is faith? O where is loyalty?
If it be banished from the frosty head,
Where shall it find a harbour in the earth?
Wilt thou go dig a grave to find out war,
And shame thine honourable age with blood? 170
Why art thou old and want'st experience,
Or wherefore dost abuse it if thou hast it?
For shame in duty bend thy knee to me,
That bows unto the grave with mickle age.

SALISBURY

My lord, I have considered with myself 175
The title of this most renownèd Duke,
And in my conscience do repute his grace
The rightful heir to England's royal seat.

KING HENRY

Hast thou not sworn allegiance unto me?

SALISBURY I have. 180

KING HENRY

Canst thou dispense with heaven for such an oath?

---

157 **indigested** unformed. This may also develop the bear imagery, since bear cubs were supposed to be licked into shape by their mothers.

159 **heat you** make you sweat (by fighting)
   anon soon
165 **spectacles** The word could mean either 'eyes' or 'eye-glasses' in Elizabethan usage: it probably means the former here, though either is possible.
167 **frosty** white with age

168 **harbour** shelter
   in the on
169 **to** only to (i.e. die in battle)
172 **abuse** misuse
174 **That** who (i.e. Salisbury)
   mickle great (a northern or north-midlands dialect form, used several times by Shakespeare, as at *Errors* 3.1.45: 'mickle blame')
177 **repute** consider
181 **dispense with** expect dispensation from. The phrase may carry overtones of the

SALISBURY

It is great sin to swear unto a sin,
But greater sin to keep a sinful oath.
Who can be bound by any solemn vow
To do a murd'rous deed, to rob a man,   185
To force a spotless virgin's chastity,
To reave the orphan of his patrimony,
To wring the widow from her customed right,
And have no other reason for this wrong
But that he was bound by a solemn oath?   190

QUEEN MARGARET

A subtle traitor needs no sophister.

KING HENRY (*to an attendant*)

Call Buckingham, and bid him arm himself.

                         Exit attendant

YORK (*to King Henry*)

Call Buckingham and all the friends thou hast,
I am resolved for death or dignity.

CLIFFORD

The first, I warrant thee, if dreams prove true.   195

192.1 *Exit attendant*] *not in* F   194 or] ROWE 1709; *and* F

'dispensation' that the Pope could provide, as when in 1570 he excommunicated Elizabeth I and thus absolved her subjects from their oaths of allegiance (see the note to ll. 182–90).
for for breaking

182–90 **It is . . . oath** This may sound like mere sophistry, as Margaret tartly points out at l. 191, but Salisbury has been presented as the most moderate and thoughtful of the Yorkist faction, and Tom McAlindon shows how the conflicting demands for oaths of loyalty by church and state in the sixteenth century, like those of the rival kings dramatized here, created crises of conscience like Salisbury's ('Swearing and Forswearing in Shakespeare's Histories', *RES* 51 (2000), 208–29). There were determined official attempts to dispose of such confusion, such as the homily 'Against Swearing and Perjury': 'But if a man . . . swear to do anything . . . against the law

of Almighty God, . . . let him take it for an unlawful and ungodly oath' (Shaheen, p. 319). It became proverbial: 'An unlawful oath is better broken than kept' (Dent O7).

187–8 These lines echo the frequent scriptural injunction to protect widows and orphans (e.g. Deuteronomy 10: 18, 27: 19).

187 **reave** deprive, bereave
patrimony inheritance

188 **customed right** a widow's right to inherit her husband's estate
customed accustomed

191 **sophister** specious reasoner (to argue for him)

194 **or** F has 'and'; which may be right: 'I shall not waver whatever comes' (McKerrow).
dignity i.e. the crown

195 **dreams** Presumably Clifford alludes to York's dreams of power, which Warwick in the next line takes as the dreams you have when asleep.

WARWICK

You were best to go to bed and dream again,
To keep you from the tempest of the field.

CLIFFORD

I am resolved to bear a greater storm
Than any thou canst conjure up today;
And that I'll write upon thy burgonet   200
Might I but know thee by thy household badge.

WARWICK

Now by my father's age, old Neville's crest,
The rampant bear chained to the ragged staff,
This day I'll wear aloft my burgonet,
As on a mountain top the cedar shows   205
That keeps his leaves in spite of any storm,
Even to affright thee with the view thereof.

CLIFFORD

And from thy burgonet I'll rend thy bear,

---

197 you] Q; thee F 201 household] Q; housed F1; houses F2 202 age] Q; badge F
207 to] Q; io F1; so F2–4

196–7 **You . . . you** F has 'thee' for the second *you*, Q has 'you' in both lines. F's 'thee' is probably a slip, but it might be intentional. Shakespeare, and the Elizabethans generally, distinguished carefully between the polite 'you' and the familiar or abusive 'thou' (or 'thee'), and Warwick might be deliberately shifting his tone. The abusive 'thou/thee' is unsurprisingly dominant in this scene.

200 **burgonet** A light helmet, topped with a crest, originating in Burgundy, hence the form (*OED a.*).

201 **Might . . . badge** if I might recognize you by your family crest (upon your closed helmet)

202 **Now by my father's age** This is Q's reading; F has 'Now by my father's badge'; otherwise Warwick's speech is identical in F and Q. Both the grammatical structure of the speech (*old Neville's crest . . . I'll wear*) and the idiom *Now by . . .*, which Dover Wilson calls a 'common Shakespearian gambit', make clear that the phrase is an oath or assertion, not that Warwick is telling Clifford that he may recognize him 'by [his] father's badge': the exact phrase does not occur

elsewhere in Shakespeare, but two plays close to *2 Henry VI* in date have 'Now by . . . My father's death' (*Richard III* 4.4.306–7) and 'by my father's reverend tomb' (*Titus* 2.3.296). Salisbury's age, in connection with oaths, is much dwelt on at ll. 162–74. F's 'badge' was almost certainly caught from the 'badge' in the preceding line.

202–3 **old Neville's . . . staff** Warwick inherited the emblem of the bear and ragged staff, and his title, not from his father (Neville) but from his father-in-law, Richard Beauchamp, Earl of Warwick.

203 **rampant** A heraldic term, meaning 'standing on its hind legs'.
ragged jagged, irregular (tree-trunk) (*OED a.*[1] 2a)

204 **aloft** on the top of

205 **cedar** Because of its height and spreading branches, the cedar was a symbol of royalty, as at *Cymbeline* 5.6.454–5. Warwick associates himself with it again at his death: 'Thus yields the cedar to the axe's edge' (*3 Henry VI* 5.2.11).

207 **affright** terrify

And tread it under foot with all contempt,
Despite the bearherd that protects the bear.   210
YOUNG CLIFFORD
And so to arms, victorious father,
To quell the rebels and their complices.
RICHARD
Fie, charity, for shame! Speak not in spite,
For you shall sup with Jesu Christ tonight.
YOUNG CLIFFORD
Foul stigmatic, that's more than thou canst tell.   215
RICHARD
If not in heaven, you'll surely sup in hell.

                                        Exeunt severally

5.2   ⌈*Alarum.*⌉ *Enter the Earl of Warwick*
WARWICK
Clifford of Cumberland, 'tis Warwick calls!
An if thou dost not hide thee from the bear,
Now, when the angry trumpet sounds alarum,
And dead men's cries do fill the empty air,
Clifford I say, come forth and fight with me!   5
Proud northern lord, Clifford of Cumberland,
Warwick is hoarse with calling thee to arms.
        Enter the Duke of York
How now, my noble lord? What, all afoot?

---

210 bearherd] F (Bearard)   216.1 *severally*] *not in* F
5.2.0.1 *Alarum*] Q *(subs.); not in* F

---

212 **complices** accomplices
213 **charity** i.e. for charity
    in spite spitefully
214 **you . . . tonight** Probably a deliberate
    echo of Christ's promise on the cross to
    the repentant thief—'today shalt thou be
    with me in paradise' (Luke 23: 43)—in
    view of Richard's liking for 'odd old ends,
    stol'n forth of Holy Writ' (*Richard III*
    1.3.335).
215 **stigmatic** (one who is branded—
    stigmatized—with a hot iron to make
    his crime known, as Richard is branded
    with deformity)
    that's . . . tell Proverbial: 'That's more
    than I know' (Dent M1155.1).
5.2 For the differences between F and Q in

both sequence and material, see the
Textual Introduction, pp. 93–5. Oxford
adopts Q's order and some of its material;
this edition follows F, which itself follows
the order of events in Hall.
1, 6 **of Cumberland** The Cliffords were not
    created Earls of Cumberland till 1525.
2 **An if** (the emphatic form of 'if')
    bear (picking up from the talk of bears at
    5.1.144–6 and especially 202–10)
3 **sounds alarum** sounds the call to arms
4 **dead** dying
7–8 Between these lines, Oxford inserts
    Clifford's line from Q: 'Warwick, stand
    still, and stir not till I come' (2136). See
    Textual Companion, p. 193.
8 **all afoot** (i.e. without your horse)

YORK

  The deadly-handed Clifford slew my steed.

  But match to match I have encountered him,   10

  And made a prey for carrion kites and crows

  Even of the bonny beast he loved so well.

     Enter Lord Clifford

WARWICK (*to Clifford*)

  Of one or both of us the time is come.

YORK

  Hold, Warwick; seek thee out some other chase,

  For I myself must hunt this deer to death.   15

WARWICK

  Then nobly, York; 'tis for a crown thou fight'st.

  (*To Clifford*) As I intend, Clifford, to thrive today,

  It grieves my soul to leave thee unassailed.   *Exit*

CLIFFORD

  What seest thou in me, York? Why dost thou pause?

YORK

  With thy brave bearing should I be in love,   20

  But that thou art so fast mine enemy.

CLIFFORD

  Nor should thy prowess want praise and esteem,

  But that 'tis shown ignobly and in treason.

YORK

  So let it help me now against thy sword,

  As I in justice and true right express it.   25

---

9 **deadly-handed** murderous

10 **match to match** one opponent to another

11 **carrion kites and crows** Kites are scavenging birds which feed on putrifying carcasses; *carrion crow* is a common name for the crow, and the adjective is transferred to apply to the *kites* as well.

12 **bonny beast** i.e. his horse. *Bonny* is a northern word for 'beautiful' (*OED a.* 1), which may have inspired Q's line 'the bonniest grey that e'er was bred in north' (2144).

13 **the time** i.e. the end of life

14–15 These lines, and the situation, are substantially repeated at *3 Henry VI* 2.4.12–13, where the younger Richard

tells Warwick that he himself will hunt the younger Clifford to death.

14 **chase** game, prey

16 **nobly** (i.e. fight nobly, well)

19–30 **What . . . will** This is the Folio's version of the encounter between York and Clifford. Oxford adopts the Quarto's, given here in Appendix A, Passage G, which is, as the editors say, 'a political emblem of the struggle between York and Lancaster' (*Textual Companion*, p. 193). F, by contrast, allows a moment of chivalry before the full horrors of civil war emerge in the next play.

20 **brave** warlike

    bearing appearance, manner

21 **fast** firmly

CLIFFORD
My soul and body on the action, both.

YORK
A dreadful lay. Address thee instantly.

CLIFFORD
La fin couronne les œuvres.
          Alarums. They fight, and York kills Clifford

YORK
Thus war hath given thee peace, for thou art still.
Peace with his soul, heaven, if it be thy will.   *Exit*   30
          Alarums, then enter Young Clifford

YOUNG CLIFFORD
Shame and confusion, all is on the rout!
Fear frames disorder, and disorder wounds
Where it should guard. O war, thou son of hell,
Whom angry heavens do make their minister,
Throw in the frozen bosoms of our part   35
Hot coals of vengeance! Let no soldier fly!
He that is truly dedicate to war
Hath no self-love; nor he that loves himself
Hath not essentially, but by circumstance,

---

28 œuvres] F2 (*subs.*); *eumenes* F1   28.1 *Alarums . . . Clifford*] Q (*subs.*); *not in* F
30.1 *Alarums . . . Clifford*] Q (*subs.*);   *Enter yong Clifford.* F

---

26 **action** (outcome of the) combat
27 **dreadful lay** awesome wager
    Address prepare
28 *La . . . œuvres* 'The end crowns the
    works' (French). The sentiment was
    proverbial: 'The end crowns all' (Dent
    E116).
29–30 **Thus . . . will** The chivalric tone
    appropriately concludes with York's
    prayer for his opponent's soul: it is imme-
    diately replaced by Young Clifford's, a
    tone which will dominate *3 Henry VI*.
31 **confusion** haphazard destruction
    on the rout in disorderly retreat
32 **frames** creates
32–3 **disorder wounds . . . guard** An image
    of chaos: so great is the *disorder* of the
    battle that soldiers are *wound*ing those
    that they should *guard*—i.e. are kill-
    ing those on their own side. For a

similarly chaotic *rout*, compare *Cymbeline*
5.5.4–51.
34 **minister** agent. The idea is that soldiers,
    by killing people in battle, are the bringers
    of divine retribution.
35 **frozen** (with fear; compare *2 Henry IV*
    1.1.198–9, where it is said of Hotspur's
    soldiers that 'This word "rebellion" . . .
    had froze them up, | As fish are in a
    pond')
    part side
36 **Hot . . . vengeance** Perhaps an echo of
    Psalm 140: 10: 'Let hot burning coals fall
    upon them.'
37 **dedicate** dedicated. See the note to
    1.1.123.
39 **essentially** by nature (as at *Hamlet*
    3.4.171–2: 'I essentially am not in mad-
    ness | But mad in craft')
    circumstance accident

The name of valour.
     He sees his father's body
           O let the vile world end,   40
And the premisèd flames of the last day
Knit earth and heaven together.
Now let the general trumpet blow his blast,
Particularities and petty sounds
To cease! Wast thou ordained, dear father,   45
To lose thy youth in peace, and to achieve
The silver livery of advisèd age,
And in thy reverence and thy chair-days, thus
To die in ruffian battle? Even at this sight
My heart is turned to stone, and while 'tis mine   50
It shall be stony. York not our old men spares;
No more will I their babes. Tears virginal

40 *He . . . body*] *not in* F

40–5 **O let . . . cease** Clifford expresses his grief and horror at his father's death by evoking the Day of Judgement. Although a passage from Ovid's *Metamorphoses* (1.254–8), in which Jupiter plans to destroy the world with fire, may have contributed to the passage, 'it is probable that "flames of the last day" is a reference to Scripture, and that the majority of his audience would have been reminded of the Bible's description of the fiery end of the world' (Shaheen, p. 321), for example 2 Peter 3: 12: 'The day of God, by which the heavens being on fire, shall be dissolved, and the elements shall melt with heat.' L. 43 alludes to the 'last trumpet' (1 Corinthians 15: 52) which 'shall blow' to summon all men to judgement.

40 **vile world** A characteristically Shakespearian phrase, recurring at Sonnet 71.4 and at the death of Cleopatra (*Antony* 5.2.308).

41 **premisèd** predestined

43 **general trumpet** (because it calls everyone, at the last judgement)

44 **Particularities** individual details (contrasted with *general* in the previous line, a distinction already drawn, punningly, by Jack Cade at 4.2.102–3)
    petty trivial (compared with that of the last trumpet)

45 **ordained** fated

46 **lose** waste

47 **livery** uniform (i.e. his white hair)
    advisèd wise, well-considered (Onions)

48 **reverence** venerable age
    chair-days i.e. last days, in which you need to sit in, or be carried in, a chair. In his grief Clifford greatly exaggerates his father's senility: the picture he presents bears little resemblance to the vigorous, belligerent old warrior we have seen on stage.

50–1 **My . . . stony** Proverbial: 'A heart as hard as a stone' (Dent H311), ultimately derived from the Bible, for example 1 Samuel 25: 37: 'His heart died within him, and he was like a stone.' Compare *Othello* 4.1.178–9: 'my heart is turned to stone; I strike it, and it hurts my hand.'

51 **stony** pitiless
    York The house of York, as *their* in the next line makes clear.

52–60 **No more . . . fame** This anticipates Clifford's slaughter of York's young son Rutland in *3 Henry VI* 1.3. In performance, this focused savagery can seem more chilling than the general butchery of the Cade scenes.

52 **virginal** This may mean 'of young girls', or more generally 'of young and innocent people' (like Rutland).

Shall be to me even as the dew to fire,
And beauty that the tyrant oft reclaims
Shall to my flaming wrath be oil and flax.   55
Henceforth I will not have to do with pity.
Meet I an infant of the house of York,
Into as many gobbets will I cut it
As wild Medea young Absyrtus did.
In cruelty will I seek out my fame.   60
Come, thou new ruin of old Clifford's house;
        He takes his father's body upon his back
As did Aeneas old Anchises bear,
So bear I thee upon my manly shoulders.
But then Aeneas bare a living load,
Nothing so heavy as these woes of mine.   65
                              Exit with the body
        Alarums. Then enter Richard and the Duke of Somerset
        to fight. Richard kills Somerset

RICHARD
    So lie thou there:

59 Absyrtus] F (*Absirtis*)   61.1 *He . . . back*] Q (*subs.*); *not in* F   65.1 *Exit . . . body*] *Exet* yoong
Clifford with his father. Q; *not in* F   65.2–3 *Alarums . . . Somerset*] *Enter Richard, and Somerset to
fight.* F

53 **dew to fire** Water drops sprinkled on to fire
    were held to make it burn more fiercely.
54 **beauty . . . reclaims** Especially after *vir-
    ginal* at l. 52, this may be a specific allu-
    sion to Marlowe's *Tamburlaine*, Part 1,
    5.1.64–206: after slaughtering four vir-
    gins of Damascus, because he has sworn
    to do so, Tamburlaine yields to the influ-
    ence of Zenocrate's beauty and spares her
    father.
    reclaims subdues, recalls to human
    feeling
55 **to . . . flax** act like oil and flax on my flam-
    ing anger (i.e. intensify it). This line com-
    bines two proverbs: 'Put not fire to flax'
    (Dent F278) and 'To add oil to the fire'
    (Dent O30).
57 **Meet I** if I meet
58 **gobbets** lumps of flesh
59 **As . . . did** The sorceress Medea, carried
    away (*wild*) with passion for Jason, fled
    with him from her father; she killed and
    cut up her brother Absyrtus, scattering
    the pieces behind her to delay her father
    who paused in his pursuit to pick them
    up. Absyrtus is mentioned by name in

Ovid's *Tristia*, 3.9.6, a work that may
have contributed to the composition
of the parting of Margaret and Suffolk
(see the note to 3.2.343–416). F's
'Absirtis' may be the author's slip or the
compositor's.
61 **new . . . house** i.e. Old Clifford's body.
    The description of a corpse in terms of
    a ruined building occurs elsewhere in
    Shakespeare, for example at *King John*
    4.3.65: 'this ruin of sweet life'.
62 **As . . . bear** In Virgil's *Aeneid* 2.707–804,
    Aeneas carries his old father Anchises on
    his back from the sack of Troy. Cassius
    uses a very similar phrase to Clifford's at
    Julius Caesar 1.2.114–16.
64 **bare** See the note to 4.10.76.
65 **heavy** (a) weighty (b) sorrowful
65.1–3 Q inserts a combat between Clifford
    and Richard, picking up from their
    verbal duel at 5.1.213–16. See the Textual
    Introduction, p. 94. In Q's text, the
    Richard/Somerset combat that follows at
    this point in F and this edition, takes place
    at the start of the battle sequence (i.e.
    before Warwick's entry at 5.2.0.1).

For underneath an alehouse' paltry sign,
The Castle in Saint Albans, Somerset
Hath made the wizard famous in his death.
Sword, hold thy temper; heart, be wrathful still;   70
Priests pray for enemies, but princes kill.

Exit ⌈with Somerset's body⌉
Alarums. Enter King Henry, Queen Margaret, and
others

QUEEN MARGARET
Away my lord, you are slow, for shame, away!

KING HENRY
Can we outrun the heavens? Good Margaret, stay.

QUEEN MARGARET
What are you made of? You'll nor fight nor fly.
Now is it manhood, wisdom, and defence,   75

71.1 *Exit . . . body*] *Exet* Q; *Fight. Excursions.* F   71.2 *Alarums*] *not in* F ; Alarmes againe, and
then enter three or foure, bearing the Duke of *Buckingham* wounded to his Tent. | Alarmes
still Q

---

67 **underneath . . . sign** In its preceding stage direction, Q says that Richard kills Somerset 'under the sign of the Castle in Saint Albans' (ll. 2112–13). Oxford comments: 'while "the sign of the Castle" may have been a stage property employed in this scene, the Q direction may equally be the reporter "literalizing" for his reader: the dialogue in both texts would make it clear to an audience that Somerset lay dead under the ale-house sign, whether that sign were actually present on stage or not' (*Textual Companion* p. 193).
paltry crude. Compare 3.2.81 and note.

68–9 **Somerset . . . death** Somerset has justified the prophecies made about him at 1.4.34–6. Richard's allusion may be a general one, or *wizard* may refer specifically to Bolingbroke, who conjured up the prophesying spirit.

70 **hold thy temper** maintain your hardness and resilience (i.e. don't break), perhaps with a pun on *temper* (remain angry), in view of the next phrase.

71 **Priests . . . enemies** A derisive reference to one of the basic tenets of Christianity, delivered by Christ during the Sermon on the Mount: 'Love your enemies'

(Matthew 5: 44).

71.1–2 Between these lines Oxford inserts a direction from Q in which Buckingham is carried wounded to his tent. There is no reference to Buckingham's fate in F, which is consistent with what seems to be F's generally uncertain treatment of Buckingham throughout the play, and which is even sustained in the opening of the next play, where he is said to be 'either slain or wounded dangerous' (*3 Henry VI* 1.1.11). Q's direction may report something in an earlier version of the play, or simply be the company's attempt to tie up a loose end. The BBC television version ties it more tightly: in the battle, Buckingham's throat is cut.

73–4 **Can we . . . fly** The contrasting personalities of Henry and Margaret are sustained in their brief final appearance in the play. Henry's line reinforces his religious cast of mind, using what Shaheen calls 'a common religious idea rather than . . . a conscious reference to scripture' (p. 322); and Margaret's exasperation with him is surely audible in her reply.

73 **outrun** escape

74 **nor . . . nor** neither . . . nor

To give the enemy way, and to secure us
By what we can, which can no more but fly.
    Alarum afar off
If you be ta'en, we then should see the bottom
Of all our fortunes; but if we haply scape—
As well we may if not through your neglect—   80
We shall to London get where you are loved,
And where this breach now in our fortunes made
May readily be stopped.
    Enter Young Clifford
YOUNG CLIFFORD (*to King Henry*)
But that my heart's on future mischief set,
I would speak blasphemy ere bid you fly;   85
But fly you must; uncurable discomfit
Reigns in the hearts of all our present parts.
Away for your relief, and we will live
To see their day and them our fortune give.
Away my lord, away!   *Exeunt*   90

5.3   *Alarum. Retreat. Enter the Duke of York, his sons*
           Edward and Richard, the Earl of Warwick, and soldiers,
           with a drummer and some bearing colours

YORK
    Of Salisbury, who can report of him,

83.1 *Young*] *not in* F
  5.3.0.2 *Edward*] Q3; *not in* F, Q1–2 0.3 *a drummer . . . colours*] Drum & Colours. F 1]
OXFORD *opens scene, after* Q: How now, boys ! Fortunate this fight hath been, | I hope, to us and
ours for England's good | And our great honour, that so long we lost | Whilst faint-heart Henry
did usurp our rights.

76 **To . . . way** to cease fighting the enemy
    (i.e. retreat)
    secure us save ourselves
77 **what** whatever means
    which . . . fly (we) who are not able to do
    anything other than take flight
78 **ta'en** taken
    bottom lowest point
79 **haply scape** by chance escape
80 Margaret's exasperation surfaces again in
    this parenthesis.
81 **where you are loved** Here the play departs
    from the chronicles: Hall says that it was
    York who had 'too many friends about the
    city of London' (p. 232). The dramatist,
    reading hastily, may have mistaken to
    whom Hall's 'he' refers.

82–3 **breach . . . be stopped** The image is of a
    hole shot in a castle's defences being
    hastily filled up again.
84 **But that** were it not for the fact that
85 **speak blasphemy** take God's name in
    vain. Again Clifford is using extreme ter-
    minology to reflect his extreme state.
    ere before
86 **uncurable** irreversible
    discomfit defeat, discouragement (*OED sb.
    obs.*)
87 **present parts** remaining forces
88 **relief** safety (from danger)
89 **To see . . . give** to gain a victory like theirs
    and give them a defeat like ours
5.3.0.1 **Retreat** A fanfare signalling the end
    of the battle.

That winter lion who in rage forgets
Agèd contusions and all brush of time,
And like a gallant in the brow of youth,
Repairs him with occasion. This happy day   5
Is not itself, nor have we won one foot
If Salisbury be lost.

RICHARD   My noble father,
Three times today I holp him to his horse,
Three times bestrid him; thrice I led him off,
Persuaded him from any further act;   10
But still where danger was, still there I met him,
And like rich hangings in a homely house,
So was his will in his old feeble body.
But noble as he is, look where he comes.

     Enter the Earl of Salisbury

SALISBURY

Now by my sword, well hast thou fought today;   15
By th' mass, so did we all. I thank you, Richard.
God knows how long it is I have to live,
And it hath pleased him that three times today

14–14.1 But noble . . . *Salisbury*] F ; *Enter the Earls of Salisbury and Warwick* | EDWARD (*to York*) | See, noble father, where they both do come— | The only props unto the house of York ! OXFORD (*after* Q)

0.2 **Edward . . . Warwick** Edward is not mentioned in F, but Q, which gives him lines to replace l. 14, confirms his presence. Q makes other changes: Warwick, for instance, does not enter at this point, but with his father Salisbury at 14.1. Oxford follows Q's arrangement, and also inserts four lines from Q at the start of the scene; in accordance with its general policy, this edition follows F.

1 **Of . . . of** The syntactical construction is acceptable Shakespearian grammar: compare *All's Well* 1.2.29: 'on us both did haggish age steal on'.

2 **winter lion** lion in the winter (i.e. at the end) of his life

3 **Agèd contusions** bruises of old age
brush attack. For the force of *brush*, compare Timon's comparison of his friends who have deserted him: 'as leaves | Do on the oak, have with one winter's brush | Fell from their boughs' (*Timon*

4.3.264–6).

4 **brow** prime

5 **Repairs . . . occasion** 'takes advantage of the opportunity to renew himself (by fighting)' (Sanders)

6 **one foot** (of ground)

8 **holp** helped

9 **bestrid him** stood over him to protect him from the enemy, as Falstaff asks Prince Hal to do at *1 Henry IV* 5.1.121–2. As Hal points out, that would have been a tricky operation for him—but also, presumably, for the crippled Richard. Like his general support and admiration for Salisbury, this detail emphasizes that, despite his sardonic mockery of God and man (5.1.213–16; 5.2.71), the Richard of this play is characterized as a brave young warrior: he is not yet the monster of *Richard III*.

10 **act** (military) action

12 **hangings** i.e. wall-hangings, tapestries
homely modest, humble

You have defended me from imminent death.
Well lords, we have not got that which we have: 20
'Tis not enough our foes are this time fled,
Being opposites of such repairing nature.

YORK

I know our safety is to follow them,
For as I hear, the King is fled to London,
To call a present court of Parliament.   25
Let us pursue him ere the writs go forth.
What says Lord Warwick, shall we after them?

WARWICK

After them? Nay, before them if we can.
Now by my hand, lords, 'twas a glorious day.
Saint Albans battle won by famous York   30
Shall be eternized in all age to come.
Sound drums and trumpets, and to London all,
And more such days as these to us befall!

⌈*Flourish.*⌉ *Exeunt*

---

32 drums] Q; Drumme F   33.1 *Flourish*] *not in* F

---

20 **we . . . have** we have not yet secured what
we have acquired (because (a) we are only
temporarily victorious; (b) we have not
yet made York king)

22 **opposites** opponents
of such repairing nature i.e. who can so
easily recover

25 **present** immediate
court of Parliament assembly of councillors and great lords (*OED, court, sb.*[1] 9).
This is presumably an emergency mea-

sure to reinforce his authority and find
ways of opposing York. In dramatic
terms, this looks forward directly to the
opening of *3 Henry VI*, when the Yorkists
break into the King's palace where 'The
Queen' (interestingly, not the King)
'holds her Parliament, | But little thinks
we shall be of her council' (1.1.35–6).

26 **writs** summonses to attend Parliament

29 **by my hand** (a common oath)

31 **eternized** immortalized

APPENDIX A

PASSAGES FROM THE QUARTO TEXT

THIS appendix gives those Quarto passages which appear to offer major alternative versions of passages in the Folio (rather than simply an imperfect recollection of the Folio lines), modernized and annotated so as to allow direct comparison with the Folio versions given in the main text of this edition. They are discussed in the Textual Introduction.

The Q line references given in parentheses are to the through line numbering of the Malone Society Reprint, ed. William Montgomery (Oxford, 1985).

A. Instead of Queen Margaret's speech at 1.1.24–31, Q (51–6) has:

> Th'excess of love I bear unto your grace
> Forbids me to be lavish of my tongue
> Lest I should speak more than beseems a woman.
> Let this suffice: my bliss is in your liking,
> And nothing can make poor Margaret miserable   5
> Unless the frown of mighty England's King.

B. After 1.4.39, Q (519–25) adds:

BOLINGBROKE
> Then down, I say, unto the damnèd pool
> Where Pluto in his fiery wagon sits
> Riding amidst the singed and parchèd smokes,
> The road of Ditis by the river Styx.
> There howl and burn for ever in those flames.   5

A.1 excess of] OXFORD; excessive Q

A.1 **Th'excess of love** Q's 'excessive' is probably a memorial error. Shakespeare only uses *excessive* once elsewhere (*All's Well* 1.1.53) but *excess of* frequently, e.g. 'excess of it will make me surfeit' (*Two Gentlemen* 3.1.219), 'excess of wine' (*Henry V* 2.2.42), 'Give me excess of it' (*Twelfth Night* 1.1.2).

A.3 **beseems** is becoming to. Shakespeare uses this word, or forms of it, frequently in the 1590s.

B. Oxford conjectures that this passage may have been added in rehearsal to cover the spirit's descent. It is written in an imitative Marlovian style, evoking the classical underworld.

B.2 **Pluto** The classical god of the underworld, also known as Dis; see the next note.

B.4 **road of Ditis** 'The genitive singular of "Dis"... came to refer more generally to the underworld itself' (Montgomery).
river Styx In classical mythology, one of the nine rivers of the underworld, over which the souls of the dead had to be ferried.

289

Rise, Jourdayne, rise, and stay thy charming spells.
Zounds, we are betrayed!

C. Instead of having the Spirit's prophecies read out by York at
1.4.58–67, Q (705–15) has them read by the King after 2.1.171:

KING HENRY (*reads*)
'First, of the King: what shall become of him?
The Duke yet lives that Henry shall depose,
Yet him outlive and die a violent death.'
God's will be done in all.
(*Reads*) 'What fate awaits the Duke of Suffolk?   5
By water shall he die, and take his end.'
SUFFOLK ⌈*aside*⌉
By water must the Duke of Suffolk die?
It must be so, or else the devil doth lie.
KING HENRY (*reads*)
'Let Somerset shun castles. For safer shall he be
Upon the sandy plains than where castles mounted stand.'   10

D. Instead of 3.1.223–330, Q (1102–62) has:

QUEEN MARGARET
Then sit we down again, my lord Cardinal,
Suffolk, Buckingham, York, and Somerset.
Let us consult of proud Duke Humphrey's fall.
In mine opinion it were good he died,
For safety of our King and commonwealth.   5
SUFFOLK
And so think I, madam, for as you know,
If our King Henry had shook hands with death,
Duke Humphrey then would look to be our king;
And it may be by policy he works
To bring to pass the thing which now we doubt.   10
The fox barks not when he would steal the lamb,
But if we take him ere he do the deed,
We should not question if that he should live.
No, let him die in that he is a fox,
Lest that in living he offend us more.   15

B.6 **stay** stop
  charming magic
D.2 **Buckingham, Somerset** Q's version
  specifically involves these characters in
  the plot against Duke Humphrey, where-

as in F's version (compare 3.1.223–81),
their presence seems to be ignored.
D.3 **consult of** deliberate about
D.10 **doubt** fear, suspect
D.13 **if that** whether

CARDINAL BEAUFORT
  Then let him die before the commons know,
  For fear that they do rise in arms for him.
YORK
  Then do it suddenly, my lords.
SUFFOLK
  Let that be my Lord Cardinal's charge and mine.
CARDINAL BEAUFORT
  Agreed, for he's already kept within my house.   20
      Enter a Messenger
QUEEN MARGARET
  How now sirrah, what news?
MESSENGER
  Madam, I bring you news from Ireland.
  The wild O'Neill, my lords, is up in arms,
  With troops of Irish kerns that uncontrolled
  Doth plant themselves within the English pale,   25
  And burns and spoils the country as they go.
QUEEN MARGARET
  What redress shall we have for this, my lords?
YORK
  'Twere very good that my lord of Somerset,
  That fortunate champion, were sent over
  To keep in awe the stubborn Irishmen,   30
  He did so much good when he was in France.
SOMERSET
  Had York been there with all his far-fetched policies,
  He might have lost as much as I.
YORK
  Ay, for York would have lost his life before
  That France should have revolted from England's rule.   35
SOMERSET
  Ay so thou might'st, and yet have governed worse than I.
YORK
  What, worse than naught? Then a shame take all.

D.23 **O'Neill** The O'Neills were famous as
a rebellious Irish family. The resonance
of the name in the 1590s was that Hugh
O'Neill, Earl of Tyrone, led a series of
rebellions against English rule from 1587
until his death in 1616.
D.24 **kerns** See the second note to 3.1.310.
D.25 **English pale** The area around Dublin

most securely subject to English
authority.
D.26 This line has been misplaced in Q,
which prints it after l. 29.
D.28–39 See the Commentary to
3.1.291–308.
D.34–5 **before** | **That** before

SOMERSET
Shame on thyself, that wisheth shame.
QUEEN MARGARET
Somerset forbear. Good York be patient,
And do thou take in hand to cross the seas   40
With troops of armèd men to quell the pride
Of those ambitious Irish that rebel.
YORK
Well madam, sith your grace is so content,
Let me have some bands of chosen soldiers,
And York shall try his fortune against those kerns.   45
QUEEN MARGARET
York, thou shalt. My lord of Buckingham,
Let it be your charge to muster up such soldiers
As shall suffice him in these needful wars.
BUCKINGHAM
Madam I will, and levy such a band
As soon shall overcome those Irish rebels.   50
But York, where shall those soldiers stay for thee?
YORK
At Bristol I will expect them ten days hence.
BUCKINGHAM
Then thither shall they come, and so farewell.   *Exit*
YORK
Adieu, my lord of Buckingham.
QUEEN MARGARET
Suffolk, remember what you have to do—   55
And you, Lord Cardinal—concerning Duke Humphrey.
'Twere good that you did see to it in time.
Come, let us go, that it may be performed.

Exeunt all but York

E. 3.2 in Q (1188–90) begins with the following stage direction:

> *Then the curtains being drawn, Duke Humphrey is discovered*
> *in his bed, and two men lying on his breast and smothering*
> *him in his bed. And then enter the Duke of Suffolk to them*

D.43 **sith** since
D.47 **muster up** assemble troops for battle
(*OED v.*[1] 8a)
D.48 **suffice** be enough for
D.51 **stay for** await

D.57 **in time** in good time, sooner rather than
later (*OED sb.* 46(b))
E. Q's version, here, focuses attention on the
murder itself, F's on its consequences.

F. After 4.7.117, Q (1834–53) adds:

Enter a Rebel

REBEL O captain, London Bridge is afire!

CADE Run to Billingsgate and fetch pitch and flax and quench it.

Enter the Butcher and a Sergeant

SERGEANT Justice, justice, I pray you sir, let me have justice of this
fellow here.

CADE Why, what has he done?   5

SERGEANT Alas sir, he has ravished my wife.

BUTCHER (*to Cade*) Why, my lord, he would have 'rested me and I
went and entered my action in his wife's proper house.

CADE Dick, follow thy suit in her common place. (*To the Sergeant*)
You whoreson villain, you are a sergeant—you'll take any man   10
by the throat for twelve pence, and 'rest a man when he's at
dinner, and hale him to prison ere the meat be out of his mouth.

F.0.1 *a Rebel*] *Robin* Q F.1 REBEL] *Robin*. Q F.2 quench] Q3; squench Q1–2 F.8 went
and] Q2; went and and Q1 proper] OXFORD; paper Q F.12 hale] This edition (*conj.* Oxford);
haue Q

F.1 **London Bridge is afire** (as Cade had
instructed at 4.6.14)

F.2 **Run . . . it** Cade's command is ironical,
for although Billingsgate was the principal water-gate in London, *pitch* and *flax*
intensify flame, rather than extinguishing
it. Compare 5.2.55 and note.

F.3–4 **justice . . . here** The phrasing and
rhythm are close to the appeals for justice
in *The Comedy of Errors* (5.1.134 and 191),
the first of several verbal links with that
play recorded in the notes that follow.

F.3 **of** on

F.7 **'rested** arrested. 'Shakespeare uses this
aphetic form four times, all in *Errors*'
(*Textual Companion*, p. 190). They occur
in an episode in which one of the
Antipholus twins is arrested by a
Sergeant.

F.8–9 **entered . . . place** These lines combine
a legal meaning (*entered my action, follow
thy suit*) with sexual innuendoes: *entered
. . . house* means 'penetrated her', and *follow . . . place* 'continue to have her'.

F.8 **proper** Oxford's emendation of Q's
'paper' seems certain : the *Textual Companion*, pp. 190–1, lists several appropriate senses, of which the principal one is
'own, private'.
house vagina. Compare its use as a verb at
Tragedy of Lear 3.2.27 : 'The codpiece that
will house . . .'

F.9 **suit** civil proceeding or action, and also

probably a homophone of *shoot*, 'An off-
shoot ; a growth or sprout from a main
stock' (*OED, shoot, sb.*¹ 2c)—i.e. erection.
common place Cade implies that many
others have preceded Dick in having the
Sergeant's wife—compare Sonnet
137.10, where the 'Dark Lady' is called
'the wide world's common place'—with a
pun on the legal 'common pleas', common law actions (i.e. *suits*).

F.10 **whoreson villain** *Whoreson* literally
means 'son of a whore', but it was widely
used as a general term of abuse, as at
Errors 4.4.25, 'Thou whoreson, senseless
villain!', shortly after Antipholus of
Ephesus has been arrested by the
Sergeant.

F.10–12 **you are . . . at dinner** 'With this
description compare Dromio of
Syracuse's (*Errors* 4.3.13–41). In
Errors Antipholus of Ephesus is arrested
by a sergeant just after his dinner (4.1)'
(*Textual Companion*, p. 191).

F.12 **hale** drag forcibly. Although Oxford
retain Q's 'have' in their text, citing *OED,
have, v.* 16, Gary Taylor's conjecture
'hale' seems preferable : it is used by the
Lieutenant at 4.1.132, just before the
murder of Suffolk, and by Cade himself
at 4.8.56, and it corresponds with the
increasing ferocity of Cade's speech, as he
instructs Dick to mutilate the Sergeant.

(*To the Butcher*) Go, Dick, take him hence: cut out his tongue for
cogging, hough him for running, and to conclude, brain him
with his own mace.   *Exit the Butcher with the Sergeant*   15

G. Instead of 5.2.19–30, Q (2153–65) has:

YORK
Now Clifford, since we are singled here alone,
Be this the day of doom to one of us,
For know my heart hath sworn immortal hate
To thee and all the house of Lancaster.

CLIFFORD
And here I stand and pitch my foot to thine,   5
Vowing not to stir till thou or I be slain.
For never shall my heart be safe at rest
Till I have spoiled the hateful house of York.
    Alarums. They fight. York kills Clifford
YORK
Now Lancaster, sit sure; thy sinews shrink.
Come fearful Henry, grovelling on thy face,   10
Yield up thy crown unto the prince of York.   *Exit*

F.14 brain] OXFORD; Braue Q   G.3 know] OXFORD; now Q   G.6 not] OXFORD; neuer Q

F.14 **cogging** cheating, lying
    hough hamstring, 'disable by cutting the
    sinew or tendons of the hough', i.e.
    behind the knee (*OED v.*[1])
    brain Q's 'braue' seems to have arisen
    through confusion with the exclamations
    'brave' and 'braver' associated with the
    displaying of the heads of Lord Saye and
    his son-in-law immediately after this
    passage (4.7.121–2), which Q does not
    include; or the error may simply be a
    compositorial misreading.
G.1 **singled** separated from others. 'The verb
    continues the deer hunt metaphor [from
    5.2.15], for "single" is also a specific hunt-
    ing term meaning to separate a deer from
    the herd (*OED v.*[1] 2)' (Montgomery).

G.3 **know** Oxford emends Q's 'now' on the
    grounds that the line is weak : 'the substi-
    tution of "now" for "know" would be an
    easy error' (*Textual Companion*, p. 193). It
    could also have been caught from the
    'Now' two lines earlier, either by the
    reporter or the compositor.
G.5 **pitch . . . to** set firmly against
G.6 **not** Oxford emends Q's 'never' because
    the 'repetition of "never" in the next line
    is suspicious, and suggests memorial
    error either there or here' (*Textual
    Companion*, p. 193).
G.8 **spoiled** destroyed
G.9 **sure** securely
    sinews shrink the forces that uphold you
    diminish

CHRONICLE SOURCES

THERE is unfortunately no complete edition of either Hall or Holinshed more recent than the reprints of 1809 (Hall) and 1807–8 (Holinshed). Since these are marginally more accessible than the originals of 1548 (Hall) and 1587 (Holinshed), page references are to these editions. Grafton and Fabyan are cited from the originals, *The Mirror for Magistrates* from Lily B. Campbell's edition (Cambridge, 1938). I have tried to allow the chronicles to speak for themselves, with the minimum of intervention, even when they present markedly different interpretations of the play's events, for example in Henry's motive for banishing Suffolk at 3.2.293–303.

1.1.1–9 **As by . . . espoused** In 1444, 'The Earl of Suffolk, made Marquis of Suffolk, . . . sailed into France for the conveyance of . . . Queen [Margaret] into the realm of England. . . . This noble company came to the city of Tours in Touraine, where they were honourably received both of the French King and of the King of Sicily, where the Marquis of Suffolk, as Procurator to King Henry, espoused the said lady. . . . There were also the Dukes of Orléans, of Calabre, of Alençon, and of Brittany, seven earls, twelve barons, twenty bishops, beside knights and gentlemen. . . . Soon after her arrival [in England in 1445], she was conveyed to the town of Southwick in Hampshire, where she with all nuptial ceremonies was coupled in matrimony to King Henry VI. . . . After which marriage, she was with great triumph conveyed to London, and so to Westminster, where . . . she with all solemnity thereunto appertaining, was crowned Queen' (Hall, pp. 204–5).

1.1.15 **The happiest gift**, 40–61 **the articles** 'The Earl of Suffolk, . . . too much affectionate to this unprofitable marriage, . . . agreed . . . that the Duchy of Anjou and the County of Maine should be released and delivered to the King her father, demanding for her marriage neither penny nor farthing, as who would say that this new affinity excelled riches and surmounted gold and precious stone. . . . A certain truce [between England and France] was concluded . . . for eighteen months' (Hall, pp. 203–4).

1.1.63 **the first Duke of Suffolk** 'This Marquis . . . by the means of the Queen was shortly erected to the estate and degree of a Duke, and ruled the King at his pleasure' (Hall, p. 207).

1.1.65 **We here discharge** See 1.3.102–15 below.

1.1.74–102 **Brave peers . . . been** 'Humphrey Duke of Gloucester, Protector of the realm, repugned and resisted as much as in him lay this new alliance' (Hall, p. 204).

1.1.110–11 **whose large style ... purse** King René 'for all his long style, had too short a purse to send his daughter honourably to the King' (Hall, p. 205).

1.1.113 **the keys of Normandy** Anjou and Maine 'are called the keys of Normandy' (Fabyan, ii. 397); Hall and Holinshed call them the 'stays and backstands'.

1.1.127–33 **I never read ... her** 'the King with her had not one penny, and for the fetching of her ... Suffolk demanded a whole fifteen, in open parliament' (Hall, p. 205).

1.1.143 **our ancient bickerings** 'the Duke of Gloucester sore grudged at the proud doings of the Cardinal of Winchester, and ... the Cardinal likewise sore envied and disdained at the rule of the Duke of Gloucester' (Hall, p. 197).

1.1.157–61 **What though ... Humphrey** 'for the noble prowess and virtue ... he was both loved of the commons and well spoken of of all men, and no less deserving the same, being called the good Duke of Gloucester' (Grafton, ii. 598).

1.1.189–91 **Warwick ... commons** 'among all sorts of people he obtained great love, much favour, and more credence, which things daily more increased by his abundant liberality and plentiful housekeeping ... that they judged him able to do all things' (Hall, pp. 231–2; the reference to housekeeping is not in Holinshed).

1.1.193 **thy acts in Ireland** In 1449 (see 3.1.282–9 below), York's 'politic governance, his gentle behaviour, to all the Irish nation ... had brought that rude and savage nation to civil fashion' (Hall, p. 219).

1.2.35–44 'For not content to be a duchess great,
    I longèd sore to bear the name of Queen. ...
    Since there was none which that time was between
    Henry the King and my good Duke his eme [uncle],
    Heir to the crown and kingdom of this realm. ...
    Alas the while to counsel I did call
    Such as would seem by skill conjectural
    Of art magic and wicked sorcery
    To deem and divine the prince's destiny.'
         (*The Mirror for Magistrates*, pp. 434–5)

1.2.75–6 **With Margery Jourdayne ... conjuror** In 1441, 'Dame Eleanor Cobham, wife to the said Duke [Humphrey], was accused of treason, for that she by sorcery and enchantment intended to destroy the King, to th'intent to advance and to promote her husband to the crown.' Her accomplices included 'Roger Bolingbroke, a cunning necromancer, and Margery Jourdayne, surnamed the Witch of Eye' (Hall, p. 202).

1.3.43-65 **My lord . . . holiness** For Hall's detailed contrast between Margaret and Henry, see the Introduction, p. 28.

1.3.47-8 **What . . . governance** 'This woman, perceiving that her husband did not frankly rule as he would, but did all thing by th'advice and counsel of Humphrey Duke of Gloucester, . . . determined with herself to take upon her the rule and regiment both of the King and his kingdom [rather than] suffer her husband, being of perfect age and man's estate, like a young scholar or innocent pupil to be governed by the disposition of another man' (Hall, p. 208).

1.3.52 **rann'st a-tilt** In 1444, at the celebrations of the proxy marriage of Margaret with Suffolk in Tours, 'there were triumphant jousts' (Hall, p. 205).

1.3.102-15, 161-5 In 1446, 'the Duke of York was established Regent of France . . . to continue in that office for the term of five years, which being expired, [York], as a man most meet to supply that room, [was] appointed . . . again as Regent of France. . . . But the Duke of Somerset, still maligning the Duke of York's advancement, . . . now wrought so, that the King revoked his grant made to the Duke of York . . . and with help of . . . Suffolk obtained that grant for himself, which malicious dealing . . . York might so evil bear, that in the end the heat of displeasure burst out into such a flame as consumed at length not only both those two noble personages, but also many thousands of others' (Holinshed, iii. 208-9; not in Hall).

1.3.119-38 The Queen was determined to 'evict' Duke Humphrey 'out of all rule and authority', supported by those who 'had borne malice to the Duke', led by Suffolk, Buckingham, the Cardinal, and the Archbishop (the play substitutes the Duke) of York. 'Divers articles . . . were laid to his charge in open council', for example that he 'had not so much advanced and preferred the commonwealth and public utility as his own private things and peculiar estate', and especially 'that he had caused men adjudged to die to be put to other execution than the law of the land had ordered' (Hall, pp. 208-9). Several of the charges against Humphrey in the play were in fact brought against Suffolk by Parliament in 1449 (Hall, pp. 217-18).

1.3.168-73 **if I be . . . lost** In 1435, 'by all ways and means possible [Somerset] both hindered and detracted [York], causing him to linger in England without dispatch, till Paris and the flower of France were gotten by the French King. . . . Each work[ed] things to the other's displeasure' (Hall, p. 179).

1.4.0.1-3, 40 In 1441, 'were arrested, as aiders and counsellors to the . . . Duchess, Thomas Southwell, priest . . . , John Hum, priest, Roger Bolingbroke, a cunning necromancer, and Margery Jourdayne, surnamed the Witch of Eye' (Hall, p. 202). The conjuring itself was probably suggested by Elizabethan drama rather than chronicle: see pp. 82–3.

1.4.34–5 **What . . . castles** See 5.2.19–90 below. The other prophecies are the dramatist's invention.

2.1.1–18 For the hawking opening, see the headnote to this scene in the Commentary.

2.1.57–155 As the King 'rode in progress, there came to the town of St Albans a certain beggar with his wife . . . saying that he was born blind and never saw in all his life, and was warned in his dream that he should come out of Berwick, where he said that he had ever dwelled, to seek Saint Alban. . . . When the King was come, and the town full of people, suddenly this blind man at Saint Alban's shrine had his sight, and the same was solemnly rung for a miracle, and *Te Deum* sung, so that nothing was talked of in all the town, but this miracle. So happened it then that Duke Humphrey of Gloucester, a man no less wise than also well learned, having great joy to see such a miracle, called the poor man unto him, and . . . looked well upon his eyen, and asked whether he could ever see anything at all in all his life before. And when as well his wife as himself affirmed fastly no, then he looked advisedly upon his eyen again and said, 'I believe you very well, for me thinketh that ye can not see well yet.' 'Yes sir', quoth he, 'I thank God and his holy martyr, I can see now as well as any man.' 'Yea, can?' quod the Duke, 'what colour is my gown?' Then anon the beggar told him. 'What colour', quod he, 'is this man's gown?' He told him also without any staying or stumbling, and told the names of all the colours that could be showed to him. And when the Duke saw that, he bade him 'walk faitour [impostor]', and made him to be set openly in the stocks, for though he could have seen suddenly by miracle the difference between divers colours, yet could he not by sight so suddenly tell the names of all these colours, except he had known them before, no more than he could name all the men whom he should suddenly see' (Grafton, ii. 597–8).

2.2.3–5 **In this . . . crown** In 1448–9, York 'began secretly to allure to his friends of the nobility and privately declared to them his title and right to the crown' (Hall, p. 210).

2.2.10–52 The clearest statement about Edward III's sons is Grafton's, who sets them out in a table. If so well-known an event as Bolingbroke's deposition of Richard II required a specific source, it could have been York's oration to Parliament in 1460, stating his claim to the throne (Hall, p. 246), which is also used in the opening scene of *3 Henry VI*. York's tracing of his mother's descent from Edward's third son borrows material and phrasing from Hall: see the Introduction, p. 31.

2.2.39–42 This Edmund . . . till he died See the Commentary for the two different Mortimers conflated here.

2.3.5–8 In 1441, 'Margery Jourdayne was burnt in Smithfield, and Roger Bolingbroke was drawn and quartered at Tyburn, . . . John Hum had his pardon, and Southwell died in the Tower before execution' (Hall, p. 202).

2.3.9–16 Duchess Eleanor was 'judged to do open penance in three open places within the city of London, and after that adjudged to perpetual prison in the Isle of Man, under the keeping of Sir John Stanley. . . . The Duke of Gloucester took all these things patiently, and said little' (Hall, p. 202).

2.3.58.1–105 In 1446, 'an armourer's servant of London appealed his master of treason, which offered to be tried by battle. At the day assigned, the friends of the master brought him malmsey and aqua vitae to comfort him withal, but it was the cause of his and their discomfort, for he poured in so much that when he came into the place in Smithfield where he should fight, both his wit and strength failed him; and so, he being a tall and a hardy personage, overladed with hot drinks, was vanquished of his servant, being but a coward and a wretch, whose body was drawn to Tyburn and there hanged and beheaded' (Hall, pp. 207–8). None of the chroniclers links this accusation of treason with York's claim to the crown: this is the dramatist's invention.

2.4.17.3 *a wax taper* '*Polychronicon* sayeth she was enjoined to go through Cheapside with a taper in her hand' (Holinshed, iii. 203; not in Hall).

2.4.60–4 I must offend . . . crimeless Humphrey 'thought neither of death nor of condemnation to die, such affiance had he in his strong truth and such confidence . . . in indifferent justice' (Hall, p. 209; not in Holinshed).

2.4.71–4 I summon . . . dealing In 1447, 'for the furtherance of their purpose [the destruction of Humphrey], a parliament was summoned to be kept at Bury' (Hall, p. 209).

3.1.84–5 For the loss of France, see 290–308 below.

3.1.97–138 On the second day of the Parliament at Bury, Humphrey 'was by the Lord Beaumont, then High Constable of England, accompanied by the Duke of Buckingham and other, arrested, apprehended, and put in ward'. For the specific accusations, see 1.3.119–38 above. 'Although the Duke . . . sufficiently answered to all things to him objected, yet because his death was determined, his wisdom little helped, nor his truth smally availed' (Hall, p. 209).

3.1.233–81 **This Gloucester . . . doom** Humphrey's enemies, 'fearing that some tumult or commotion might arise if a prince so well beloved of the people should be openly . . . put to death, determined to trap and undo him ere he thereof should have knowledge or warning' (Hall, p. 209).

3.1.282–9, 309–30 In 1448, 'a new rebellion began in Ireland, . . . for repressing whereof Richard Duke of York, with a convenient number of men, was sent thither as lieutenant to the King' (Hall, p. 213).

3.1.290–308 **That Somerset . . . shame** In 1450 Somerset, as Regent of France, 'moved with the dolour of his wife and love of his children', surrendered Caen to the French King, on condition that he 'and all his might depart in safeguard with all their goods and substance . . . , which thing kindled so great a rancour in [York's] heart and stomach that he never left persecuting . . . Somerset, till he had brought him to his fatal point and extreme confusion' (Hall, pp. 215–16).

3.1.355–78 **And for a minister . . . arms** 'To th'intent that it should not be known that the Duke of York or his friends were the cause of the sudden rising, a certain young man of a goodly stature and pregnant wit was enticed to take upon him the name of John Mortimer, although his name were John Cade' (Hall, p. 220). Cade's association with the Irish wars may have been suggested by Holinshed's gloss that Cade was 'an Irishman, as *Polychronicon* sayeth' (iii. 220).

3.2 At the Parliament of Bury in 1447, Duke Humphrey 'the night after his imprisonment was found dead in his bed, and his body showed to the lords and commons, as though he had died of a palsy or impostume; but all indifferent persons well knew that he died of no natural death but of some violent force: some judged him to be strangled; some affirm that a hot spit was put in at his fundament; other write, that he was stifled or smouldered [smothered] between two feather beds' (Hall, p. 209). Holinshed adds: 'some have affirmed that he died of very grief, for that he might not come openly to his answer' (iii. 211). For the wider consequences of Duke Humphrey's murder, see the Introduction, p. 40.

3.2.245–71 **Dread lord . . . life** In 1450, the people 'began to make exclamation against the Duke of Suffolk, affirming him to be the only cause of the delivery of Anjou and Maine, the chief procurer of the death of the good Duke of Gloucester, the very occasion of the loss of Normandy, the most swallower-up and consumer of the King's treasure . . . and worthy to be put to most cruel punishment' (Hall, p. 217).

3.2.293–303 **O Henry . . . to thee** 'The Queen, which entirely loved the Duke, fearing that some commotion and trouble might rise if he were let go unpunished, caused him to be committed to the Tower'; but he was soon released, which 'incensed the fury of the mutable commons much more than before. . . . When King Henry perceived that the commons were thus

... bent against the Queen's darling, William Duke of Suffolk, he ... banished ... Suffolk as the abhorred toad and common nuisance of the realm of England for the term of five years, meaning by this exile to appease the furious rage of the outrageous people, and that pacified, to revocate him into his old estate, as the Queen's chief friend and counsellor' (Hall, pp. 218–19).

3.3 In 1447, Winchester, 'called the rich Cardinal, departed out of this world. ... This man was son to John of Gaunt, Duke of Lancaster, descended of an honourable lineage, but born in bast[ardy], more noble of blood than notable in learning, haut in stomach and high in countenance, rich above measure of all men, and to few liberal, disdainful to his kin and dreadful to his lovers, preferring money before friendship. ... His covetous[ness] insatiable and hope of long life made him both to forget God, his prince, and himself in his latter days; for Doctor John Baker, ... his chaplain, wrote that he, lying on his death bed, said these words: "Why should I die, having so much riches? If the whole realm would save my life, I am able either by policy to get it, or by riches to buy it. Fie, will not death be hired, nor will money do nothing? ... But I see now the world faileth me, and so I am deceived: praying you all to pray for me."' (Hall, pp. 210–11.)

4.1 In 1450, when the banished Suffolk took ship, 'intending to be transported into France, he was encountered with a ship of war appertaining to the Duke of Exeter ... called "The Nicholas of the Tower". The captain of the same barque with small fight entered into the Duke's ship, and perceiving his person present, brought him to Dover road, and there on the one side of a cock-boat caused his head to be stricken off, and left his body with the head upon the sands of Dover, which corpse was there found by a chaplain of his, and conveyed to Wingfield College in Suffolk, and there buried. This end had William de la Pole, first Duke of Suffolk, as men judge by God's punishment: for above all things he was noted to be the very organ, engine, and deviser of the destruction of Humphrey the good Duke of Gloucester, and so the blood of the innocent man was with his dolorous death recompensed and punished' (Hall, p. 219).

4.2 Cade's rebellion of 1450 is supplemented with details of the Peasants' Revolt of 1381.

4.2.63 **All the realm shall be in common** In 1381, John Wall or Ball preached that 'matters go not well ... nor shall not do until everything be common' (Grafton, ii. 330).

4.2.71 **let's kill all the lawyers** In 1381, the rebels beheaded 'all such men of law, justices, and jurors as they might catch ... without respect of pity or remorse of conscience' (Holinshed, ii. 737).

4.2.78–101 The Clerk of Chatham . . . neck in 1381, 'it was dangerous among them to be known for one that was learned, and more dangerous if any man were found with a penner and inkhorn at his side; for such seldom or never escaped from them with life' (Holinshed, ii. 746).

4.2.112–4.3.0.1 In 1450, Cade, 'intending to bring the King farther within the compass of his net, broke up his camp and retired backward to the town of Sevenoaks in Kent. . . . The Queen . . . sent Sir Humphrey Stafford . . . and William his brother . . . to follow the chase of the Kentishmen, thinking that they had fled, but verily they were deceived, for at the first skirmish both the Staffords were slain' (Hall, p. 220).

4.2.125 Adam was a gardener The preacher John Ball used the couplet 'When Adam delved and Eve span, | Who was then a gentleman?' (cited by Holinshed, ii. 749).

4.2.144 the Duke . . . this See 3.1.355–78 above.

4.2.146–51 tell the King . . . Maine Cade promised his followers 'that if . . . they might once take the King, the Queen, and other their councillors . . . they would honourably entreat the King and so sharply handle his councillors that neither fifteens should hereafter be demanded nor once any impositions or tax should be spoken of' (Hall, p. 220).

4.2.150–1 the Lord Saye . . . Maine 'the commons . . . beseeched the King that such persons as assented to the release of Anjou and . . . Maine might be extremely punished and . . . they accused . . . Lord Saye and divers other' (Hall, p. 219).

4.2.167–70 Proclaim . . . doors Perhaps suggested by a message sent by the King to York just before the battle of St Albans in 1455: any rebels will 'be hanged, drawn, and quartered, . . . in example to make all such traitors to beware for to make any rising of people within mine own land' (Holinshed, iii. 239; not in Hall).

4.3.9.1–12 *He apparels . . . to London* After Cade had slain the Staffords, 'he apparelled himself in their rich armour, and so with pomp and glory returned again toward London' (Hall, p. 220; Holinshed's detail that Sir Humphrey's breastplate was 'set full of gilt nails' (iii. 224) comes from Fabyan's account, but the play does not use it).

4.3.14–16 If we . . . Fear not that Cade 'broke up the jails of the King's Bench and Marshalsea and set at liberty a swarm of gallants both meet for his service and apt for his enterprise' (Hall, p. 222).

4.4.8–12 I'll send . . . general The King sent to Cade 'the Archbishop of Canterbury and Humphrey Duke of Buckingham to commune with him of his griefs and requests. These lords found him sober in communication, wise in disputing, arrogant in heart, and stiff in his opinion, and by no ways possible to be persuaded to dissolve his army except the King in person would come to him' (Hall, pp. 220–1).

4.4.26 **the rebels are in Southwark,** 38 **retire to Kenilworth** 'The King, . . . having daily report of the concourse and access of people which continually resorted to [Cade], . . . departed in all haste to the castle of Kenilworth in Warwickshire. . . . [Cade], being advertised of the King's absence, came first into Southwark' (Hall, p. 221).

4.5.0.1 *Lord Scales* The King left 'only behind him the Lord Scales to keep the Tower of London' (Hall, p. 221).

4.5.4, 10 **The Lord Mayor . . . Matthew Gough** The Mayor and magistrates, determined 'to repel and expulse this mischievous head and his ungracious company', asked Scales for help: 'The Lord Scales promised them his aid, . . . and Matthew Gough was by him appointed to assist the Mayor and the Londoners, because he was both of manhood and experience greatly renowned' (Hall, p. 221).

4.6.0.1–1 *Enter . . .* **city** Cade 'entered into London, . . . striking his sword on London Stone, saying "Now is Mortimer lord of this city"' (Hall, p. 221).

4.7.0.1–2 In the battle between the citizens of London and the rebels for London Bridge, 'the multitude of the rebels drove the citizens from the stoops [posts] at the bridge foot to the drawbridge . . . and slew . . . Matthew Gough, a man of great wit, much experience in feats of chivalry, the which in continual wars had valiantly served the King and his father' (Hall, p. 222).

4.7.1–2 **now go . . . them all** In 1381, the rebels burnt John of Gaunt's palace, the Savoy, 'and then came unto the Temple and other Inns of Court, and spoiled the books of law' (Grafton, ii. 335).

4.7.12–14 **burn . . . England** In 1381, the rebels 'purposed to burn and destroy all records, evidences, court-rolls, and other muniments'. Wat Tyler said, 'putting his hands to his lips, that within four days all the laws of England should come forth of his mouth' (Holinshed, ii. 737, 740).

4.7.18–128 **Here's the Lord Saye . . . kiss** In 1450, Cade 'caused Sir James Fiennes, Lord Saye, and Treasurer of England, to be brought to the Guildhall of London, and there to be arraigned, which being before the King's justices put to answer, desired to be tried by his peers, for the longer delay of his life. [Cade,] perceiving his dilatory plea, by force took him from the officers and brought him to the Standard in Cheap[side] and there, before his confession ended, caused his head to be cut off and pitched it on a high pole, which was openly borne before him through the streets. And this cruel tyrant, not content with the murder of the Lord Saye, went to Mile End and there apprehended Sir James Cromer, then sheriff of Kent and son-in-law to the said Lord Saye, and him, without confession or excuse heard, caused there likewise to be headed, and his head to be fixed on a pole, and with these two heads this bloody butcher entered into the city again, and in despite caused them in every street kiss together, to the great detestation of all the beholders' (Hall, p. 221). See the Introduction, p. 55.

4.7.20 one-and-twenty fifteens See 4.2.146–51 above.

4.7.125–6 defer . . . night When Cade first arrived in Southwark, he prohibited 'to all men murder, rape, or robbery, by which colour he allured to him the hearts of the common people' (Hall, p. 221)—not quite the same as deferring the spoil of the city until night!

4.8.1–2 Down Saint Magnus' Corner . . . Thames During the battle for London Bridge, 'fearful women with children in their arms . . . leapt into the river' and 'the Londoners were beat back to the stoops at St Magnus' Corner' (Hall, p. 222).

4.8.6–69 When the weary rebels retreated from London Bridge into Southwark, the Archbishop of Canterbury and the Bishop of Winchester seized their opportunity, 'bringing with them under the King's Great Seal a general pardon unto all the offenders, which they caused to be openly proclaimed and published. Lord, how glad the poor people were of this pardon . . . and how they accepted the same, in so much that the whole multitude, without bidding farewell to their captain, retired the same night. . . . A proclamation [was] made that whosoever could apprehend the said Jack Cade should have for his pain a thousand marks' (Hall, p. 222). The bishops are replaced in the play by Buckingham and Clifford, but Buckingham accompanied Canterbury to the first meeting with Cade: see 4.4.8–12 above. Clifford's patriotic appeal to the memory of Henry V is the dramatist's invention.

4.8.24–5 the White Hart in Southwark When Cade first arrived in London, he 'came first into Southwark, and there lodged at the White Hart' (Hall, p. 221).

4.9.15–21 this day . . . countries 'The King himself came into Kent, and there sat in judgement upon the offenders, and if he had not mitigated his justice with mercy and compassion, more than five hundred by the rigour of his law had been justly put to execution; but he considered both their fragility [Grafton: simplicity] and innocency, and how they with perverse people were seduced and deceived, and so punished the stubborn heads, and delivered the ignorant and miserable people, to the great rejoicing of all his subjects' (Hall, p. 222).

4.9.25–31 The Duke of York . . . traitor In 1451, York returned from Ireland 'to consult with his special friends', especially Salisbury and Warwick. They decided 'that the Duke should raise an army of men, under a pretext to remove divers councillors about the King', above all Somerset, 'for that it was well known that he would be altogether against the Duke of York in his challenge . . . to the crown' (Holinshed, iii. 229; the last point is not in Hall).

4.9.37–41 **Buckingham . . . from him** See 5.1.12–55 below.

4.10 'John Cade, . . . seeing his company thus . . . suddenly depart, mistrusting the sequel of the matter, departed secretly . . . into Sussex [where] one Alexander Iden, esquire of Kent, found him in a garden, and there in his defence manfully slew the caitiff Cade and brought his dead body to London, whose head was set on London Bridge' (Hall, p. 222).

5.1 The play drastically condenses and simplifies a series of confrontations between York and Henry from 1450 until the first battle of St Albans in 1455 into one continuous sequence.

5.1.12–55 **Whom . . . tent** In 1452, the armies of York and Henry faced one another. The King sent the Bishops of Winchester and Ely to negotiate with York, who answered that 'his intent was to remove from [the King] certain evil-disposed persons of his council . . . amongst whom he chiefly named Edmund Duke of Somerset, whom if the King would commit to ward . . . he promised not only to dissolve his army . . . but also offered himself, like an obedient subject, to come to the King's presence and to do him true and faithful service. . . . The King, perceiving that without great bloodshed he could not bridle [York], nor without war he could not appease the furious rage of the common people . . . , caused the Duke of Somerset to be committed to ward . . . till the fury of the people were somewhat assuaged and pacified. Which thing done, [York] dissolved his army, and broke up his camp, and came to the King's tent' (Hall, p. 226). In the play, these negotiations are conflated with those before the battle of St Albans in 1455, where Buckingham is the King's ambassador (as in Holinshed, but not in Hall).

5.1 83–92 **Somerset . . . abuse** In 1455, after a second arrest of Somerset, 'the King, either of his own mind or by the Queen's procurement, caused the Duke of Somerset to be set at liberty' (Hall, p. 232).

5.1.93–108 **'King' . . . grace** In 1453, York laid 'great offences to King Henry, saying that he was a man neither of wit nor stomach, neither meet to be a king nor apt to govern a commonwealth' (Hall, p. 231). In 1452, when York went to the King's tent (see 5.1.12–55 above), 'contrary to the promise made by the King, he found the Duke of Somerset set . . . at liberty, whom the Duke of York boldly accused of treason, of bribery, oppression, and many other crimes. The Duke of Somerset not only made answer to the Duke's objections, but also accused him of high treason toward the King his sovereign lord. . . . The King removed straight to London, and the Duke of York as a prisoner' (Hall, p. 226).

5.1.111 call ... bail While York was a prisoner, 'a rumour sprang throughout London that Edward Earl of March, son and heir apparent to [York], accompanied with a strong army of Marchmen, was coming toward London, which tidings sore appalled the Queen and the whole council [who] set ... York at liberty' (Hall, p. 227).

5.1.144-7 Call ... to me In 1453, York 'fastened his chain between these two strong ... pillars', Salisbury and Warwick (Hall, p. 232).

5.2.0.1 *Enter the Earl of Warwick* In 1455, the battle of St Albans began as the King was still negotiating with York: 'the Earl of Warwick with the Marchmen entered at the other gate of the town and fiercely set on the King's forward, and them shortly discomfited' (Hall, p. 232).

5.2.19-90 'Then came the Duke of Somerset and all the other lords with the King's power, which fought a sore and a cruel battle. . . . The King's army was ... dispersed. . . . For there died under the sign of the Castle, Edmund Duke of Somerset, who long before was warned to eschew all castles, and beside him lay ... John Lord Clifford. . . . Buckingham, being wounded ... , seeing Fortune's lowering chance, left the King post alone, and with a great number fled away' (Hall, pp. 232-3). See the Commentary to 5.2.71.1-2.

ALTERATIONS TO LINEATION

1.1.206	And . . . cause] POPE; *as two lines in* F, *divided after* 'York'
207	Then . . . main] Q; *as two lines in* F, *divided after* 'away'
208	Unto . . . lost] Q; *as two lines in* F, *divided after* 'main'
1.3.219–21	Away . . . away] CAPELL; *as prose* F
1.4.24–7	Asmodeus . . . hence] CAPELL; *divided after* 'God', 'at', *and* 'speak' *in* F
35–6, 66–7	Let . . . stand] OXFORD (*conj.* Vaughan); *as three lines in* F, *divided after* 'castles' *and* 'plains'
60–1	Why . . . posse] CAMBRIDGE; *as one line in* F
68–9	Come . . . understood] OXFORD (*conj.* Hibbard; *see collation*); *three lines in* F, *divided after* 'lord' (Lords F) *and* 'attain'd'
72	Thither . . . them] POPE; *as two lines in* F, *divided after* 'news'
76	At . . . ho] CAPELL; *as two lines in* F, *divided after* 'lord'
2.1.23	What . . . peremptory] POPE; *as two lines in* F, *divided after* 'Cardinal'
24–5	*Tantaene . . . malice*] THEOBALD; *divided after* 'hot' *in* F
32–3	I . . . Queen] MALONE; *as one line in* F
41–2	Ay . . . grove] THEOBALD; *as three lines in* F, *divided after* 'peep' *and* 'evening'
45	We . . . sword] POPE; *as two lines in* F, *divided after* 'sport'
46–7	True . . . grove] THEOBALD; *divided in* F *after* 'advised'
50	Now . . . this] POPE; *as two lines in* F, *divided after* 'priest'
51–2	*Medice . . . yourself*] THEOBALD; *as one line in* F
53	The . . . lords] Q; *as two lines in* F, *divided after* 'high'
83	Poor . . . thee] POPE; *as two lines in* F, *divided after* 'soul'
86–7	Tell . . . shrine] POPE; *as three lines in* F, *divided after* 'fellow' *and* 'devotion'
88–91	God . . . thee] POPE; *as five lines in* F, *divided after* 'devotion', 'oftener', 'Alban' *and* 'shrine'
92–3	Most . . . so] POPE; *as three lines in* F, *divided after* 'forsooth' *and* 'voice'
101–2	Alas . . . life] POPE; *as prose* F
108–9	Why . . . of] CAPELL; *as one line* F
109–10	Black . . . jet] CAPELL; *as one line* F
123–8	Then . . . impossible] HANMER; *as eight lines in* F, *divided after* 'there', 'Christendom', 'blind', 'names', 'wear', 'colours', *and* 'all'; *as prose* Q

134	Have . . . whips] OXFORD; *as two lines in* F, *divided after* 'town'
146–7	Come . . . quickly] POPE; *as one (verse?) line in* F
2.2.34–5	The . . . daughter] POPE; *as three lines in* F, *divided after* 'Clarence' *and* 'crown'
45–6	Married . . . fifth son] CAPELL; *as three lines in* F, *divided after* 'Cambridge' *and* 'Langley'
47–50	By . . . Clarence] THEOBALD; *as five lines in* F, *divided after* 'kingdom', 'March', 'Mortimer', *and* 'daughter'
64–5	We . . . stained] POPE; *as three lines in* F, *divided after* 'lords' *and* 'crowned'
2.3.1	Stand . . . wife] POPE; *as two lines in* F, *divided after* 'Cobham'
22–5	Stay . . . feet] POPE; *as five lines in* F, *divided after* 'Gloucester', 'staff', 'be', *and* 'guide'
71–2	Be . . . prentices] ROWE; *as verse in* F, *divided after* 'master'
2.4.72	holden . . . month] Q; *verse in* F
84–5	And . . . farewell] POPE; *divided after* 'her' *in* F
106	Madam . . . sheet] POPE; *as two lines in* F, *divided after* 'done'
3.1.104	'Tis . . . France] POPE; *as two lines in* F, *divided after* 'lord'
107	Is . . . it] POPE; *as two lines in* F, *divided after* 'so'
223	Free . . . beams] POPE; *as two lines in* F, *divided after* 'lords'
3.2.238	Why . . . drawn] POPE; *as two lines in* F, *divided after* 'lords'
4.1.71	Pole . . . dirt] OXFORD; *as two lines in* F, *divided before* 'Ay' (*see collation*)
116	Come . . . death] ROWE 1714; *as prose in* F
117–18	*paene . . . fear*] OXFORD; *as one line in* F
4.2.126–7	Marry . . . not] Q; *as prose in* F
141–2	And . . . what] POPE; *as prose in* F
145	He . . . myself] OXFORD; *as prose in* F
4.4.7	What . . . supplication] OXFORD; *perhaps prose in* F
4.5.2–5	No . . . rebels] POPE; *as verse in* F, *divided after* 'slain', 'bridge', 'them', *and* 'Tower'
4.6.1–6	Now . . . Mortimer] POPE; *as verse in* F, *divided after* 'city', 'Stone', 'cost', 'wine', 'reign', *and* 'any'
13–15	Come . . . away] POPE; *as verse in* F, *divided after* 'them', 'fire', *and* 'too'
4.7.15–16	Then . . . out] POPE; *as verse in* F, *divided after* 'statutes'
121–8	But . . . Away] THEOBALD; *as verse in* F, *divided after* 'braver', 'well', 'again', 'up', 'Soldiers', 'night', 'maces', *and* 'corner'
4.8.3–4	What . . . kill] HANMER; *as verse in* F, *divided after* 'hear' *and* 'parley'

32–3	We'll . . . Cade] POPE; *as verse in* F, *divided after* 'Cade'
53–4	A . . . and Clifford] POPE; *as verse in* F, *divided* A Clifford! | We'll
4.9.42	My . . . willingly] OXFORD; *as two lines in* F, *divided after* 'lord'
5.2.19	What . . . pause] POPE; *as two lines in* F, *divided after* 'York'

APPENDIX A

C.9–10	Let . . . stand] OXFORD; *as three lines in* Q, *divided after* 'castles' *and* 'plains'
D.32–3	far-fetched policies, | He] This edition; far-fetched | Policies, he Q
F.7–8	Why . . . house] OXFORD; *as verse in* Q, *divided after* 'me'
9–16	Dick . . . mace] OXFORD; *as verse in* Q, *divided after* 'place', 'you'll', 'pence', 'dinner', 'mouth', 'cogging', *and* 'conclude'

:

INDEX

THIS is a selective guide to the Commentary and the Introduction, though it does not duplicate the section headings of the latter. Citations from other texts are not normally included. Characters in the play are only listed if their names (e.g. Sander Simpcox) or their historical counterparts (e.g. Henry VI or Duke Humphrey) are discussed. Asterisks identify entries which supplement the information given in *OED*. 'App.' = Appendix A.